日本の中国学専門家ハンドブック

JAPANESE SCHOLARS OF CHINA

A Bibliographical Handbook

日本の中国学専門家ハンドブック

JAPANESE SCHOLARS OF CHINA

A Bibliographical Handbook

Compiled by

John Timothy Wixted

The Edwin Mellen Press
Lewiston/Queenston/Lampeter

Library of Congress Cataloging-in-Publication Data

Wixted, John Timothy.
    Japanese scholars of China : a bibliographical handbook = [Nihon
no Chūgokugaku senmonka handobukku] / compiled by John Timothy
Wixted.
       p.   cm.
    Includes bibliographical references and indexes.
    ISBN 0-7734-9571-1
    1. Sinologists--Japan--Handbooks, manuals, etc. I. Title.
II. Title: Nihon no Chūgokugaku senmonka handobukku.
DS734.8.W58 1992
951'.007202'252--dc20   92-25299
                                                  CIP

A CIP catalog record for this book
is available from the British Library.

The Edwin Mellen Press   The Edwin Mellen Press
Box 450   Box 67
Lewiston, New York   Queenston, Ontario
USA 14092   CANADA L0S 1L0

Edwin Mellen Press, Ltd.
Lampeter, Dyfed, Wales
UNITED KINGDOM SA48 7DY

Printed in the United States of America

CONTENTS

PREFACE

This volume has developed out of a general project by the compiler to develop a broad range of materials introducing Japanese sinology to Western scholars. The types of material already available about Japanese sinology—whether published in Japanese or in Western languages—generally fall into three distinct categories, which might better be thought of as "axes." One axis is based on the **time-period** covered (e.g., bibliographies of Japanese scholarship on T'ang-period China). Another axis is based on the **discipline** covered (e.g., a bibliography of post-World War II Japanese studies on Chinese literature). And the third axis is based on the specific **scholars** doing research. The lattermost is the focus of this volume. Although there is some overlapping of categories, most available reference works are based on one of these axes. Of course, all three complement each other, being different ways in effect of slicing the same cake, each in turn producing different cross-sections of ultimately the same material.

The compiler decided to complete this volume first for a combination of reasons. In 1979 and 1980, three reference works appeared that <u>Japanese Scholars of China: A Bibliographical Handbook</u> both serves as an index to and supplements, as well as another title that was most useful for its compilation. The <u>Handbook</u> makes these works more accessible, while going beyond them in ways that complement them.

Over the past quarter of a century, a truly outstanding generation of Japanese China scholars has retired and, in many cases, passed away. The amount of material that has appeared concerning them, including bibliographies of their work, <u>Festschriften</u> dedicated to them, reprints of their collected writings, roundtable discussions of their scholarship, and reminiscences about or even by them, has been considerable. This seemed the optimum time to bring such disparate information together and to complete this volume dealing with one axis of information.

Tempe, Arizona
May 1992

ACKNOWLEDGMENTS

The help of several individuals in the preparation of this volume is gratefully acknowledged. Two scholars in Japan, Prof. Shiba Yoshinobu of The Institute of Oriental Culture, Tokyo University, and Prof. Kim Bunkyō (Kim Moonkyung) of Keiō University, kindly read through the manuscript and offered numerous corrections and suggestions. Prof. Nagatomi Masatoshi of Harvard University was extremely helpful in clarifying the background of scholars in Buddhist studies. The following also saw an earlier version of the manuscript and supplied important emendations: Prof. Joshua A. Fogel, University of California-Santa Barbara; Prof. Linda Grove, Sophia University; Dr. Joseph P. McDermott, Cambridge University; and Prof. Matsumaru Michio, The Institute of Oriental Culture, Tokyo University. None is responsible for errors that remain.

Others who provided necessary encouragement for the project and/or helped in other ways include: Dr. Glen W. Baxter, Harvard University; Prof. Timothy C. Wong, Ohio State University; Dr. Ronald C. Egan, University of California-Santa Barbara; Prof. David R. Knechtges, University of Washington; Prof. William H. Nienhauser, Jr., University of Wisconsin; Prof. Jack L. Dull, University of Washington; Prof. Hok-lam Chan, University of Washington; Mr. Frank Joseph Shulman, University of Maryland; Prof. James T.C. Liu, Princeton University; Prof. Laurence G. Thompson, University of Southern California; and Prof. Tanaka Issei, The Institute of Oriental Culture, Tokyo University.

Mr. Aoki Toshiyuki of Harvard-Yenching Library, Mr. Weiying Wan of the Asia Library at the University of Michigan, and Ms. Yoshimura Yoshiko and Mr. Nishioka Takeo of the Library of Congress provided assistance at their respective institutions.

Grant support from the Research Resources Program of the National Endowment for the Humanities made completion of the Handbook possible. Modest travel stipends from the following were also of benefit: Faculty Grant-in-Aid Program, Arizona State University; Center for Chinese Studies, University of Michigan; Center for Japanese Studies, University of Michigan; Center for Far Eastern Studies, University of Chicago; Stanford East Asian National Resource Center, Stanford University; and Northeast Asia Council, Association for Asian Studies.

Acknowledgments

The ongoing support of Dr. Julia L. Wixted and the encouragement of Ms. Claire Tierney Knapp are especially appreciated.

Calligraphy for the volume was done by Ms. Hino Ayumi of Arizona State University.

ABBREVIATIONS AND SYMBOLS

Under the names of most entrants in <u>Japanese Scholars of China: A Bibliographical Handbook</u>, one or more of the following three abbreviations appear, all explained (with full bibliographical citation) in Section III of the "Introduction"--

Lit = **Literature** volume: <u>Chūgoku bungaku semmonka jiten</u> [A Dictionary of Japanese Specialists on Chinese **Literature**].

Teng = **Teng** Ssu-yü, <u>Japanese Studies on Japan and the Far East: A Short Bibliographical and Biographical Introduction</u>.

Yen = **Yen** Shao-tang, <u>Jih-pen ti Chung-kuo hsueh-chia</u> [China Scholars of Japan].

Before each bibliographical citation under a scholar's name, one or more of the following symbols are used. They indicate that the entry that follows consists of--

   + = A bibliography of the scholar's work.

   * = A bibliography of the scholar's <u>major</u> works, a short bibliography, or bibliographical information included in a <u>nempu</u> (chronological biography) of the scholar.

        For explanation of "Buddhist studies*," see Intro., Sect. VIII, Part 1.

   • = Supplementary material on the scholar's life or work: <u>in memoriam</u> notices, personal memoirs by the scholar or by the scholar's students, roundtable discussions of the entrant's work, etc.

   ø = A <u>Festschrift</u>: a volume of articles dedicated to the scholar, including (unless otherwise indicated) a bibliography of the scholar's work. (For discussion, see Intro., Sect. VI.)

   Σ = A <u>zenshū</u> (complete edition) or other multi-volume selection of the scholar's work, including a bibliography of the scholar's publications (unless otherwise indicated).

   ∈ = A **book-length** Western-language work **BY** the scholar.

   ∋ = A Western-language book, article, or review **ABOUT** the scholar.

Within individual entries under a scholar's name, the following symbols or abbreviations may be used to indicate--

NNO = The work is "analyzed" in <u>**N**ihon **n**i **o**keru Tōyōshi rombun mokuroku</u> [Japanese Studies on Asian History]. (For explanation, see Intro., Sect. VI.)

TRNS = The work is "analyzed" in <u>Tōyōgaku ronshū naiyō sōran</u> [A Guide
            to the Contents of <u>Festschriften</u> and Other Collections of
            Articles Published in Japan concerning Oriental Studies].
            (For explanation, see Intro., Sect. VI.)
{E}   = The work contains an English- or other Western-language summary
            (or summaries) at the end of the volume.

Immediately after the names of some main entrants in the body of the <u>Handbook</u>,
the following abbreviation appears--
   NC = No Chinese characters are being given for the name in this
            entry. (For explanation, see Intro., Sect. VIII, Part 4.)

At the end of a series of entries under a scholar's name, the following abbrevi-
ations may appear--
 Intro. = "Introduction."
                ("Intro. #12" refers to cited work #12 in the "Introduc-
                tion"; "Intro., Sect. III" refers to Section III of the
                "Introduction.")
Collected Articles = "Additional Collected Articles concerning China,"
                i.e., the "Appendix."
                ("Collected Articles #24" refers to entry #24 in the "Appen-
                dix.")

INTRODUCTION

A GUIDE TO THE WORK

I

The Handbook Summarized

Japanese Scholars of China: A Bibliographical Handbook--hereafter referred to as the **Handbook**--is a reference work that leads to a wealth of bibliographical and biographical information about more than 1,500 twentieth-century Japanese scholars of China. The work serves a variety of purposes.

First, the **Handbook** offers accurate readings of the names of Japanese scholars of China.

Second, it gives short characterizations of each scholar's area of specialization.

Third, it serves as an index to, and is intended to be used in concert with, four important reference works (entries #3, #4, #5, and #12 in the "Introduction"). Three of these works give useful biographical and bibliographical information about Japanese sinological scholars; the fourth lists article-by-article (with page numbers) the contents of Festschriften and other collections of articles dealing with China.

Fourth, the **Handbook** includes as many bibliographies as possible of the work of individual Japanese China scholars. These bibliographies may appear as separate volumes, individual journal articles, appendices to scholarly studies, sections of Festschriften, or parts of complete editions of scholars' work (zenshū 全集).

Fifth, the **Handbook** lists many Japanese-language books and articles (especially those published from 1960 through 1988) that tell about China scholars in Japan. They include material such as in memoriam notices, round-table discussions of scholars' work, biographical and autobiographical sketches, and chronological biographies (nempu 年譜).

Sixth, special attention is paid to English- and other Western-language material of two kinds: 1) **articles and books** in Western langugues **ABOUT** Japanese sinologists, and 2) **book-length** volumes **BY** Japanese China scholars **in Western languages**. Furthermore, English- and other European-language materials (such as articles, book summaries, or synopses of articles) included in Japanese-language books cited are noted. Several Western-language book reviews of Japanese-language studies by scholars in Japan are also noted.

Seventh, the work has several useful indexes. The one to the surnames of Japanese scholars included in the <u>Handbook</u>, arranged alphabetically by romanized Chinese reading (Index A), should be especially helpful when checking an unfamiliar surname. (The Japanese reading can be determined in Index A by those knowing the Chinese reading for the name, and then all entries with that surname can be checked in the body of the <u>Handbook</u>.) The extensive subject index (Index H) can lead the reader to listings of Japanese scholars active in specific fields of China study. The table of books and monographs in Western languages on China by Japanese scholars (Index E), as well as the roster of non-Japanese cited in the <u>Handbook</u> (Index B), while useful to those familiar with the largely English-language work they represent, will be particularly helpful to scholars less familiar with Japanese scholarship on China or less able to utilize Japanese-language sources. And the romanized listing of the names, together with Chinese characters, of publishers cited in the <u>Handbook</u> (Index F) should help readers cite such material.

Eighth, the <u>Handbook</u> can benefit many students of **Japan, Korea, and other parts of Asia.** Numerous scholars included in the work are of importance to the study of these areas, some of them primarily so.

In sum, the <u>Handbook</u> is a guide that leads the reader to entries in other reference works containing bibliographical and biographical information about most of the scholars cited.[1] It also leads the reader to specific information about bibliographies of individual scholars' work, books and articles concerning them, and <u>Festschriften</u> dedicated to them. Furthermore, the guide may help with a variety of additional information: the correct reading of Japanese sinological scholars' names, the names of Japanese scholars active in one's field of China research, a variety of Western-language material about Japanese scholarship on China, and the proper romanization of publishers' names in Japan.

---

[1]Hence, the <u>Handbook</u> is not a bibliography of individual China scholars' work. Nor does it offer synopses of their work. Individual book titles by scholars are sometimes listed, but only because they include bibliographies of their work, contain additional biographical information about them, or comprise book-length Western-language versions of their scholarship.

II

Which Scholars Are Included in the Handbook?

The following Japanese scholars of China are included in the body of the Handbook.

A) **All entrants** appearing in Chūgoku bungaku semmonka jiten [A Dictionary of Specialists on Chinese **Literature**] and in the volume compiled by **Yen** Shao-tang, Jih-pen ti Chung-kuo hsueh-chia [China Scholars of Japan]--called respectively the "**Lit**" and "**Yen**" volumes in the Handbook (see below, Intro. #3 and #4, for full citation). Note that only entrants in these two volumes are **all** included in the Handbook.

B) Those scholars for whom two or more publications on China are listed in **Teng** Ssu-yü, Japanese Studies on Japan and the Far East: A Short Biographical and Bibliographical Introduction--termed the "**Teng**" volume in the Handbook (see below, Intro. #5, for full citation).

C) All Japanese scholars of China for whom bibliographies, in memoriam notices, or other bibliographical or biographical items are listed in annual issues of the annual "Kyoto Bibliography" for the years 1960 through 1988 (the most recent volume, for 1988, having been published in 1991):

#1   Tōyōgaku bunken ruimoku [Annual Bibliography of Oriental Studies].

東洋学文献類目

Kyōto Daigaku Jimbun Kagaku Kenkyūjo, ed. & publ.   Kyoto, 1963-, annual.

[From 1934 to 1960, the bibliography was entitled Tōyōshi kenkyū bunken ruimoku. Issues for 1961 and 1962 appear as Tōyōgaku kenkyū bunken ruimoku.]

[An absolutely invaluable series, its annual volumes list relevant scholarship for a given year on China and other parts of "Asia" (exclusive of Japan), arranged by discipline (with separate listings for articles and books in both East Asian- and Western-language sections). Each bibliography analyzes hundreds of Chinese, Japanese, and Korean-language journals, while at the same time covering a wide range of Western-language sources. Includes book reviews.]

D) Those scholars dealing with China who are listed in the following work:

#2 <u>Tōyōgaku chosaku mokurokurui sōran</u> [A Survey of Bibliographies of Writings by Japanese Scholars of Oriental Studies].

東洋学著作目録類総覧

By Kawagoe Yasuhiro. Tokyo: Chūsekisha, 1980. 108 pp. [Includes hundreds of bibliographies listed under scholar-entrants' names--as arranged in Japanese "alphabetical" (<u>gojū-on</u>) order--the readings for which are also given in <u>hiragana</u>. Date of publication and name of publisher (or journal title) are provided for bibliographies cited, but no page numbers. The work's coverage is incorporated into (and considerably supplemented by) the <u>Handbook</u>. See also p. xx, n. 3, and p. xxxviii, n. 19, below.]

E) Those Japanese sinologists whose collected writings (<u>zenshū</u>) have been published separately or whose multi-volume selected work (normally, four volumes or more) has been reprinted.

F) Those Japanese sinologists for whom a <u>Festschrift</u> has been published (see Intro., Sect. VI).

G) Japanese scholars of China who have written BOOK-LENGTH **Western-language** studies of China or whose translated work has appeared as separate BOOK-LENGTH **Western-language** works or monographs.

H) An additional one hundred Japanese China scholars, whose names and fields of study have been added to help offset the imbalance that necessarily follows from using the above criteria (see Intro., Sect. III).

I) Japanese translators, editors, and contributors cited in the <u>Handbook</u> under main entries for the above, as well as Japanese names in works cited in the "Introduction" and "Appendix." Thus, the body of the work serves as an index to all Japanese cited in the <u>Handbook</u> (complemented by Index B, "Non-Japanese Cited in the <u>Handbook</u>"), even though many of the individuals in this category are not China scholars.

· · · · ·

The <u>Handbook</u> contains only a fraction of the total number of twentieth-century Japanese scholars who have published material on China. An important volume cited below, <u>Nihon ni okeru Tōyōshi rombun mokuroku</u> (Intro. #7), which gives complete listings of article titles published in major Japanese "Oriental

Studies" journals from the late 1800s until 1962, has an index of nearly 10,000 contributors, roughly 80 percent of whom deal with China (the remainder being concerned with other parts of Asia). A large number of scholars have become active in the nearly three decades since that work appeared, not to mention those who do not fall within its purview. One can thus surmise that the pool of twentieth-century Japanese China scholars approaches 15,000.

The Handbook includes 1,644 main-entry names (namely, entries for whom a short characterization of their field of study is given), well over 90 percent of whom are concerned with China.[2] Given the criteria for inclusion, the work treats virtually all of the giants among the century's Japanese scholars of China, most major figures, a large number of well-known scholars, and a variety of less important or comparatively minor figures.

III

Reference Guides to Japanese Scholars of China

The "Lit," "Yen," and "Teng" Volumes

The Handbook is directly keyed to the following three important reference works, all dealing with Japanese scholars of China.

#3 Chūgoku bungaku semmonka jiten [A Dictionary of Japanese Specialists on Chinese Literature].

中国文学専門家事典

Nichigai Asoshieetsu, ed. & publ. Tokyo, 1980. 12,288 pp.

[Hereafter referred to as the "Lit" volume.]

#4 Jih-pen ti Chung-kuo hsueh-chia [China Scholars of Japan].

日本的中国学家

By **Yen** Shao-tang 严紹璗 . Peking: Chung-kuo She-hui K'o-hsueh Ch'u-pan-she, 1980. 7,708 pp.

[Hereafter referred to as the "**Yen**" volume.]

---

[2]If alternate name-readings and other indexed crosslistings of names are added, there are 1,915 entries in the Handbook.

#5 Japanese Studies on Japan and the Far East: A Short Biographical and Bibliographical Introduction.

By **Teng** Ssu-yü [鄧嗣禹], with the collaboration of Masuda
Kenji and Kaneda Hiromitsu. Hong Kong: Hong Kong University
Press, 1961. 10,485 pp.

[Hereafter referred to as the **"Teng"** volume.]

The following is an outline of the arrangement of the three volumes, with
discussion of the strengths and weaknesses of each. The **"Lit"** volume is an
exceptionally fine work that covers a wide range of Japanese scholars, not only
of Chinese literature but also of Chinese thought. Entries are arranged in
Japanese "alphabetical" (gojū-on 五十音) order. Normally, they include information about the field of study of a scholar, as well as the person's date of
birth, place of graduation, institutional affiliation, and other information
current at the time of its publication: home address, phone number, and a list
of professional organizations to which the entrant belongs. Following this
information is a listing of the scholar's publications: first, general writings
related to Chinese literature (and thought, broadly defined), as well as Chi-
nese-Japanese comparative studies; then, writings arranged by period of subject
matter (e.g., pre-Han, Sung, Ming, post-1949 period, etc.). Book entries
generally include date of publication, publisher, and total number of pages.
Journal articles normally include article and journal title, issue number, date
of publication, and page numbers. The "Lit" volume is a reference work that can
be used with facility, thanks both to the arrangement of publication entries
under each scholar's name by period of subject and the clear layout of the
volume. It is also quite reliable.

The **"Yen"** volume is something of a mixed bag. The extraordinary amount of
information contained within the work makes it a useful, even indispensable,
work. But the work includes entries for politicians (including some Diet
members), journalists, novelists, and others who merely have some public interest in China. Their names are all included in the Handbook, however, **so that
the Handbook can serve as a comprehensive name-entry index to the "Yen" work,
just as it does for the "Lit" volume.** Scholars are listed alphabetically in the
"Yen" volume according to the pinyin romanization of the first character of
their surnames. The work gives the date of birth, current institutional affiliation, and areas of interest for each of its numerous entrants. There follows
a generally long section outlining the career and activities of the person in

question; then comes a listing of the entrant's important works, mostly book titles. Unfortunately, all titles, whether of books or articles, are translated into Chinese, making the problem of looking up specific works by a given scholar in Western or Japanese libraries more difficult. This is especially true since editors of volumes (when different from the entrants) or joint editors are not listed. Indeed, sometimes titles are given to articles in a book edited by someone else, without mention of either the book title or editor (only the publisher being listed), which renders the task of tracking down certain entries quite frustrating. (The reader must use the name index of the annual "Kyoto Bibliography" [Intro. #1] for the year of publication cited to find further bibliographic details.) The romanized readings of scholars' names in the "Yen" volume are inaccurate with great frequency in ways that go beyond mere misprints. For different reasons--the long sections on entrants' careers, the inclusion of numerous people active in promoting Sino-Japanese friendship who have published little, and the poor method of citing Japanese scholarly writings--one suspects that the work was compiled as much to be a guide for Chinese to "visiting firemen" from Japan (academics, journalists, political figures), as it was to be a serious research tool. Notwithstanding the very real drawbacks to the volume, the "Yen" work is uniquely broad in coverage. It is an important and useful tool, especially if used in conjunction with other reference works and with the expectation of some inconvenience and inaccuracy.

The **"Teng"** bibliography, although thirty years old, is still quite valuable as a reference tool. Scholars are arranged by general field of research interest. (Half of the volume is devoted to Japanese scholars of Japanese history, literature, etc., who are not included in the Handbook.) The work gives the date of birth of each scholar, a short synopsis of the entrant's career and area of scholarly interest, and a generous sampling of the scholar's publications. The title of each publication is given in Japanese, in romanization, and in English translation (page numbers also being provided). The "Teng" volume has unique strengths. For example, it is easier for most Western scholars to scan this book's bibliographical citations than many other sources, since English translations are supplied for all titles. Those who have dealt with the sometimes highly specialized titles of Japanese scholarship on China can appreciate how helpful it is to have the subject areas of titles outside one's area of specialization clarified by a scholar of Teng Ssu-yü's standing. The meticu-

lous romanization of cited Japanese titles can also help in two ways: familiar-
izing readers with the Japanese readings of Chinese personal names, place names,
book titles, and terminology in their field of interest, and enabling them to
cite such material accurately.   The current usefulness of this handsomely
prepared volume is limited by its being dated, but it is extremely helpful in
what it does survey and often refers to forthcoming work that has since materi-
alized.

Whenever possible, **all three volumes** should be consulted for quick reference concerning an individual scholar, as these works, which account for most of
the names included in the Handbook, both overlap in treatment and reflect
certain tendencies.   The "Lit" volume is quite good in its treatment of mid-
level and older scholars of Chinese literature and thought.   The "Teng" volume,
although very helpful for the many Chinese history scholars it treats, because
of its date of publication only includes scholars who are now either quite
senior or deceased.   And the "Yen" volume, as noted, while idiosyncratic in
coverage, works from a broad base.

*   *   *   *   *

The other criteria used for inclusion of scholars in the Handbook also
contribute to the same result--coverage of scholars who are generally older,
more established, or deceased.   Scholars are included if A) bibliographies of
their work have been published, B) Festschriften have been dedicated to them, C)
their collected writings (zenshū) have been published, D) book-length work of
theirs has appeared in a Western language, or E) in memoriam notices, etc.,
about them were published from 1960 to 1988.

If only these criteria were used, few younger Japanese China scholars
would be included, and the coverage of mid-level scholars would be skewed: many
of those in Chinese literature and thought would be included (since they appear
in the "Lit" volume), whereas comparatively few in Chinese history and other
fields would appear.   As a partial corrective to this imbalance, the compiler,
in consultation with scholars noted in the "Acknowledgments," has added the
names of one hundred Japanese China scholars to the Handbook, mostly in Chinese
history.   Unlike other main entries in the volume, these names do not lead to
additional bibliographical or biographical information about the scholar in
question, other than a characterization of the entrant's field of study.   For
additional bibliographical information, the reader should check under the

person's name both in recent issues of the annual "Kyoto Bibliography" (Intro. #1) and in the card catalogs of major sinological collections (including more recently published ones for Harvard-Yenching Library and the University of Michigan).

IV

Personal Names and Fields of Study of Japanese Scholars of China

Personal Names

Proper readings of the names of Japanese scholars of China, like the readings for Japanese names in general, are difficult to determine. A final reading for each of the scholars included in the Handbook was determined by first consulting the following four reference works:

#6   <u>Japanese Researchers in Asian Studies</u>.

Enoki Kazuo, ed. Tokyo: The Centre for East Asian Cultural Studies (Directories No. 2), 1963. 5,281 pp.

[Arranged by discipline, the work gives the name (in Japanese and romanization), date of birth, institutional affiliation, date of university graduation (along with the name of the institution and of the academic faculty from which the person graduated), and area of scholarly interest for hundreds of scholars of "Asian Studies." The name index in the back (pp. 229-266) is especially useful.]

#7   <u>Nihon ni okeru Tōyōshi rombun mokuroku</u>   [Japanese Studies on Oriental History].

日本における東洋史論文目録

Tōyōshi Kenkyū Rombun Mokuroku Henshū Iinkai, ed. Tokyo: Nihon Gakujutsu Shinkōkai, 1964-67. 4 vols.

[Referred to in the Handbook as **"NNO."**]

[An article-by-article listing of all studies concerning "Oriental History" (exclusive of Japan) in major periodicals and other collective publications in Japan from ca. 1880 to 1962. Vol. 4 (1967) is invaluable as an index to the names of Japa-

nese scholars of Asian studies included in the preceding three
volumes. Names are listed in alphabetical order, romanized and
with characters. See also Intro., Sect. VI.]

#2 Tōyōgaku chosaku mokurokurui sōran [A Survey of Bibliographies
     of Writings by Japanese Scholars of Oriental Studies], dis-
     cussed above (p. xiv).[3]

#3 The "Lit" volume, Chūgoku bungaku semmonka jiten [A Dictionary
     of Japanese Specialists on Chinese Literature], discussed above
     (pp. xv-xvi).

What is important about these four works is that, being specialized
compilations about Japanese sinologists, they are far more reliable as sources
of readings than other reference materials. They are prime sources for the
readings of scholars' names in the Handbook, and even they differ among themselves in a significant number of cases.

For the proper reading of names of modern China scholars in Japan, the
following two works proved particularly helpful:

#8 Kindai Chūgoku kankei bunken mokuroku: 1945-1978 nen [A Bibli-
     ography of Studies on Modern China: 1945-1978].

     近代中国関係文献目録 ─ 1945-1978年 ─

     Kindai Chūgoku Kankei Bunken Mokuroku Kankō Iinkai, ed. Tokyo:
     Chūō Kōron Bijutsu Shuppan, 1980. 7,640 pp.

     [Arranged by scholars' names in gojū-on order, this major ref-
     erence tool lists almost all scholarship on modern Chinese
     history published in Japan from the end of World War II until
     1978.]

#9 "Modern China Studies in Japan."

     Mori Masao, ed. Tokyo: The Centre for East Asian Cultural
     Studies, 1982. Pamphlet. 7,45 pp.

---

[3]Notwithstanding the helpfulness of this work, there are bibliographies of
individual scholars' work omitted from it that have been included in the Handbook. Most came from checking the annual issues of the "Kyoto Bibliography"
(Intro. #1). Appendix A ("Bibliography of Works of Individual Scholars," pp.
171-180) of the following work also yielded a few items:
     Bibliography of Bibliographies of East Asian Studies in Japan.
     Goto Kimpei, ed. Tokyo: The Centre for East Asian Cultural Studies,
     1964. (Directories No. 3.) 1,2,190,16 pp.

[This pamphlet gives in English only, without any Japanese, the names, addresses, institutional affiliations, and areas of specialization of 315 Japanese scholars of modern China. Entrants are arranged according to general field, with an alphabetical index to all included.][4]

The following two works also served as important authorities for the readings of many names:

#10 Kokuritsu Kokkai Toshokan choshamei tenkyoroku: Meiji ikō Nihon jimmei [A Source Authority for Authors' Names in the National Diet Library: Post-Meiji Japanese Names].

国立国会図書館著者名典拠録一明治以降日本人名一

Kokuritsu Kokkai Toshokan Shūshū Seiribu, ed. Tokyo: Kinokuniya. 4 vols.

Vol. 1 1979 A-M. 5,1520 pp.

Vol. 2 1979 N-Z. pp. 1521-3045.

Vol. 3 1981 Tsuiroku 追録 (Apr. 1978-March 1981). 1,592 pp.

Vol. 4 1979 Index to Vols. 1 and 2. 1,84 pp.

[The volumes are arranged alphabetically by old-style romanization: e.g., Matsumura Takashi is listed under "Matumura Takasi."]

---

[4]There are two drawbacks to the booklet, both remedied in the Handbook for entries it treats: no Chinese characters are given for scholars' names, and long marks are not included in the romanization of names.
    Two additional works are invaluable for presenting English-language introductions to and summaries of Japanese scholarship on modern Chinese history. They can also serve as sources for the readings of scholars' names for the modern China field:
    Japanese Studies of Modern China: A Bibliographical Guide to Historical and Social-Science Research on the 19th and 20th Centuries. By John King Fairbank, Banno Masataka, and Yamamoto Sumiko. Rutland, Vt. and Tokyo: Charles E. Tuttle, 1955; rpt. 1971. 9,331 pp.
And--
    Japanese Studies of Modern China since 1953: A Bibliographical Guide to Historical and Social Science Research on the Nineteenth and Twentieth Centuries, Supplementary Volume for 1953-1969. By Kamachi Noriko, John K. Fairbank, and Ichiko Chūzō. Cambridge, East Asian Research Center, Harvard University, 1975. 23,603 pp.

#11 <u>Kenkyūsha, kenkyū kadai sōran, 1984-nempan: Jimbun, shakai</u>

<u>kagaku hen</u> [A Compendium of Researchers and Research Subjects,

1984 Edition: Volumes for the Humanistic and Social Sciences.]

研究者・研究課題総覧 1984年版 ―人文・社会科学編―

Mombushō Gakujutsu Kokusai-kyoku, ed.   Tokyo: Nihon Gakujutsu

Shinkōkai, 1984. 2 vols.

  Vol. 1 Jimbun kagaku. 1,5,1,1568 pp.

  Vol. 2 Shakai kagaku, Sakuin.   1 p., pp. 1569-2123, and

          1,119,1,136,172 pp.

[This set of volumes can be used roughly as one would consult <u>A</u>

<u>Directory of American Scholars</u>. Eighth edition. (New York: R.R.

Bowker, 1982.) 4 vols.]

Additional sources of readings included the following: the comments of
Japanese sinologists who read the <u>Handbook</u> in draft form (see the "Acknowledg-
ments"), catalog cards for the library collections used in compiling the <u>Hand</u>-
<u>book</u>, English-language tables of contents of Japanese journals cited, and
English-language title-pages added to book-length studies in Japanese.

    When more than one reading for a scholar's name emerged, a final rendering
was determined by looking at the number of sources using each reading and taking
into account their relative reliability. The other readings were then **crosslisted** in the <u>Handbook</u>. These crosslisted readings include ones that may or may
not be "correct"--correctness being a thornier question than one might think.
Additionally, some exceptional readings were added, including ones that appear
in the "Teng" volume (Intro. #5) as well as a few from the catalog cards of
major libraries, simply because users of the <u>Handbook</u> will have to deal with
them on a practical basis.[5] Thus, the compiler was more interested in listing
a scholar in the <u>Handbook</u> under a reliable, accurate reading of that person's
name, while crosslisting other attested readings (and even some doubtful ones)
for the practical situations that a user of the work would likely encounter,

---

[5]The Library of Congress, for example, files works by Uno Tetsuto under
"Uno Tetsujin," and the National Diet Library lists Mikami Tsugio's writings
under "Mikami Tsuguo"--readings found attested nowhere else.

than in trying to delimit a <u>single</u> (sometimes ultimately elusive) final reading.[6]

Fields of Study

The characterization of a scholar's area of specialization that appears
after the entrant's name in <u>Handbook</u> main entries is intended simply to be a
rough index to the scholar's field of study. Descriptions found in <u>Japanese
Researchers in Asian Studies</u> (Intro. #6) were used as the basis for many of
these characterizations. For most entrants, material found in the reference
works cited after their names was summarized. This has resulted in acceptable
characterizations of well-known scholars, as they are cited in more than one
general reference guide, and bibliographies of their work are often available as
a further aid. For scholars whose names appear in the <u>Handbook</u> with only a
"Lit," "Yen," or "Teng" reference after their name, material about them found in
those works was summarized. Although in such cases the compiler of the <u>Handbook</u>
was basically a hostage to the three sources each with its own limitations of
coverage, this procedure has the virtue at least of putting forward a scholar's
name in an initial context and of leading the reader to the type of material
indicated. Whether or not it gives a rounded characterization of the scholar's
work, however, depends in each case.

For several entrants listed in the <u>Handbook</u>, there are published collected
works (<u>zenshū</u>) of ten, fifteen, or twenty volumes of wide-ranging scholarship.
Others included here may have fewer than five articles to their name. The
characterizations of both can appear vague (e.g., "Chinese thought"), because
the writings of the one may be so broad and those of the other so unfocused.
This is to say nothing of the vast majority of scholars who fall somewhere
in-between.

Too much specificity in characterizing a scholar can be equally mislead-
ing. To cite an example: three Japanese scholars, in particular, are associated with the study of the thirteenth-century Chinese poet, Yuan Hao-wen. Two of
them, Oguri Eiichi and Suzuki Shūji, have written books on Yuan Hao-wen; one,

---

[6]The readings of names in the "Yen" volume (Intro. #4) were not relied upon
at all. While serving as an index to that work, the <u>Handbook</u> also corrects its
innumerable misreadings and misromanizations of Japanese scholars' names.

Nakamura Yoshihiro, has written a handful of articles on the figure. Since Nakamura's writings have been almost solely on Yuan Hao-wen, his field of interest can be easily specified: "Chinese poetry, Chin period, Yuan Hao-wen." Oguri Eiichi's published interests are sufficiently wider to warrant classifying him as follows: "Chinese literature, Chin and Yuan periods." But Suzuki Shūji, the scholar who has published the most on the poet, is the author of several other books on Chinese poetry and literature; thus, the characterization of him becomes "Chinese literature, esp. traditional poetry." The result is that description of only one of the three scholars' work refers specifically to Yuan Hao-wen, and that person's studies are not necessarily the most noteworthy or extensive of the three.[7] The example points up a more general problem. It would be impractical (easily doubling the size of the Handbook), and would defeat the purpose of the short encapsulations, to expand the characterizations with too many specific examples. For the same reasons, in Index H ("Scholars in the Handbook, Listed by Fields of Study") the categories are purposely kept fairly broad.

In characterizing scholars' fields of study--both in the body of the work and in Index H--"Classical Chinese thought" refers to the study of classical texts through the Han period; "Modern Chinese history" signifies the period from the Opium War until the present; and "Chinese vernacular fiction" refers to premodern fiction in the vernacular language, as distinct from "Modern Chinese literature" (from ca. 1917 to the present).[8]

---

[7]Given the criteria for inclusion, a fourth younger scholar was left out of the Handbook whose work on Yuan Hao-wen merits as much attention as the writing of Nakamura Yoshihiro.

[8]Note that periods of history treated in areas adjacent to China are sometimes given in sinocentric terms: e.g., "Mongolian history, Ming period."

V

Sample Entries from the <u>Handbook</u>

The following three sample entries should help clarify the use of the <u>Handbook</u>. Other explanatory material concludes the section.

SAMPLE ONE

Morohashi Tetsuji 諸橋 轍次 Chinese thought, classical and Sung periods. Chinese language and lexicography.

Lit 264, Yen 631, Teng #671.

- <u>"Dai Kan-Wa jiten" o yomu</u> [293,1 pp.].
  『大漢和辞典』を読む
  Kida Jun'ichirō, ed. Tokyo: Taishūkan Shoten, 1986.
  [Among various articles on Morohashi's monumental Japanese dictionary of Chinese is one by the editor (pp. 11-62), telling how Morohashi actually compiled the work.]

- * Shibun 87 (1983), 86 pp.
  [The entire issue is devoted to <u>in memoriam</u> notices and reminiscences about Morohashi; a short bibliography of his major works appears on p. 6.]

Σ <u>Morohashi Tetsuji chosakushū</u>, vol. 10 (1977), 627-631.
  Tokyo: Taishūkan Shoten, 1975-1977. 10 vols.

- * Kambun kyōshitsu 75 (March 1966), 13.

- Ibid., 16-38.

- Tōhōgaku 26 (July 1963), 108-128, and 27 (Feb. 1964), 118-133.

ø <u>Morohashi hakushi koki shukuga kinen rombunshū</u> [2,3,17,3, 730,3 pp.], 13-17.
  Morohashi Tetsuji sensei koki shukuga kinenkai, ed. & publ.
  Tokyo, 1953.
  TRNS #237, NNO 3:419-420.

Morohashi Tetsuji's name is given in both its romanized and Japanese forms, along with a short characterization of his area of specialization. He is listed as being included in all three general reference works about Japanese sinologists to which the Handbook is keyed (see Intro., Sect. III): on pages 264 and 631 respectively of the "Lit" and "Yen" volumes, and as entry #671 of the "Teng" volume.

A symbol precedes each of the entries that follow (note "Abbreviations and Symbols," pp. ix-x). The "•" tells the reader that an entry contains supplementary material on the scholar's life or work: in memoriam notices, memoirs by or about the scholar, roundtable discussions of the entrant's work, and the like. An asterisk "*" precedes an entry containing abbreviated bibliographical information about the scholar. The "Σ" indicates a "zenshū" entry, i.e., a multi-volume reprint of the scholar's works. And the "ø" points to a Festschrift dedicated to the scholar (see Intro., Sect. VI).

All "Σ" (zenshū) and "ø" (Festschriften) entries, unless otherwise specified, include bibliographies of their subjects' work. The specific volume and page numbers cited in zenshū entries indicate a bibliography of the scholar-entrant's work. Thus, a bibliography of the writings of Morohashi Tetsuji is found on pp. 627-631 of volume 10 of his zenshū (the entry preceded by an "Σ"). Similarly, the specific page numbers cited in a Festschrift entry--namely, the unbracketed page numbers that follow the listing of a work's total page count (in brackets)--always indicate a bibliography for the dedicatee of the Festschrift. Thus, a bibliography of Morohashi Tetsuji's work appears on pp. 13-17 of the Festschrift cited here (the entry preceded by an "ø"), as indicated by the unbracketed numbers that follow the total page count for the volume: 2,3,17,3,730,3 pp. (the bibliography being comprised of pp. 13-17 of the 17-pp. section).[9]

No Chinese characters are given for zenshū titles or for most Festschrift main titles. Only subject-significant (titles or) subtitles of Festschriften are transcribed in Japanese in the body of the Handbook (see Intro., Sect. VI). The title of the first volume cited above is given in Japanese, as are all such titles that otherwise might be unclear if only romanized. The characters making up the other two book titles, as well as those for the editor and publisher of the Festschrift (other than characters for the name "Morohashi Tetsuji"), can be found readily in Index C ("Japanese Phrases Cited in the Handbook, with Chinese

---

[9]The same convention is followed in citing bibliographies of scholars' works that appear in books by or about the scholar: the unbracketed page numbers after the total page count refer to the bibliography.

Characters and English Equivalents"). The characters for the editor of the first volume, Kida Jun'ichirō, can be found by looking up his name in the body of the Handbook, which acts as an index to all Japanese cited in the Handbook. Index D ("East Asian-Language Journals Cited, with Chinese Characters") gives the Chinese characters for the more than 200 Japanese-language journals cited in the volume, as well as several Chinese-language journals; one can find there the Japanese for Shibun, Kambun kyōshitsu, and Tōhōgaku.[10] The characters for Taishūkan Shoten, the publisher of two of the works listed, appear in Index F ("Publishers of East Asian-Language Books Cited, with Chinese Characters").

There are two Kambun kyōshitsu entries, because the cited sections of the journal (p. 13 and pp. 16-38) are separated by two pages. If the sections had run continuously, they would have been conflated into one citation, with the dual symbols "•*" preceding it and a single set of page numbers cited--as was the case for the Shibun citation near the beginning of the entry. Note, however, that for journal articles having **both** a full bibliography **and** supplementary material about an author, the following rule was followed: if the two parts combined total **ten or fewer pages**, they become a single entry in the Handbook preceded by a "+" (the symbol normally used to indicate a **separate bibliography** of a scholar's writing); if they total **more than ten pages**, the material is divided into separate "+" and "•" entries.

Note the "**TRNS**" and "**NNO**" numbers at the end of the Festschrift entry cited in this sample. These indicate that, both in entry #237 of Tōyōgaku ronshū naiyō sōran (i.e., "TRNS," Intro. #12), and on pp. 419-420 of volume 3 of Nihon ni okeru Tōyōshi rombun mokuroku (i.e., "NNO," Intro. #7), there are complete listings of the authors, article titles, and article page-numbers of the Asia-related scholarly contributions in this volume. (For fuller discussion, see Intro., Sect. VI.)

As is true throughout the Handbook, **entries are in reverse chronological order**: that is, most recent publications come first.[11] Hence, the Morohashi

---

[10]Note that journal titles in East Asian languages appear with such frequency in the Handbook that they are not underlined, except in running text.

[11]The only exceptions to this are series of citations from different issues of the same journal, which are listed together, and citations of two-part contributions (like the Tōhōgaku entry cited here), which only nominally fall out of reverse chronological order.

Tetsuji citations are dated as follows: 1986, 1983, 1975-77, 1966, 1963-64, and 1953.

SAMPLE TWO

Sanetō Keishū   実藤惠秀   Modern Sino-Japanese historical rela-
                                 tions. Modern Chinese language and
                                 literature.

Lit 124, Yen 386, Teng #579.

• Shakai kagaku tōkyū (Waseda Daigaku) 33.1 (Sept. 1987), 33-59.

• Tōyō bungaku kenkyū 16 (March 1968), 29-31.

+ Gakujutsu kenkyū (Jimbun kagaku, shakai kagaku hen) 16 (1967), 209-210.

+ Kokubungaku kenkyū (Waseda Daigaku) 36 (Oct. 1967), 129-130.

• Ibid., 1-15.

Also listed under Collected Articles #31.

Certain items distinguish this sample entry from the preceding one. Bibliographies of the scholar's writings are indicated by the two **plus** "+" prefixes. This is the standard symbol throughout the Handbook preceding an entry for a **separate bibliography of a scholar's writings** (other than Festschriften or zenshū, prefixed "ø" and "Σ," which are automatically assumed to include scholars' bibliographies). Thus, full bibliographies of Sanetō Keishū's writings appear on pp. 209-210 and pp. 129-130 of the respective issues of the two journals cited. **"Also listed under Collected Articles #31"** leads the reader to the "Appendix" of the Handbook ("Additional Volumes of Collected Articles concerning China"), where Sanetō Keishū is listed under entry #31 as the editor of a volume of articles published in 1942 entitled Kindai Shina shisō.

SAMPLE THREE

Hoshi Ayao   星斌夫   Chinese socio-economic history, Ming and
                               Ch'ing periods, esp. Grand Canal
                               transportation.

Yen 532, Teng #484.

ø Hoshi hakushi taikan kinen Chūgokushi ronshū [23,422,3 pp.],
   5-18.

中国史論集

Hoshi Ayao sensei taikan kinen jigyōkai, ed. & publ. Yamagata,
1978.

TRNS #223.

+ Yamagata Daigaku kiyō (Jimbun kagaku) 9.1 (Feb. 1978), 3 pp.

∈ Idem, The Ming Tribute Grain System [3,112 pp.].

Translated by Mark Elvin. Ann Arbor: Center for Chinese Studies, University of Michigan, 1969.

The following should be noted in this sample. First, there is no entry
for Hoshi Ayao in the "Lit" volume; he appears only in the "Yen" and "Teng"
reference works. Second, Chinese characters (as discussed in Intro., Sect. VI)
are supplied only for the subject-significant subtitle of the Hoshi Festschrift,
Chūgokushi ronshū. (The characters for the discrete words in the rest of the
title, other than Hoshi's name, can be looked up in Index C: "Japanese Phrases
Cited in the Handbook, with Chinese Characters and English Equivalents.")
Third, the prefix "∈" indicates a book-length Western-language volume BY the
scholar. Finally, the "Idem" in this entry, as elsewhere in the Handbook,
refers to the scholar-entrant under whom it is listed (i.e., Hoshi Ayao) and not
to the author or editor of a work that might fall between the scholar-entrant's
name and the entry where "Idem" appears.

Other Explanatory Material

No attempt has been made to rank the material under scholars' names in the
Handbook, other than to identify with a symbol the nature of an entry and to
list items in reverse chronological order. There are various reasons for this.
The items listed are diverse and their ranking would depend on the end a re-
searcher had in mind: e.g., the compilation of a bibliography, the preparation
of a biography, or research on a "school" or group of scholars. The supplementary material in many cases is unique and difficult to categorize, to say
nothing of prioritize; and some readers would want to sort through all available material for themselves in any case. Finally, multiple bibliographies,

although seemingly redundant, often complement or overlap each other in cover-age.   Even with bibliographies that are virtually identical, it is best to provide as complete a listing as possible, since only one may be available at a reader's library.[12]

In the <u>Handbook</u>, all materials are listed that turned up as a result of following the procedures outlined in Section II of the "Introduction."   The entries that have resulted, when consulted, would in turn lead to still more items about an entrant, and so on.   For example, the <u>Handbook</u> lists those items concerning Takahashi Kazumi that resulted from taking the steps indicated, and makes a special point of noting listings they contain of additional material about him.   But no attempt is made to try to include all of the items that these listings refer to, for this would result in a virtually endless proliferation of material.   The <u>Handbook</u> serves its function by leading to such material about the scholars it treats, noting special listings therein of additional readings.

To update material about any scholar listed in the <u>Handbook</u>--be the point of departure the "Lit," "Yen," or "Teng" volumes and/or bibliographies of the scholar's work cited in the <u>Handbook</u>--the reader should check under the en-trant's name in those issues of the annual "Kyoto Bibliography" (Intro. #1) that postdate the last reliable information available from these initial sources.

VI

<u>Festschriften</u> and Collected Articles concerning China

<u>Festschriften</u> are volumes of collected articles contributed by students, friends, and colleagues in honor of a distinguished scholar.[13]   Although they usually commemorate a festive occasion, such as a seventy-seventh birthday, the term is used here to include also collections of articles published in posthu-mous honor of a scholar.

The publishing of <u>Festschriften</u> is a popular custom in Japan.   Many important articles of Japanese scholarship on China are located in these vol-

---

[12]The compiler of the <u>Handbook</u> personally examined more than 90 percent of the items cited in the <u>Handbook</u>.

[13]<u>Festschriften</u> is the plural form of the word, <u>Festschrift</u> the singular.

umes.   As _Festschriften_ usually include bibliographies of the dedicatees' writings, and often other biographical information as well, they are important sources of information on Japanese scholars.   Also, because much of Japanese scholarship revolves around groups or coteries of scholars, _Festschriften_ help identify those individuals who might be grouped together.   In addition, much interesting sinological work in Western languages, by Japanese and non-Japanese alike, lies virtually buried in these volumes.

Usually, a single word in the title of a _Festschrift_ will tell the reader the occasion that prompted its compilation.   If the title contains one of the following words, the work will be in honor of the dedicatee's--

beiju	米寿	88th birthday
hakuju	白寿	99th birthday
kakō	華甲	61st birthday
kanreki	還暦	60th birthday
kiju	喜寿	77th birthday
koki	古稀	70th birthday
shōju	頌寿	long life
taikan	退官	retirement
taikyū	退休	retirement

Every effort has been made in the _Handbook_ to identify as many _Festschriften_ dedicated to China scholars in Japan as possible, to give information about bibliographies and biographical material they contain, and to highlight whatever Western-language material (articles or synopses of articles) they include.

Fortunately, a comparatively recent Japanese publication complements the _Handbook_ in this undertaking.   It prints out article-by-article (giving the initial page number for each citation) the contents of 254 volumes of collected scholarly articles published in Japan, listing only those articles whose subject matter is related to Asia (i.e., _Tōyōgaku_, "Oriental Studies" exclusive of Japan):

#12 <u>Tōyōgaku ronshū naiyō sōran</u> [A Guide to the Contents of <u>Fest-</u>
<u>schriften</u> and Other Collections of Articles Published in Japan
concerning Oriental Studies].

東洋学論集内容総覧

Kokusho Kankōkai, ed. & publ. Compiled by Kawagoe Yasuhiro and
Iwashige Hidemaru. Tokyo, 1980. 2,10,1,184,28 pp.

[Hereafter referred to as **"TRNS."**]

Many volumes listed in the "TRNS" work are <u>Festschriften</u>. As they are
associated with individual scholars and usually include bibliographies of their
work, they are listed, with appropriate "TRNS" entry numbers, in the body of the
<u>Handbook</u> under their dedicatees' names (e.g., in the sample entry in Sect. V
above, "TRNS #237" is given under the Morohashi Tetsuji <u>Festschrift</u>).

Volumes listed in the "TRNS" work that are not <u>Festschriften</u> dedicated to
individual scholars (e.g., volumes commemorating the twenty-fifth and fiftienth
anniversaries of the founding of the Tōhō Gakkai) are listed, with appropriate
"TRNS" entry numbers, in the "Appendix" to the <u>Handbook</u> ("Additional Volumes of
Collected Articles concerning China"), as long as such volumes contain at least
three China-related articles.

The "TRNS" work offers important advantages. It enables the user to scan
the contents of dozens of volumes having a wide range of articles about China,
especially those volumes unavailable at the user's own library. Utilizing its
index of contributors, one can readily check the titles of articles by scholars
in one's field of interest. And a reader can track down the title of a volume
seen earlier, for which there is no other recollection than the name of one of
its contributors.

There are two drawbacks to the "TRNS" work, both largely remedied by the
<u>Handbook</u>. First, there is no index to the dedicatees of <u>Festschriften</u>: entries
are simply arranged in Japanese <u>gojū-on</u> order according to the full title of the
work in question. Since such titles generally omit the first names of scholars
who are being honored, there is no way of telling which of sometimes several
possible scholars with the same surname is being honored by the <u>Festschrift</u>.
For example, listing #200 in the "TRNS" work, <u>Hashimoto hakushi koki kinen</u>
<u>Tōyōgaku ronshū</u> [In Commemoration of the Seventieth Birthday of Dr. Hashimoto:
A Collection of Articles on Oriental Studies], does not tell the user if the
Japanese scholar of Asian studies to whom the work is dedicated is Hashimoto

Hōkei, Hashimoto Jun, Hashimoto Mantarō, Hashimoto Masukichi, Hashimoto Takakatsu, Hashimoto Takashi, or some other Hashimoto. The Handbook clarifies this
by listing the volume under Hashimoto Jun.

Second, the works analyzed in "TRNS" are listed under only one title; the
subtitles (or "co-titles") of these collections are often as important as the
nominal full title under which one finds them in "TRNS." Subtitles often give
the only clue to the contents of a volume, and sub- and co-titles are sometimes
understandably but misleadingly used by scholars and librarians when citing and
cataloging these works. For example, it is the sub- or co-title to the Festschrift dedicated to Aoyama Sadao, Aoyama hakushi koki kinen Sōdaishi ronsō [In
Commemoration of the Seventieth Birthday of Dr. Aoyama: A Collection of Articles on Sung-Period History], that tells the user what the subject matter of the
volume is. In scholarly writings one sees the work cited in both its full and
abbreviated (Sōdaishi ronsō) forms.

In the Handbook, this problem is handled in two ways. The titles of
Festschriften are given in the body of the Handbook in full romanization, but
Chinese characters and underlined romanization are provided for only those parts
of titles that indicate subject matter.[14] For example, the volume just noted
is listed in the Handbook under Aoyama Sadao as--

Aoyama hakushi koki kinen Sōdaishi ronsō
宋代史論叢

The complete title is given in romanization, but only the subject-significant
part of it is underlined and given in Japanese. And in the "Appendix," which
includes several problematic titles, numerous crosslistings are provided.

More than sixty Festschriften are cited in the body of the Handbook that
are not found in the "TRNS" work, about half of which do not postdate the
compilation of that work. Basically, three additional resources were used to
supplement the "TRNS" volume: the annual "Kyoto Bibliography" for the years
1960 through 1988 (Intro. #1); the compiler's own scanning of titles in East

---

[14]The entire title of any Festschrift without a subject-significant co- or
subtitle is underlined. Chinese characters for the phrasings in these titles,
if not supplied with the entry, can be found in Index C.

Asian collections, especially Harvard-Yenching Library; and other bibliographies that yielded a few titles that would otherwise have been omitted.[15]

Since it is of importance to know if a <u>Festschrift</u> or other collection of articles is analyzed in the "TRNS" volume, whenever one is not it is indicated as follows: "**TRNS:oo.**" Another work that, like the "TRNS" volume, gives the complete contents (authors, article titles, and article page-numbers) for several <u>Festschriften</u> and other collections of articles concerning China is the "**NNO**" volume: <u>Nihon ni okeru Tōyōshi rombun mokuroku</u> [Japanese Studies on Oriental History] (Intro. #7). This information appears at the back of Volume 3 of the four-volume work. For the reader's convenience, the <u>Handbook</u> notes which volumes of collected articles are also analyzed in the "NNO" work. (See, for example, the sample entry in Sect. V above: "NNO 3:419-420" appears, in addition to the "TRNS" number [#237], for the Morohashi Tetsuji <u>Festschrift</u> cited.)

Not all of the 254 <u>Festschriften</u> analyzed in the "TRNS" volume are included in the <u>Handbook</u>. Those dealing with South Asia, the Near or Middle East, Southeast Asia, and Korea are omitted. However, any volumes that contain three or more articles about China are listed. In those instances where <u>Festschriften</u> are dedicated to scholars totally outside the China field but the volume contains the requisite number of China-related articles, the scholar's name and the <u>Festschrift</u> title appear in the <u>Handbook</u>. However, the scholar's field of specialization is enclosed <u>in parentheses</u>, and page numbers for any bibliography of that person's work are omitted.[16]

---

[15]Namely--
"Festschriften für japanische Wissenschaftler in der ostasiatischen Sammlung der Staatsbibliothek Preussischer Kulturbesitz."
By Eva Kraft. Berlin: Staatsbibliothek Preussischer Kulturbesitz, 1972. Pamphlet. 1,22,1 pp.
And--
<u>Author Catalogues of Western Sinologists</u>.
By Donald Leslie and Jeremy Davidson. Canberra: Department of Far Eastern History, Research School of Pacific Studies, Australian National University, 1966. 57,1,257,1 pp.

[16]By way of example, under the main entry for Kanazawa Shōzaburō, the scholar's field of specialization, "History of Japanese language," is given in parentheses. Such characterizations help suggest the subject area of any China-related articles in the <u>Festschrift</u> cited: for example, in the volume noted any China-related articles are likely to be on the Chinese language--a surmise that can be easily verified, even if the Festschrift is not readily available, by checking the "TRNS" and "NNO" volumes as cited under the entry.

Individual journal issues dedicated to scholars are normally already included in the <u>Handbook</u> because they contain bibliographical and/or biographical information about the scholar. However, they are <u>not</u> listed as <u>Festschriften</u> (with the prefix "ø"), unless published as separate books or unless analyzed separately in the "TRNS" or "NNO" works.

The works listed in the "Appendix" ("Additional Volumes of Collected Articles concerning China") complement the more than 150 <u>Festschriften</u> cited in the body of the <u>Handbook</u> by listing collections of articles that are not dedicated to individual scholars. These two types of work, a) <u>Festschriften</u> and b) other volumes of collected articles by several authors, are "of the same cloth" for sinological purposes for three reasons: Japanese scholars and librarians treat the two the same (one term is used for both, <u>ronshū</u> 論集); the reference tool that optimizes their use (the "TRNS" volume) treats them together; and both tend to reflect scholarly coteries in their groupings of contributors. The "Appendix" includes only those volumes listed in the "TRNS" work that contain the requisite three China-related articles. Referred to as "Collected Articles" when cross-referenced elsewhere in the <u>Handbook</u>, the "Appendix" contains helpful information on numerous works particularly troublesome to check in library collections.

Although there may be some minor inconsistencies in citation, the "publisher" given for <u>Festschriften</u> and other volumes of collected articles is normally the <u>hakkōsho</u> 発行所 (issuing agency) listed on the publication information page, and not the <u>hatsubaisho</u> 発売所 (distributor) or <u>insatsujo</u> 印刷所 (printer), should these differ from the former.

VII

Book-Length Western-Language Works of Japanese Sinology

In order to make more accessible the writings of Japanese scholars of China, the <u>Handbook</u> lists as many of their **Western-language BOOKS AND MONOGRAPHS** as possible. (To also include **Western-language ARTICLES** by these scholars would result in a listing of **well over a thousand** titles; Western-language **articles BY** scholars named in the <u>Handbook</u> are **NOT** included.) English- and other European-language articles (and several reviews) are included in the <u>Handbook</u>

only when they are **about** scholars and their work, not **by** them. Even though some of the books and monographs cited in the Handbook are shorter than many substantial Western-language articles published by the same scholars, it is simplest for bibliographical purposes to keep the distinction being made here, since books, monographs, and edited volumes appear individually in library catalogs and book listings. Note Index E ("China-Related Western-Language Books and Monographs by Japanese Scholars of China"), arranged alphabetically by author, which gives the titles of all such Western-language books and monographs cited in the Handbook.[17] (Many Western-language books not related to China by scholars in the Handbook are noted at the end of individual entries, but are neither cited in full nor included in Index E.)[18]

The following book-length Western-language translations of Japanese scholarship on China are **not** included in the body of the Handbook, as they are collections of translated articles by several scholars and are not identifiable with any specific Japanese author or editor. They are listed here alphabetically:

#13 "Chinese Fiction and Drama." Acta Asiatica 32 (1977). Entire issue.

#14 "Historical Studies on Central Asia in Japan." Acta Asiatica 34 (1978). Entire issue.

#15 "Japanese Studies in Social and Economic History of the Ming Dynasty." Acta Asiatica 38 (1980). Entire issue.

#16 A Pictorial Encyclopedia of The Oriental Arts. Vol. 1: China.

  Pt. 1 The Yin, Chou, and Warring States Period - The Six Dynasties Period (c. 1355 B.B.-588 A.D.). 32 pp. plus 193 pl.

  Pt. 2 The Sui and T'ang Periods - The Ming and Ch'ing Periods (589-1912). 31 pp. plus 177 pl.

Kadokawa Shoten, ed. New York: Crown Publishers, 1969.

---

[17]The names of Japanese authors, publishers, translators, etc., of Western-language works are cited in the Handbook as they appear in the original Western-language publications, regardless of inconsistencies in romanization or in the use of long marks.

[18]For example, see the entries under Hirakawa Akira and Satō Masahiko.

#17 <u>State and Society in China: Japanese Perspectives on Ming-Qing</u>
    <u>Social and Economic History</u>.
    Linda Grove and Christian Daniels, eds. Tokyo: University of
    Tokyo Press, 1984. 520 pp.

#18 "Studies in Social and Political History of the Yüan Dynasty."
    <u>Acta Asiatica</u> 45 (1983). Entire issue.

#19 "Studies in the History of Chinese Science." <u>Acta Asiatica</u> 36
    (1979). Entire issue.

#20 "Taoism." <u>Acta Asiatica</u> 27 (1974). Entire issue.

#21 <u>Transport in Transition: The Evolution of Traditional Shipping</u>
    <u>in China</u>.
    Translated by Andrew J. Watson. Ann Arbor: Center for Chinese
    Studies, University of Michigan, 1972. 5,7,93,1 pp.

#22 "Viewpoints on T'ang China." <u>Acta Asiatica</u> 55 (1988). Entire
    issue.

Two additional volumes of collected articles by Japanese scholars of China,
<u>Chinese Calligraphy</u> and <u>Chinese Painting</u>, are listed in the body of the <u>Handbook</u>
under their respective editors, Nakata Yūjirō and Miyagawa Torao.

VIII

Some Conventions Followed in the <u>Handbook</u>

1. Buddhist Studies

A distinction is drawn in the <u>Handbook</u> when characterizing scholars of
Buddhism, both in the body of the work and in Index H ("Scholars in the <u>Hand-</u>
<u>book</u>, Listed by Fields of Study"). "Buddhist studies*"--with an asterisk--
indicates a scholar of Buddhism whose work appears to be <u>secondarily related to</u>
<u>China</u>. Other references to the study of Buddhism--without an asterisk--point to
scholars whose work seems more concerned with **Buddhism in China**. This is not a
qualitative distinction. There are scholar-giants and comparatively minor
figures in both categories. It is simply intended to help initial users of the

guide sort through dozens of names in a field that uniquely encompasses South, Southeast, and East Asia.[19]

2. Capitalization: Journal and Book Titles

The capitalization of Japanese journal titles cited in the Handbook follows the conventions used by Harvard-Yenching Library: namely, in addition to initial words, the organizational, institutional, and place name components in titles are also capitalized: e.g., "Kyōto Daigaku Bungakubu kenkyū kiyō." It is a system that helps clarify meaning.[20] The same conventions are followed when capitalizing Japanese book titles and the titles of Chinese journals.

3. Capitalization: Names of Institutional Editors

In the body of the Handbook, the capitalization of names of institutional editors of volumes is avoided. Only personal names, university and department names, and words like Chūgoku, Nihon, and Bukkyō are capitalized. In the "Introduction" and "Appendix," however, capitals are used for institutional editors because of the special nature of many of the titles included there (especially in the "Appendix").

---

[19]Readers should also note that Tōyōgaku chosaku mokurokurui sōran (Intro. #2) lists numerous bibliographies of individual Japanese Buddhologists' writings as appearing in the following:
　　Nihon Indogaku Bukkyō Gakkai gakkai-shō jushōsha meibo [A List of Names of Association Prize-Winners of the Japanese Association of Indian and Buddhist Studies].
日本印度学仏教学会学会賞受賞者名簿
　　Nihon Indogaku Bukkyō Gakkai, ed. & publ. Tokyo, 1974.
Because the above listing was unavailable to the compiler, these entries are not found in the Handbook since it was not possible to determine which entrants should be included.

[20]The following listing that adopts this system includes many of the journal titles cited in the Handbook:
　　Aoki Toshiyuki, "Current Japanese-Language Serials in the Social Sciences and Humanities," Harvard-Yenching Library Occasional Reference Notes 10 (March 1980), entire issue; and "Supplement," Ibid. 11 (Sept. 1980), pp. 24-32.

4. Chinese Characters: Main Entrants / Cross References

The names of most main entrants are given in both romanization and Japanese transcription in the body of the <u>Handbook</u>, which serves as an index to all Japanese cited. This obviates the need to give a person's name in Japanese more than once in the volume. (Thus, for example, although Kawagoe Yasuhiro is cited in Intro. #2 and #12, without his name being given in Chinese characters, the reader can find his name in Japanese in the body of the <u>Handbook</u>, listed alphabetically.)

Chinese characters are not provided under alternate readings of entrants' names as long as the cross-referenced reading is only one entry removed from the main listing for the scholar. If the cross-referenced alternate reading is more than one entry away, Chinese characters are supplied for both.

Characters are not given for some of the Japanese names listed in the body of the work. This usually results from the name having appeared in a Western-language publication that does not supply them. The abbreviation **"NC"**--"no characters [are being provided]"--is added to clarify such cases.

5. Indexes: Japanese / Non-Japanese Cited

All Japanese names cited in the "Introduction" and "Appendix" are cross-listed in the body of the book (usually together with transcription in Japanese), so as to make the latter **an index to all Japanese** in the <u>Handbook</u>.

At the end of many main entries in the body of the work, one finds the designation, **"Also listed under . . . ,"** directing the reader to other places in the volume where additional work by a scholar is cited. For indexing purposes, Japanese translators, editors, and contributors whose names would otherwise only appear under other scholars' names are also given separate entries in the body of the text, even though many are not China scholars; after their names, one finds **"Listed under . . . ,"** directing readers to where they are cited.

Index B, "Non-Japanese Cited in the <u>Handbook</u>," complements the body of the text by completing the indexing of names appearing in the work. Included are Westerners and Chinese cited in the <u>Handbook</u>, not only editors, translators, authors, and book reviewers, but also non-Japanese contributors of Western-language articles noted as appearing in <u>Festschriften</u> cited in the <u>Handbook</u>.

When deciding whether to place an entrant with a Japanese surname in one of the two indexes (in the body of the text, or in Index B), the following distinction was drawn. If a subject has a Japanese surname but **a non-Japanese first name** (like Wake A. Fujioka), the person is listed in Index B, "Non-Japanese Cited in the Handbook," and necessarily referred to in Western-language word order (i.e., surname last). If the party has **a Japanese surname and a Japanese first name** (like Kataoka Tetsuya), even if the only cited work by the entrant is in English and the entrant's name is not additionally given in Japanese transcription, the person is included in the body of the work and consistently referred to in Japanese word order (i.e., surname first).

The few non-Japanese who are listed as main entrants in the Handbook appear because they fall under the criteria for inclusion in the work (see Intro., Sect. II). Note that even though such ethnic Chinese or Korean main entrants are listed in the body of the Handbook according to the Japanese readings of their names (e.g., Chin Shunshin), the Chinese or Korean readings of their names are also crosslisted both there and in Index B ("Non-Japanese Cited in the Handbook").

6. Pagination: Arabic Numerals

No roman numerals are used when citing book pages. The conglomeration of sections of many books, especially collective volumes--for example, the "2,3, 17,3,730,3 pp." of the Morohashi Tetsuji Festschrift cited in the sample entry above--reflects the problem. It is not at all uncommon to find two different sets of roman-numeral pages at different ends of the same Festschrift volume, another set of numbers for the Japanese text in the "front" part of the book, still another set for the English text at the "back" of the book (with the latter paginated from the outside of the book inward), and the publication page tucked away in-between the different-language texts. Therefore, the Handbook lists in arabic numerals the total pages in each section of a book, going from the Japanese title page to the back cover of the book, regardless of whether the numerals are arabic, roman, or sinitic (unnumbered printed pages found in-between numbered sections are also counted and included). Such a listing serves the two ends of helping identify where the cited page numbers of bibliographies fall, and of telling how large the text is for potential xeroxing purposes. The same principle is followed for Western-language books.

7. Place Names

Although the Chinese characters for major East Asian cities are doubtless familiar to most users of the Handbook, Index G ("Places of Publication Cited, with Chinese Characters") lists all place names mentioned for book publishers. (The characters for places names cited to clarify journal titles appear in parentheses after those titles in Index D: "East Asian-Language Journals Cited, with Chinese Characters.") Index G includes entries that might not be readily familiar: e.g., Yono in Saitama Prefecture, or Keijō (the Japanese pre-1945 rendering for Seoul).

8. Romanization: Modified Wade-Giles System

The Wade-Giles system of romanization is used in the Handbook for Chinese personal names and for the titles of Chinese books and journals. A modification of the system, as used in publications by the Council on East Asian Studies of Harvard University, is followed: namely, umlauts appear only in those syllables where it is critical to distinguish between readings (e.g., between yü and yu), and they are dropped where unnecessary (e.g., in yuan and hsun).

9. Romanization: Ombin (Sound Changes)

Throughout the Handbook, Japanese names, journal titles, etc., are romanized as they are spoken--i.e., in "m"-sounding combinations, "rombun, Kambun, Shimmura" are transcribed rather than "ronbun, Kanbun, Shinmura," and the like. This is in keeping with the stress throughout the work on the actual Japanese readings of names, journals, book titles, and publishers. The reader should note, however, that library catalogs normally use "n" in these combinations. This should not prove an inconvenience, as -m combinations appear alphabetically where -n ones would, and vice versa.

10. Same-Name Scholars

There are **two** entries in the Handbook for each of the following names, as **two different scholars** have the **same romanized name**--with different Chinese characters, except for Satō Ichirō--Kamata Shigeo, Kobayashi Hideo, Mori Masao, Nakajima Toshio, Nakamura Takashi, Oda Takeo, Satō Ichirō, Shimada Masao, Tanaka Masami, and Yokoyama Hiroshi.

11. Simplified Chinese Characters

A few older forms of characters are used when transcribing <u>personal names</u> in the <u>Handbook</u> (for <u>ryū</u> 龍 , <u>den</u> 傳 , and a few other <u>Kanji</u>).   Otherwise, forms now current in Japan are used.

12. Western-Language Book Reviews

Although several Western-language reviews of Japanese scholars' **Japanese-language books** are included in the <u>Handbook</u>, such listings are not intended to be comprehensive. They are included because they can be particularly helpful in introducing and summarizing a scholar's work. No entries are listed, however, for reviews of **Western-language books** by Japanese scholars of China: e.g., <u>An Introduction to Sung Poetry</u> by Yoshikawa Kōjirō, <u>The Ming Tribute Grain System</u> by Hoshi Ayao, and <u>Medieval Chinese Society and the Local "Community"</u> by Tanigawa Michio. Such titles are assumed to be better known and more accessible to Western readers. To find reviews for these latter works, readers should turn to relevant volumes of the annual "Kyoto Bibliography" (Intro. #1), checking issues for the year the work was first published and for immediately succeeding years. (The same procedure will turn up reviews, in East Asian as well as in Western languages, for other book-length works cited in Japanese or Western languages.)

日本の中国学専門家ハンドブック

JAPANESE SCHOLARS OF CHINA

A Bibliographical Handbook

Abe Chōichi 阿部肇一 History of Chinese Buddhism, Sung period.
 Yen 3.

Abe Hiroshi 阿部 洋 Modern Chinese history, esp. Japanese educational activities in China before World War
 II.

Abe Kaneya 阿部兼也 Chinese literature, T'ang and Sung periods.
 Chinese vernacular fiction.

 Lit 9, Yen 2.

Abe Ken'ya
 see Abe Kaneya.

Abe Masao 阿部正雄
 Listed under Suzuki Daisetsu.

Abe Ryūichi 阿部隆一 Chinese bibliography. Japanese thought, Edo
 period.
 Yen 2, Teng #462.
 Σ Abe Ryūichi ikōshū.
 Tokyo: Kyūko Shoin, 1985-86. 4 vols.
 •* Shidō bunko ronshū 19 (1983), 441-452.

Abe Seitoku 安部成得 Chinese poetry, traditional.
 Lit 10.

Abe Shōjirō 阿部正次郎 Chinese literature, pre-T'ang period.
 Lit 9.

Abe Takeo 安部健夫 Asian, incl. Central Asian, history, esp.
 Yuan period.
 Teng #550.
 + Tōyōshi kenkyū 18.3 (Dec. 1959), 215-217.

Abe Tomoji   阿部知二   Modern Chinese literature.
    Yen 3.
    Σ Abe Tomoji zenshū. No biblio.
        Tokyo: Kawade Shobō, 1974-75. 13 vols.

Abe Yasuki   阿部泰記   Chinese vernacular fiction and drama.
    Lit 10.

Abe Yoshio   阿部吉雄   Classical Chinese thought. Neo-Confucianism.
                               Confucianism in Korea and Japan.
    Lit 11, Yen 1, Teng #696.
    + Jissen kokubungaku 14 (1978), 86-91.
    • Ibid., 64-85.
    + Han 5.5-6 (May-June 1976), 4-20.
    + Jimbun Kagakuka kiyō (Tōkyō Daigaku) 39 (Dec. 1966), 200-204.
    + Tōkyō Shinagaku hō 12 (1966), 17-20.

Abe Yukio   阿部幸夫   Modern Chinese literature. Classical Chinese
                               thought.
    Lit 10.

Adachi Ikutsune   安達生恒   Chinese economy, incl. agricultural and com-
                               mercial economy.
    Teng #69.

Adachi Keiji   足立 啓二   Chinese socio-economic history, late Ch'ing
                               and early Republican periods.

Adachi Toshio   足立 利雄   Contemporary Chinese economy.
    Yen 646.

Adachibara Yatsuka 足立原 八束 Chinese vernacular fiction and drama.
    Lit 8.

Adachihara Yatsuka
    see Adachibara Yatsuka.

Aihara Shunji   相原 俊二   Chinese history, pre-Han period.
        Yen 496.

Aiko Katsuya   愛甲 勝矢   Chinese agricultural economics. Chinese eco-
                                nomic theory.

        Yen 4.

Aiura Takashi   相浦 杲   Modern Chinese language, grammar and phonolo-
                                gy. Chinese vernacular fiction. Modern Chi-
                                nese literature.

        Lit 1, Yen 496.

Akamatsu Toshihide   赤松 俊秀   Buddhist studies.* History of Japanese Bud-
                                dhism and culture, medieval period.

        Yen 52.

Akao Yoshinori   赤尾 善徳   Contemporary Chinese politics.
        Yen 52.

Akasaka Mitsuo   赤坂 三男   Contemporary Chinese politics.
        Yen 51.

Akatsuka Kiyoshi   赤塚 忠   Classical Chinese thought. Chinese epigraphy.
        Lit 2, Yen 53.
        Σ Akatsuka Kiyoshi chosakushū.
           Tokyo: Kenkyūsha. 1985-89. 7 vols.
        + Shibun 88 (1984), 36-37.
        ∋ David N. Keightley, "Akatsuka Kiyoshi and the Culture of Early
           China: A Study in Historical Method," Harvard Journal of Asiatic
           Studies 42.1 (June 1982), 267-320.

[Review article of Akatsuka Kiyoshi, <u>Chūgoku kodai no shūkyō to bun-</u>
<u>ka: In ōchō no saishi</u> 中国古代の宗教と文化 一殷王朝の祭祀一 , To-
kyo: Kadokawa Shoten, 1977. 2,8,869 pp.]
  + Chūtetsubun Gakkai hō 1 (Oct. 1974), 38-44.

Akeno Yoshio   明野義夫   Contemporary Chinese economy.
     Yen 275.

Akiba Takashi   秋葉 隆   Ethnology of Korea and Manchuria.
     + Chōsen gakuhō 9 (March 1956), 314-322.

Akioka Ieshige   秋岡 家栄   Contemporary China.
     Yen 326.

Akisada Jitsuzō   秋貞 実造
     see Tamura Jitsuzō.

Akita Nariaki
     see Akita Shigeaki.

Akita Shigeaki   秋田 成明   History of Chinese thought and customs. Chi-
                                         nese ethnology and religion.
     Lit 3, Yen 330.

Akiyama Kenzō   秋山 謙蔵   Sino-Japanese historical relations.
     Yen 329.

Akiyama Motohide   秋山 元秀   Chinese historical geography.

Akiyama Terukazu   秋山 光和   History of art: Japan, China, East Asia.
     Yen 328.
     ∈ <u>Arts of China</u>. 3 vols.
        Vol. 1: <u>Neolithic Cultures to the T'ang Dynasty: Recent Discoveries</u>.
        By Akiyama Terukazu et al. Coordinated by M. Tregear. Tokyo and
        Palo Alto, Calif.: Kodansha International, 1968. 5,1,245 pp.

[Includes chapters by several Japanese scholars of Chinese art
history.]
Vol. 2: <u>Buddhist Cave Temples: New Researches</u>.
By Akiyama Terukazu and Matsubara Saburō. Translated by Alexander
C. Soper. Tokyo and Palo Alto, Calif.: Kodansha International,
1969. 248 pp.
Vol. 3: <u>Paintings in Chinese Museums: New Collections</u>.
[Chapters by Yonezawa Yoshiho and Kawakita Michiaki.]
Translated by George Hatch. Tokyo, New York, and San Francisco:
Kodansha, 1970. 235 pp.

[Book-length Western-language work by Akiyama on Japanese painting is
not listed here.]

Akiyama Yoshiteru   秋山 良照 Modern and contemporary Chinese history,
incl. World War II.

Yen 329.

Akiyoshi Kukio   秋吉 久紀夫 Modern Chinese literature. Chinese literature, Ming period.

Lit 3, Yen 327.

Akizuki Kan'ei   秋月 観暎 History of Chinese religion, Taoism.
Yen 330, Teng #481.
+ Tōyōshi ronshū (Tōhoku Daigaku) 3 (Jan. 1988), 188-191.

Akizuki Ryōmin   秋月 龍珉   Ch'an Buddhism, Japan and China.
Σ <u>Akizuki Ryōmin chosakushū</u>. No biblio.
Tokyo: San'ichi Shobō, 1978-80. 15 vols.
∋ P. Demiéville, Review of Akizuki's translation of the <u>Lin-chi lu</u>,
<u>Rinzai roku</u> 臨済録 (Tokyo: Chikuma Shobō, 1972. 4,6,256,18 pp.
[Zen no goroku #10]), in <u>T'oung Pao</u> 59 (1973), 301-302.
Also listed under Suzuki Daisetsu.

Akizuki Ryūmin
see Akizuki Ryōmin.

Amagai Kenzaburō 天海 謙三郎 Chinese economic history.

+ Idem, <u>Chūgoku tochi monjo no kenkyū</u> [4,3,13,4,8,866,6 pp.], 857-862.

中国土地文書の研究

Tokyo: Keisō Shobō, 1966. {E}

Amano Motonosuke 天野 元之助 Chinese economic history, esp. agricultural
                                              history, premodern and modern.

Yen 448, Teng #482.

• Chikaki ni arite 3 (March 1983), 72-76 & 55.

+ Chūgokushi kenkyū (Ōsaka Shiritsu Daigaku) 7 (1982), 80-83.

• Ibid., 1-2 & 79.

• Nung-shih yen-chiu (Peking) 2 (March 1982), 46.

∋ Ramon H. Myers, "Amano Motonosuke (1901-1980)," <u>Journal of Asian</u>
    <u>Studies</u> 40.2 (Feb. 1981), 443-444.

• UP (Tōkyō Daigaku) 4.1 (#27), 4.2 (#28), 4.3 (#29); (Jan., Feb.,
    March 1975); pp. 28-33, 18-22, 24-29, respectively.

+ Jimbun kenkyū 12.8 (Sept. 1961), 8-15.

• Ibid., 1-7.

Amano Shizuo   天野 鎮雄 Classical Chinese thought, esp. Taoism.
    Lit 11, Yen 447, Teng #654.

Amenomiya Yōzō 雨宮 庸蔵 Contemporary international relations. Contem-
                                              porary Chinese politics.

Yen 581.

Ami Yūji   網 祐次 Chinese literature, Six Dynasties and T'ang
                                    periods.

Lit 12, Yen 472, Teng #582.

Anami Korehiro 阿南 惟敬 Manchurian history.
    + Bōei Daigakkō kiyō 33 (Sept. 1976), 5 pp.

Anazawa Tatsuo 穴沢 辰雄 Classical Chinese thought.
    Lit 8, Yen 538, Teng #655.

Andō Hikotarō   安藤彦太郎   Modern Chinese economic history. Modern Sino-
                                  Japanese relations.

   Yen 6, Teng #70.

   ∋ Idem, <u>Peking</u> [150 pp.].
     Tokyo and Palo Alto: Kodansha International, 1968;   London: Ward
     Lock, 1968.

Andō Kōsei   安藤更生   East Asian art and archaeology.

   Yen 7, Teng #175.

   * Bijutsushi kenkyū (Waseda Daigaku) 9 (1972), 71.

  +* <u>Andō Kōsei nempu chosaku mokuroku</u> [91,19 pp.], 19 pp.
     Andō Kōsei nempu sakusei iinkai, ed.   Tokyo: Andō Kiyo 安藤きよ,
     1972.

Andō Makoto   安東諒   Chinese literature, Six Dynasties period.
   Lit 15.

Andō Shunroku   安東俊六   Chinese poetry, T'ang period.
   Lit 15, Yen 11.

Andō Takatsura   安藤孝行   Philosophy. Chinese literature, traditional.
   Yen 9.

Andō Tomonobu   安藤智信   History of Chinese Buddhism.
   Yen 10.

Andō Toshio   安藤俊雄   History of Chinese Buddhism, esp. T'ien-t'ai
                                  Buddhism.

   Yen 8, Teng #720.

   + Idem, <u>Tendaigaku ronshū: Shikan to Jōdo</u> [9,525,29 pp.], 3-7.
     天台学論集 ― 止観と浄土 ―
     Tokyo: Heirakuji Shoten, 1975.

   ●* Ōtani gakuhō 54.1 (June 1974), 52-57.

Andō Yōko   安藤陽子   Modern Chinese literature.
        Yen 8.

Aochi Shin   青地 晨
        see Aoki Shigeru.

Aoe Shunjirō   青江舜二郎
        Listed twice under Naitō Konan.

Aoki Masaru   青木正児   Chinese literature and the arts. Chinese dra-
                                ma. Chinese literary and art theory. Histo-
                                ry of Chinese food.

        Lit 1, Yen 320, Teng #583.

        Σ Aoki Masaru zenshū, vol. 10 (1975), 417-426.
            Tokyo: Shunjūsha, 1969-75. 10 vols.

        + Ritsumeikan bungaku 245 (Nov. 1965), 120-129.

        • Ibid., 118-119.

        • Tōhōgaku 31 (Nov. 1965), 158-179.

        • Shūkan Tōyōgaku 13 (May 1965), 93-97.

        ø Aoki Masaru hakushi kanreki kinen Chūka rokujū meika genkōroku [2,
            5,311 pp.]. No biblio.
            中華六十名家言行録
            Yoshikawa Kōjirō, ed. Tokyo: Kōbundō, 1948.
            TRNS:oo, NNO 3:403.

Aoki Shigeru   青木 滋   Modern Japanese history. Contemporary Asian
                                affairs: Japan, Korea, China.
        Yen 321.

Aoki Tomitarō   青木富太郎   Asian, esp. Mongolian, history.
        Yen 319, Teng #495.

        + Kainan shigaku 7 (1969).

Aoki Toshiyuki   青木利行
        Listed under Intro., Footnote 20.

Aoyama Hiroshi   青山宏   Chinese poetry, T'ang- and Sung-period <u>tz'u</u>.
    Lit 2, Yen 323.

Aoyama Kōryō   青山公亮   Korean history, Koryo period. Chinese histo-
                                       ry, incl. Yuan period.

    Yen 322, Teng #710.

    + Chōsenshi Kenkyūkai rombunshū 18 (1981), 174-176.

    + Ibid. 2 (1966).

    + Shundai shigaku (Meiji Daigaku) 19 (Sept. 1966), 3-6.

Aoyama Sadao   青山定雄   Chinese history, T'ang and Sung periods. Chi-
                                         nese historical geography.

    Yen 322, Teng #525.

    ø Aoyama hakushi koki kinen <u>Sōdaishi ronsō</u> [20,491,3 pp.], 9-14.
        宋代史論叢
        Aoyama hakushi koki kinen kankōkai, ed. Tokyo: Seishin Shobō, 1974.
        TRNS #007.

    + Chūō Daigaku Bungakubu kiyō 72 (Shigakuka 19) (March 1974), 185-192.

Ara Matsuo   荒松雄   Indian history, thought, and society.
    Yen 182.

    + Tōyō Bunka Kenkyūjo kiyō (Tōkyō Daigaku) 88 (March 1982), 8 pp.

Arai Ken   荒井健   Chinese literature, esp. poetry and poetics.
    Lit 12, Yen 185.

Arai Shin'ichi   荒井信一   Modern Chinese history, World War II.
    Yen 186.

Arai Takeo   荒井宝雄   Contemporary Chinese politics.
    Yen 529.

Arai Yoshio   荒井瑞雄   Chinese literature.
    Yen 186.

Araki Kengo　　　荒木見悟　　Chinese thought. Neo-Confucianism, incl. Japan.

   Lit 13, Yen 183, Teng #687.

+　Tetsugaku nempō 41 (1982), 6 pp.

ø　Araki kyōju taikyū kinen　Chūgoku tetsugakushi kenkyū ronshū　[12,705
pp.], 8-12.

中国哲学史研究論集

Araki kyōju taikyū kinenkai, ed.　Fukuoka: Ashi Shobō, 1981.

TRNS:oo.

Araki Osamu　　　荒木　修　　Modern Chinese thought, literature, and language.

   Lit 13, Yen 184, Teng #697.

Araki Toshikazu　　荒木敏一　　Chinese history, Sung period. Chinese bibliography.

   Yen 184, Teng #536.

Arao Sei　　　荒尾　清　　Late nineteenth-century commercial adventurer
in China.

∋　Paul Scott, "The Etymology of Cooperation: Sino-Japanese Relations
and Arao Sei, Sino-Japanese Studies Newsletter 1.2 (March 1989), 13-
17.

∋　Paul Scott, Japan-China: Arao Sei and the Paradox of Cooperation
(Osaka: Kansai University of Foreign Studies, 1988).　11,163 pp.

Araya Junkō　　　阿頼耶順宏　Modern Chinese literature, drama, and film.
Modern Chinese language.

   Lit 14, Yen 4.

Arimitsu Kyōichi　有光教一　Asian, esp. Korean, archaeology.
   Yen 570, Teng #711.

Arimitsu Norikazu

   see Arimitsu Kyōichi.

Arisaka Hideyo   有坂秀世   Chinese and Japanese languages, historical
                                   phonology.

  + Chūgokugo-gaku 231 (Oct. 1984), 76-86.

Arita Kazuo   有田知夫   Modern Chinese thought. Chinese bibliography.

   Yen 571.

Arita Tadahiro   有田忠弘   Chinese language. Chinese literature, Ch'ing-
                                   period vernacular fiction.

   Lit 14, Yen 571.

Aritaka Iwao   有高巖   East Asian history, incl. Mongolia and Korea.
                                   Chinese history, esp. T'ang and Yuan peri-
                                   ods. Chinese social history. History of
                                   Chinese legal thought.

   Yen 569.

  • Rekishi kyōiku 16.4 (Apr. 1968), 108-109.

  + Risshō shigaku 32 (1968), 1 p.

  • Ibid., 1 p. and 107-114.

Asai Atsushi   浅井敦一   Contemporary Chinese law.
   Yen 318.

Asai, B.   NC
   Listed under Collected Articles #81.

Asai Motoi   浅井紀   Chinese history, Ming and Ch'ing periods,
                                   religious uprisings.

Asai Shigenori   浅井茂紀   Classical Chinese thought.
   Lit 6.

Asai Torao   浅井虎夫   Chinese legal history.

+ Idem, <u>Shina ni okeru hōten hensan no enkaku</u> [10,2,13,417 pp.], 410-

416.

支那二於ケル法典編纂ノ沿革

Tokyo: Kyūko Shoin, 1977.

[The body of the book, but not the bibliography, is a reprint of the

1911 edition published by Kyōto Hōgakkai as vol. 7 of <u>Hōritsu keizai-</u>

<u>gaku kenkyū sōsho</u>.]

Asakawa Kenji   浅川謙次   Modern Chinese history. Chinese economic ge-

ography.

Yen 316.

+ Idem, <u>Kokuun o hiraki seiten o miru: Asakawa Kenji tsuitō ikōshū</u> [357

pp.], 346-355.

披黒雲睹青天 ― 浅川謙次追悼遺稿集 ―

Asakawa Kenji tsuitō ikōshū kankō iinkai, ed. & publ. Tokyo, 1977.

Asakura Hisashi   朝倉尚   Chinese literature, esp. Sung period.
Lit 6.

Asami Kazuo   浅海一男   Contemporary Chinese politics.
Yen 317.

Asano Michiari   浅野通有   Chinese literature, thru Han period, esp.
                               <u>Ch'u-tz'u</u>.

Lit 6.

+ Kambun Gakkai kaihō (Kokugakuin Daigaku) 29 (Feb. 1984).

Asano Yūichi   浅野裕一   Classical Chinese thought.
Lit 7.

Ashida Shigeyuki   芦田茂幸   Modern Chinese literature.
Lit 7.

Ashida Takaaki   芦田孝昭   Chinese vernacular fiction. Modern Chinese literature.

     Lit 8, Yen 265.

Ashidate Ichirō   芦立一郎   Chinese poetry, T'ang period.
     Lit 8.

Ashikaga Atsuuji   足利惇氏   Buddhist studies.* Sanskrit language and lit-erature.

     Yen 647, Teng #753.

     •   Indogaku shiron shū 6-7 (March 1965), 1-4, and 196-199.
     +   Seinan Ajia kenkyū (Kyōto Daigaku) 13 (Dec. 1964), 3-6.

Ashizawa Shinji   芦沢新二   Chinese political relations with Southeast Asia.

     Yen 265.

Asō Isoji   麻生磯次   Japanese literature, Edo period. Sino-Japa-nese literary relations.

     Yen 267, Teng #389.

Asobe Kyūzō   遊部久蔵   Economics. Modern Chinese economic history.
     Teng #73.

Ayabe Tsuneo   綾部恒雄   Social anthropology, Southeast Asia, incl. Thailand. Chinese minorities.

     Yen 260.

Baba   馬場
     see also Bamba.

Baba Akio   馬場明男   Modern Chinese political economy. Sociology, social stratification.

     Yen 266.

Bamba   馬場

    see also Baba.

Bamba Nobuya   馬場伸也   Modern Japanese history, incl. Sino-Japanese
                                                relations.

    Yen 266.

   ∈ Idem, <u>Japanese Diplomacy in a Dilemna: New Light on Japan's China</u>
     <u>Policy, 1924-1929</u> [440 pp.].

     Kyoto: Minerva Press, 1972; Vancouver: University of British Colum-
     bia Press, 1972.

     [Additional book-length English-language studies co-edited by Bamba,
     on modern Japanese history, are not listed here.]

Banno Junji   坂野潤治   Modern Japanese history and thought. Modern
                                                Sino-Japanese relations.

Banno Masataka   坂野正高   Modern Chinese diplomatic history. Chinese
                                                bibliography.

    Yen 22, Teng #163.

  + Ajia bunka kenkyū (Asian Cultural Studies) 25.2 (1987).

  • Li-shih hsueh-pao (Taipei) (Kuo-li Shih-fan Ta-hsueh) 9 (1981), 365-
   374.

  ∈ Idem, <u>China and the West, 1858-1861: The Origins of the Tsungli Yamen</u>
    [8,2,1,367,1,45 pp.].

    Cambridge, Mass.: Harvard University Press, 1964.

    Also listed under Intro., Footnote 4.

Banno Ryōkichi   坂野良吉   Modern Chinese history, Republican period.

Bekki Atsuhiko   別枝篤彦   Historical geography, East and Southeast
                                                Asia.

    Yen 31.

    [A short English-language volume by Bekki on life in Japan is not listed
    here.]

Bitō Masahide   尾藤正英   Japanese thought, Edo period. Sino-Japanese
                                    relations.

    Yen 480.

Ch'en Hsin-ming   陳新銘
    see Izumi Kiyoshi.

Ch'en Shun-ch'en   陳舜臣
    see Chin Shunshin.

Chida Kuichi
    see Chida Kyūichi.

Chida Kyūichi   千田九一   Chinese vernacular fiction. Modern Chinese
                                    literature.

    Lit 173, Yen 318.

Chihara Katsumi   千原勝美   Classical Chinese thought.
    Teng #656.

Chihara Masayoshi
    see Chihara Katsumi.

Chikashige Masumi   近重真澄   History of science in Japan and China.
    ∈ Idem, <u>Alchemy and Other Chemical Achievements of the Ancient Orient:</u>
    <u>The Civilization of Japan and China in Early Times as Seen from the</u>
    <u>Chemical Point of View</u> [7,102 pp.].
    Tokyo: Rakuho Uchida (sic) [内田老鶴圃], 1936.

Chikusa Masaaki   竺沙雅章   Chinese social history, T'ang and esp. Sung
                                    period. History of Chinese Buddhism.

    Yen 643.

Chin Shunshin   陳舜臣   Modern Chinese history. Historical novelist.
    Yen 51.

∈ Idem, <u>Murder in a Peking Studio (Pekin Yūyūkan)</u> [14,181,1 pp.]
   Translated, with an introduction, by Joshua A. Fogel. Tempe: Center
   for Asian Studies, Arizona State University, 1986.

∃ Joshua A. Fogel, "The Historical Fiction of Chin Shunshin," <u>Chinese
   Republican Studies Newsletter</u> 4.2 (Feb. 1981), 17-19.

Chūbachi Masakazu 中鉢雅量   Chinese literature, esp. vernacular fiction,
                                        Ming period.

   Lit 174, Yen 610.

Denda Akira   傳田章   Chinese drama, Yuan period, esp. <u>Hsi-hsiang
                                        chi</u>.

   Lit 177, Yen 59.

Dohi Yoshikazu   土肥義和   Chinese history, esp. T'ang period, Tun-huang
                                        and Turfan.

   Yen 465.

Doi Akio   土居明夫   Contemporary Chinese politics.
   Yen 465.

Doi Akira   土井章   Contemporary Chinese economics. Sino-Japanese
                                        historical relations. Chinese vernacular
                                        fiction, late Ch'ing period.

   Yen 465.

Doi Hisaya   土井久弥   Buddhist studies.* Hindi language and litera-
                                        ture.

   Yen 466.

Doi Kenji   土井健司   Chinese poetry, T'ang period.
   Lit 178.

Doi Kyūya   土井久弥
   see Doi Hisaya.

Ebata Shin'ichirō   江幡真一郎   Early Chinese thought and history.
    Yen 207.

Ebisawa Tetsuo   海老沢哲雄   Mongolian history, Yuan period.

Edayoshi Isamu   枝吉勇   Economic history: China, Manchuria, South
                                                    Asia.
    Yen 607.

Egami Namio   江上波夫   Asian archaeology and anthropology.
    Yen 208, Teng #138.

+ "A Bibliography of N. Egami (to 1983)," <u>Kodai Oriento Hakubutsukan</u>
<u>kiyō</u> (Bulletin of The Ancient Orient Museum) 5 (1983), 8-20.

∋ "Main Field Works of N. Egami," <u>Ibid</u>., 7.

+ Jōchi shigaku 22 (1977).

ø <u>Egami Namio kyōju koki kinen ronshū</u>, vol. 1 (1976), 40 pp. 3 vols.

    Vol. 1: Kōko, bijutsu hen [56,455 pp.] 考古・美術篇
    Vol. 2: Minzoku, bunka hen [11,535 pp.] 民族・文化篇
    Vol. 3: Rekishi hen [10,661 pp.] 歴史篇

Egami Namio kyōju koki kinen jigyōkai, ed. Tokyo: Yamakawa Shuppansha, 1976-77.

TRNS #029.

+ Tōyō Bunka Kenkyūjo kiyō (Tōkyō Daigaku) 43 (March 1967) , 21-34.

Egashira Hiroshi   江頭広   Chinese social history, pre-Han period.
    Yen 207.

Eguchi Keiichi   江口圭一   Modern Japanese history. Sino-Japanese histo-
                                                    ry, 1930s.
    Yen 207.

Ehata Shin'ichirō   江幡真一郎
    see Ebata Shin'ichirō.

Ejima Hisao   江嶋寿夫   Chinese history, Ming period, esp. horse
                                            trade.

Endō Motoo   遠藤元男   Japanese history, medieval period. Sino-Japa-
                                            nese historical relations.
      Yen 591, Teng #215.

Endō Saburō   遠藤三郎   Modern Chinese history. Sino-Japanese histor-
                                            ical relations, World War II.
      Yen 590.

Endō Tetsuo   遠藤哲夫   Classical Chinese thought.
      Yen 590.

Enoki Kazuo   榎一雄   Central Asian and Chinese history. East-West
                                            historical relations. Chinese bibliography.
      Yen 664, Teng #139.
      ø Enoki hakushi shōju kinen Tōyōshi ronsō [540 pp.], 3-76.
         東洋史論叢
         Enoki hakushi shōju kinen Tōyōshi ronsō hensan iinkai, ed.   Tokyo:
         Kyūko Shoin, 1988.
         TRNS:oo.
      ø Enoki hakushi kanreki kinen Tōyōshi ronsō [46,498,14 pp.], 16-46.
         東洋史論叢
         Enoki hakushi kanreki kinen hensan iinkai, ed. Tokyo: Yamakawa Shup-
         pansha, 1975.
         TRNS #030.
      Also listed under Intro. #6, Ishida Mikinosuke (twice), Iwai Hirosato
      (twice), Katō Shigeshi, and Wada Sei (twice).

Etani Toshiyuki   恵谷俊之   Central Asian and Indian history.
      + Tōkai shigaku 6 (1970), 37-38.

Etō Shinkichi   衛藤瀋吉   Modern Chinese history. Contemporary Chinese
                                            politics and international relations.
      Yen 474, Teng #565.

+ Shakai kagaku kiyō (Tōkyō Daigaku) 33 (1984), 28-33.

Also listed under Miyazaki Tōten and Suzue Gen'ichi.

[The book co-edited by Etō, of articles on the 1911 Revolution, is not
listed here.]

Etō Shun   衛藤駿   History of art, incl. China.

Yen 474.

Etō Toshio   衛藤利夫   Mongolian history.

+ Toshokan zasshi 48.10 (Oct. 1954), 19-22.

+ Shūsho geppō 74 (1942).

Ezoe Toshio   江副敏生   Contemporary Chinese economy.

Yen 206.

+ Shōgaku ronsan (Chūō Daigaku) 24.5-6 (March 1983), 333-337.

Ezure Takashi   江連隆   Chinese literature, esp. literary imagery of
                                the moon.

Lit 49.

Fuji Masaharu   富士正晴   Modern Japanese writer. Chinese literature,
                                incl. vernacular fiction (Hung-lou meng)
                                and Six Dynasties poetry (T'ao Ch'ien).

Yen 124.

Also listed under Yoshikawa Kōjirō.

Fujieda Akira   藤枝晃   Asian, incl. Chinese, history. Mongolian lan-
                                guage. Tun-huang documents.

Yen 446, Teng #467.

∋* "Major Publications of Professor FUJIEDA Akira," Cahiers d'Extrême-
    Asie 3 (1987).

+ Tōhō gakuhō 49 (Feb. 1977), 393-401.

Fujii Eizaburō   藤井栄三郎 Chinese language.

Yen 440.

Fujii Hiroshi   藤井 宏   Chinese socio-economic history, Ming and
                                    Ch'ing periods.
    Yen 440, Teng #551.

Fujii Mamoru   藤井 守   Chinese poetry, Six Dynasties period, esp.
                                    <u>yueh-fu</u> and Pao Chao.
    Lit 228.

Fujii Matsuichi   藤井 松一   Japanese history, incl. Russo-Japanese War.
                                    Modern Chinese history, Sino-Japanese War.
    Yen 440.

Fujii Sen'ei   藤井 専英   Classical Chinese thought, <u>Hsun-tzu</u>.
    Yen 442.

Fujii Shōzō   藤井 昇三   Contemporary Chinese politics and interna-
                                    tional relations. Modern Chinese history
                                    and thought, Republican period.
    Yen 441.
    Also listed under Ozaki Hostumi.

Fujiie Reinosuke   藤家 礼之助   Chinese history, Han and Six Dynasties peri-
                                    ods.
    Yen 439.

Fujikawa Masakazu   藤川 正数   Chinese customs and manners, Han and Six Dy-
                                    nasties periods. Classical Chinese thought.

    Yen 436, Teng #657.
    + Chūgoku bungaku ronsō (Ōbirin Daigaku) 13 (March 1987), 1-5.

Fujimoto Akira   藤本 昭   Contemporary economy, China and U.S.S.R.
    Yen 436.

Fujimoto Kōzō　　藤本幸三　　Chinese history. Modern Chinese literature.
　　　Lit 230, Yen 435.

Fujimura Michio　　藤村道生　　Modern Chinese history, Sino-Japanese War.
　　　　　　　　　　　　　　　　Japanese history, Russo-Japanese War.
　　　Yen 437.

Fujino Iwatomo　　藤野岩友　　Chinese literature, thru the Han period, esp.
　　　　　　　　　　　　　　　　Ch'u-tz'u. Chinese lexicography.
　　　Lit 229, Yen 444, Teng #584.
　　+　Kambun Gakkai kaihō (Kokugakuin Daigaku) 22 (Nov. 1976), 165-170.
　　●　Ibid., 1.
　　+　Ibid. 10 (Jan. 1959), 2 pp.

Fujioka Katsuji　　藤岡勝二　　(Linguistics.)
　　ø　Fujioka hakushi kōseki kinen Gengogaku rombunshū [2,3,589,106 pp.].
　　言語学論文集
　　　Fujioka hakushi kōseki kinenkai, ed.　Tokyo: Iwanami Shoten, 1935.
　　　[Includes an English-language article by N. Fukushima on Tokharian.]
　　　TRNS #216, NNO 3:419.

Fujioka Shōji
　　　see Fujioka Katsuji.

Fujisawa Makoto　　藤沢誠　　Chinese thought, esp. Sung period.
　　　Yen 445, Teng #688.

Fujisawa Yoshimi　　藤沢義美　　History of ethnology, Yunnan. Chinese histo-
　　　　　　　　　　　　　　　　ry, T'ang period, Nan-chao kingdom.
　　　Yen 445, Teng #526.

Fujita Hideo　　藤田秀雄　　Chinese poetry, thru T'ang period.
　　　Lit 228, Teng #585.
　　+　Saga Daigaku Kyōyōbu kenkyū kiyō 1 (1969), 3 pp.

Fujita Kunio   藤田国雄   Chinese art and archaeology.
    Yen 442.

Fujita Masanori   藤田正典   Modern Chinese history. Chinese bibliography.

    Yen 443.

Fujita Motoharu   藤田元春   Chinese history. Chinese archaeology. Sino-
                                Japanese historical relations.

    +   Yamanashi Daigaku Gakugei Gakubu kenkyū hōkoku 6 (1955), 9-14.

    •   Ibid., 1-8 and 43-54.

Fujita Ryōsaku   藤田亮策   Korean archaeology.

    +   Tōhōgaku 64 (July 1982), 201-207.

    •   Ibid., 173-201.

    +   Chōsen gakuhō 20 (July 1961), 159-178.

    •   Ibid., 149-158.

    +   Shigaku 33.3-4 (April 1961), 189-191.

Fujita Toyohachi   藤田豊八   East-West historical relations. Chinese lit-
                                erature.

    +   Tōhōgaku 63 (Jan. 1982), 199-202.

    •   Ibid., 162-198.

    •   Tōyō Bunko shohō 13 (1981), 40-49.

    +   Jen-wen yueh-k'an (Shanghai) 4.6 (Aug. 1933), 13-17 (separate pagina-
        tion).

    •   Ibid., 1-13 (separate pagination).

    +   Idem, <u>Tōzai kōshōshi no kenkyū,</u> vol. 1, 31-40. 2 vols.

            Vol. 1: Nankai hen   [40,700 pp.]   西海篇
            Vol. 2: Seiiki hen   [521,265,47 pp.]   西域篇
        [Note that Vol. 2 includes a 265-page supplement comprised of Fuji-
        ta's studies of early Chinese literature.]

        Tokyo: Oka Shoin, 1933; rpt. Ogihara Seibunkan, 1943.

    +   Yen-ching hsueh-pao (Peking) 8 (Dec. 1930), 1649-1654.

+ Idem, <u>Kempō isō</u> [7,98,5, pp.], 5 pp.

剣峯遺草

Ikeuchi Hiroshi, ed. Tokyo: Fujita Kinnojō 藤田金之丞 , 1930.

+ Shigaku zasshi 40.9 (Sept. 1929), 119-125.

Fujita Yūken   藤田裕賢 Chinese literature, Ch'ing-period fiction,
                                        esp. <u>Liao-chai chih-i.</u>

   Lit 228, Yen 443.

Fujiwara Kōdō   藤原弘道 (Japanese Buddhism.)

   ø Fujiwara Kōdō sensei koki kinen <u>Shigaku Bukkyōgaku ronshū.</u>
      史学仏教学論集
      Fujiwara Kōdō sensei koki kinenkai, ed. & publ. Kyoto, 1973.   2
      vols. 14,755 pp., and pp. 756-1475 plus 2,5 pp.
      TRNS:oo.

Fujiwara Riichirō 藤原利一郎 Southeast Asian history, Vietnam. Sino-Viet-
                                     namese historical relations.

   Yen 447, Teng #140.

   + Shisō (Kyōto Joshi Daigaku) 43 (March 1986), 77-80.

Fujiwara Sadamu   藤原定
   see Fujiwara Tei.

Fujiwara Shō   藤原尚
   see Fujiwara Takashi.

Fujiwara Sosui   藤原楚水 Chinese calligraphy.
   •* Tōhōgaku 68 (July 1984), 187-208.

Fujiwara Takao   藤原高男 Classical Chinese thought, esp. <u>Lao-tzu.</u>
   Lit 230.

Fujiwara Takashi   藤原尚   Chinese poetry, <u>fu.</u>
   Lit 230.

Fujiwara Tei   藤原定   Modern Chinese thought.
    Teng #698.

Fujiyoshi Jikai   藤吉慈海   Buddhist studies.*
    Yen 439, Teng #723.
    + Zengaku kenkyū (Hanazono Daigaku) 65 (1986), 2-8.

Fujiyoshi Masumi 藤善真澄   Chinese history, esp. T'ang and Sung periods.
                             Chinese historical geography.
    Yen 442.

Fujizuka Chikashi 藤塚鄰   Sino-Korean cultural history, Ch'ing period.
                             Classical Chinese thought, Analects.
    + Tōhōgaku 69 (Jan. 1985), 193-194.
    • Ibid., 168-192.

Fukada Kyūya   深田久弥   Modern Japanese writer, esp. about mountains,
                               incl. Himalayas. Central Asia, Silk Road.
    Yen 382.

Fukatsu Tanefusa 深津胤房 Classical Chinese thought.
    Lit 222, Yen 382.
    Also listed twice under Katō Jōken.

Fukaura Seibun
    see Fukaura Shōbun.

Fukaura Shōbun   深浦正文 Buddhist studies. Indian Buddhism.
    * Idem, Bukkyō bungaku gairon [521 pp.], 518-520.
    仏教文学概論
       Kyoto: Nagata Bunshōdō, 1970.

Fukihara Shōshin 富貴原章信 Buddhist studies.* Indian Buddhism.
    Teng #724.
    •* Ōtani gakuhō 55.2 (Sept. 1975), 71-74.

Fukino Yasushi   吹野安   Classical Chinese thought. Chinese poetry,
                                             T'ang period.
    Lit 223.

Fukuda Jōnosuke   福田襄之介   History of Chinese language, <u>Shuo-wen chieh-
                                             tzu</u>.
    Yen 119.

Fukuhara Ryōgon   福原亮巖   Buddhist studies.
    + Bukkyōgaku kenkyū 32-33 (March 1977), 8 pp.

Fukuhara Ryūzō   福原龍藏   Classical Chinese thought. Chinese poetry,
                                             T'ang period.
    Lit 227.

Fukui Fumimasa   福井文雅   Chinese thought and religion, esp. classical
                                             and medieval periods. Chinese bibliography.

    Lit 224, Yen 118.

Fukui Haruhiro   NC
    Listed under Ishikawa Tadao.

Fukui Kōjun   福井康順   Asian thought. Taoism. Buddhist literature,
                                             Six Dynasties period.
    Lit 224, Yen 117, Teng #648 and #765.
    ø Fukui hakushi shōju kinen <u>Tōyō bunka ronshū</u> [39,1218,90,16 pp.],
       29-39.
       東洋文化論集
       Fukui hakushi shōju kinen rombunshū kankōkai, ed.   Tokyo: Waseda
       Daigaku Shuppanbu, 1969.
       [Includes two articles in Western languages: R.A. Stein, "Un example
       de relations entre Taoïsme et religion populaire," pp. 79-90; and
       Miyamoto Shōson, "The Middle Path Concept in History and Society,"
       pp. 35-58.]
       TRNS #211.

ø Fukui hakushi shōju kinen <u>Tōyō shisō ronshū</u> [4,823,34,2 pp.]. No
   biblio.

東洋思想論集

   Fukui hakushi shōju kinen rombunshū kankōkai, ed. & publ. Tokyo,
   1960.

   [Includes two articles in English: Miyamoto Shōson, "Is <u>Nirvana</u>
   Nichts or Peace?" pp. 1-27; and Masunaga Reihō, "Philosophy of Full
   Function," pp. 28-34.]

   TRNS #210, NNO 3:418-419.

Fukui Shigemasa   福井重雅   Chinese thought, Han period.
   Yen 118.

Fukukawa Shōzō   福川正三
   Listed under Collected Articles #64.

Fukumoto Masaichi
   see Fukumoto Masakazu.

Fukumoto Masakazu   福本雅一   Chinese poetry, esp. Yuan, Ming, Ch'ing peri-
                                 ods. Chinese painting and calligraphy.

   Lit 227, Yen 115.

Fukunaga ?   NC   Buddhist studies.
   ø <u>Fukunaga sensei kakō kinen ronshū</u>.
   Fukunaga sensei kakō kinenkai, ed. Tenri: Tenri Daigaku Shuppanbu,
   1962.
   TRNS #180.

Fukunaga Mitsuji   福永光司   Classical Chinese thought, esp. Taoism.
   Lit 226, Yen 121.
   ∋ Livia Knaul, "The Habit of Perfection: A Summary of Fukunaga Mitsu-
      ji's Studies on the <u>Chuang tzu</u> Tradition," <u>Cahiers d'Extrême-Asie</u> 1
      (1985), 71-85.
   + Chūtetsubun Gakkai hō 4 (1979), 21-30.

Fukusawa   福沢
    see Fukuzawa.

Fukushima Masao   福島正夫   Japanese law, esp. family registration law.
                                       Chinese law.

    Yen 116.
    + Tōyō Bunka Kenkyūjo kiyō (Tōkyō Daigaku) 43 (March 1967), 35-44.
    Also listed twice under Niida Noboru.

Fukushima, N.   NC
    Listed under Fujioka Katsuji and Ogiwara Unrai.

Fukushima Shun'ō   福島俊翁   Chinese thought.
    + Zengaku kenkyū (Hanazono Daigaku) 58 (1970), 9 pp.

Fukushima Yoshihiko 福島吉彦   Chinese poetry, thru T'ang period. Chinese
                                   historical texts, Shih-chi.
    Lit 226, Yen 115.

Fukushima Yutaka   福島裕   Contemporary Chinese economy and society,
                                   incl. communes.
    + Keizaikei (Kantō Gakuin Daigaku) 86 (Feb. 1971), 166-168.
    • Ibid., 145-165.

Fukutake Tadashi   福武直   Sociology, social structure of villages,
                                   incl. China.
    Yen 120, Teng #119.
    Σ Fukutake Tadashi chosakushū, Suppl. vol. (1976), 427-468.
       Tokyo: Tōkyō Daigaku Shuppankai, 1975-76. 10 vols., and one supple-
       mentary volume (bekkan).
    [Book-length Western-language books by Fukutake on the sociology of
    Japan and of other parts of Asia are not listed here.]

Fukuyama Toshio   福山敏男   Asian architectural and art history.
    Yen 119.

Fukuzawa Sōkichi   福沢宗吉   Chinese socio-economic history, T'ang period.
                                 History of Asian education.
        Yen 122, Teng #527.

Fukuzawa Yokurō   福沢与九郎   Chinese history, esp. T'ang- and Sung-period
                                 socio-economic history.
        Yen 122, Teng #528.

Fuma Susumu   夫馬 進   Chinese social history, Ming and Ch'ing peri-
                                 ods.

Fumoto Yasutaka   麓 保孝   Chinese thought, incl. Neo-Confucianism.
        Lit 232, Yen 262, Teng #699.
        + Bōei Daigakkō kiyō 26 (March 1973), 1-7.
        + Idem, Kansen Koharadai shibunshō.
           寒泉小原台詩文抄
           Tokyo: Shunjūsha, 1973.

Funaki Katsuma   船木勝馬   History of North China, Six Dynasties period.
        Yen 58.
        Also listed under Toriyama Kiichi.

Funakoshi Taiji   船越 泰次   Chinese history, T'ang period.
        Yen 59.

Funatsu Tomihiko   船津富彦   Chinese poetry and poetics, esp. Six Dynas-
                                 ties period.
        Lit 231, Yen 58.

Furumaya Tadao   古厩忠夫   Modern Chinese labor history.
        Yen 154.

Furuno Kiyoto   古野清人   Sociology of religion. Taoism. Ethnology.
        Yen 156.
        • Minzokugaku kenkyū 44.2 (Sept. 1979), 216-220.

Σ <u>Furuno Kiyoto chosakushū</u>.   No biblio.

Tokyo: San'ichi Shobō, 1972-74.   8 vols.

Furusawa Michio   古沢 未知男 Sino-Japanese literary relations.

Yen 157.

Furushima Kazuo   古島 和雄   Modern Chinese economic history.

Yen 153, Teng #74.

+ Shakai kagaku kenkyū (Tōkyō Daigaku) 33.4 (Nov. 1981), 281-283.

• Ibid., 251-280.

Furushima Toshio   古島 敏雄   Japanese agricultural history. Agricultural

economics, incl. Chinese village problems.

Yen 153.

Furuta Gyō   NC
Listed under Inoue Yasushi.

Furuta Keiichi   古田 敬一   Chinese poetics. Chinese literature, Six Dy-

nasties, esp. <u>Shih-shuo hsin-yü</u>.

Lit 232, Yen 155, Teng #726.

Furuta Shōkin   古田 紹欽   Buddhist studies, incl. Zen.
Yen 155.
Also listed twice under Suzuki Daisetsu.

Furuya Tsugio   古屋 二夫   Chinese language, esp. proverbs in vernacular

fiction.

Lit 233, Yen 154.

Giga Sōichirō   儀我 壮一郎 Contemporary Chinese economy.
Yen 563.

+ Keiei kenkyū (Ōsaka Shiritsu Daigaku) 33.5-6 (March 1983), 229-247.

Goi Naohiro   五井直弘   Chinese history, Han period.
    Yen 484.

    ∋ Joshua Fogel, Review of Goi Naohiro, <u>Kindai Nihon to Tōyōshigaku</u>
       近代日本と東洋史学   (Tokyo: Aoki Shoten, 1976. 13,260 pp.), in
       <u>Journal of Asian Studies</u> 37.1 (Nov. 1977), 145-146.

Gotō Akinobu   後藤秋正   Chinese poetry, Six Dynasties.
    Lit 107.

Gotō Kimpei   後藤均平   Chinese history. Sino-Vietnamese history.
                                Bibliography.
    Yen 187.
    Also listed under Intro., Footnote 3.

Gotō Motomi   後藤基巳   Chinese thought.
    Lit 108, Yen 188.
    + Idem, <u>Min Shin shisō to Kirisuto-kyō</u> [4,270 pp.], 247-252.
       明清思想とキリスト教
       Tokyo: Kenkyū Shuppan, 1979.
    + Shirayuri Joshi Daigaku kenkyū kiyō 13 (1977).

Gotō Nobuko   後藤延子   Modern Chinese thought, esp. May Fourth Move-
                                ment.
    Lit 107.

Gotō Shunzui   後藤俊瑞   Chinese thought, Neo-Confucianism.
    Teng #689.
    • Tetsugaku (Hiroshima) 13 (Oct. 1961), 135-138.

Gotō Sueo   後藤末雄   Chinese history, esp. Ch'ing period.
    Yen 188.

Gotō Tomio   後藤富男   History of Mongolian society.
    Yen 187.

Gotō Toshimizu   後藤 俊瑞
    see Gotō Shunzui.

Gōyama Kiwamu   合山 究   Chinese literature, esp. Sung period.
    Lit 106.

Gushima Kanesaburō
    see Gushima Kenzaburō.

Gushima Kenzaburō 具島 兼三郎 International relations, incl. China.
    Yen 236, Teng #50.

Hachiya Kunio   蜂屋 邦夫 Chinese thought, Six Dynasties period.

Hadani Ryōtai   羽溪 了諦
    see Hatani Ryōtai.

Hadano Hakuyū   羽田野伯猷 Buddhist studies.* Indian and Tibetan Bud-
                                        dhism.
    Yen 583.

Haga Kōshirō   芳賀 幸四郎 Japanese cultural history, medieval period.
                                 History of Chinese studies in medieval Ja-
                                 pan.
    Yen 114, Teng #281.

Haga Noboru   芳賀 登   Chinese and Japanese history, nineteenth cen-
                                 tury.
    Also listed under Tanaka Masami.

Hagio Chōichirō   萩尾長一郎 Chinese vernacular fiction.
    Lit 203.

Hagiwara Jumpei   荻原淳平   Chinese history, Yuan and Ming periods. Mon-
                                golian and Manchurian history.

    Yen 102, Teng #552.

    + Tōyōshi kenkyū 42.4 (March 1984), 1-8.

Hakeda Yoshito   羽毛田義人

    Listed under Yoshikawa Kōjirō.

Hama Kazue   濱一衛   History of Chinese drama.

    Lit 211, Yen 32, Teng #622.

    + Chūgoku bungaku ronshū (Kyūshū Daigaku) 4 (May 1974), 3-7.

    + Bungaku ronshū (Kyūshū Daigaku) 20 (March 1973), 4 pp.

Hama Ryūichirō   濱隆一郎   Chinese poetry, traditional.

    Lit 212.

Hamada Kōsaku   濱田耕作   Chinese archaelology and art history.

    + Tōhōgaku 67 (Jan. 1984), 201-207.

    • Ibid., 159-201.

    ø Hamada Kōsaku sensei tsuioku <u>Kodai bunka ronkō</u> [5,5,270,2 pp.]. No
       biblio.

       古代文化論考

       Kodaigaku kyōkai, ed. & publ. Kyoto, 1969. {E}

       [Note the evaluations of Hamada's work, pp. 1-9.]

       TRNS:oo.

    • Kodaigaku 16.2-4 (Dec. 1969), 108-111.

    + <u>Hamada sensei tsuitōroku</u> [11,70,498 pp.], 35-70.

       Kyōto Teikoku Daigaku Bungakubu Kōkogaku Kenkyūshitsu, ed. & publ.
       Kyoto, 1939.

       [Apart from the bibliography of Hamada's writings, this volume con-
       sists solely of reminiscences of the scholar, including one in Eng-
       lish by Serge Elisséeff, pp. 493-495, and one in German by Otto
       Kummel, pp. 495-496.]

    + Hōun 24 (June 1939), 119-120.

    • Ibid., 93-119.

*   Nihon kosho tsūshin #117 (April 1939), 38-39.

∋+ S. Elisséef, "Hamada Kōsaku," <u>Harvard Journal of Asiatic Studies</u> 3
     (1938), 407-429.

+   Kōkogaku ronsō 8.2 (Dec. 1937-Aug. 1938), 14-36.

•   Ibid., 1-13.

+   Shirin 23.4 (Oct. 1938), 257-263.

+   Tōyōshi kenkyū 3.6 (July-Aug. 1938), 80-87.

Hamaguchi Shigekuni 濱口重国   Chinese social and institutional history,
                                          Ch'in thru T'ang periods.

    Yen 32, Teng #483.

+   Idem, <u>Shin Kan Zui Tō shi no kenkyū</u>, vol. 2, 1003-1008.
     秦漢隋唐史の研究
     Tokyo: Tōkyō Daigaku Shuppankai, 1966. 2 Vols. 4,5,681 pp., and pp.
     682-1008 plus 88 pp.

Hamashima Atsutoshi 濱島敦俊 Chinese socio-economic history, esp. Ming and
                                       Ch'ing periods.

Hamashita Takeshi   濱下武志 Chinese economic history, esp. monetary his-
                                       tory, Ming, Ch'ing, and Republican periods.

Hanabusa Hideki   花房英樹 Chinese poetry, Six Dynasties and T'ang peri-
                                       ods, esp. Po Chü-i.

    Lit 210, Yen 181.

Hanabusa Nagamichi 英 修道 Modern East Asian diplomatic history.
    Yen 565, Teng #165.

Hanai Hitoshi   花井等 Contemporary international relations.
    Yen 182.

Hanaoka Kyoko   NC
    Listed under Satō Masahiko.

Hanayama Shinshō   花山信勝   Buddhist studies.* Japanese Buddhism.
　　Teng #728.

　　Listed under Miyamoto Shōson, Nanjō Bun'yū, Ogiwara Unrai, Suzuki
　　Daisetsu, Takakusu Junjirō, and Watanabe Kaigyoku.

Hanazaki Saien   花崎采琰   Chinese poetry, esp. Sung tz'u.
　　Lit 210.

Haneda Akira   羽田 明   Central Asian history.
　　Yen 582.

　　Also listed under Tamura Jitsuzō.

Haneda Tōru   羽田 亨   Central and Northern Asian history.
　　• Tōhōgaku 51 (Jan. 1976), 141-156.
　　• Ibid. 50 (July 1975), 129-144.
　　+ Ibid. 11 (Oct. 1955), 157-162.
　　• Ibid. 11 (Oct. 1955), 135-156.
　　∋* Charles C.S. Gardner and Ching-ying Lee Mei (Mrs. Kuang-ti Mei),
　　　"Haneda Tōru," Bibliographies of Fourteen Non-American Specialists on
　　　the Far East. Mimeographed. Cambridge, Mass., 1960 [separate pagi-
　　　nation for each entry], 4 pp.
　　+ Tōyōshi kenkyū 14.3 (Nov. 1955), 81-84.
　　• Ibid., 1-80.
　　+ Shirin 38.4 (July 1955), 68-74.
　　ø Haneda hakushi shōju kinen Tōyōshi ronsō [26,1003,37 pp.], 15-21.
　　東洋史論叢
　　　Haneda hakushi kanreki kinenkai, ed. Kyoto: Tōyōshi Kenkyūkai, 1950.
　　　{E}
　　　TRNS #204, NNO 3:417-418.
　　Also listed under Naitō Konan.

Haniya Yutaka   埴谷雄高   (Modern Japanese novelist.)
　　Listed under Takahashi Kazumi.

Hara Kakuten   原 覚天   International economics, Asia. Modern Chinese
                                      history, Manchuria.

∋ Ramon H. Myers, Review of Hara's collection of articles, <u>Gendai Ajia</u>
<u>kenkyū seiritsu shiron: Mantetsu Chōsabu, Tōa Kenkyūjo, IPR no kenkyū</u>
現代アジア研究成立史論－満鉄調査部・東亜研究所・IPRの研究－
(Tokyo: Keisō Shobō, 1984. 18,982 pp.), in <u>Journal of Asian Studies</u>
46.3 (Aug. 1987), 644-645.

Hara Sanshichi   原 三七   Chinese traditional drama.
    Yen 586.

Hara Tomio   原 富男   Classical Chinese thought.
    Lit 215, Teng #649.

Harada, J.   NC
    Listed under Mizuno Seiichi (twice) and Nagahiro Toshio (twice).

Harada Ken'yū   原田憲雄
    see Harada Norio.

Harada Kinjirō   原田謹次郎 Chinese art history.
    ∈ Idem, <u>The Pageant of Chinese Painting</u>, or <u>Shina meiga hōkan</u> [3,8,41
      pp., 1000 pl., plus 30 pp.].
      支那名画宝鑑
      Tokyo: The Otsuka-kogeisha, 1936.

Harada Masami   原田正巳   Chinese thought, esp. modern period.
    Lit 217, Yen 588
    + Tōyō no shisō to shūkyō (Waseda Daigaku) 1 (June 1984), 115-117.

Harada Matsusaburō 原田松三郎 Chinese language.
    Yen 587.

Harada Minoru   原田稔   Modern Chinese thought and language. Chinese
                                      lexicography.
    Yen 589.

Harada Norio   原田憲雄   Chinese poetry, T'ang period.
   Lit 215.

Harada Taneshige   原田種成   Classical Chinese thought. Chinese historical
                               texts, T'ang and Sung periods, esp. Chen-
                               kuan cheng-yao.
       Lit 216, Yen 588.
       + Daitō Bunka Daigaku Kangakkai shi 24 (March 1985), 1-8.

Harada Toshiaki   原田敏明   Japanese religion, incl. Chinese influences.
   Yen 586.

Harada Yoshito   原田淑人   East Asian archaeology. History of Chinese
                               social customs, esp. clothing.
       Yen 587, Teng #1.
       • Shigaku zasshi 84.2 (Feb. 1975), 86-87.
       + Idem, Tōa kobunka setsuen [482 pp.], 464-481.
         東亜古文化説苑
         Harada Yoshito sensei beiju kinenkai, ed. & publ. Tokyo, 1973.
       • Tōhōgaku 25 (March 1963), 122-138.
       Also listed under Torii Ryūzō.

Hasebe Gakuji   長谷部楽爾 Chinese art history, ceramics.
       Yen 43.
       ∈ Chinese Ceramics [95 pp.].
         By Hayashiya Seizo and Hasebe Gakuji. Translated by Charles A.
         Pomeroy. Rutland, Vt.: Charles E. Tuttle Co., 1966.

Hasebe Rakuji
       see Hasebe Gakuji.

Hasegawa Hiroshi   長谷川 寛   Modern Chinese language.
       Yen 42.

Hasegawa Ryōichi　長谷川 良一　　Modern Chinese language and literature.
　　Lit 205, Yen 41.

Hashikawa Bunsō　　橋川 文三　　Japanese politics and political thought. Mod-
　　　　　　　　　　　　　　　　　　　ern Sino-Japanese relations.

　　Yen 316.

Hashikawa Bunzō
　　see Hashikawa Bunsō.

Hashikawa Tokio　　橋川 時雄　　Chinese literature, esp. Six Dynasties and
　　　　　　　　　　　　　　　　　　T'ang periods. Modern Chinese history, Re-
　　　　　　　　　　　　　　　　　　publican period.
　　Lit 204, Yen 315.
　　• Tōhōgaku 35 (Jan. 1968), 203-227.

Hashimoto Hōkei　　橋本 芳契　　Buddhist thought.* Japanese Buddhism.
　　ø Hashimoto hakushi taikan kinen　Bukkyō kenkyū ronshū　[992 pp.],
　　　8-18.
　　　仏教研究論集
　　　Hashimoto hakushi taikan kinen Bukkyō kenkyū ronshū kankōkai, ed.
　　　Osaka: Seibundō, 1975.
　　　TRNS:oo.

Hashimoto Jun　　橋本 循　　Chinese poetry, thru T'ang period, also
　　　　　　　　　　　　　　　　Ch'ing-period poetry.
　　Lit 204, Yen 314, Teng #586.
　　ø Hashimoto hakushi kiju kinen　Tōyō bunka ronsō　[6,2,3,534,2 pp.],
　　　4-6.
　　　東洋文化論叢
　　　Ritsumeikan Daigaku jimbun gakkai, ed. & publ. Kyoto, 1967.
　　　TRNS #201.

ø Hashimoto hakushi koki kinen <u>Tōyōgaku ronsō</u>   [4,1,3,486,2 pp.], 4
   pp.
   東洋学論叢
   Ritsumeikan Daigaku jimbun gakkai, ed. & publ. Kyoto, 1960.
   TRNS #200.
+ Ritsumeikan bungaku 180 (June 1960), 1-4.

Hashimoto Keizō   橋本 敬造 History of astronomy in China, Ming and
                                        Ch'ing periods.

∈ Idem, <u>Hsü Kuang-ch'i and Astronomical Reform: The Process of the</u>
   <u>Chinese Acceptance of Western Astronomy, 1629-1635</u> [246 pp.].
   Suita: Kansai University Press, 1988.

Hashimoto Mantarō   橋本 欣太郎 Modern Chinese language and linguistics.
   Yen 313.
+ Ajia Afurika gengo bunka kenkyū 35 (March 1988), 201-212.
∈ Idem, <u>The Hakka Dialect: A Linguistic Study of Its Phonology, Syntax</u>
   <u>and Lexicon</u> [26,580 pp.].
   Cambridge: Cambridge University Press, 1973.

Hashimoto Masukichi 橋本 増吉 East Asian history, esp. early periods. Man-
                                        churia.
+ Shigaku 29.4 (March 1957), 110-114.
• Ibid., 102-110.

Hashimoto Mineo   橋本 峰雄
   Listed under Suzuki Daisetsu.

Hashimoto Takakatsu 橋本 高勝 Classical Chinese thought.
   Yen 313.

Hashimoto Takashi   橋本 堯 Chinese vernacular fiction and drama, Ming
                                        period.

   Lit 205, Yen 315.

Hasumi Shigeyasu   蓮実重康   Chinese art history, esp. Sung and Yuan periods.

     Yen 248.

Hata Ikuhiko   秦 郁彦   Modern Chinese history and international relations.

     Yen 319.

Hatachi Masanori   畑地正憲   Chinese history, Five Dynasties and Sung periods.

Hatada Takashi   旗田巍   Korean and Japanese history. Mongolian history. Chinese rural society. History of
peoples in China.

     Yen 307, Teng #712.

     * Senshū shigaku 11 (1979), 74-92.

     + Jimbun gakuhō (Tōkyō Toritsu Daigaku) 89 (March 1-20.

     [A book-length English-language translation of Hatada's history of Korea
is not listed here.]

Hatani Ryōtai   羽溪了諦   Buddhist studies.* Central Asian Buddhism.

     ø Hatani hakushi beiju kinen <u>Bukkyō ronsetsu senshū</u> [862 pp.], 5-8.

     仏教論説選集

       ed.? Tokyo: Daitō Shuppansha, 1971.

       TRNS:oo.

Hatani Ryōtei

     see Hatani Ryōtai.

Hatano Tarō   波多野太郎   Traditional Chinese drama and vernacular fiction. Modern Chinese literature. Chinese
language and linguistics. Tun-huang texts.

     Lit 205, Yen 34, Teng #637.

     + Yokohama Shiritsu Daigaku ronsō (Jimbun kagaku keiretsu) 28.2-3
       (March 1977), 179-190.

     • Ibid., 191-205.

Hatano Yoshihiro　波多野善大　Modern Chinese history, esp. economic histo-
                                        ry.

   Yen 33, Teng #566 and #788.

  +　Nagoya Daigaku Tōyōshi kenkyū hōkoku 6 (Aug. 1980), 276-278.

  •　Ibid., 1-28.

  +　Nagoya Daigaku Bungakubu kenkyū ronshū 56 (Shigaku 19) (1972), 1-3.

Hattori Masayuki　服部昌之　Modern Chinese language. Chinese vernacular
                                        fiction.

   Yen 124.

Hattori Ryūzō　服部隆造　Modern Chinese literature.

   Lit 210.

Hattori Shirō　服部四郎　Altaic languages, esp. Mongolian. History of
                                        Chinese language.

   Yen 123, Teng #206.

  ∅∋　<u>Studies in General and Oriental Linguistics Presented to Shirō Hat-</u>
     <u>tori on the Occasion of His Sixtieth Birthday</u> [36,694 pp.], 14-36.
     Roman Jakobson and Kawamoto Shigeo, eds. Tokyo: TEC Company, Ltd.,
     1970.
     [All titles in "A Bibliography of Books and Articles by Shirō Hat-
     tori" are given in English; most are accompanied by a one-phrase or
     one-sentence English summary.]
     TRNS:oo.

  ∋　Shibata Takeshi, "Hattori Shirō," Translated by W.A. Grootaers, <u>Orbis</u>
     (Louvain) 7 (1958), 281-286.

Hattori Takeshi　服部健　Asian ethnology. Gilyak language.
   Yen 122, Teng #207.

Hattori Unokichi　服部宇之吉　Chinese thought. Chinese institutions, Ch'ing
                                        period. Chinese law.

  •　Shakai kagaku tōkyū (Waseda Daigaku) 34.2 (#99) (Dec. 1988), 31-54.

  •　Bunka 45.1-2 (Sept. 1981), 1-32.

- Shih-chieh hua-hsueh chi-k'an (Taipei) 2-3 (Sept. 1981), 41-73.
  [Chinese translation of preceding entry.]

•* Tōyōgaku no sōshisha-tachi [320 pp.], 119-168.

東洋学の創始者たち

  Yoshikawa Kōjirō, ed. Tokyo: Kōdansha, 1976.
  [Except for a somewhat different nempu, a reprint of the Tōhōgaku material listed below.]

- Tōhōgaku 46 (July 1973), 163-186.
- Shibun 58 (Oct. 1969), 27-33.
+ Ibid. 20.5 (Apr. 1938), 45-55.
ø Hattori sensei koki shukuga kinen rombunshū [57,2,2,6,1034 pp.], 50-57.

  Hattori sensei koki shukuga kinen rombunshū kankōkai, ed. Tokyo: Fuzambō, 1936.

  TRNS #203, NNO 3:416-417.

See also the Stefan Tanaka entry under Shiratori Kurakichi.

Hattori Yasushi   服部 端   Chinese poetry, traditional.
     Lit 209.

Hayakawa Kōzaburō   早川 光三郎   Sino-Japanese literary relations.
     Lit 212.

Hayakawa Michisuke   早川 通介   Chinese language.
     Yen 593.

Hayashi Hideichi   林 秀一   Classical Chinese thought.
     Lit 213, Yen 250, Teng #658.
   + Idem, Hayashi Hideichi hakushi sonkō [15,238], 232-236.

林秀一博士存稿

     Hayashi Hideichi sensei koki kinenkai, ed. Okayama: Hayashi Hideichi Sensei Koki Kinen Shuppankai, 1974.

Hayashi Kensaku   林 謙作
     Listed under Collected Articles #3.

Hayashi Kenzō   林 謙三   History of East Asian music.
    Teng #197.

Hayashi Megumi   林 恵海   Japanese sociology. Chinese rural society.
    Teng #120.

Hayashi Minao   林 巳奈夫   Chinese archaeology and epigraphy.
    Yen 249.

Hayashi Morimichi 林 盛遙   Chinese literature.
    Lit 213, Yen 251.

Hayashi Taisuke   林 泰輔   Chinese history, esp. pre-Han period.
    + Idem, Shina jōdai no kenkyū [25,4,522,52,5,7 pp.], 1-7.
       支那上代之研究
        Tokyo: Kōfūkan, 1927; rpt. 1944.
    See also the Stefan Tanaka entry under Shiratori Kurakichi.

Hayashi Tomoharu   林 友春   History of education in Asia.
    Teng #107.
    Also listed under Collected Articles #33.

Hayashi Yukimitsu 林 雪光   Chinese language. Chinese songs, Yuan period.

    Lit 214, Yen 249.

Hayashida Shinnosuke 林田 慎之助   Chinese poetry and poetics, esp. Six Dynas-
                                        ties period.
    Lit 214, Yen 252.

Hayashiya Seizō   林屋 晴三   Chinese art history, esp. ceramics.
    ∈ Chinese Ceramics [95 pp.].
        By Hayashiya Seizo and Hasebe Gakuji. Translated by Charles A.
        Pomeroy. Rutland, Vt.: Charles E. Tuttle Co., 1966.

Hayashiya Tatsusaburō   Japanese cultural history, incl. theatrical
　　　　林屋 辰三郎   arts. Sino-Japanese historical relations.
　　Yen 251, Teng #284.

Hayashiya Tatsuzaburō
　　see Hayashiya Tatsusaburō.

Hazama Naoki   狭間直樹   Modern Chinese history, esp. May Fourth Move-
　　　　　　　　　　　　　　　　　ment.

　　Yen 494.

Hemmi Baiei   逸見 梅栄   Asian art history.
　　Yen 564.

Hibino Takeo   日比野丈夫   Chinese historical geography. Chinese histo-
　　　　　　　　　　　　　　　　　ry.

　　Yen 333, Teng #468.
　　+　Tōhō gakuhō 50 (Feb. 1978), 519-524.
　　Also listed under Mizuno Seiichi.

Hidaka Rokurō   日高 六郎   Sociology and education. Contemporary Chinese
　　　　　　　　　　　　　　　　　politics and society.

　　Yen 334.

Higaonna Kanjun   東思納 寛惇　Okinawa. Sino-Japanese historical relations.
　　Yen 104.

Higashi Ichio
　　see Higashi Kazuo.

Higashi Kazuo   東 一夫   Chinese history, Sung period.
　　Yen 106.
　　+˙ Shikai (Tōkyō Gakugei Daigaku) 21-22 (1975).
　　+　Tōyō kodai chūsei shi kenkyū (Tōkyō Gakugei Daigaku) 3 (1974).

Higashionna Kanjun 東恩納 寛惇
    see Higaonna Kanjun.

Higashiyama Kaii   東山魁夷   Modern Japanese painter. Contemporary China
                                   interest.
    Yen 104.

Higo Kazuo   肥後和男   Japanese cultural history, incl. folklore and
                                   mythology. Sino-Japanese historical rela-
                                   tions.
    Yen 114, Teng #237 and #790.

Higuchi Susumu   樋口 進   Modern Chinese literature.
    Lit 217, Yen 463.
    ∅ Higuchi Susumu sensei koki kinen Chūgoku gendai bungaku ronshū.
      中国現代文学論集
      Higuchi Susumu sensei koki kinen kankōkai, ed.   Fukuoka: Chūgoku
      Shoten, 1990.
      TRNS:oo.

Higuchi Takayasu   樋口 隆康   Asian archaeology. Chinese art history.
    Yen 462, Teng #3.
    ∅ Tembō Ajia no kōkogaku Higuchi Takayasu kyōju taikan kinen ronshū
      [648 pp.], 627-646.
      展望アジアの考古学
      Idem et al., eds.   Tokyo: Shinchōsha, 1983.
      TRNS:oo.

Hihara Toshikuni   日原 利国   Classical Chinese thought.
    Lit 219, Yen 335.
    ∋ M. Kalinowski, Review of Hihara's dictionary of Chinese thought,
      Chūgoku shisō jiten 中国思想辞典 (Tokyo: Kembun Shuppan, 1984.
      452 pp.), in T'oung Pao 71 (1985), 293-294.
    ∋ Benjamin A. Elman, Review of the same work (Chūgoku shisō jiten), in
      Journal of Asian Studies 45.1 (Nov. 1985), 120-121.
    + Chūgoku shisōshi kenkyū (Kyōto Daigaku) 7 (1984), 115-123.

Hijikata Teiichi   上方定一   Fine arts. History of art, China and Japan.
    Yen 464.

    Σ Hijikata Teiichi chosakushū. No biblio.
       Tokyo: Heibonsha, 1976-77. 12 vols.

Himeda Mitsuyoshi   姫田光義   Modern Chinese history.

Himeta Mitsuyoshi
    see Himeda Mitsuyoshi.

Hino Kaisaburō   日野開三郎 Chinese socio-economic history, T'ang and
                                      Sung periods. History of Manchuria.
    Yen 335, Teng #537.

    ø Ronshū: Chūgoku shakai seido bunka shi no shomondai Hino Kaisaburō
       hakushi shōju kinen [623 pp.], 5-20.
       論集一中国社会・制度・文化史の諸問題
       Hino Kaisaburō hakushi shōju kinen ronshū kankōkai, ed.   Fukuoka:
       Chūgoku Shoten, 1987.
       TRNS:oo.

    Σ Tōyōshigaku ronshū. No biblio.
       東洋史学論集
       Tokyo: San'ichi Shobō, 1980-84. 10 vols.

    + Shien (Kyūshū Daigaku) 109 (Nov. 1972), 101-104.

    Also listed under Shigematsu Shunshō.

Hino Kaizaburō
    see Hino Kaisaburō.

Hino Tatsuo   日野龍夫 Sino-Japanese literary relations.
    Yen 334.

Hirai Hidebumi
    see Hirai Hidefumi.

Hirai Hidefumi   平井秀文   Chinese literature, T'ang-period fiction.
    Teng #587.

Hirai Hisayuki   平井尚志
    Listed under Komai Kazuchika.

Hirakawa Akira   平井彰   Buddhist studies.* Indian Buddhism.
    Yen 300.

    ø Hirakawa Akira hakushi kanreki kinen ronshū Bukkyō ni okeru hō no
       kenkyū [19,664,1 pp.], 7-16.
       仏教における法の研究
       Hirakawa Akira hakushi kanreki kinenkai, ed. Tokyo: Shunjūsha, 1975.
       TRNS:oo.

    [A book-length English-language translation of a history of Indian
    Buddhism by Hirakawa is not listed here.]

Hiraki Kōhei   平木康平   Chinese thought, Six Dynasties period.
    Lit 221.

Hirako Takurei   平子鐸嶺   Buddhist art history.
    * Idem, (Zōtei) Bukkyō geijutsu no kenkyū [2,6,791,32 pp.], 20-28.
       (増訂) 仏教芸術の研究
       Tokyo: Kokusho Kankōkai, 1976.
       [An expanded version (with a nempu for Hirako) of the 1914 (or 1923)
       edition of Bukkyō geijutsu no kenkyū: Tokyo: Sanseisha, 1914.
       2,6,770,21 pp.]
    + Takurei Hirako Hisashi sensei chosaku nempyō ryakureki [1,41 pp.], 6-
       40.
       鐸嶺平子尚先生著作年表略歴
       Noda Nobuta, ed. Tokyo: Hasshūkai, 1974.

Hiranaka Reiji   平中苓次   Chinese taxation system and criminal law,
                                esp. Ch'in and Han periods.
    Yen 307.

- Ritsumeikan bungaku 331-333 (March 1973), 180.
- Tōhōgaku 45 (Jan. 1973), 159-160.

Hirano Ken'ichirō 平野 健一郎 Modern Chinese political thought and history.
   Yen 304.

Hirano Kenshō 平野 顕照 Buddhist influence on Chinese literature, Six
                              Dynasties and T'ang periods.
   Lit 221, Yen 304.

Hirano Tadashi 平野 正 Modern Chinese history, Republican period.
   Yen 305.

Hirano Yoshitarō 平野 義太郎 Contemporary Chinese politics and economy.
                              Sino-Soviet relations.
   Yen 304, Teng #567.

Hiraoka Kentarō 平岡 健太郎 International trade. Sino-Japanese trade.
   Yen 303.

Hiraoka Masaaki 平岡 正明 Modern Chinese history, World War II.
   Yen 302.

Hiraoka Takeo 平岡 武夫 Chinese literature and history, esp. T'ang
                              period.
   Lit 220, Yen 301, Teng #529.
   + Kangaku kenkyū (Nihon Daigaku) 20 (Feb. 1983), 3-14.
   • Ibid., 1-3.
   + Tōhō gakuhō 46 (March 1974), 357-359.

Hiraoka Teikichi 平岡 禎吉 Classical Chinese thought.
   Teng #659.

  + <u>Satsuma Hantō no sōgōteki kenkyū</u> [5,600 pp.], 599-600.

薩摩半島の総合的研究

     Sasaki Heigorō and Saitō Takeshi, eds.   Tokyo: Gendai Jaanarizumu
     Shuppankai, 1971.

Hirase Minokichi   平瀬巳之吉   Modern Chinese economic history.
     Teng #75.

Hirata Sakae   平田 栄   Chinese thought. Neo-Confucianism.
     Yen 304.

Hirata Yutaka   NC
     Listed under Mikami Yoshio.

Hiratsuka Masunori 平塚 益徳   History of education: Japan, China, and else-
                                   where.
     Yen 306, Teng #108.

Hirayama Hisao   平山 久雄   Chinese language, esp. phonetics and phonol-
                                   ogy.
     Yen 303.

Hiroike Chikurō   廣池千九郎   East Asian legal history.
     + Morarojii kenkyū 10 (June 1981), 151-158.
     • Ibid., 97-151 and 159-166.
     ø <u>Seitan hyakunen Hiroike hakushi kinen ronshū</u>.
        Uchida Tomoo, ed.   Kashiwa (Chiba): Hiroike Gakuen Shuppanbu, 1967;
        Hiroike Gakuen Jigyōbu, 1973.
        [Note that the 1973 edition is an expanded version (14,496 pp.) of
        the 1967 edition (10,372 pp.), both compiled by the same editor and
        published under the same auspices. The combined curriculum vitae and
        bibliography for Hiroike is the same in both editions: pp. 367-370
        (1967), and pp. 489-493 (1973).]
        TRNS #208 (1967).

Σ <u>Hiroike hakushi zenshū</u>. No biblio. 4 vols.

Kashiwa (Chiba): Hiroike Gakuen Shuppanbu, 1937; rpt. 1968-69.

[Vols. 2 and 3 deal with China. Note the index of cited Chinese works (listed chapter by chapter under each cited work): vol. 3, 835-866.]

Hiroike Senkurō

see Hiroike Chikurō.

Hirotsune Jinsei 廣常人世   Chinese thought.

Lit 222, Yen 162.

Hisae Fukusaburō 久重福三郎 Chinese economics, incl. currency. Chinese agriculture. International economics.

+ Nagoya Gakuin Daigaku ronshū (Shakai kagaku hen) 7.1 (March 1970), 195-197.

ø Hisae Fukusaburō sensei Sakamoto Ichirō sensei kanreki kinen <u>Chūgoku</u> <u>kenkyū</u> [1,196 pp.], 151-159.

中国研究

Hisae Fukusaburō sensei Sakamoto Ichirō sensei kanreki kinen gyōji jumbi iinkai, ed. & publ. Kobe, 1965.

TRNS:oo.

Hisamatsu Shin'ichi 久松真一

Listed under Suzuki Daisetsu.

Hishinuma Tōru 菱沼透 Modern Chinese literature and language.

Lit 218.

Hiyama Hisao 檜山久雄 Modern Chinese literature.

Lit 219, Yen 165.

Hō Takushū 彭沢周 Modern Chinese history, late Ch'ing period. Modern Sino-Japanese and Sino-Korean relations. Chinese Communist Party.

Honda Megumu   本多 恵   Indian philosophy. Chinese language.
    Yen 30.

Honda Osamu   本田 治   Chinese socio-economic history, Sung and Yuan
                                         periods.

Honda Shigeyuki   本田 成之   Chinese thought.
    + Shinagaku, Vol. 10 special issue [vol. 13 in rpt. ed.] (Apr. 1942),
       827-830.

Honda Wataru   本田 済   Chinese thought, classical and medieval peri-
                                         ods.
        Lit 235, Yen 30, Teng #660.

Hora Tomio   洞 富雄   Japanese history. Modern Chinese history.
    Yen 106, Teng #219.

Hori Toshikazu   堀 敏一   Chinese socio-economic history, esp. Han thru
                                         T'ang periods.
    Yen 237.

Horie Eiichi   堀江英一   Japanese socio-economic history, Edo period.
                                         Modern Chinese economic history.
        Teng #76.

Horiike Nobuo   堀池信夫   Classical Chinese thought and early Chinese
                                         science.
    Lit 235.

Horikawa Takeo   堀川武夫   Modern Chinese history.
    Yen 238.

Horikawa Tetsuo   堀川哲男   Modern Chinese history, Boxer Rebellion and
                                         Sun Yat-sen.
    Yen 238.

Hoshi Ayao   星 斌夫   Chinese socio-economic history, Ming and Ch'ing periods, esp. Grand Canal transportation.

     Yen 532, Teng #484.

   ø   Hoshi hakushi taikan kinen <u>Chūgokushi ronshū</u> [23,422,3 pp.], 5-18.

     中国史論集

     Hoshi Ayao sensei taikan kinen jigyōkai, ed. & publ. Yamagata, 1978.

     TRNS #223.

   +   Yamagata Daigaku kiyō (Jimbun kagaku) 9.1 (Feb. 1978), 3 pp.

   ∈   Idem, <u>The Ming Tribute Grain System</u> [3,112 pp.].

     Translated by Mark Elvin. Ann Arbor: Center for Chinese Studies, University of Michigan, 1969.

Hoshikawa Kiyotaka 星川 清孝   Chinese poetry, thru T'ang period. Chinese prose, T'ang thru Ming periods. Chinese literary thought, Six Dynasties.

     Lit 233, Yen 532.

   ø   Hoshikawa hakushi taikyū kinen <u>Chūgoku bungaku ronsō</u> [3,7,391 pp.], 4-7.

     中国文学論叢

     Ishikawa Tadahisa, ed. Machita: Ōbirin Daigaku Bungakubu Chūgokugo Chūgoku Bungaku-ka, 1979.

     [Note the articles about Hoshikawa, pp. 371-390.]

     TRNS:oo

   +   Chūgoku bungaku ronsō (Ōbirin Daigaku) 7 (March 1979), 1-7.

   •   Ibid., 372-390.

Hosoda Mikio   細田三喜夫   Chinese poetry, traditional.

     Lit 234, Teng #588.

   +   Jimbun kagaku kenkyū hōkoku (Nagasaki Daigaku Kyōiku Gakubu) 23 (1974), 2 pp.

Hosokawa Haruma   細川鄗真   Chinese language.

     Yen 493.

Hosoya Sōko   細谷草子   Modern Chinese literature.
    Lit 235.

Hosoya Yoshio   細谷良夫   Chinese history, Ch'ing period.
    Yen 493.

Hozumi Fumio   穂積文雄   Chinese economic history. Chinese thought.
    Yen 432, Teng #77.
    + Keizai ronsō (Kyōto Daigaku) 97.1 (Jan. 1966), 145-150.

Ichien Kazuo   一円一億   Japanese (and Chinese) law.
    Yen 563.

Ichihara Kōkichi
    see Ichihara Kyōkichi.

Ichihara Kyōkichi   市原亨吉   Chinese literature, T'ang and Ming periods.
    Lit 22, Yen 406.
    + Tōhō gakuhō 48 (Dec. 1975), 359.

Ichikawa Mototarō   市川本太郎   Classical Chinese thought.
    Lit 21, Teng #661.

Ichikawa Yasuji
    see Ichikawa Yasushi.

Ichikawa Yasushi   市川安司   Chinese thought, esp. Chuang-tzu. Neo-Confu-
                                      cianism.
    Lit 21, Yen 402.
    + Jimbun Kagakuka kiyō (Tōkyō Daigaku) 55 (May 1972), 4 pp.
    + Tōkyō Shinagaku hō 16 (1971), 45-48.

Ichiko Chūzō   市古宙三   Modern Chinese history. Chinese bibliography.
                                      Contemporary China.
    Yen 404.

+ Ajia-shi kenkyū (Chūō Daigaku) 8 (1984), 3-7.

+ Chūō Daigaku Bungakubu kiyō 112 (Shigakuka 29), 207-211.

ø <u>Ronshū: Kindai Chūgoku kenkyū</u> [12,1,633,5 pp.], 626-632.

論集 ー近代中国研究ー

Ichiko Chūzō kyōju taikan kinen ronsō henshū iinkai, ed.   Tokyo:
Yamakawa Shuppansha, 1981.

[Note Ichiko's remarks on his career in modern Chinese studies, pp.
611-632.]

TRNS:oo.

+ Ochanomizu shigaku 22 (1978), 1-4.

● Ibid., 107-110.

Also listed under Intro., Footnote 4.

Ichiko Shōzō   市古尚三   Chinese economic history, Ch'ing period.
    Yen 404.

Ichimura Kinjirō   市村金次郎   Modern Chinese language.
    Yen 403.

Ichimura Kisaburō   市村其三郎   Early Japanese history. Sino-Japanese histor-
                                                 ical relations.

    Yen 404, Teng #238.

Ichimura Sanjirō   市村瓚次郎 Chinese history.
    ●* Tōhōgaku 53 (Jan. 1977), 151-170.
    ø Ichimura hakushi koki kinen   <u>Tōyōshi ronsō</u>   [3,18,9,5,1,4,2,1214
       pp.], 18 pp.

    東洋史論叢

    Ichimura hakushi koki kinen Tōyōshi ronsō kankōkai, ed.   Tokyo:
    Fuzambō, 1933.

    TRNS #018, NNO 3:405-406.

Ichinosawa Torao   市野沢寅雄 Chinese poetry, T'ang period, Tu Mu. Chinese
                                                 poetics, <u>Ts'ang-lang shih-hua</u>.

    Lit 22, Yen 405.

Idachi Yoshitsugu　伊地智善継　Modern Chinese language and linguistics.
 Lit 22, Yen 553.

 ø Idachi Yoshitsugu, Tsujimoto Haruhiko ryō kyōju taikan kinen <u>Chūgoku</u>
   <u>gogaku bungaku ronshū</u> [9,4,513,1 pp.].   No biblio.
   中国語学文学論集
   Idachi Yoshitsugu, Tsujimoto Haruhiko ryō kyōju taikan kinen ronshū
   kankōkai, ed.   Tokyo: Tōhō Shoten, 1983.
   TRNS:oo.

Ide Tatsurō　　　　井手達郎　Chinese socio-economic history, esp. Sung
                                          period.
 Teng #538.

Igarashi Masakazu　五十嵐正一　Chinese educational history.
 + Idem, <u>Chūgoku kinsei kyōiku shi no kenkyū</u> [19,458,7 pp.], 7-9.
   中国近世教育史の研究
   Tokyo: Kokusho Kankōkai, 1979.
 +* <u>Igarashi Masakazu sensei: Sono hito to kyōiku</u>.
   五十嵐正一先生―その人と教育―
   Igarashi rekishi seminaaru, ed. Ko Igarshi Masakazu sensei chosaku
   kankōkai, publ. Tokyo?, 1979.
 + <u>Ko Igarashi Masakazu sensei chosho rombun ichiran</u>.
   Ko Igarashi Masakazu sensei chosho kankōkai, ed. & pub.   Tokyo?,
   1977.

Igarashi Shōichi
 see Igarashi Masakazu.

Ihara Hiroshi　　　伊原 弘　Chinese history, Sung period.　　　　　　　.

Ihara Kōsuke　　　伊原 弘介　Chinese socio-economic history, Ch'ing period.

Ihara Takushū　　伊原 沢周
 see Hō Takushū.

Iida Kichirō   飯田吉郎
    see Iida Yoshirō.

Iida Rigyō   飯田利行
    see Iida Toshiyuki.

Iida Sugashi   飯田須賀斯   History of Chinese architecture and fine
                                      arts. Sino-Japanese cultural relations.
    Yen 110, Teng #193.

Iida Tadao   飯田忠雄   Chinese law. Maritime law.
    Yen 111.

Iida Toshiyuki   飯田利行   Chinese historical linguistics.
    Yen 110, Teng #638.
    ø Iida Toshiyuki hakushi koki kinen <u>Tōyōgaku ronsō</u> [3,625,3 pp.],
       613-625.
    東洋学論叢
    Iida Toshiyuki hakushi koki kinen rombunshū kankōkai, ed.   Tokyo:
    Kokusho Kankōkai, 1980.
    TRNS:oo.

Iida Yoshirō   飯田吉郎   Modern Chinese literature. Chinese vernacular
                                        literature. Sino-Japanese literary rela-
                                        tions, late Ch'ing period.
    Lit 16.

Iijima Shunkei   飯島春敬   East Asian calligraphy.
    Yen 110.

Iikura Shōhei   飯倉照平   Modern Chinese literature, incl. minorities
                                        literature. Comparative Sino-Japanese folk-
                                        tales.
    Lit 15, Yen 111.

Iizuka Akira   飯塚朗   Modern Chinese literature. Chinese vernacular
                                            fiction.

    Lit 16, Yen 112, Teng #623.

    + Iizuka Akira sensei taikan kinen shōsatsu.

    Iizuka Akira sensei taikan kinen jigyōkai, ed. & publ. Tokyo, 1971.

Iizuka Kōji   飯塚浩二 Human geography. Economic and cultural as-
                                            pects of Asia.

    Yen 112, Teng #130.

    Σ Iizuka Kōji chosakushū, vol. 10 (1976), 597-613.

       Tokyo: Heibonsha, 1974-76. 10 vols.

    + Chirigaku hyōron 44.2 (Feb. 1971), 148-151.

    + Tōyō Bunka Kenkyūjo kiyō (Tōkyō Daigaku) 43 (March 1967), 1-20.

Ijichi Yoshitsugu 伊地智義継
    see Idachi Yoshitsugu.

Ikeda Daisaku   池田大作 Contemporary   Japanese   politician.   Asian
                                            thought, Buddhism.

    Yen 55.

    ∈ Idem, The Flower of Chinese Buddhism [10,225 pp.].

       Translated by Burton Watson. New York: Weatherhill, 1986.

    [Additional book-length English-language volumes of Ikeda's writings are
    not listed here.]

Ikeda Makoto   池田誠 Chinese socio-economic history, T'ang and
                                            Sung periods. Modern Chinese history. Con-
                                            temporary Chinese politics. Chinese bibli-
                                            ography.

    Yen 57, Teng #539.

Ikeda On   池田温 Chinese socio-economic and legal history,
                                            esp. T'ang period.

    Yen 56.

∋ M. Soymié, Review article on Ideda On's study of Chinese household registers, <u>Chūgoku kodai sekichō kenkyū: Gaikan rokubun</u> 中国古代 籍帳研究—概觀・録文— (Tokyo: Tōkyō Daigaku Tōyō Bunka Kenkyū-jo, 1979. 7,669,4 pp.) in <u>T'oung Pao</u> 68 (1982), 340-346.

Ikeda Suetoshi 池田 末利 Early Chinese thought and religion.

Lit 17, Yen 55, Teng #662.

ø Ikeda Suetoshi hakushi koki kinen <u>Tōyōgaku ronshū</u> [23,1,1022,57, 5,4 pp.], 5-17.

東洋学論集

Ikeda Suetoshi hakushi koki kinen jigyōkai, ed. & publ. Hiroshima, 1980.

[Includes an article by L. Vandermeersch, "Note sur les inscriptions oraculaires de Fengchucun," 1-15.]

TRNS:oo.

Ikeda Takeo 池田武雄 Chinese language.

Yen 56.

Ikeda Tomohisa 池田知久 Classical Chinese thought.

Lit 18, Yen 57.

Ikeda Yūichi 池田雄一 Early Chinese history.

Yen 57.

Ikegami Teiichi 池上貞一 Contemporary Chinese political and legal history.

Yen 54.

Ikeuchi Hiroshi 池内宏 Korean and Inner Asian history.

•* <u>Tōyōgaku no sōshisha-tachi</u> [320 pp.], 263-320.

東洋学の創始者たち

Yoshikawa Kōjirō, ed. Tokyo: Kōdansha, 1976.

[A reprint of the <u>Tōhōgaku</u> material listed below, with a list of Ike-uchi's major works omitted.]

●* Tōhōgaku 48 (July 1974), 115-142.

+   Idem, <u>Ikeuchi Hiroshi isō</u> [2,43,10 pp.], 10 pp.
    No ed. or publ. Tokyo?, 1952.

ø   Ikeuchi hakushi kanreki kinen <u>Tōyōshi ronsō</u> [9,6,2,3,912 pp.], 9
    pp.
    東洋史論叢
    Ikeuchi hakushi kanreki kinen kankōkai, ed. Tokyo: Zayūhō Kankōkai,
    1940.
    TRNS #013, NNO 3:404.
Also listed under Fujita Toyohachi and Shiratori Kurakichi.

Ikkai Tomoyoshi   一海知義   Chinese poetry, esp. Six Dynasties and T'ang
                                 periods. Chinese historical texts, <u>Shih-
                                 chi</u>.
Lit 22, Yen 562.

Imabori Seiji   今堀 誠二
    see Imahori Seiji.

Imaeda Jirō   今枝二郎   Chinese literature, pre-T'ang period.
    Lit 33.

Imahama Michitaka 今濱通隆   Chinese literature, pre-T'ang period.
    Lit 35.

Imahori Seiji   今堀 誠二   Chinese socio-economic history: modern, Sung,
                                 and Ch'ing periods.
    Yen 213, Teng #485.

+   <u>Hiroshima Daigaku zaishokuchū ni okeru kenkyū gyōseki mokuroku 1939-
    1977</u> [2,1,50 pp.], 50 pp.
    広島大学在職中に於ける研究業績目録 1939-1977
    Imahori Seiji hakushi gyōseki kankōkai, ed. & publ. Tokyo, 1977.

Imai Keiichi   今井 啓一   Early Japanese history. Sino-Japanese histor-
                                ical relations.
    Yen 212, Teng #239.

Imai Kiyoshi   今井 清   Chinese literature, T'ang period.
    Lit 33.

Imai Seiichi   今井 清一   Chinese geography, cities.
    Also listed under Ozaki Hotsumi.

Imai Usaburō   今井 宇三郎   Chinese classics, Sung period. <u>I-ching</u>.
    Lit 33, Yen 212.

Imaizumi Juntarō   今泉 潤太郎   Modern Chinese language. Chinese lexicogra-
                                    phy.
    Yen 214.

Imamura Yoshio   今村 与志雄   Modern Chinese literature. Chinese fiction.
                                    Chinese vernacular fiction.
    Lit 35, Yen 210.

Imanaga Seiji   今永 清二   History of Islam. Chinese agricultural soci-
                                    ety. Modern Chinese history.
    Yen 215.

Imanishi Haruaki
    see Imanishi Shunjū.

Imanishi Shunjū   今西 春秋   Chinese and Manchurian history, Ming and
                                    Ch'ing periods.
    Yen 214, Teng #496.

Imataka Makoto   今鷹 真   Chinese literature, pre-T'ang period. Chinese
                                    historical texts, <u>Shih-chi</u>.
    Lit 34, Yen 215.

Imatomi Masaki   今富 正巳   Modern Chinese language.
    Yen 211.

Imazeki Tenhō   今関 天彭
     see Imazeki Toshimaro.

Imazeki Toshimaro   今関 寿麿   Chinese poetry, traditional. Sino-Japanese
                                  historical relations.
     Lit 34, Yen 211.
     ●* Tōhōgaku 33 (Jan. 1967), 157-175.

Inaba Ichirō   稲葉一郎   Chinese thought, T'ang period. Chinese eco-
                                  nomic history.
     Yen 99.

Inaba Iwakichi   稲葉岩吉   Asian history, incl. Central Asia.
     ø Inaba hakushi kanreki kinen Man Sen shi ronsō [1,4,1,18,2,769 pp.].
        No biblio.
        満鮮史論叢
        Inaba hakushi kanreki kinenkai, ed. & publ. Keijō [Seoul], 1938.
        [Note Inaba's discussion of his own work, pp. 1-28.]
        TRNS #019, NNO 3:406.
     + Idem, Shakkei [5,126,15 pp.], 15 pp.
        釈椋
        Osaka: Ōsaka Yagō Shoten, 1936.

Inaba Seiichi   稲葉誠一   Chinese history and literature, Ch'ing peri-
                                  od.
     Lit 29, Yen 98.

Inaba Shōji   稲葉昭二 Modern Chinese literature, Yü Ta-fu.
     Lit 29.

Inaba Shōju   稲葉正就   Tibetan language and culture. Modern Chinese
                                  history, Sino-Japanese War.
     Yen 99, Teng #729.

Inada Masatsugu   稲田正次   Law, esp. constitutional law, Japan and China.

Yen 98, Teng #31.

Inada Osamu   稲田尹   Chinese vernacular fiction. Taiwanese folk-
songs.

Lit 28, Teng #624.

Inada Takashi   稲田孝   Chinese literature: poetry and vernacular
fiction. Chinese myth and legend.

Lit 29, Yen 97.

Inahata Kōichirō   稲畑耕一郎   Chinese literature, pre-T'ang period. Chinese
poetry, fu.

Lit 30.

Inami Ritsuko   井波律子   Chinese literature, Six Dynasties period.
Lit 30, Yen 225.

Inoguchi Atsushi   猪口篤志   Classical Chinese though... Chinese poetry,
Shih-ching.

Lit 32, Yen 633.

+ Daitō Bunka Daigaku Kangakkai shi 26 (1987), 1-4.

Inoi Makoto   家井真   Early Chinese thought. Chinese poetry, Shih-
ching.

Lit 31.

Inokuchi Akira   井口晃   Modern Chinese literature.
Lit 32.

Inokuma Bunhei

see Inokuma Fumiaki.

Inokuma Fumiaki   猪熊 文炳   Modern Chinese language.
    Yen 634.

Inokuma Kaneshige   猪熊 兼繁   Japanese history: manners, customs, court
                                      ceremonies. East Asian law.
        Yen 633, Teng #32.

Inomata Shōhachi   猪俣庄八   Modern Chinese literature. Chinese vernacular
                                      fiction.
        Lit 32, Yen 634.
        + Hokkaidō Daigaku Bungakubu kiyō 17.2 (Nov. 1969), 28-29.

Inosaki Takaoki   井崎 隆興   Chinese history, Yuan period.
    Teng #540.

Inoue Gengo   井上 源吾   Chinese thought.
    Lit 31, Yen 229.
        + Jimbun kagaku kenkyū hōkoku (Nagasaki Daigaku Kyōiku Gakubu) 24
           (1975), 2 pp.

Inoue Hideo   井上 秀雄   Korean history. East Asian ethnological his-
                                      tory.
        Yen 229.

Inoue Hiromasa   井上 裕正   Modern Chinese history, esp. Sino-British
                                      relations, Opium War.
    Also listed under Naitō Konan.

Inoue Kiyoshi   井上 清   Modern Japanese history. Contemporary Sino-
                                      Japanese relations. Modern Chinese economy.
        Yen 227, Teng #299.
        • Li-shih chiao-hsueh (T'ien-chin) 197 (May 1980), 55.

Inoue Masamichi   井上 順理   Classical Chinese thought. Sino-Japanese cul-
                                      tural relations.
        Yen 228, Teng #110.

Inoue Mitsusada   井上 光貞   Early Japanese history. Sino-Japanese historical relations.

Yen 225, Teng #241.

Inoue Sonken   井上 選軒

see Inoue Tetsujirō.

Inoue Tetsujirō   井上 哲次郎 Japanese and Chinese thought, Confucianism.

ø <u>Inoue sensei kiju kinen bunshū</u> [1,12,686 pp.], 4-5.

Sonken kai, ed. Tokyo: Fuzankai, 1931.

TRNS #020.

See also the Stefan Tanaka entry under Shiratori Kurakichi.

Inoue Yasushi   井上 靖   Japanese novelist and short-story writer.
Writer of historical fiction set in
premodern China and Central Asia.

Yen 226.

∈ Idem, <u>Wind and Waves</u> [11,201 pp.].

Translated by James T. Araki. Honolulu: University of Hawaii Press,
1989.

∈ Idem, <u>Tun-huang</u> [12,201 pp.].

Translated by Jean Oda Moy. Tokyo: Kodansha International, 1978.

∈ Idem, <u>The Roof Tile of Tempyo</u> [17,140 pp.].

Translated by James T. Araki. Tokyo: University of Tokyo Press,
1975.

∈ Idem, <u>Journey beyond Samarkand</u> [130 pp.].

Translated by Furuta Gyo and Gordon Sager. Tokyo and Palo Alto,
Calif.: Kodansha International, 1971.

∋ James T. Araki, "Yasushi Inoué and His 'Tempyō,'" <u>Books Abroad</u> 44.1
(Winter 1970), 55-59.

∈ Idem, <u>Flood</u> [195 pp.].

Translated by John Bester. Tokyo: Hara Shobo, 1964.

[Japanese text and English translation. "Flood," pp. 7-75. Another
story, unrelated to China, appears on pp. 77-195.]

∈ Idem, Lou-lan [229 pp.].

Translated by E. Seidensticker. Tokyo: Hara Shobo, 1964.

[Japanese text and English translation. "Lou-lan," pp. 8-123.

Another story, unrelated to China, appears on pp. 125-229.]

[Additional book-length Western-language translations of Inoue's work
that do not deal with China are not listed here.]

Inui Kazuo   乾 一夫   Classical Chinese thought. Chinese poetry,
                                      Shih-ching. Chinese fiction, T'ang period.

Lit 30, Yen 313.

Inuki Gunji   井貫軍二   Modern Chinese literature.
      Lit 31.

Irie   入江

      see also Iriye.

Irie Keishirō   入江啓四郎   Chinese international relations. Modern Chi-
                                         nese history.

Yen 336, Teng #166.

Iritani Sensuke   入谷 仙介   Chinese poetry, traditional.
      Lit 37.

Iriya Yoshitaka   入矢 義高   Chinese literature, incl. drama, vernacular
                                       fiction, and Ch'an Buddhist literature.

      Lit 37, Yen 338, Teng #589.

      + Zen Bunka Kenkyūjo kiyō (Nagoya) 15 (Dec. 1988), 3-24.

      ø Iriya kyōju Ogawa kyōju taikyū kinen Chūgoku bungaku gogaku ronshū

         [4,2,5,23,797,35,4,3 pp.], 17-23.

         中国文学語学論集

      Iriya kyōju Ogawa kyōju taikyū kinenkai, ed. & publ. Kyoto, 1974.

      [Includes a preface in English by Burton Watson, 3 pp.]

      TRNS #021.

∈ <u>The Recorded Sayings of Layman P'ang: A Ninth-Century Zen Classic</u>
[109 pp.].
Translated from the Chinese by Ruth Fuller Sasaki, Yoshitaka Iriya,
and Dana R. Fraser. New York and Tokyo: Weatherhill, 1971.

Iriye   入江
see also Irie.

Iriye Akira   入江 昭
Listed under Naitō Konan.
[Book-length Western-language studies by Iriye on modern Japanese
history and foreign policy are not listed here.]

Ise Sentarō   伊瀬 仙太郎 Central Asian history. East-West historical
relations.
Yen 553, Teng #141.
+ Shikai (Tōkyō Gakugei Daigaku) 23-24 (1977), 51-59.

Ishibashi Hideo 石橋 秀雄   Chinese history, Ch'ing period.
Yen 394.

Ishibashi Keijūrō 石橋 啓十郎 Chinese art history, calligraphy.
Yen 393.

Ishibashi Ushio   石橋 丑雄   Japanese diplomat. History of Peking, esp.
Altar of Heaven.

Ishida Eiichirō   石田 英一郎 Cultural anthropology and comparative ethnol-
ogy: esp. Japan, also Asia and Latin Ameri-
ca.
Teng #16.
Σ <u>Ishida Eiichirō zenshū</u>, vol. 8 (1972), 571-599.
Tokyo: Chikuma Shobō, 1970-72. 8 vols.
* Idem, <u>Ningen to bunka no tankyū</u> [506 pp.], 506.
人間と文化の探究
Tokyo: Bungei Shunjūsha, 1970.

+ Nihon Bunka Kenkyūjo kenkyū hōkoku (Tōhoku Daigaku) 3 (March 1967),
  315-328.

Ishida Hiroshi   石田 博   Japanese literature. Chinese literature. <u>Kam-
                                     bun</u>.

+ Kambun Gakkai kaihō (Kokugakuin Daigaku) 29 (Feb. 1984), 126-132.
+ Ibid. 19 (Feb. 1974), 61-65.
• Ibid., 1.

Ishida Ichirō   石田 一郎   Chinese thought.
       b. 1914.
Yen 397.
Cf. next entry.

Ishida Ichirō   石田 一良   Japanese cultural history and thought, incl.
                                     neo-Confucianism.

    b. 1913.
  Yen 398, Teng #221.
  Cf. preceding entry.

Ishida Kōdō   石田公道   Chinese literature, Six Dynasties period.
                                  Chinese classics in Japan.

Lit 20.

+ Gogaku bungaku (Hokkaidō Kyōiku Daigaku) 15 (1977), 2 pp.
• Ibid., 69-70.

Ishida Kōhei   石田興平   Modern Chinese economic history, incl. Man-
                                   churia.

Yen 397.

+ Osaka Daigaku keizaigaku 16.2-3 (Dec. 1966), 137-146.
+ Hikone ronsō (Jimbun kagaku tokushū) 17 (Oct. 1965), 80-84.
• Ibid., 69-79.

Ishida Mikinosuke 石田 幹之助 East Asian history, incl. T'ang-period China.
East-West historical relations. Chinese bibliography.

Yen 394, Teng #142.

• Kodai bunka 35.8 (Aug. 1983), 33-42.

+ Kokugakuin zasshi 77.3 (March 1976), 257-282.

• Ibid. 76.3 (March 1975), 51-53.

• Shih-huo yueh-k'an (fu-k'an) (Taipei) 5.5 (Aug. 1975), 50-53.

• Tōhōgaku 49 (Jan. 1975), 129-163.

• Ibid. 32 (June 1966), 182-195.

• Ibid. 29 (Feb. 1965), 146-181.

• Kokushigaku 94 (Nov. 1974), 61-68.

+ Shisō (Nihon Daigaku) 18 (Sept. 1974).

• Ibid., 79-84.

• Shoshigaku 24-25 (July 1974), 82-84.

* Nihon kosho tsūshin 39.7 (#363) (July 1974), 11.

ø Ishida hakushi shōju kinen Tōyōshi ronsō [6,28,2,1,4,570 pp.], 28 pp.

東洋史論叢

Ishida hakushi koki kinen jigyōkai, ed. & publ. Tokyo, 1965.

TRNS #014.

ø Ishida, Wada, Ryō, Yamanaka yon sensei shōju kinen Shigaku rombunshū [41,585 pp.], 3-9.

石田・和田・龍・山中四先生頌寿記念 史学論文集

Shōju kinen rombunshū kankō iinkai, ed. Tokyo: Nihon Daigaku Shigakkai Shōju Kinen Rombunshū Kankō Iinkai, 1962.

TRNS #015.

∋+ K. Enoki, "Writings of Dr. Mikinosuke ISHIDA," Memoirs of the Research Department of the Toyo Bunko 20 (1961), 5-26.

∋ K. Enoki, "Dr. Mikinosuke ISHIDA and Dr. Hirosato IWAI," Ibid., 1-3.
Also listed under Shiratori Kurakichi, and Collected Articles #63a and #81.

Ishida Moriaki   石田 保昭   Contemporary Chinese politics and history.
Modern Indian history.

Yen 395.

Ishida Mosaku   石田茂作   History of art: Japan, also China. Japanese
                                archaeology.
   Yen 396, Teng #4.
   ø <u>Nihon rekishi kōkogaku ronsō</u>, vol. 1, 708-726.
      日本歴史考古学論叢
      Nihon rekishi kōko gakkai, ed. Tokyo: Yoshikawa Kōbunkan, 1966. 2
      vols. 8,731 pp., and 431 pp.
      TRNS:oo.

Ishida Seiichi   石田精一   Contemporary Chinese politics.
   Yen 398.

Ishida Takeo   石田武夫   Chinese language. Modern Chinese literature,
                                esp. poetry.
   Lit 20, Teng #639.
   + Hikone ronsō (Shiga Daigaku) 122-123 (March 1967), 122-127.

Ishida Yasuaki   石田保昭
   see Ishida Moriaki.

Ishida Yoneko   石田米子   Modern and contemporary Chinese history.
   Yen 396.

Ishiguro Noritoshi 石黒宣俊   Study of the Chinese classics, late Ch'ing
                                period, esp. <u>Kung-yang chuan</u> (<u>Ch'un-ch'iu</u>).
   Lit 19, Yen 393.

Ishiguro Shun'itsu 石黒俊逸   Classical Chinese thought.
   Teng #663.

Ishihama Juntarō   石濱純太郎 Premodern Chinese history. Central Asian his-
                                tory and languages.
   Yen 387.
   • Kodai bunka 35.8 (Aug. 1983), 33-42.
   • Kaitoku 42 (Oct. 1972), 5-20.

- Shisen 37 (July 1968), 54-55.
- Hakuen (Kansai Daigaku) 7 (June 1968), 1-4.
- Kansai Daigaku Chūgoku Bungakkai kiyō 1 (March 1968), 36.
- ø Ishihama sensei koki kinen <u>Tōyōgaku ronsō</u> [18,4,1,671,131 pp.], 18 pp.

  東洋学論叢

  Ishihama sensei koki kinenkai, ed. & publ. Suita, 1958.

  TRNS #017, NNO 3:404-405.

- ø <u>Ishihama sensei kanreki kinen rombunshū</u>. No biblio.

  Kansai Daigaku Tōzai Gakujutsu Kenkyūjo, ed. & publ. Suita, 1956.

  2 vols.

  [Consists of articles separately paginated.]

  TRNS #016.

  Also listed under Collected Articles #81.

Ishihara Akira   NC   East Asian medical history, incl. Taoism and
                                    sexuality.

- ∈ <u>The Tao of Sex</u> [1,2,1,1,2,241 pp.].

  Translated by Ishihara Akira and Howard S. Levy. Illustrator, Takata Shōjirō. Yokohama: Shibundō, 1968. 2nd rev. ed., Yokohama: Shibundō, 1969. First paperback ed., New York: Harper & Row, 1970. 3rd rev. ed., Lower Lake, Calif.: Integral Publishing, 1989.

  [Subtitle: (An Annotated Translation of the Twenty-eighth Section of) <u>The Essence of Medical Prescriptions</u> (<u>Ishimpō</u>).]

  [Note the annotated bibliography of studies of sex in China (pp. 193-215) and in Japan (pp. 216-228).]

  [Note also the review of the volume by André Levy, <u>T'oung Pao</u> 57 (1971), 213-220.]

Ishihara Michihiro 石原 道博 Sino-Japanese historical relations.

  Yen 399, Teng #553.

- + Idem, <u>Mimmatsu Shinsho Nihon kisshi no kenkyū</u> [3,6,2,542 pp.], 529-542.

  明末清初日本乞師の研究

  Tokyo: Fuzambō, 1945.

Ishii Masatoshi   石井正敏   Sino-Japanese historical relations.
      Yen 393.

Ishii Takashi   石井孝   Japanese diplomatic history. Sino-Japanese
                                      historical relations.
           Yen 392, Teng #287.

Ishijima Kairyū   石島快隆   Chinese thought, Taoism.
           Lit 19, Yen 393.

Ishijima Noriyuki 石島紀元   Modern Chinese history, Republican period.

Ishikawa Misao   石川三佐男 Chinese poetry, Shih-ching.
      Lit 19.

Ishikawa Shigeru   石川　滋   Economics: China, Taiwan, Southeast Asia.
      Yen 391.
      • Hitotsubashi ronsō 87.5 (May 1982), 125-146.

Ishikawa Tadahisa 石川 忠久   Chinese poetry, Six Dynasties period.
      Lit 18, Yen 389.
      Also listed under Hoshikawa Kiyotaka.

Ishikawa Tadao   石川 忠雄   Modern Chinese political history. Contempo-
                                      rary Chinese politics.
      Yen 390, Teng #54.
      ø Ishikawa Tadao kyōju kanreki kinen rombunshū   Gendai Chūgoku to
      sekai: Sono seijiteki tenkai   [6,1071 pp.], 999-1007.
      現代中国と世界 ― その政治的展開 ―
      Ishikawa Tadao kyōju kanreki kinenkai rombunshū henshū iinkai, ed.
      Tokyo: Keiō Tsūshin, 1982.
      [Note the article in Japanese by Nakajima Mineo (pp. 217-242) about
      current research on China in France and about the image of China
      among French intellectuals.]

[Note also the English-language review of this volume by Fukui Haruhiro, Journal of Asian Studies 42.4 (Aug. 1983), 925-927.]
TRNS:oo.

Ishikawa Tatsuzō 石川達三 Modern Japanese novelist. Sino-Japanese historical relations, World War II.
Yen 388.

Ishikawa Umejirō 石川梅次郎 Chinese poetry, traditional. Chinese thought.
Lit 18, Yen 389.

Isobe Takeo 磯辺武雄
Listed under Taga Akigorō.

Itano Chōhachi 板野長八 Classical Chinese thought.
Lit 21, Yen 24, Teng #700.

Itō Akio 伊東昭雄
see Itō Teruo.

Itō Chūta 伊東忠太 History of Chinese and Japanese architecture.
∋ Joshua A. Fogel, "New Publication of Interest," Sino-Japanese Studies
2.2 (March 1990), 2-3.
[Reports (with one sample reproduction) the reprint of a volume of
drawings by Itō of historic buildings in China.]

Itō Fumisada 伊藤文定 Chinese thought, Six Dynasties.
Teng #590.

Itō Hisaaki 伊藤久秋
Listed under Mutō Chōzō.

Itō Katsu 伊藤克 Modern Chinese literature.
Yen 557.

Itō Keiichi   伊藤 敬一   Modern Chinese literature and language.
    Lit 23, Yen 556.
    + Gaikokugo-ka kenkyū kiyō (Tōkyō Daigaku) 34.5 (1986), 155-159.

Itō Masafumi   伊藤 正文   Chinese literature, Six dynasties and T'ang
                                    periods.
    Lit 27, Yen 560.

Itō Masanobu
    see Itō Masafumi.

Itō Michiharu   伊藤 道治   Chinese history, pre-Han period. Chinese epi-
                                    graphy.
    Yen 554, Teng #5.
    ∋ David N. Keightley, Review of a volume by Itō Michiharu et al.,
        Kōkotsu moji: Hito, mono, kokoro 甲骨文字ー人・物・心ー (Nara?: Tenri-
        kyō Doyūsha, 1987. 190,69 pp.), in Harvard Journal of Asiatic Studies
        50.1 (June 1990), 378-383.
    ∋ David N. Keightley, Abstract of Itō Michiharu, Chūgoku kodai ōchō no
        keisei 中国古代王朝の形成   (Tokyo: Sōbunsha, 1975. 3,370,16
        pp.), in Early China 1 (Fall 1975), 8-9.

Itō Michiji
    see Itō Michiharu.

Itō Norio   伊藤 徳男
    see Itō Tokuo.

Itō Seiji   伊藤 清司   Early Chinese history and ethnology. History
                                    of Chinese art. Chinese mythology.
    Lit 24, Yen 557.

Itō Shūichi   伊藤 秀一   Modern international relations in Asia, incl.
                                    Sino-Russian relations.

Itō Sōhei   伊藤 漱平   Chinese literature, Ch'ing period. Chinese
                                vernacular fiction, <u>Hung-lou meng</u>. Modern
                                Chinese literature.

Lit 24, Yen 558.

ø Itō Sōhei kyōju taikan kinen   <u>Chūgokugaku ronshū</u>   [8,13,1,1,1109,5
    pp.], 7-13.

中国学論集

Itō Sōhei kyōju taikan kinen Chūgokugaku ronshū kankō iinkai, ed.
Tokyo: Kyūko Shoin, 1986.

TRNS:oo.

Itō Takao   伊東 隆夫   Southeast (also East) Asian history. Religion
                                in China, Ming-period Catholicism.

Yen 552, Teng #143.

Itō Takeo   伊藤 武雄   Modern Chinese society and politics, incl.
                                economics. Modern Sino-Japanese relations.

Yen 559.

∈ <u>Life along the South Manchurian Railway: The Memoirs of Itō Takeo</u>
    [31,241 pp.].

Translated with an Introduction by Joshua A. Fogel. Armonk, N.Y.:
M.E. Sharpe, 1988.

[Note the prefatory section by the translator (pp. vii-xxxi): "Introduction: Itō Takeo and the Research Work of the South Manchurian
Railway Company."]

Itō Teruo   伊東 昭雄   Modern Chinese thought.
   Lit 26.

Itō Tokuo   伊藤 徳男   Chinese history, esp. Han period.

Itō Tomio   伊藤 富雄   Chinese literature, traditional.
   Lit 26.

Itō Tomoatsu   伊東倫厚   Classical Chinese thought.
      Lit 26, Yen 552.

Itō Toramaru   伊藤虎丸   Modern Chinese literature, incl. comparisons
                                          with Japan and Korea.
      Lit 26, Yen 555.

Iuchi Hirobumi   井内弘文   Modern Japanese economic thought. Modern Chi-
                                          nese economic history.
      Teng #79.

Iuchi Hirofumi
      see Iuchi Hirobumi.

Iwai Hirosato   岩井大慧   Asian history. Sino-Japanese historical rela-
                                          tions. East Asian religion.
      Yen 543, Teng #17.
      ø Iwai hakushi koki kinen Tenseki ronshū [29,70,879,32 pp.], 29 pp.
         典籍論集
         Iwai hakushi koki kinen jigyōkai, ed. & publ. Tokyo, 1963.
         [Includes a German-language article on Zen Buddhism by Masunaga
         Reiho, pp. 26-32.]
         TRNS #022.
      ∋+ K. Enoki, "Writings of Dr. Hirosato IWAI," Memoirs of the Research
         Department of the Toyo Bunko 20 (1961), 27-34.
      ∋ K. Enoki, "Dr. Mikinosuke ISHIDA and Dr. Hirosato IWAI," Ibid., 1-3.
      Also listed under Yanai Wataru.

Iwaki Hideo   岩城秀夫   History of Chinese drama, esp. Sung thru Ming
                                          periods.
      Lit 39, Yen 541.

Iwami Hiroshi   岩見宏   Chinese socio-economic history and Chinese
                                          thought, Ming and Ch'ing periods.
      Yen 542, Teng #554.

Iwamura Michio   岩村三千夫   Modern Chinese history.
    Yen 540, Teng #568.
    +• Chūgoku kenkyū geppō 351 (May 1977), 1-4 and 12.

Iwamura Shinobu   岩村忍   History of Mongolia and Islam. Chinese his-
                                                tory, Yuan period. East-West historical
                                                relations.
    Yen 539, Teng #541.
    + Tōhō gakuhō 41 (March 1970), 765-767.
    Also listed under Mizuno Seiichi and Nagahiro Toshio.

Iwao Kobori   NC
    Listed under Collected Articles #44.

Iwao Seiichi   岩生成一   Japanese history, early Edo period. History
                                                of Japanese and Chinese activity in South-
                                                east Asia. East-West historical relations.
    Yen 544, Teng #289.
    + Hōsei shigaku 26 (1974), 107-112.

Iwasa Seiichirō   岩佐精一郎 Central Asian history.
    + Idem, Iwasa Seiichirō ikō [4,1,2,3,2,252 pp.], 2 pp.
       Wada Sei, ed. Tokyo: Iwasa Den'ichi 岩佐傳一   , 1936.

Iwasaki Fukuo   岩崎富久男 Modern Chinese history, anti-Japanese cam-
                                                paigns. Modern Chinese language.
    Yen 544.

Iwashige Hidemaru   岩重日出丸
    Listed under Intro. #12.

Izumi Kiyoshi   和泉清   Chinese bibliography.
    Yen 168.

Izumi Takayuki   泉 鴻元   Chinese international relations. Contemporary
                                    Chinese economy.

    Yen 331.

Izutsu Toshihiko   井筒 俊彦   Semitic languages, esp. Arabic. Comparative
                                    philosophy, incl. classical Chinese
                                    thought.

∈ Idem, <u>Sufism and Taoism: A Comparative Study of Key Philosphical
    Concepts</u> [493 pp.].

    Tokyo: Iwanami Shoten, 1983;   Berkeley: University of California
    Press, 1984.

    [Additional book-length English-language works by Izutsu on the Koran
    and on Japanese aesthetics are not listed here.]

Izushi Masahiko

    see Izushi Yoshihiko.

Izushi Yoshihiko   出石 誠彦   East Asian history. Early Chinese history.
                                    Chinese myth and legend.

+ Idem, <u>Shina shinwa densetsu no kenkyū</u> [5,2,2,6,862,16 pp.], 834-840.
    支那神話伝説の研究
    Tokyo: Chūō Koronsha, 1973.   Revised and expanded from the 1943
    edition.

    [Note the evaluation of Izushi's work, pp. 841-862.]

ø Izushi Yoshihiko sensei tsuitō <u>Tōyōgaku kenkyū</u> [2,2,168 pp.], 33-
    38.
    東洋学研究
    Tōyōgaku Dōkōkai, ed.   Tokyo: Fujii Shoten, 1943.

    [<u>Tōyōgaku kenkyū</u> #1 (Nov. 1943).]

    TRNS #161.

Jinnouchi Yoshio   陳内 宣男   Modern Chinese literature. Sino-Japanese cul-
                      陳内   tural relations.

    Lit 141, Yen 605.

Kaga Eiji   加賀 栄治   Classical Chinese thought. Six Dynasties in-
                                terpretation of the classics. History of
                                Chinese language.

    Lit 80, Yen 198.

    ø Kaga hakushi taikan kinen <u>Chūgoku bun- shi- tetsugaku ronshū</u> [11,
       1234,6 pp.]. No biblio.

    中国文史哲学論集

    Kaga hakushi taikan kinen ronshū kankōkai, ed.   Tokyo: Kōdansha,
    1979.

    [Note the section by Kaga on his career, pp. 1213-1231.]

    TRNS:oo.

    Also listed under Naitō Konan.

Kagawa Shun'ichirō 香川 俊一郎   Contemproary Chinese economics.
    Teng #80.

Kageyama Seiichi   影山 誠一   Chinese economic history. Chinese history,
                                Ch'ing period. Chinese social customs.

    Yen 566.

    * Daitō Bunka Daigaku Kangakkai shi 14 (1975), 2 pp.

Kageyama Takeshi
    see Kageyama Tsuyoshi.

Kageyama Tsuyoshi 影山 剛   Early Chinese history. Chinese economic his-
                                tory, Han period.

    Yen 565, Teng #502.

Kaihara Fumio   甲斐原 文夫   Modern Chinese political history.
    Yen 202.

Kaionji Chōgorō   海音寺 潮五郎 Author of Japanese historical novels with
                                themes such as the Mongol invasion.

    Yen 166.

Kaizuka Shigeki   貝塚茂樹   Early Chinese history. Chinese epigraphy.
        Yen 25, Teng #503 and #787.

    •   Seiji no hendōki ni okeru gakusha no ikikata [1,5,377 pp.].
        政治の変動期における学者の生き方
        By Uehara Tadamichi. Uehara Tadamichi o yomu kai, ed. Tokyo: Kenkyū
        Shuppan, 1980.
        [Note the two articles on Kaizuka's research: pp. 184-221 and 222-
        241.]
        [The work is vol. 1 of Uehara Tadamichi chosakusen.]

    Σ   Kaizuka Shigeki chosakushū, vol. 10 (1978), 413-471.
        Tokyo: Chūō Kōronsha, 1976-78. 10 vols.

    +   Tōhō gakuhō 40 (March 1969), 421-425.

    ∈   Idem, Confucius [192 pp.].
        Translated by Geoffrey Bownas. London: George Allen & Unwin, 1956;
        New York: The Macmillan Company, 1956.

        Also listed under Mizuno Seiichi.

Kaji Nobuyuki   加地伸行   Classical Chinese thought. Chinese historical
                                          texts, Shih-chi.
        Lit 83, Yen 197.

Kaji Tetsujō   加地哲定   Chinese Buddhism.
        Yen 198.

Kaji Wataru   鹿地亘   Modern Chinese literature.
        Lit 83, Yen 263, Teng #625.

Kajima Morinosuke   鹿島守之助   Japanese diplomatic history. International
                                          relations. Sino-Japanese historical rela-
                                          tions.
        Yen 263.

Kakehi   筧
        see Kakei.

Kakei Fumio   筧 文生   Chinese poetry, T'ang and Sung periods. Mod-
                                      ern Chinese literature.

    Lit 81, Yen 203.

Kakei Kumiko   寛 久美子   Modern Chinese language and literature. Chi-
                                      nese poetry, T'ang and Ch'ing periods, Li
                                      Po and Huang Tsun-hsien.

    Lit 133, Yen 204.

    [Same person as Shimada Kumiko 島田久美子.]

Kamachi Kan'ichi   蒲池歡一   Chinese literature, esp. Ming period, and
                                      modern Chinese poetry.

    Lit. 89.

Kamachi Noriko   蒲地典子   Modern Chinese history. Japanese bibliography
                                      on China.

  ∈ Idem, <u>Reform in China: Huang Tsun-hsien and the Japanese Model</u> [16,
    384 pp.].

    Cambridge, Mass.: Council on East Asian Studies, Harvard University,
    1981.

    Also listed under Intro., Footnote 4.

Kamada   鎌田

    see Kamata.

Kamata Shigeo   鎌田重雄   Chinese history, esp. Ch'in and Han periods.
    Yen 247, Teng #504.

  ∋ A.H. [A.F.P. Hulsewé], "Nécrologie," <u>T'oung Pao</u> 55 (1969), 316.

  ø Kamata hakushi kanreki kinen <u>Rekishigaku ronsō</u> [20,4,660 pp.], 8-
    20.

    歴史学論叢

    Kamata sensei kanreki kinenkai, ed. & publ. Tokyo, 1969.

    TRNS #044.

  * Shisō (Nihon Daigaku) 14 (1970).

    Cf. next entry.

Kamata Shigeo   鎌田茂夫   Buddhist studies in China, Korea, and Japan.
    Yen 246.
    + Tōyō Bunka Kenkyūjo kiyō (Tōkyō Daigaku) 106 (March 1988), 11-24.
    Cf. preceding entry.

Kamata Tadashi   鎌田 正   Chinese thought, incl. classics, esp. <u>Tso</u>
                                <u>chuan</u>. Chinese poetry, traditional.
    Lit 88, Yen 247, Teng #591.

Kamaya Osamu   鎌田 修   Modern Chinese literature.
    Lit 89.

Kambayashi Ryūjō   神林隆淨
    Listed under Ogiwara Unrai.

Kambe Teruo   神戸輝夫   Chinese history, Ch'ing period, minorities in
                                Southwest China.

Kamei Katsuichirō 亀井勝一郎   Contemporary Japan, commentary. Contemporary
                                Sino-Japanese relations.
    Yen 163.

Kamei Takashi   亀井 孝   History of Japanese and Chinese languages.
    Yen 164, Teng #210.

Kamio Ryūsuke   上尾龍介   Chinese poetry, T'ang period. Modern Chinese
                                literature and thought.
    Lit 90.

Kamioka Kazuyoshi 上岡一嘉   Economy of overseas Chinese. Business manage-
                                ment.
    Yen 376.

Kamiya Masao   神谷正男   Modern Chinese thought.
    Yen 383.

Kamo Giichi   加茂 儀一   Cultural history. History of technology.
    Yen 199.

Kanakura Enshō   金倉 円照   Buddhist studies.* Indian philosophy.
    Yen 216, Teng #754.
    ø Kanakura hakushi koki kinen Indogaku Bukkyōgaku ronshū [3,4,8,5,
    532,460,4,3 pp.], 8 pp.
    印度学仏教学論集
    Kanakura hakushi koki kinen rombunshū kankōkai, ed. Kyoto: Heirakuji
    Shoten, 1966.
    [Includes English-language articles, mostly on Indian Buddhism, but
    also one by J. Rahder, "Old Turkish and Mongolian BURXAN (BURQAN),"
    pp. 111-119.]
    TRNS:oo.

Kanamaru Kunizō   金丸 邦三   Chinese language and literature. Modern Chi-
                             nese thought.
    Lit 86, Yen 219.

Kanaoka Shōkō   金岡 照光   Chinese Buddhist literature. Tun-huang mate-
                             rials, esp. pien-wen literature. Chinese
                             poetry, Sung period, Su Shih.
    Lit 84, Yen 217.

Kanaya Osamu   金谷 治   Classical Chinese thought.
    Lit 86, Yen 218, Teng #664.
    + Bunka 46.3-4 (Feb. 1983), 80-83

Kanazawa Shōzaburō 金沢庄三郎 (History of Japanese language.)
    ø Kanazawa hakushi kanreki kinen Tōyō gogaku no kenkyū [3,1,3,708,4
    pp.].
    東洋語学乃研究
    Kanazawa hakushi kanreki shukugakai, ed. Tokyo: Sanseidō, 1932.
    TRNS #043, NNO 3:409.

Kanda Hideo   神田秀夫   Early Japanese literature. Sino-Japanese lit-
                                    erary relations.

        Yen 384.

Kanda Kiichirō   神田喜一郎   Chinese bibliography. East Asian history.
                                    Chinese art history, esp. calligraphy. Chi-
                                    nese language.

        Lit 93, Yen 385, Teng #706.

    +   Tōhōgaku 73 (Jan. 1987), 246-248.

    Σ   Kanda Kiichirō zenshū.   No biblio.

        Kyoto: Dōhōsha, 1983-90.   9 vols.

    •   Biburia 83 (Oct. 1984), 48-51.

    ø   Kanda hakushi kanreki kinen Shoshigaku ronshū   [793 pp.], 783-793.
        書誌学論集
        Kanda hakushi kanreki kinenkai, ed.   Tokyo: Heibonsha, 1957.

        TRNS #045.

    Also listed under Sugimura Kunihiko.

Kanda Nobuo   神田信夫   Chinese history, Ming and Ch'ing periods.
                                    Manchurian history.

        Yen 384, Teng #555.

Kaneda Hiromitsu NC
        Listed under Intro. #5.

Kaneda Jun'ichirō   金田純一郎   Chinese literature, esp. Shih-ching and ver-
                                    nacular fiction.

        Lit 87.

Kanegae Nobumitsu   鐘ケ江信光   Modern Chinese language and lexicography.
        Yen 627.

Kaneko Jirō   金子二郎   Modern Chinese language and literature. Chi-
                                    nese vernacular fiction, Hung-lou meng.

        Lit 87, Yen 220.

Kaneko Noboru   金子 昇   Modern Chinese thought and religion. Chinese
                                    minorities.

    Yen 220.

Kaneko Ryōta

    see Kaneko Ryōtai.

Kaneko Ryōtai   金子 良太   Tibetan studies.
   + Tōyō gakuhō 61.1-2 (Dec. 1979), 208-216.

Kaneko Shūichi   金子 修一   Chinese social history, T'ang period.

Kaneto Mamoru   金戸 守   Classical Chinese thought, Lun-yü.
    Lit 88.

Kani Hiroaki   可児 弘明   Overseas Chinese, esp. migration. Hong Kong.

Kanō   狩野

    see Kano.

Kano Gunkatsu   鹿野 軍勝
    Listed under Yoshikawa Kōjirō.

Kano Naoki   狩野直喜   Chinese thought and literature.
  •* Tōyōgaku no sōshisha-tachi [320 pp.], 169-219.
    東洋学の創始者たち
    Yoshikawa Kōjirō, ed. Tokyo: Kōdansha, 1976.
    [A reprint of the Tōhōgaku material listed below.]
  • Tōhōgaku 42 (Aug. 1971), 130-158.
  • Nihon Gakushiin kiyō 6.2-3 (Nov. 1948), 203-204.
  • Tōkō 5 (Apr. 1948), 7-98.
  ø Kano kyōju kanreki kinen Shinagaku ronsō [8,2,3,998,41 pp.], 8 pp.
    支那学論叢
    Suzuki Torao, ed. Kyoto: Kōbundō, 1928.

[Includes three articles in French (by S. Lévi, P. Demiéville, and
M.C. Haguenauer) and one in English (by N. Nevsky).]
TRNS #039, NNO 3:410.

Kano Naosada   狩野 直禎   Chinese history and literature, Six Dynasties
                                        period.

    Yen 406.

Kano Naoyoshi

    see Kano Naosada.

Kano Tadao   鹿野 忠雄   Ethnography, Taiwan.
    ∈ <u>An Illustrated Ethnography of Formosan Aborigines</u>.   3 vols.
    By Kano Tadao and Segawa Kokichi.
        Vol. 1 <u>The Yami</u> [5,456 pp.].
    Rev. ed., Tokyo: Maruzen Co., 1956. Rev. and enlarged ed., Taipei:
    Southern Materials Center, 1986.
        Vol. 2 <u>The Tsuo</u>, and Vol. 3 <u>The Bunnu</u>.
    To be published by the Southern Materials Center (Taipei).

Kanokogi Noboru   鹿子木 昇   Contemporary Asian economy.
    Yen 265.

Karashima Noboru   辛島 昇   Asian, esp. Indian, history.
    Yen 534.

Karashima Takeshi   辛島 驍   Modern Chinese literature. Chinese poetry,
                                        T'ang period.
    Lit 90, Teng #626.

Karube Jion   軽部慈恩   Korean and Chinese archaeology.
    Teng #713.
    • Gekkan kōkogaku jaanaru 51 (Dec. 1970), 19.

Kasahara Chūji　　笠原 仲二　　Classical Chinese thought.
    Lit 81, Yen 243, Teng #665.

Kasahara Tokushi　　笠原 十九司　　Modern Chinese history, May Fourth period.

Kashiwa Sukekata　　柏 祐賢　　Chinese (and East Asian) agricultural econo-
                                                    my.

    Teng #82.

Kataoka Masao　　片岡 政雄　　Chinese literature, Six Dynasties and T'ang
                                                  periods.

    Lit 82.

Kataoka Shibako　　片岡 芝子　　Chinese economic history, Ming and Ch'ing
                                                  periods.

Kataoka Tetsuya　　NC　　Modern Chinese history, Communist movement.
    ∈　Idem, <u>Resistance and Revolution in China: The Communists and the
       Second United Front</u> [13,326 pp.].
       Berkeley: University of California Press, 1974.

Katayama Sen　　片山 潜　　Japanese socialist and labor movements. Sino-
                                                  Japanese relations.
    ∋* Hyman Kublin, "A Bibliography of the Writings of Sen Katayama in
       Western Languages," <u>Far Eastern Quarterly</u> 11.1 (Nov. 1951), 71-77.

Katayama Tetsu　　片山 哲　　Chinese poetry, T'ang period.
    Yen 299.

Katayama Tomoyuki　　片山 智行　　Modern Chinese literature. Modern Chinese
                                                thought, May Fourth period.

    Lit 82, Yen 300.

Katō Genchi　　加藤 玄智
    Listed under Collected Articles #46.

Katō Jōken   加藤常賢   Early Chinese thought. Chinese epigraphy.
    Lit 84, Yen 199, Teng #666.

* Iken Katō Jōken: Gakumon to sono hōhō [422 pp.].
  維軒加藤常賢—学問とその方法—
  Fukakatsu Tanefusa, ed. Kawasaki: Katō Sada 加藤さだ , 1984.
* Iken Katō Jōken: Gakumon to sono omoide [454 pp.].
  維軒加藤常賢—学問とその思いで—
  Fukatsu Tanefusa, ed. Kawasaki: Katō Sada, 1980.
  [Pp. 306-361 are devoted to articles on Katō's achievements and
  writings, pp. 362-401 to in memoriam notices for him, pp. 405-415 to
  material about his library, and pp. 416-456 to his life.]
+ Kōkotsugaku 12 (Aug. 1980), 3-8.
* Tōhōgaku 39 (March 1970), 166-192.
+ Tōkyō Shinagaku hō 1 (1955), 49-54.

Katō Kyūzō   加藤九祚   History of Manchuria. Siberia.
    Yen 200.

Katō Shigeru   加藤繁   Chinese economic history.
** Tōhōgaku 55 (Jan. 1978), 134-162.
* Tōyō Bunko shohō 6 (1974), 1-16, and 7 (1975), 13-36.
+ Idem, Shina keizaishi kōshō, vol. 2, 880-896.
  支那経済史考証
  Tokyo: Tōyō Bunko, 1953. {E} 2 vols. 8,3,697,10 pp., and 8,924,56
  pp.
+ Idem, Chūgoku keizaishi no kaitaku [268 pp.], 247-264.
  中国経済史の開拓
  Enoki Kazuo, ed. Tokyo Ōkiku Shoin, 1948.
ø Katō hakushi kanreki kinen Tōyōshi shūsetsu [1,1,1,16,5,1,4,952
  pp.], 5-16.
  東洋史集説
  Katō hakushi kanreki kinen kankōkai, ed. Tokyo: Fuzambō, 1941.
  TRNS #038, NNO 3:409.

Katō Shigeshi
    see Katō Shigeru.

Katō Shūichi   加藤周一   Japanese literary and cultural history. Chi-
                                    nese thought.

    Yen 201.

    See Addenda, p. 279.

    [English-language translated volumes of Katō's works on Japanese lit-
    erature are not listed here.]

Katō Yūzō   加藤祐三   Modern Chinese history.
    Yen 202.

Katsumura Tetsuya 勝村哲也   Chinese bibliography. Chinese history, Six
                                    Dynasties period.

    Yen 386.

Kawabata Genji   河鰭源治   Modern Chinese history, incl. T'ai-p'ing Re-
                                    bellion and history of Taiwan.

Kawabe Toshio   河部利夫   Southeast Asian history. Thai history and
                                    language. Overseas Chinese in Southeast
                                    Asia.

    Yen 170.

    + Ajia Afurika gengo bunka kenkyū 14 (Dec. 1977), 247-249.

Kawachi Jūzō   河地重蔵   Modern Chinese history and economics. Chinese
                                    socio-economic history, Han and Six Dynas-
                                    ties periods.

    Yen 170, Teng #505.

Kawachi Shōen   河内昭円   Chinese literature and Buddhism, T'ang peri-
                                    od.

    Lit 93, Yen 171.

Kawachi Yoshihiro 河内良弘   East Asian archaeology and ethnology. Chinese
                                history, Chin period.
        Yen 171.

Kawada Tadashi   川田 侃   Asian international relations.
        Yen 66.

Kawagoe Yasuhiro   川越 泰博
        Listed under Intro. #2 and #12.

Kawaguchi Akira   川口 晃   Modern Chinese language.
        Yen 62.

Kawaguchi Hisao   川口 久雄   Sino-Japanese literary relations.
        Yen 60, Teng #592.

Kawahara Masahiro   河源正博   History of South China and Southeast Asia,
                                incl. Sino-Vietnamese historical relations.
                                Chinese history, Sung period.
        Yen 172, Teng #542.
    +   Hōsei shigaku 35 (1983), 73-74.
    •   Ibid., 74-83.

Kawahara Yoshirō   河原由郎   Chinese economic history, Sung period.
        Yen 172.
    +   Idem, Sōdai shakai keizaishi kenkyū [3,349 pp.], 343-346.
        宋代社会経済史研究
        Tokyo: Keisō Shobō, 1980.
    +   Fukuoka Daigaku keizaigaku ronsō 23.3-4 (March 1979), 5 pp.

Kawahide   河鰭
        see Kawabata.

Kawai Kōzō   川合康三   Chinese literature, T'ang period.
        Lit 90.

Kawai Teikichi　　　川合貞吉　　　Modern Chinese history.
　　Yen 63.

Kawakami Hisatoshi 川上久寿
　　see Kawakami Kyūju.

Kawakami Kei　　　　川上淫　　　Chinese art history.
　　Yen 65.

Kawakami Kōichi　　河上光一　　Chinese history, Sung period, incl. tea and
　　　　　　　　　　　　　　　　salt monopolies.

Kawakami Kyūju　　　川上久寿　　Modern Chinese language and literature, esp.
　　　　　　　　　　　　　　　　Lu Hsun. Soviet studies of modern Chinese
　　　　　　　　　　　　　　　　literature.
　　Lit 91, Yen 65.
　　+　Otaru Shōka Daigaku jimbun kenkyū 56 (Dec. 1978), 201-203.

Kawakatsu Ken'ryō 川勝賢亮
　　see Kawakatsu Mamoru.

Kawakatsu Mamoru　　川勝守　　Chinese socio-economic history, Ming and
　　　　　　　　　　　　　　　　Ch'ing periods.

Kawakatsu Yoshio　川勝義雄　Chinese history, esp. Six Dynasties period.
　　Yen 64, Teng #517.
　　+　Tōhō gakuhō 57 (March 1985), 741-742.
　　∋　John Lee, "Kawakatsu Yoshio (1922-1984)," Journal of Asian Studies
　　　　44.1 (Nov. 1984), 257.

Kawakita Michiaki　NC
　　Listed under Akiyama Terukazu.

Kawakita Yasuhiko 川北泰彦　Chinese poetry, T'ang period.
　　Lit 92, Yen 60.

Kawakubo Teirō   川久保悌郎   Chinese and Manchurian history, Ch'ing peri-
                                                    od.
   Yen 62.

Kawamoto Kunie   川本邦衛   Chinese language. Vietnamese language and
                                                    literature.
   Yen 60.

Kawamoto Shigeo   川本茂雄
   Listed under Hattori Shirō.

Kawanishi Masaaki   川西政明
   Listed under Takahashi Kazumi.

Kawano Shigetō   川野重任   Economy of Asia. Agriculture in Southeast
                                                    Asia.
   Yen 67.

Kawarasaki Chōjūrō
   see Kawarazaki Chōjūrō.

Kawarazaki Chōjūrō   河原崎長十郎   Japanese playwright who employs Chinese
                                                    themes.
   Yen 171.

Kawasaki Hideji   川崎秀二   Contemporary China.
   Yen 62.

Kawasaki Takaharu   河崎孝治   Classical Chinese thought.
   Lit 92.

Kawase Kazuma   川瀬一馬   Japanese and Chinese bibliography, incl. Chi-
                                                    nese books in Japan.
   Yen 63, Teng #463.

Kawata Teiichi   河田 悌一   History of Chinese thought, Ch'ing and modern
                                                periods.

    Lit 92.

Kawazoe Shōji   川添 昭二   Sino-Japanese relations, Yuan period.
    Yen 67.

Kegasawa Yasunori 気賀沢 保規   Chinese history, T'ang period.

Keimatsu Mitsuo   慶松 光雄   History of natural sciences in China. Earth-
                                                quake studies. Chinese gazeteers.

    Teng #556.
    + Jishin (Daini-shū) 29.4 (Dec. 1976), 8 pp.
    + Hokuriku shigaku (Kanazawa Daigaku) 20 (1972), 70-72.

Kezuka Eigorō   毛塚 栄五郎   Chinese poetry, traditional.
    Lit 104, Yen 268.

Kida Jun'ichirō   紀田 順-郎
    Listed under Morohashi Tetsuji.

Kida Tomoo   沐田 知生   Chinese history, Sung period, esp. urban cul-
                                                ture.

Kikuchi Hideo   菊地 英夫   Chinese history, Six Dynasties, T'ang, and
                                                Five Dynasties periods, incl. military sys-
                                                tem.

    Yen 234.

Kikuchi Masanori   菊地 昌典   Contemporary international relations.
    Yen 234.

Kikuchi Saburō   菊地 三郎   Modern Chinese literature.
    Lit 94, Yen 235.

Kikuchi Takaharu   菊池貴晴   Modern Chinese history.
  Yen 233, Teng #569.

  ø <u>Chūgoku kingendai-shi ronshū</u> Kikuchi Takaharu sensei tsuitō ronshū
   [606 pp.], 595-602.
   中国近現代史論集
   Shingai Kakumei Kenkyūkai, ed. Tokyo: Kyūko Shoin, 1985.
   TRNS:oo.

Kikuchi Yūji   菊地雄二
  Listed under Yoshikawa Kōjirō.

Kikuta Masanobu   菊田正信   Modern Chinese language and linguistics.
  Yen 235.

Kim Bunkyō   金文京   Chinese drama and vernacular fiction.

Kim Moonkyung
  see Kim Bunkyō.

Kimata Tokuo   木全徳雄   Chinese thought and literature, Six Dynasties
            period.
  Lit 95.

Kimishima Hisako   君島久子   Chinese literature, esp. children's litera-
            ture. Chinese legends.
  Lit 95.

Kimura Eiichi   木村英一   Chinese thought, incl. Taoism and neo-Confu-
            cianism.
  Lit 96, Yen 280, Teng #650.

  ø <u>Chūgoku tetsugakushi no tembō to mosaku</u> [2,4,1,1006,6 pp.].   No
  biblio.
   中国哲学史の展望と模索
   Kimura Eiichi hakushi shōju kinen jigyōkai, ed. Tokyo: Sōbunsha,
   1976.
   TRNS #132.

∍ Leon Hurvitz, "A Recent Japanese Study of Lao-tzu," <u>Monumenta Serica</u>
   20 (1961), 311-367.

   [A review of Kimura Eiichi, <u>Rōshi no shin kenkyū</u> 老子の新研究 ,
   Tokyo: Sōbunsha, 1959. 7,2,633,9,25 pp.]

   [Hurvitz does much more than review the work. He translates the
   entire <u>Tao-te ching</u>, noting different textual points Kimura makes in
   his study, which has its own 9-pp. English summary.]

Kimura Hiroshi   木村 泛   International relations: Sino-Soviet and
                                                      Sino-Japanese.

       Yen 277.

Kimura Ihee   木村 伊兵衛   Modern China: photography and travel.
       Yen 279.

Kimura Kihachirō   木村 禧八郎   Contemporary Sino-Japanese relations.
       Yen 278.

Kimura Kiyotaka   木村 清孝   Chinese Buddhism.
       Yen 278.

Kimura Masao   木村 正雄   Chinese socio-economic history, premodern
                                                      period, incl. land system.

       Yen 279.

   + Idem, <u>Chūgoku kodai nōmin hanran no kenkyū</u> [6,487,17 pp.], 481-484.
       中国古代農民叛乱の研究
       Tokyo: Tōkyō Daigaku Shuppankai, 1979.

   ∅ Kimura Masao sensei taikan kinen <u>Tōyōshi ronshū</u> [8,3,3,512 pp.], 3-
      8.
       東洋史論集
       Kimura Masao sensei taikan kinen jigyōkai, ed.   Tokyo: Kyūko Shoin,
       1976.

       TRNS #048.

Kimura Masutarō   木村 増太郎 Modern Chinese economy, Republican period.
  + Shokō (Mantetsu) 6 (Sept. 1929), 4, and 7 (Oct. 1929), 3.

Kimura Taiken   木村 泰賢 Buddhist studies.*
  Σ <u>Kimura Taiken zenshū</u>, vol. 6 (1937), 501-511.
    Tokyo: Meiji Shoin, 1936-37; rpt. Tokyo?: Daihōrin-kaku, 1968.   6
    vols.
  + Shūkyō kenkyū 7.4 (July 1930), 103-115.
  • Ibid., 7-102 and 116-120.

Kin Bunkyō   金 文京
  see Kim Bunkyō.

Kinami Takuichi   水南 卓一   Chinese thought, neo-Confucianism.
  Lit 95, Yen 281.

Kindaichi Kyōsuke   金田一 京助 (Linguistics and ethnology.)
  ø Kindaichi hakushi koki kinen <u>Gengo minzoku ronsō</u> [12,1442 pp.].
  言語民族論叢
    Kindaichi hakushi koki kinen bunshū kankōkai, ed. Tokyo: Sanseidō,
    1953.
    TRNS #063, NNO 3:411.

Kinugawa Tsuyoshi 衣川 強   Chinese history, Sung and Yuan periods. Chi-
                                         nese bibliography.
  Yen 560.

Kishibe Shigeo   岸辺 成雄   History of East Asian music.
  Yen 11, Teng #199.
  + Jimbun Kagakuka kiyō (Tōkyō Daigaku) 61 (Rekishi to bunka 9, Rekishi-
    gaku kenkyū hōkoku 15) (March 1975), 217-222.

Kishimoto Mio   岸本美緒 Chinese economic history, Ming and Ch'ing
                                         periods.

Kitagawa Hidenori　北川 秀則　Indian philosophy. Tibetan studies.
    Yen 28, Teng #755.

Kitagawa Momoo　北川 桃雄　East Asian art history.
    Yen 27.

Kitamura Hajime　北村 甫　Sino-Tibetan languages.
    Yen 29.
    + Ajia Afurika gengo bunka kenkyū 31 (March 1986), 177-181.

Kitamura Hironao　北村 敬直　Chinese economic and social history, Ch'ing
                                    and modern periods.
    Teng #85.
    + Tōyō shien (Ryūkoku Daigaku) 30-31 (1988), 3-8.
    + Ryūkoku shidan 79 (March 1981), 251-254.
    + Keizaigaku zasshi (Ōsaka Shiritsu Daigaku) 73.5-6 (Dec. 1975), 124-
        129.

Kitamura Hirotada
    see Kitamura Hironao.

Kitamura Minoru　北村 稔　Modern and contemporary Chinese political
                                    history.

Kitaoka Masako　北岡 正子　Modern Chinese literature.
    Lit 94, Yen 28.

Kitayama Yasuo　北山 康夫　Modern Chinese and Korean history.
    Yen 28, Teng #570.
    + Rekishi kenkyū (Ōsaka Kyōiku Daigaku) 14 (1976), 3 pp.

Kitō Kiyoaki　鬼頭 清明　Japanese history. Sino-Japanese historical
                                    relations.
    Yen 164.

Kitō Yūichi   鬼頭有一   History of Chinese language. Chinese poetry,
                                        traditional.
        Lit 95, Yen 165.

Kiyama Hideo   木山英雄   Modern Chinese literature.
        Lit 96, Yen 282.

Kiyokoba Azama   清木庭東   Chinese history, Sung period.

Kiyose, Gisaburo N. NC   See Addenda, p. 279.

Kiyozawa Manshi   清沢満之
        Listed under Suzuki Daisetsu.

Kobata Atsushi   小葉田淳   Japanese economic history, incl. Sino-Japa-
                                        nese trade.
        Yen 520, Teng #265.

Kobayashi Fumio   小林文男   Contemporary Chinese economy and thought.
        Yen 511.

Kobayashi Hajime   小林元   History of Islam.
        Yen 513.

Kobayashi Hideo   小林秀雄   (History.)
        ø Kobayashi kyōju kanreki kinen Shigaku rombunshū [3,4,3,2,629 pp.].
        史学論文集
           Rikkyō Daigaku Shigakkai, ed. & publ. Tokyo, 1938.
           TRNS #073.
           [Cf. the following.]
        ø Shien (Rikkyō Daigaku) 11.3-4 (March 1938).
           [Contains the same material, entitled Shigaku ronsō 史学論叢, as
           in the preceding.]
        Cf. the next entry.

Kobayashi Hideo   小林英夫   Contemporary East Asian political and economic history. Modern Sino-Japanese historical
relations.

    Yen 513.
    Cf. the preceding entry.

Kobayashi Kazumi   小林一美   Modern Chinese history. History of popular
movements.

Kobayashi Kōji   小林弘二   Contemporary Chinese politics, incl. collec-
tivization policy.

    Yen 510.

Kobayashi Noboru   小林昇   Chinese thought and history, Six Dynasties
period.

    Lit 111, Yen 510, Teng #667.
    ●* Philosophia (Firosofia) (Waseda Daigaku) 69 (1981), 203-207.

Kobayashi Nobuaki   小林信明   Chinese thought. Chinese poetry, T'ang period.

    Lit 111, Yen 511, Teng #701.

Kobayashi Shimmei
    see Kobayashi Nobuaki.

Kobayashi Susumu   小林進   Contemporary Chinese economy, incl. Hong
Kong.

    Yen 510.

Kobayashi Taichirō 小林太市郎   Chinese art history. Chinese poetry, T'ang
period, Wang Wei.

    Lit 110, Yen 512.
    Σ Kobayashi Taichirō chosakushū. No biblio.
        Kyoto: Tankōsha, 1973-74. 8 vols.
    ● Hōkō 13 (March 1967), 20 pp.

　　　• Kindai (Kōbe Daigaku) 37 (July 1965), 28-33.

　　　+ Kenkyū (Kōbe Daigaku) 34 (March 1964), 2-21.

Kobayashi Takashi 小林 多加土　　Modern Chinese thought and politics.
　　　Yen 509, Teng #543.

Kobayashi Takashirō 小林 高四郎　　Mongolian history and literature. Chinese
　　　　　　　　　　　　　　　　　　　history, Yuan period. East-West historical
　　　　　　　　　　　　　　　　　　　relations.
　　　Yen 509.

Kobayashi Takeshi　　小林 健志　　Japanese art history. Chinese poetry and po-
　　　　　　　　　　　　　　　　　　　etics, esp. T'ang period.
　　　Lit 110, Teng #177.

Kobayashi Toshio　　小林 俊雄　　Chinese textual studies, esp. Meng-tzu.
　　　Lit 110.

Kōchi Sō　　　　高 知 聡
　　　Listed under Takahashi Kazumi.

Kodama Rokurō　　児 玉 六郎　　Classical Chinese thought, esp. Hsun-tzu.
　　　Lit 107.

Kodama Shinjirō　　小玉 新次郎　Premodern Central Asian history.

Koga Noboru　　古 賀 登　　Chinese political and social history, esp.
　　　　　　　　　　　　　　　　Han and T'ang periods.
　　　Yen 154.

Koizumi Fumio　　小泉文夫　　East Asian music.
　　　Yen 514.

Kojima Masami　　小島正巳　　Contemporary Chinese economy.
　　　Yen 505.

Kojima Masao   小嶋 政雄   Chinese literature, pre-Han period. Chinese
                                  thought. Early Chinese science.

    Lit 106.

    * Daitō Bunka Daigaku Kangakkai shi 14 (1975), 2 pp.

Kojima Noriyuki   小島 憲之   Early Japanese poetry. Sino-Japanese literary
                                  relations.

    Yen 504, Teng #331.

Kojima Reeitsu

    see Kojima Reiitsu.

Kojima Reiitsu   小島 麗逸   Modern and contemporary Chinese and Asian
                                  economy and politics.

    Yen 504.

    ∈ Urbanization and Urban Problems in China [10,142 pp.]
      By Reeitsu Kojima. Tokyo: Institute of Developing Economies (IDE
      Occasional Paper Series #22), 1987.

Kojima Shinji   小島 晋治   Modern Chinese history, T'ai-p'ing Rebellion.
    Yen 503.

Kojima Sukema   小島 祐馬
    see Ojima Sukema.

Kojima Yoshio   小島 淑男   Chinese socio-economic history, late Ch'ing
                                  and Republican periods.

Kōma Miyoshi   高馬 三良   Chinese Taoist literature.
    Lit 106, Yen 134.

Kōma Saburō

    see Kōma Miyoshi.

Komada Shinji   駒田信二   Chinese vernacular literature, Ming period.
                                Sino-Japanese literary relations. Modern
                                Chinese literature.
        Lit 111, Yen 232.

Komai Kazuchika   駒井和愛   East Asian archaeology.
        Yen 231, Teng #8.
    +   Idem, Rōkan: Komai Kazuchika hakushi zuihitsushū [31,2,5,535 pp.],
        18-42.
        琅玕一駒井和愛博士随筆集一
        Komai Kazuchika hakushi kinenkai, ed. & publ. Tokyo, 1977.
        [Note the 31-pp. section about Komai, plus photos, at the beginning
        of the volume.]
    •   Idem, Rōkan (Ho) [160 pp.].
        琅玕（補）
        Komai Kazuchika hakushi kinenkai, ed. & publ. Tokyo, 1978.
    •   Shikan 85 (March 1972), 83.
    •   Tōhōgaku 43 (Jan. 1972), 15-16.
    +   Komai Kazuchika sensei chosaku mokuroku [3,29 pp.], 3 pp. and 1-28.
        Hirai Hisayuki and Nakagawa Shigeo, eds. Tokyo: Rikkyō Daigaku Haku-
        butsukan-gaku Kenkyūshitsu, 1966.

Komatsu Hideo   小松英生   Chinese literature, Six Dynasties period.
        Lit 112.

Komatsu Tadashi   小松忠志   Chinese poetry, T'ang period, Li Po.
        Lit 112.

Komatsu Yoshitaka   小松芳喬
        Listed under Nomura Kentarō.

Kominami Ichirō   小南一郎   Chinese literature, esp. Ch'u-tz'u and Six
                                Dynasties fiction. Classical Chinese
                                thought.
        Lit 113, Yen 514.

Komine Kimichika　小峰王親　　Modern Chinese literature.
　　Lit 113, Yen 506.

Komori Ikuko　　　小守郁子　　Chinese poetry, Six Dynasties period.
　　Lit 113.

Kondō Haruo　　　近藤春雄　　Chinese literature, esp. T'ang-period fiction
　　　　　　　　　　　　　　　　　and poetry.
　　Lit 114, Yen 222.
　　　• Setsurin 27 (Feb. 1979), 17-18.

Kondō Hideki　　　近藤秀樹　　Chinese history, Ch'ing period.

Kondō Hideo　　　近藤英雄　　Chinese poetry, Shih-ching.
　　Lit 116.

Kondō Kuniyasu　　近藤邦康　　Modern Chinese thought.
　　Lit 114, Yen 221.

Kondō Mitsuo　　　近藤光男　　Chinese literature, esp. traditional poetry.
　　　　　　　　　　　　　　　　　Chinese thought, Ch'ing period.
　　Yen 222.
　　　+ Chūgoku Bungakkai hō (Ochanomizu Daigaku) 6 (1987), 5-14.

Kondō Yasunobu　　近藤康信　　Classical Chinese thought and neo-Confucian-
　　　　　　　　　　　　　　　　　ism.
　　　Lit 116, Yen 224.

Kondō Yasuo　　　近藤康男　　Contemporary Chinese and Japanese agricultur-
　　　　　　　　　　　　　　　　　al economy.
　　Yen 224.

Konishi Jin'ichi　小西甚一　　Japanese literature, incl. poetry. Chinese
　　　　　　　　　　　　　　　　　literary theory. Sino-Japanese literary
　　　　　　　　　　　　　　　　　relations.
　　Yen 519, Teng #346.

[English-language translated volumes of Konishi's history of Japanese literature are not listed here.]

Konishi Noboru   小西 昇   Chinese literature, Six Dynasties period, esp. yueh-fu and Hsieh Ling-yun. Modern Chinese literature.

   Lit 108.

Konishi Teruo   小西 輝夫
   Listed under Tsukamoto Zenryū.

Kōno Rokurō   河野 六郎   Korean language. Sino-Korean linguistic relations.

   Yen 173.

Konose Tsuneyasu   許勢 常安   Chinese language. Chinese thought, late Ch'ing period, esp. Liang Ch'i-ch'ao.

   Lit 109, Yen 538.

Korenaga Shun   是永 駿   Modern Chinese literature, esp. Mao Tun.
   Lit 114.

Kōsaka Jun'ichi   香坂 順一   Chinese language. Chinese lexicography: terms in vernacular fiction and modern language and literature.

   Lit 104, Yen 497.

Kōsaka Torizō   上坂 酉三   Contemporary Chinese economy, trade.
   Yen 375.

Koshimizu Masaru   輿水 優   Modern Chinese language.
   Yen 573.

Kosugi Kazuo   小杉 一雄   Chinese art history.
   Yen 514.

Koyama   小山

   see also Oyama.

Koyama Fujio   小山富士夫 Chinese art history, esp. ceramics.

   Yen 515.

    ∋ G.St.G.M. Gompertz, "A Further Appreciation of Fujio Koyama (Died 7th October, 1975)," <u>Oriental Art</u> N.S. 22.1 (Spring 1976), 108-109.

    ∋ John Figgess, "Fujio Koyama: An Appreciation," <u>Oriental Art</u> N.S. 21.4 (Winter 1975), 324-327.

    ∈ <u>Two Thousand Years of Oriental Ceramics</u> [379 pp.].
     By Fujio Koyama and John Figgess. New York: Abrams, 1961.

    ∈ <u>Chinese Ceramics: One Hundred Selected Masterpieces from Collections in Japan, England, France, and America</u> [5,62 pp. plus 112 plates].
     Koyama Fujio, ed. Tokyo: Nihon Keizai, 1960.

    ∈ Idem, <u>Keramik des Orients: China, Japan, Korea, Südostasien, Naher Osten</u> [411 pp.].
     Vorwort und Übersetzung von Dietrich Seckel. Tokyo: Bijutsu Shuppan-sha, 1959.

Koyama Masaaki   小山正明

   see Oyama Masaaki.

Kōzen Hiroshi   興膳宏   Chinese literature and literary theory, Six Dynasties.

   Lit 105, Yen 533.

   Also listed under Yoshikawa Kōjirō.

Kōzuma Takae   上妻隆栄 Contemporary Chinese economy.

   Yen 376.

   + Tōa keizai kenkyū 47.1-2 (March 1980), 165-168.

Kubo Noritada   窪徳忠   Chinese religion, incl. Taoism.

   Yen 467, Teng #486.

   + Tōyō Bunka Kenkyūjo kiyō (Tōkyō Daigaku) 64 (March 1974), 1-13.

Kubota Bunji   久保田文次   Modern Chinese history, 1911 Revolution.

Kubota Takeshi   久保田 剛   Early Chinese cultural history.
    Yen 230.

Kubozue Yoshifumi   窪添慶文   Chinese history, Six Dynasties thru T'ang
                                   periods.

Kudō Naotarō   工藤直太郎   See Addenda, p. 279.

Kudō Takamura   工藤篁   Chinese literature and language.
    Lit 98, Yen 144.
    • Ajia Afurika Gengo Bunka Kenkyūjo tsūshin 24 (Aug. 1975), 1-4.
    + Chūtetsubun Gakkai hō 1 (Oct. 1974), 45-47.

Kudō Toyohiko   工藤豊彦   Chinese thought.
    Yen 144.

Kumagai Nobuo   熊谷宣夫   Chinese art history.
    Yen 535.
    •* Bukkyō geijutsu 89 (Dec. 1972), 100.

Kumagai Norio
    see Kumagai Nobuo.

Kumagai Osamu   熊谷治   Early Chinese history and legend.
    Lit 98.

Kumano Shōhei   熊野正平   Modern Chinese thought and society.
    Teng #702.

Kumashiro Yukio   熊代幸雄   Chinese agriculture. Chinese agricultural
                                   law.
    Yen 534.
    • Chūgoku kenkyū geppō 378 (Aug. 1979), 34-36.

Kume Kunitake　　久米邦武
　　　see the Stefan Tanaka entry under Shiratori Kurakichi.

Kunieda Minoru　　国枝　稔　　Chinese poetry, T'ang period.
　　　Lit 98.

Kurai Ryōzō　　蔵居良造　　Contemporary Chinese politics. Overseas Chi-
　　　　　　　　　　　　　　　nese.

　　　Yen 592.

Kuraishi Takeshirō　倉石武四郎　Chinese language and literature. Chinese bib-
　　　　　　　　　　　　　　　liography and lexicography.

　　　Lit 99, Yen 37, Teng #640.

　　• Ajia Afurika Gengo Bunka Kenkyūjo tsūshin 27 (July 1976), 1-3.

　　• Tōhōgaku 40 (Sept. 1970), 154-173.

　　ø Kuraishi hakushi kanreki kinen　Chūgoku no meicho　[2,5,421 pp.],
　　　419-421.
　　　中国の名著

　　　Tōkyō Daigaku Chūgoku Bungaku Kenkyūshitsu, ed.　Tokyo: Keisō Shobō,
　　　1961.

　　　[Consists of articles on major Chinese writers and literary works.]
　　　TRNS:oo.

　　+ Tōkyō Shinagaku hō 4 (1958), 15-23.

Kuramitsu Uhei　　倉光卯平　　Chinese literature, esp. Ming and Ch'ing pe-
　　　　　　　　　　　　　　　riods.

　　　Lit 101, Yen 37.

　　+ Seinan Gakuin Daigaku bunri ronshū 6.2 (Feb. 1966), 4-7.

Kurata Junnosuke　倉田淳之助　Chinese literature, esp. Sung-period poetry.
　　　　　　　　　　　　　　　Chinese bibliography.

　　　Lit 100, Yen 39, Teng #707.

Kurata Sadayoshi　倉田貞美　Modern Chinese poetry. Chinese poetry, late
　　　　　　　　　　　　　　　Ch'ing period.

　　　Lit 100, Yen 38, Teng #627.

Kure Shichirō   呉 七郎   Modern Chinese literature.
     Lit 101.

Kuribayashi Nobuo   栗林宣夫   Chinese history, Ming and Ch'ing periods.
     Yen 243.

Kuribayashi Norio
     see Kuribayashi Nobuo.

Kurihara Keisuke   栗原圭介   Classical Chinese thought.
     Yen 245.
     • Daitō Bunka Daigaku Kangakkai shi 27 (1988).

Kurihara Masuo   栗原 益男   Chinese political and social history, esp.
                                      T'ang and Sung periods.
     Yen 245.

Kurihara Tomonobu   栗原 朋信   Chinese history, esp. Ch'in and Han periods.
     Yen 244, Teng #506.
     + Shikan 102 (March 1980), 92-104.
     • Ibid., 81-91.
     ø Chūgoku zen-kindaishi kenkyū   Kurihara Tomonobu hakushi tsuitō kinen
        [303 pp.]. No biblio.
        中国前近代史研究
        Waseda Daigaku Bungakubu Tōyōshi Kenkyūshitsu, ed. Tokyo: Yūzankaku
        Shuppan, 1980.
        TRNS:oo.
     Also listed under Collected Articles #13.

Kurita Naomi   栗田直躬   Early Chinese thought.
     Yen 243, Teng #668.
     Also listed under Tsuda Sōkichi.

Kuroda Hisao   黒田寿男   Contemporary Chinese politics.
     Yen 174.

Kuroiwa Kanō
    see Kuroiwa Yoshinori.

Kuroiwa Yoshinori　黒岩嘉納　Chinese poetry, Shih-ching.
    Lit 101.

Kurokawa Yōichi　黒川洋一　Chinese poetry, T'ang period, esp. Tu Fu.
                     Sino-Japanese literary relations.
    Lit 101, Yen 174.

Kurosaka Mitsuteru　黒坂満輝　Chinese thought, Ch'ing period, esp. Wang
                     Fu-chih and T'an Ssu-t'ung.
    Yen 173.

Kusakabe Fumio　日下部文夫　Japanese and Chinese languages.
    Teng #212.

Kusamori Shin'ichi　草森紳一　Chinese poetry, T'ang period, esp. Li Ho.
                     Chinese historical texts, Shih-chi.
    Lit 97, Yen 40.

Kusano Fumio　草野文男　Chinese political economy, esp. contemporary
                     period.
    Yen 40.

Kusano Yasushi　草野靖　Chinese socio-economic history, Sung period.

Kushida Ryōkō　櫛田良洪　(History of Japanese Buddhism.)
   ø　Kushida hakushi shōju kinen　Kōsōden no kenkyū　[6,877 pp.].
    高僧伝の研究
    Kushida kyōju hakushi shōju kinenkai, ed.　Tokyo: Sankibō Busshorin,
    1973.
    TRNS:oo.

Kusumoto Masatsugu 楠本正継   Chinese thought, neo-Confucianism.
    Yen 287, Teng #651.

    ●* Tōhōgaku 62 (July 1981), 153-182.

    + Tetsugaku nempō 23 (1961), 3 pp.

Kusuyama Haruki   楠山春樹   Chinese thought, Lao-tzu and Huai-nan tzu.
    Lit 98, Yen 288.

Kuwabara Jitsuzō   桑原隲蔵   East Asian and Inner Asian history.
    ●* Tōyōgaku no sōshisha-tachi [320 pp.], 221-262.
       東洋学の創始者たち
       Yoshikawa Kōjirō, ed. Tokyo: Kōdansha, 1976.
       [A reprint of the Tōhōgaku material listed below.]
    ●* Tōhōgaku 49 (Jan. 1975), 109-128.
    Σ Kuwabara Jitsuzō zenshū, vol. 5, 551-561.
       Tokyo: Iwanami Shoten, 1968. 5 vols., and 1 suppl. vol.
    + Shirin 16.3 (July 1931), 189-195.
    ● Ibid., 184-189.
    ø Kuwabara hakushi kanreki kinen Tōyōshi ronsō [1,2,1,10,3,1368 pp.],
       10 pp.
       東洋史論叢
       Kuwabara hakushi kanreki kinen shukugakai, ed. Kyoto: Kōbundō, 1931.
       TRNS #064, NNO 3:411.

Kuwabara Takeo   桑原武夫   French literature. Chinese thought and lit-
                                       erature.
    Yen 345.
    Σ Kuwabara Takeo zenshū. No biblio.
       Tokyo: Asahi Shimbunsha, 1968-72. 8 vols.
    Also listed under Yoshikawa Kōjirō.
    [A book-length English-language volume of essays by Kuwabara comparing
    Japan and the West is not listed here.]

Kuwata Rokurō   桑田六郎   Chinese religion, incl. Islam and Christianity, Ming and Ch'ing periods. Southeast
Asian history. East-West historical relations.

    Yen 345, Teng #144.

    • Tōyō gakuhō 69.3-4 (March 1988), 217-219.

Kuwayama Ryūhei   桑山龍平   Chinese literature, incl. poetry, esp. Ch'u
tz'u. Modern Chinese literature. Sino-Japa-
nese literary relations.

    Lit 103, Yen 344, Teng #593.

    • Tenri Daigaku gakuhō (Gakujutsu Kenkyūkai shi) 37.2 (#148) (March
1986), 1-2.

Kyo Shukushin   許淑真
    Listed under Suzue Gen'ichi.

Kyōguchi Motokichi   京口元吉   Japanese history. Early Sino-Japanese historical relations.

    Teng #168.

Mabuchi Tōichi   馬淵東一   Social anthropology: Southeast Asia, Taiwan,
Okinawa.

    Yen 267.

    + Jimbun gakuhō (Tōkyō Toritsu Daigaku) 87 (March 1972), 6-16.

    • Ibid., 1-5.

Machida Kōichi   町田甲一   East Asian art history.
    Yen 103, Teng #178.

Machida Saburō   町田三郎   Chinese thought and literature, thru Han period.

    Lit 241, Yen 103.

Maeda Egaku   前田恵学   Buddhist studies.* Pali language and litera-
                                            ture.

      Yen 310.

Maeda Masana   前田正名   Chinese and Central Asian historical geogra-
                                            phy.

      Teng #578.

Maeda Naonori   前田直典   Chinese history, Yuan period.
      + Idem, Genchōshi no kenkyū [11,358,32 pp.], 354-357.
         元朝史の研究
         Tokyo: Tōkyō Daigaku Shuppankai, 1973.
      • Ibid., 347-354 and 357-358.

Maeda Toshiaki   前田利昭   Modern Chinese literature.
         Lit 237, Yen 309.

Maegawa Yukio   前川幸雄   Chinese poetry, T'ang period.
         Lit 236.

Maejima Shinji   前嶋信次   Central and Western Asian history. East-West
                                            historical relations.

      Yen 308, Teng #145.
      + Shigaku 44.4 (Oct. 1971), 115-135.
      • Ibid., 112-114.

Maeno Naoaki   前野直彬   Chinese poetry, traditional. Chinese fiction.
                                         Chinese vernacular fiction.

      Lit 237, Yen 311, Teng #594.
      + Chūtetsubun Gakkai hō 6 (1981), 17-26.

Maida Shūichi   毎田周一   Buddhist studies.*
      Σ Maida Shūichi zenshū, vol. 13 (1971), 7-83.
         Maida Shūichi zenshū kankōkai, ed. & publ. Nagano, 1969-71.   12
         vols., plus 2 vols. (vol. 12 supplement and vol. 13).

Maiya Ken'ichirō   米谷健一郎   Contemporary China.
    Yen 272.

Makino Tatsumi   牧野巽   Chinese sociology, the family. Chinese reli-
                              gion. Chinese ethnology.

    Yen 284, Teng #122.

   Σ   <u>Makino Tatsumi chosakushū</u>.   No biblio.

      Tokyo: Ochanomizu Shobō, 1979-80.   3 vols.

   +   Tōyō Bunka Kenkyūjo kiyō (Mukyūkai) 10 (March 1978), 3-8.

   •   Tōyō bunka (Mukyūkai) 41-42 (Apr. 1977), 72-76.

   •   Ibid. 37 (Sept. 1975), 63-65.

Makio Ryōkai   牧尾良海   Chinese thought and literature, traditional.
    Yen 282.

   ø   <u>Chūgoku no shūkyō shisō to kagaku</u>   Makio Ryōkai hakushi shōju kinen

      ronshū   [8,11,5,605,45,10 pp.], 8-11.

      中国の宗教思想と科学

      Makio Ryōkai hakushi shōju kinen ronshū kankōkai, ed.   Tokyo: Kokusho

      Kankōkai, 1984.   {E}

      [Includes an article in English by Terry F. Kleeman, "Land Contracts

      and Related Documents," pp. 1-34.]

      TRNS:oo.

Makita Eiji   牧田英二   Modern Chinese history and language.
    Yen 284.

Makita Tairyō   牧田諦亮   History of Chinese Buddhism.
    Yen 283, Teng #735.

   +   Tōhō gakuhō 50 (Feb. 1978), 515-517.

Makita Teiryō

    see Makita Tairyō.

Makito Kazuhiro   牧戸和宏   Modern Chinese literature.
    Lit 239.

Mano Eiji   間野英二   Premodern Central Asian history.

Mano Sen'ryū   間野潜龍   Chinese thought, incl. religious thought,
                                     Ming and Ch'ing periods. Neo-Confucianism.
     Yen 202, Teng #557.

Maruo Tsuneki   丸尾常喜   Modern Chinese literature.
     Lit 248, Yen 472.

Maruyama Masao   丸山真男   History of thought, Japan and East Asia.
     Yen 470, Teng #59.

     [Book-length Western-language translations of Maruyama's studies of
     Japanese intellectual history are not listed here.]

Maruyama Matsuyuki 丸山松幸   Classical Chinese thought. Chinese historical
                                     texts, Shih-chi. Modern Chinese thought and
                                     literature.
     Yen 469.

Maruyama Noboru   丸山昇   Modern Chinese literature.
     Lit 249, Yen 471.

Maruyama Shigeru   丸山茂   Chinese poetry, T'ang period.
     Lit 249.

Masubuchi Tatsuo   増淵龍夫   Chinese history, pre-Han and Han periods.
     Yen 598, Teng #507.

     ø Chūgokushi ni okeru shakai to minshū Masubuchi Tatsuo sensei taikan
        kinen ronshū [16,342 pp.], 1-14.
        中国史における社会と民衆
        Masubuchi Tatsuo sensei taikan kinen ronshū kankōkai, ed.   Tokyo:
        Kyūko Shoin, 1983.
        TRNS:oo.
     + Hitotsubashi ronsō 83.3 (March 1980), 162-171.
     • Ibid., 159-161.

Masuda Hajime   増田 渉
    see Masuda Wataru.

Masuda, J.   NC
    Listed under Ogiwara Unrai.

Masuda Kenji   NC
    Listed under Intro. #5.

Masuda Kiyohide   増田清秀   Chinese poetry, Six Dynasties and T'ang peri-
                                 ods, esp. yueh-fu.

    Lit 239, Yen 596.

    + Gakudai kokubun (Ōsaka Kyōiku Daigaku) 24 (1981), 7-12.

Masuda Wataru   増田 渉   Modern Chinese literature. Chinese vernacular
                                 fiction. East-West historical relations.

    Lit 240, Yen 597, Teng #628.

    ∈ Idem, <u>The Eastern Spread of Western Learning: Notes on "Various</u>
<u>Books"</u>.

        Translated by Joshua A. Fogel. In <u>Sino-Japanese Studies</u>:

          [Part 1]   2.2 (May 1990), 20-46.
          Part 2   3.1 (Nov. 1990), 36-63.
          Part 3   3.2 (Apr. 1991), 30-52.

        [Eleven chapters translated.]

    • Tu shu (Peking) 1981.10 (Oct. 1981), 146-149.

    + Jimbun kenkyū 29.7 (Nov. 1977), 1-5.

    + Ibid. 19.10 (March 1968), 1-6.

    + Ia 8 (May 1977), 29-36, and 9 (Nov. 1977), 77-78.

    • Ibid. 8 (May 1977), 11-22, and 9 (Nov. 1977), 1-8.

    • Bungaku (Iwanami Shoten) 45.5 (May 1977), 548-552.

    • Gendai no me 18.5 (May 1977), 146-151.

Masui Tsuneo   増井経夫   Modern Chinese history. Chinese historical
                                 texts, Shih-t'ung.

    Yen 595, Teng #469.

    + Hokuriku shigaku (Kanazawa Daigaku) 20 (1972), 72-77.

Masumura Hiroshi   増村宏   Chinese socio-economic history, Six Dynasties
                                    period.
    Yen 595, Teng #519.

Masunaga Reihō   増永霊鳳
    Listed under Fukui Kōjun and Iwai Hirosato.

Matake Naoshi   真武直   Chinese language, history of phonology.
    Yen 604.

Matano Tarō   俣野太郎   Classical Chinese thought. Chinese historical
                                    texts, Shih-chi.
    Lit 241.

Matsubara Saburō   松原三郎   East Asian art history, esp. Chinese Buddhist
                                    sculpture.
    Yen 430.
    Also listed under Akiyama Terukazu.

Matsuda Fukumatsu NC
    Listed under Tsuda Sōkichi.

Matsuda Hiroshi   松田弘   Classical Chinese thought.
    Lit 246.

Matsuda Hisao   松田寿男   Central Asian history. Historical geography.
    Yen 425, Teng #146.
    ø Tōzai bunka kōryūshi [487 pp.], 456-484.
        東西文化交流史
        Matsuda Hisao hakushi koki kinen shuppan iinkai, ed. Tokyo: Yūzan-
        kaku Shuppan, 1975.
        [Note Matsuda's discussion of his own scholarship, pp. 435-453.]
        TRNS #156.
    + Shikan 89 (March 1974), 77-96.

Matsuda Kazuo   松田和夫   Modern Chinese literature and language.
    Yen 426.

Matsuda Minoru   松田稔   Chinese thought, pre-T'ang period.
    Lit 246.

Matsuda Mitsugu   NC
    Listed under Shiba Yoshinobu.

Matsueda Shigeo   松枝茂夫   Chinese literature, esp. modern period and
                                    vernacular fiction. Sino-Japanese literary
                                    relations.
    Lit 243, Yen 428, Teng #629.
    + Gakujutsu kenkyū 24 (1975):
       [All three of the following bibliographies are the same.]
          Chirigaku, rekishigaku, shakai kagaku hen, 49-51.
          Kokugo, kokubungaku hen, 1-3.
          Kyōiku, shakai kyōiku, kyōiku shinri, taiiku hen, 67-69.
    + Jimbun gakuhō (Tōkyō Toritsu Daigaku) 78 (March 1970), 2-4.

Matsui Hiromi
    see Matsui Hiromitsu.

Matsui Hiromitsu   松井博光   Modern Chinese literature.
    Lit 241, Yen 422.

Matsui Shūichi   松井秀一   Chinese history, esp. T'ang period.
    Yen 423.

Matsui Takeo   松井武男   Modern Chinese language.
    Yen 423.

Matsumaru Michio   松丸道雄   Chinese epigraphy. Early Chinese history.
    Yen 426.

Matsumoto Akira   松本 昭   Chinese language: phonetics and philology.
                                            Chinese history, T'ang period.
    Yen 418.

Matsumoto Bunzaburō 松本 文三郎   Buddhist studies.
    + Ōtani gakuhō 11.2 (May 1930), 173-176.

Matsumoto Eiichi   松本 栄一   Chinese art history, incl. Tun-huang caves.
    Yen 416, Teng #179.

Matsumoto Masaaki   松本 雅明   Early Chinese thought. Chinese poetry, esp.
                                            Shih-ching. Japanese history and archaeol-
                                            ogy.
    Lit 247, Yen 418, Teng #669.
    + Hōbun ronsō (Kumamoto Daigaku) (Shigaku hen) 41 (March 1978), 152-
       167.
    + Idem, Chūgoku kodai ni okeru shizen shisō no tenkai [410 pp.], 359-
       389.
        中国古代における自然思想の展開
       Tokyo: Chūō Kōron Jigyō Shuppan, 1973.

Matsumoto Nobuhiro 松本 信広   Japanese, and East Asian, mythology. Ethnol-
                                            ogy and culture of East Asia, Southeast
                                            Asia, and India.
    Yen 417, Teng #20.
    + Shigaku 40.2-3 (Nov. 1967), 374-398.
    • Ibid., 371-373.

Matsumoto Yoshimi   松本 善海   Chinese history, history of local administra-
                                            tive system.
    Yen 417, Teng #470.

Matsumoto Yukio   松本 幸男   Chinese poetry, Six Dynasties period. Chinese
                                            fiction, T'ang period.
    Lit 248.

Matsumura Jun 松村 潤 Inner Asian history and philology. Chinese history, Ch'ing period.

Yen 420, Teng #558.

Matsumura Kazundo
see Matsumura Kazuto.

Matsumura Kazuto 松村 一人 Modern Chinese thought. Contemporary Chinese politics.

Yen 421.

Matsumura Takashi 松村 昴 Chinese literature, esp. traditional poetry.
Lit 246, Yen 419.

Matsumura Takeo 松村 武雄 Mythology, incl. China and Japan.
Yen 420.

Matsunaga Masao 松永 雅生 Chinese history, T'ang period.

Matsuno Shōji 松野 昭二 Modern Chinese history, incl. economic history. Contemporary Chinese economics.

Yen 430.

Matsuo Takayoshi 松尾 尊允 Modern East Asian history.
Yen 427, Teng #304.
Also listed under Yoshino Sakuzō.

Matsuo Takeji 松尾 武次
Listed under Collected Articles #64.

Matsuoka Yōko 松岡 洋子 Contemporary China, incl. politics.
Yen 421.

Matsushima Takahiro 松島 隆裕 Chinese thought, Han period.
Lit 245.

Matsushita Tadashi 松下忠   Japanese literature, Edo period. Chinese po-
                                   etics, Ming period. Sino-Japanese literary
                                   relations.

    Lit 245, Yen 428, Teng #595.

    + Kangaku kenkyū (Nihon Daigaku) 18-19 (#20) (Aug. 1980), 10-14.

    • Ibid., 1-10.

Matsushita Takaaki 松下隆章   Chinese art history.
    Yen 427.

Matsuura Akira   松浦明   Sino-Japanese historical relations, Ming pe-
                                   riod.

Matsuura Tomohisa 松浦友久   Chinese poetry, esp. T'ang period.
    Lit 242, Yen 423.

Matsuzaki Haruyuki 松崎治之   Chinese literature, Ch'ing period.
    Lit 244.

Matsuzaki Hisakazu 松崎寿和   Chinese archaeology.
    Yen 424.

    ø Kōko ronshū Keishuku Matsuzaki Hisakazu sensei rokujūsan-sai bunshū
       [6,672,3 pp.], 667-672.

      考古論集
      Matsuzaki Hisakazu sensei taikan kinen jigyōkai, ed. & publ. Hiro-
      shima, 1977.

      TRNS:oo.

Mekada Makoto   目加田誠   Chinese literature, esp. traditional poetry
                                   and poetics.

    Lit 260, Yen 285, Teng #596.

    Σ Mekada Makoto chosakushū. No biblio.
      Tokyo: Ryūkei Shosha, 1981-86. 8 vols.

ø Mekada Makoto hakushi koki kinen <u>Chūgoku bungaku ronshū</u> [14,522,
    22,13 pp.], 8 pp.

中国文学論集

Tokyo: Ryūkei Shosha, 1974. {E}

TRNS #234.

+ Bungaku kenkyū (Kyūshū Daigaku) 65 (1968), 13-16.

● Ibid., 5-13 and 17-28.

ø Mekada Makoto hakushi kanreki kinen <u>Chūgokugaku ronshū</u> [12,485
    pp.], 1-5.

中国学論集

Tokyo: Daian, 1964.

TRNS #233.

Mekata Makoto

    see Mekada Makoto.

Michibata Ryōshū   道端 良秀 History of Chinese Buddhism.
    Yen 99.

Michihata Ryōshū

    see Michibata Ryōshū.

Mikami Masatoshi   三上 正利 Historical geography. Siberia. Sino-Russian
                                        historical relations.

    Yen 343.

    + Rekishigaku chirigaku nempō 2 (1978), 1-4.

Mikami Seijirō   三上 誠治郎 Classical Chinese thought.
    Lit 250.

Mikami Taichō   三上 諦聴 Modern Chinese history, incl. Chinese Commu-
                                        nist party.

    Teng #571.

    + Shisen (Kansai Daigaku) 42 (March 1971), 1-4.

Mikami Tsugio   三上 次男   Archaeology: China, Manchuria, and Korea.

Chinese history, esp. Chin period.

Yen 342, Teng #508 and #789.

ø Mikami Tsugio hakushi kiju kinen rombunshū. Kōko hen, 377-443.

    Kōko hen   考古編   443 pp.

    Rekishi hen   歴史編   430 pp.

    Tōji hen   陶磁編   380 pp.

Mikami Tsugio hakushi kiju kinen rombunshū henshū iinkai, ed. Tokyo:
Heibonsha, 1985. 3 vols.

Σ Mikami Tsugio chosakushū.

Tokyo: Ochanomizu Shobō, 1979-80. 3 vols.

ø Mikami Tsugio hakushi shōju kinen ronshū   Tōyōshi kōkogaku ronshū
    [7,642,103,125 pp.], 31-125.

東洋史考古学論集

Mikami Tsugio hakushi shōju kinen ronshū henshū iinkai, ed. Kyoto:
Hōyū Shoten, 1979.

TRNS:oo.

∋ Herbert Franke, Reviews of Mikami's three-volume Kinshi kenkyū 金史
研究 (Tokyo: Chūō Kōron Bijutsu Shuppan), in T'oung Pao 59 (1973),
311-314 (for vol. 1); T'oung Pao 57 (1971), 320-325 (for vol. 2);
and T'oung Pao 60 (1974), 182-186 (for vol. 3):

vol. 1 Kindai Joshin shakai no kenkyū [1972. 481,11,1,3 pp.].
        金代女真社会の研究

vol. 2 Kindai seiji seido no kenkyū [1970. 572,9,7 pp.].
        金代政治制度の研究

vol. 3 Kindai seiji shakai no kenkyū [1973. 486,9,5 pp.].
        金代政治社会の研究

[Note also the English-language table of contents in each volume, 3,
7, and 5 pp., respectively.]

• Jimbun Kagakuka kiyō (Tōkyō Daigaku) 43 (Rekishi to bunka 9, Rekishigaku kenkyū hōkoku 13) (Aug. 1967), 299-301.

Also listed under Collected Articles #13.

Mikami Tsuguo

    see Mikami Tsugio.

Mikami Yoshio   三上義夫   Chinese and Japanese mathematics and astron-
                                            omy.

∋* Joseph Needham, <u>Science and Civilisation in China</u>, Vol. 3: <u>Mathe-</u>
<u>matics and the Sciences of the Heavens and the Earth</u>, pp. 734-735.
Cambridge: Cambridge University Press, 1959.
[Needham cites and translates 23 titles by Mikami.]

∋+ S. Yajima, "Yoshio Mikami," <u>Actes du VIIe Congrès International</u>
<u>d'Histoire des Sciences</u>, Jerusalem 4-12 Août, 1953, 646-658.
[Translation into French from the <u>Kagakushi kenkyū</u> entries below.]

+ Kagakushi kenkyū 18 (Apr. 1951), 9-11, and 22 (May 1952), 45-47.
[Cf. the preceding entry.]

• Ibid. 18 (Apr. 1951), 1-9.

∋* Hirata Yutaka, "Yoshio Mikami," <u>Isis</u> 42.2 (#128) (June 1951), 144.

Mino Yutaka   NC   East Asian art, esp. Chinese ceramics.

∈ <u>Ice and Green Clouds: Traditions of Chinese Celadon</u> [240 pp.].
By Mino Yutaka and Katherine R. Tsiang. Indianapolis: Indianapolis
Museum of Art, and Bloomington: Indiana University Press, 1987.

∈ <u>Beauty and Tranquility: The Eli Lilly Collection of Chinese Art</u> [368
pp.].
By Mino Yutaka and James Robinson. Indianapolis: Indianapolis Museum
of Art, 1983.

∈ <u>Freedom of Clay and Brush through Seven Centuries in Northern China:</u>
<u>Tz'u-chou Type Wares, 960-1600 A.D.</u> [264 pp. plus 353 add'l. plates].
By Mino Yutaka, with the assistance of Katherine S. Tsiang. Indianapolis: Indianapolis Museum of Art, and Bloomington: Indiana University Press, 1980.

∈ Idem, <u>Pre-Sung Dynasty Chinese Stonewares in the Royal Ontario Museum</u>
[1,1,2,104 pp.].
Toronto: The Royal Ontario Musem, 1974.

∈ Idem, <u>Ceramics in the Liao Dynasty: North and South of the Great Wall</u>
[86 pp.].
New York: China House Gallery and China Institute in America, 1973.

∈ An Index to Chinese Ceramic Kiln Sites from the Six Dynasties to the
    Present [3,103 pp.].

    By Mino Yutaka and Patricia Wilson.   Toronto: The Royal Ontario
    Museum, 1973.

    [A pamplet-length English-language exhibition catalog by Mino on Japa-
    nese ceramic incense boxes is not listed here.]

Misaki Ryōshū   三崎 良周   Buddhist studies.
    Yen 341.

Misawa Reiji   三沢 玲爾   Chinese poetry, thru Han period.
    Lit 251.

Mishima Hajime   三島 一   Chinese history, esp. economic history, T'ang
                                       period.
    Yen 340.

    + Idem, Chūgokushi to Nihon [421 pp.], 381-388.
       中国史と日本
       Tokyo: Shin Hyōron, 1977.

    • Chūgoku kenkyū geppō 312 (Feb. 1974), 30-31.

    + Senshū shigaku 1 (May 1968), 126-131, and 2 (Feb. 1970), 86-87.

    • Gakumon e no michi [3,107 pp.], 67-107.
       学問への道
       Senshū Daigaku Keizai Gakkai, ed. & publ. Tokyo, 1968.

Mishina Akihide

    see Mishina Shōei

Mishina Shōei   三品彰英   Mythology, history, and ethnology of East
                                       Asia, incl. Korea.
    Teng #714.

    Σ Mishina Shōei rombunshū. No biblio.
       Tokyo: Heibonsha, 1970-74. 6 vols.

    + Bukkyō Daigaku Daigakuin kenkyū kiyō 3 (March 1973), 293-300.

    • Ibid., 289-292.

*   Chōsen gakuhō 65 (Oct. 1972), 141-143.
●   Minzokugaku kenkyū 37.1 (July 1972), 66-67.
+   Kodai bunka 24.3 (March 1972), 91-100.

Mitamura Taisuke   三田村 泰助 Chinese history, esp. Ming and Ch'ing periods. Manchurian and Mongolian history.

Yen 343, Teng #497.
+   Ritsumeikan bungaku 418-421 (July 1980), 1-7.
∈   Idem, Chinese Eunuchs: The Structure of Intimate Politics [176 pp.].
**Translated by Charles A. Pomeroy. Rutland, Vt. and Tokyo: Charles E.
Tuttle Co., 1970.**
Also listed under Naitō Konan.

Mitani Taichirō   三谷太一郎   Modern Japanese history and government. Modern Sino-Japanese relations.

Mitani Takashi   三谷 孝   Modern Chinese history, twentieth-century
popular movements.

Mitarai Masaru   御手洗 勝   Ancient Chinese myth and legend. Chinese
thought.

Lit 253, Yen 584.

Mitsumori Sadao   三森 定男   Japanese and Chinese archaeology.
+   Kodai bunka 29.6 (June 1977), 2-7.
●   Ibid., 9-26.
●   Gakuen ronshū (Hokkai Gakuen Daigaku) 21 (Oct. 1972), 50-55.
●   Ibid., 3 pp.

Mitsuoka Gen   光岡 玄   Contemporary Chinese politics and economy.
Modern Chinese history.

Yen 162.

Miura Isshū   三浦一舟   Ch'an Buddhism, China and Japan.

∈ Zen Dust [22,574 pp.].

By Miura Isshū and Ruth Fuller Sasaki. Kyoto: The First Zen Institute of America in Japan, 1966; New York: Harcourt, Brace & World,
(1966) 1967.

[Subtitle: The History of the Koan and Koan Study in Rinzai (Lin-
chi) Zen.]

[The volume is an expanded version of the authors' The Zen Koan: Its
History and Use in Rinzai Zen (New York: Harcourt, Brace & World,
1965). 18,156 pp.]

[Note the review by P. Demiéville in T'oung Pao 56 (1970), 290-297.]

Miura Kunio   三浦国雄   Chinese thought, incl. neo-Confucianism, esp.
                                   Chu Hsi.

Yen 341.

Miyagawa   宮川
see also Miyakawa.

Miyagawa Torao   宮川寅雄   East Asian art and archaeology, esp. paint-
                                   ing.

Yen 147.

∈ Chinese Painting [228 pp.].

Miyagawa Torao, general editor. Translated and adapted by Alfred T.
Birnbaum. New York, Tokyo, and Kyoto: Weatherhill/Tankosha, 1983.

[Includes chapters by several Japanese scholars of Chinese painting.]

[A book-length English-language study by Miyagawa of modern Japanese
painting is not listed here.]

Miyakawa   宮川
see also Miyagawa.

Miyakawa Hisayuki 宮川尚志   History of Chinese society and religion,
                                   incl. Six Dynasties period.

Yen 147, Teng #520.

Also listed under Naitō Konan and Collected Articles #20b.

Miyakawa Kiyoshi   宮川 澄   Contemporary China.
   Yen 146.

Miyake Takeo   三宅 武雄   Economics, incl. Japan and Taiwan.
   Yen 344.

Miyake Yonekichi   三宅 米吉   Asian history.
   + Shichō 70 (Nov. 1959), 63-67.
   • Ibid., 56-62 and 68-92.
   ø Miyake hakushi koki shukuga kinen rombunshū [73,830 pp.], 52-67.
      Ōtsuka Shigakkai, ed. Tokyo: Oka Shoin, 1929.
      [Note the biography of Miyake, pp. 7-44.]
      TRNS #229, NNO 3:419.
   See also the Stefan Tanaka entry under Shiratori Kurakichi.

Miyamoto Katsu   宮本 勝   Classical Chinese thought.
   Yen 145.

Miyamoto Shōsen
   see Miyamoto Shōson.

Miyamoto Shōson   宮本 正尊   Buddhist studies.*
   Yen 145, Teng #736.
   • Tōhōgaku 41 (March 1971), 136-163.
   ø Miyamoto Shōson kyōju kanreki kinen rombunshū Indogaku Bukkyōgaku
      ronshū [618,1 pp.] No biblio.
      印度学仏教学論集
      Hanayama Shinshō et al., eds. Tokyo: Sanseidō, 1954.
      TRNS:oo
   Also listed under Fukui Kōjun (twice), Suzuki Daisetsu, Ui Hakuju, and
   Yūki Reimon.

Miyamoto Shōzaburō NC
   Listed under Yonezawa Yoshiho.

Miyasaka Yūshō   宮坂宥勝   Buddhist studies.* Indian philosophy.
　　Yen 146.

　+　Nagoya Daigaku Bungakubu kenkyū ronshū 93 (Tetsugaku 31) (1985), 1-9.

　+　SAṂBHĀṢĀ 6 (Nagoya Daigaku) (Jan. 1985), 1-9.

Miyashita Tadao   宮下忠雄   Modern Chinese economy: currency and trade.
　　Yen 151, Teng #88.

　+　Kokumin keizai zasshi 126.4 (Oct. 1972), 113-125.

　•　Ibid., 91-112.

　∈　Idem, The Currency and Financial System of Mainland China [8,278
　　pp.].
　　Translated by J.R. McEwan. Tokyo: Institute of Asian Economic Af-
　　fairs, 1966.

Miyata Ichirō   宮田一郎   Chinese vernacular fiction, Ch'ing period.
　　　　　　　　　　　　　　　　　　　Chinese language.
　　Lit 255, Yen 150.

　+　Jimbun kenkyū (Ōsaka Shiritsu Daigaku) 37.3 (Dec. 1985), 3-5.

Miyauchi Tamotsu   宮内 保   Chinese literature, incl. vernacular fiction.
　　Lit 254.

Miyazaki Hiroshi   宮崎ひろし   Modern Chinese literature.
　　Lit 255.

Miyazaki Ichisada   宮崎市定   Chinese history, esp. Six Dynasties thru Yuan
　　　　　　　　　　　　　　　　　　　periods.
　　Yen 148, Teng #471.

　•　Kodai bunka 37.4 (Apr. 1985), 35-38, and 37.5 (May 1985), 33-37.

　∈　Idem, China's Examination Hell: The Civil Service Examinations of
　　Imperial China [145 pp.].
　　Translated by Conrad Schirokauer. Tokyo and New York: Weatherhill,
　　1976.

　+　Tōyōshi kenkyū 29.4 (March 1971), 29 pp.

　+　Seinan Ajia kenkyū (Kyōto Daigaku) 14 (June 1965), 3-12.

Miyazaki Seryū   宮崎世龍   Contemporary Chinese politics and economy.
    Yen 150.

Miyazaki Tōten   宮崎滔天   Romantic revolutionary in China. Sun Yat-sen's contact for Japanese assistance to the 1911 Revolution.

∈   Idem, <u>My Thirty-three Years' Dream: The Autobiography of Miyazaki Tōten</u> [28,298 pp.].
   Translated, with an introduction, by Etō Shinkichi and Marius B. Jansen.   Princeton: Princeton University Press, 1982.

Σ   <u>Miyazaki Tōten zenshū</u>.
   Tokyo: Heibonsha, 1971-77.   5 vols.

Miyazaki Torazō   宮崎寅蔵
    see Miyazaki Tōten.

Miyazawa Masayori   宮沢正順   Chinese religious thought, Six Dynasties.
    Lit 255.

Miyazawa Seijun
    see Miyazawa Masayori.

Miyoshi Hajime   三好一   Modern Chinese literature.
    Yen 340.

Miyuki Mokusen   NC
    Listed under Yūki Reimon.

Mizoguchi Yūzō   溝口雄三   Chinese thought, esp. Ming period.
    Yen 152.

Mizuhara Ikō   水原渭江   Early Chinese thought, incl. music, calligraphy, painting, poetry, and poetics.
    Lit 252.

Mizuhara Shigemitsu 水原重光   Sino-Russian historical relations.
        Yen 412.

Mizukami Sanae   水上早苗   Chinese poetry, traditional. Chinese vernac-
                                    ular fiction.
        Lit 251.

Mizukami Shizuo   水上静夫   Ancient Chinese botany. Chinese bibliography.
        Yen 409.

    ∋ Jeffrey R. Riegel, Review article on Mizukami's study of ancient
      Chinese botany, Chūgoku kodai no shokubutsugaku no kenkyū 中国古代の
      植物学の研究   (Tokyo: Kadokawa Shoten, 1977. 782 pp.), in Har-
      vard Journal of Asiatic Studies 46.1 (June 1986), 317-323.

Mizuno Kōgen   水野弘元   Buddhist studies.* Pali language and litera-
                                    ture.
        Yen 409.

Mizuno Seiichi   水野清一   Chinese art and archaeology.
        Yen 410, Teng #9.

    +• Mizuno Seiichi hakushi tsuiokushū [176 pp.].
       Kaizuka Shigeki and Hibino Takeo, eds. Kyoto: Kyōto Daigaku Jimbun
       Kagaku Kenkyūjo Nai Mizuno Seiichi Hakushi Tsuiokushū Kankōkai, 1973.

    ∋ J. Edward Kidder, Jr., "Seiichi Mizuno, 1905-1971," Artibus Asiae
      35.1-2 (1973), 163-164.

    • Kodai bunka 23.7 (July 1971), 159-160.

    • Bukkyō geijutsu 80 (June 1971), 116.

    + Tōhō gakuhō 40 (March 1969), 425-430.

    + Idem, Chūgoku no Bukkyō bijutsu [38,489 pp.], 466-487.
      中国の仏教美術
      Tokyo: Heibonsha, 1968.

    ∈ Yün-kang: The Buddhist Cave-temples of the Fifth Century A.D. in
      North China.
      By Mizuno Seiichi and Nagahiro Toshio. Kyoto: Jimbunkagaku Kenkyu-
      sho, Kyoto University, 1951- . Translators: Caves 1-4: J. Harada

and P.C. Swann; Cave 7: M. Nagao and W. Fernström-Flygare; Cave 8: J. Harada; Cave 9: S. Iwamura; Cave 10: P.C. Swann.

[Subtitle: Detailed report of the archaeological survey carried out by the mission of the Tohobunka Kenkyusho, 1938-45, by Seiichi Mizuno and Toshio Nagahiro.]

∈ <u>A Study of the Buddhist Cave-temples at Lung-men, Honan</u> [12,17,16, 482,103,28 pp.].

By Seiiti Miduno [Mizuno Seiichi] and Tosio Nagahiro [Nagahiro Toshi-o]. Tokyo: Zauho Press, 1941.

[Note Appendix I, by Zenryū Tukamoto (Tsukamato Zenryū): "Buddhism under the Northern Wei dynasty as seen in the cave-temples at Lung-men" (in Japanese and English).]

[A book-length English-language study by Mizuno of Asuka-period Japanese art is not listed here.]

Mizuno Suzuhiko   水野 銑彦   Modern Chinese language.
    Yen 409.

Mizuno Yoshitomo   水野 美知   Chinese literature, T'ang-period fiction.
    Lit 252.

Mizusawa Toshitada 水沢 利忠   Chinese historical texts, <u>Shih-chi</u>.
    Lit 251, Yen 411.

Mizutani Shinjō   水谷 真成   Chinese language, historical phonology.
    Lit 252, Yen 408, Teng #738.

Mizutani Shinsei
    see Mizutani Shinjō.

Mochizuki Katsumi   望月 勝美   East Asian geology. Physical geography.
    Teng #134.

Mochizuki Shinkō 望月信亨   Buddhist studies.

+ Idem, <u>Mochizuki Bukkyō daijiten</u>, vol. 10 (1963), 13-19.

望月仏教大辞典

Tokyo: Sekai Seiten Kankō Kyōkai, 1931-63. 10 vols.

• Ibid., vol. 10, 1-12.

Mochizuki Shinkyō

see Mochizuki Shinkō.

Mochizuki Yasokichi 望月八十吉 History of Chinese language. Modern Chinese
                                      language.

Lit 261, Yen 473.

Momose Hiromu   百瀬 弘   Chinese socio-economic history, Ming and
                                      Ch'ing periods. Modern Chinese history.

Yen 19, Teng #572.

Momose Hiroshi

see Momose Hiromu.

Mori Akira   森 亮   Chinese poetry, traditional.
Lit 262.

Mori Katsumi   森 克巳   Sino-Japanese historical relations and Chi-
                                      nese history, T'ang thru Ming periods.
                                      Japanese history, medieval period.

Yen 347, Teng #170.

Σ <u>Mori Katsumi chosaku senshū</u>. No biblio.

Tokyo: Kokusho Kankōkai, 1975-76. 6 vols.

+ Chūō Daigaku Bungakubu kiyō 72 (Shigakuka 19) (March 1974), 171-184.

• Ibid., 165-171.

+ <u>Mori Katsumi hakushi nempu chosaku mokuroku</u>.

Mori Katsumi hakushi koki kinenkai, ed. Tokyo: Yoshikawa Kōbunkan,

1974.

ø (Shigaku ronshū) *Taigai kankei to seiji bunka*.   No biblio.

（史学論集）対外関係と政治文化
Mori Katsumi hakushi koki kinenkai, ed.   Tokyo: Yoshikawa Kōbunkan,
1974.   3 vols.

    Vol. 1:   Relations Abroad.   15,501,1 pp.

    Vol. 2:   Political Culture: Ancient and Medieval.   11,660,1 pp.

    Vol. 3:   Political Culture: Early Modern and Modern.   11,544,1
      pp.

TRNS #092.

ø Mori Katsumi hakushi kanreki kinen rombunshū *Taigai kankei to sha-*
kai keizai [672 pp.], 663-672.

対外関係と社会経済
Mori hakushi kanreki kinenkai, ed.   Tokyo: Hanawa Shobō, 1968.

TRNS #113.

Mori Masao   護　雅夫   Central Asian history. East-West historical
                                   relations.

  Yen 180.

  Also listed under Intro. #9.

  Cf. next entry.

Mori Masao   森　正夫   Chinese socio-economic history, Ming and
                                   Ch'ing periods.

  Yen 349

  Cf. preceding entry.

Mori Mikisaburō   森三樹三郎   Chinese thought, thru Six Dynasties period.
  Lit 261, Yen 348, Teng #670.

  ø Mori Mikisaburō hakushi shōju kinen *Tōyōgaku ronshū* [7,5,1402,7
    pp.], 4-7.

    東洋学論集
    Mori Mikisaburō hakushi shōju kinen jigyōkai, ed.   Kyoto: Hōyū Sho-
    ten, 1979.

    TRNS:oo.

Mori Ryō   森 亮
    see Mori Akira.

Mori Shikazō   森 鹿三   Chinese historical geography. Chinese histo-
                                    ry, esp. Han and Six Dynasties periods.
    Yen 347, Teng #472.
    +   Ōryō shigaku 8 (Feb. 1982), 3-4.
    +   Ibid. 3-4 (July 1977), 16 pp.
    ø   Mori Shikazō hakushi shōju kinen rombunshū [18,586 pp.], 3-15.
        Mori Shikazō hakushi shōju kinenkai, ed. Kyoto: Dōhōsha, 1977.
        TRNS #236.
    +   Tōhō gakuhō 42 (March 1971), 343-346.

Mori Yasutarō   森 安太郎   Early Chinese history, myth, and legend.
    Lit 262.

Morikawa Kyūjirō 森川 久次郎 Modern Chinese language.
    Yen 350.

Morimoto Jun'ichirō 守本 順一郎 History of political thought, Japan and Chi-
                                    na.
    +   Nagoya Daigaku hōsei ronshū 77 (Sept. 1978), 583-587.

Morino Shigeo   森野 繁夫   Chinese literature, Six Dynasties period.
    Lit 262, Yen 350.

Morita Akira   森田 明   History of Chinese water control.

Moritani Katsumi 森谷 克巳   Chinese and Korean economic history.
    Teng #89.
    ●* Musashi Daigaku ronshū 13.1-2 (June 1965), 147-154.

Moriya Mitsuo   守屋 美都雄 Chinese institutional and social history,
                                    incl. Six Dynasties period.

    Lit 263, Yen 407, Teng #509.

  + Idem, <u>Chūgoku kodai no kazoku to kokka</u>. <u>Bessatsu furoku</u>.

中国古代の家族と国家 別冊附録

    Kyoto: Kyōto Daigaku Bungakubu Tōyōshi Kenkyūkai, 1968.

    [Whereas the supplementary volume contains the bibliography, the
    volume proper (1,11,656,13 pp.) consists of reprints of articles by
    Moriya (original publication information for which is given on p.
    655).]

  + Hōseishi kenkyū 17 (1967), 269-271.

  + Ōsaka Daigaku Indo Tōnan-Ajia Kenkyū Sentaa ihō 4 (1967), 3-10.

Moriyasu Takao   森安 孝夫   History of Manchuria, Mongolia, and Tibet,
                                      T'ang thru Yuan periods.

Morohashi Tetsuji 諸橋轍次 Chinese thought, classical and Sung periods.
                                    Chinese language and lexicography.

    Lit 264, Yen 631, Teng #671.

  • <u>"Dai Kan-Wa jiten" o yomu</u> [293,1 pp.].

『大漢和辞典』を 読む

    Kida Jun'ichirō, ed. Tokyo: Taishūkan Shoten, 1986.

    [Among the various articles on Morohashi's monumental Japanese dic-
    tionary of Chinese is the one by the editor (pp. 11-62), telling how
    Morohashi actually compiled the work.]

  •* Shibun 87 (1983), 86 pp.

    [The entire issue is devoted to <u>in memoriam</u> notices and reminiscences
    about Morohashi; a short bibligraphy of his major works appears on
    p. 6.]

  Σ <u>Morohashi Tetsuji chosakushū</u>, vol. 10 (1977), 627-631.
    Tokyo: Taishūkan Shoten, 1975-77. 10 vols.

  * Kambun kyōshitsu 75 (March 1966), 13.

  • Ibid., 16-38.

  • Tōhōgaku 26 (July 1963), 108-128, and 27 (Feb. 1964), 118-133.

ø <u>Morohashi hakushi koki shukuga kinen rombunshū</u> [2,3,17,3,730,3 pp.],
13-17.
Morohashi Tetsuji sensei koki shukuga kinenkai, ed. & publ. Tokyo,
1953.
TRNS #237, NNO 3:419-420.

Moroi Kōji   諸井耕二   Chinese literature, esp. T'ang-period fiction.
Lit 264.

Moroi Yoshinori   諸井慶徳   Religion, incl. China.
 • Tōhō shūkyō 17 (Aug. 1961), 66-67.

Moroto Tatsuo   諸戸立雄   History of Chinese Buddhism.
Teng #530.

Mugifu Tomie   麦生登美江   Chinese vernacular fiction, Ch'ing period.
Lit 256.

Mukai Akira   向井章   Chinese economy.
Teng #90.

Mukōjima Shigeyoshi 向嶋成美   Chinese poetry, Six Dynasties and T'ang periods.
Lit 256.

Mukōyama Hiroo   向山寛夫   Chinese law, esp. labor law. Contemporary
Chinese politics.
Yen 498.
 • Chūō keizai 25.4 (Oct. 1976), 2-7.
 + Idem, <u>Chūgoku rōdōhō no kenkyū</u> [5,6,498,11,4 pp.], 485-486.
中国労働法の研究
Tokyo: Chūō Keizai Kenkyūjo, 1968. {E}
[Note the glossary of Chinese terms used for labor law, pp. 487-498.]

Munakata Kiyohiko   NC   Chinese art history, incl. calligraphic theory.

∈ Idem, <u>Ching Hao's "Pi-fa-chi": A Note on the Art of the Brush</u> [5,56 pp.].

Ascona, Switz.: Artibus Asiae, 1974.

Murakami Masatsugu 村上 正二   Mongolian history. Chinese history, Yuan period.

Yen 72, Teng #544.

+ Jimbun gakuhō (Tōkyō Toritsu Daigaku) 118 (Feb. 1977), 9 pp.

Murakami Naojirō   村上直次郎   Japanese history, history of foreign trade (incl. China), Edo period.

•* Tōhōgaku 57 (Jan. 1979), 151-178.

Murakami Tetsumi   村上哲見   Chinese poetry, T'ang and Sung periods, esp. <u>tz'u</u>.

Lit 256, Yen 71.

Murakami Tomoyuki 村上 知行   Chinese vernacular fiction.
Yen 72.

Murakami Yoshihide 村上 嘉英   Chinese language: history and dialects.
Yen 71.

Murakami Yoshimi   村上 嘉実   Chinese thought and religion, Six Dynasties period.

Lit 257, Yen 70, Teng #690.

+ Kansai Gakuin shigaku 16 (1975).

Muramatsu Akira
see Muramatsu Ei.

Muramatsu Ei   村松 暎   Chinese literature, esp. vernacular fiction, Ch'ing period.

Lit 258, Yen 68.

Muramatsu Kazuya　村松一弥　Modern Chinese folk culture, literature, and
music.

　　Lit 259, Yen 69.

Muramatsu Yūji　村松 祐次　Modern Chinese socio-economic history.
　　Yen 70, Teng #91.

ø　Ko Muramatsu Yūji kyōju tuitō rombunshū　Chūgoku no seiji to keizai
　　[4,253 pp.], 245-253.

中国の政治と経済

Ko Muramatsu kyōju tsuitō jigyōkai, ed.　Tokyo: Tōyō Keizai Shimbunsha, 1975.

[Includes articles in Western languages by Michel Cartier, Marianne
Bastid, Ramon H. Myers, Dwight H. Perkins, and Stuart R. Schram.]
TRNS #134.

•　Tōyō gakuhō 56.2-4 (March 1975), 275-281.

∋　Arthur F. Wright, "Remembering Yūji: In Memory of Muramatsu Yūji
村松祐次," Ch'ing-shih wen-t'i 3.1 (Nov. 1974), 1-2.

∋　Ramon H. Myers and Benjamin I. Schwartz, "Yūji Muramatsu, 1911-1974,"
Journal of Asian Studies 33.4 (Aug. 1974), 651-653.

+　Hitotsubashi ronsō 72.1 (July 1974), 144-155.

Murata Jirō　村田治郎　Asian architectural history.
　　Yen 73, Teng #194.

Murata Toshihiro　村田俊裕　Modern Chinese literature.
　　Lit 258.

Murayama Shichirō　村山七郎　Altaic languages, esp. Mongolian and Turkish.

　　+　Bungaku kenkyū (Kyūshū Daigaku) 70 (1973), 19-28.

Murayama Yoshihiro　村山吉広　Chinese poetry, T'ang and Ch'ing periods, and
Shih-ching.

　　Lit 259.

Mutō Chōzō   武藤長蔵   (Economic history.)

ø   Mutō kyōju zaishoku sanjūnen kinen rombunshū [4,423,9,17 pp.]

Itō Hisaaki, ed.   Nagasaki: Nagasaki Kōtō Shōgyō Gakkō Kenkyūkan, 1937.

[Includes an English-language article by R. van Gulik, "Chinese Literary Music and Its Introduction into Japan," pp. 123-160.]

TRNS #232.

Naba Toshisada   那波利貞   Chinese history, T'ang period. Tun-huang documents.

Lit 194, Yen 286.

+   Idem, Tōdai shakai bunka shi kenkyū [3,3,691,9 pp.], 682-691.

唐代社会文化史研究

Tokyo: Sōbunsha, 1974.

+   Shisō (Kyōto Joshi Daigaku) 30 (Oct. 1971), 105-111.

•   Ibid., 113-128.

•   Tōhōgaku 36 (Sept. 1968), 159-177.

+   Tōyōshi kenkyū 12.5 (Sept. 1953), 97-102.

Nagahara Keiji   永原慶二

Listed under Collected Articles #52.

Nagahiro Toshio   長広敏雄   Chinese art, esp. Buddhist art, incl. Yun-kang and Tun-huang caves.

Yen 43, Teng #180.

+   Tōhō gakuhō 41 (March 1970), 768-771.

∈   Yün-kang: The Buddhist Cave-temples of the Fifth Century A.D. in North China.

By Mizuno Seiichi and Nagahiro Toshio.   Kyoto: Jimbunkagaku Kenkyu-sho, Kyoto University, 1951- .   Translators: Caves 1-4: J. Harada and P.C. Swann; Cave 7: M. Nagao and W. Fernström-Flygare; Cave 8: J. Harada; Cave 9: S. Iwamura; Cave 10: P.C. Swann.

[Subtitle: Detailed report of the archaeological survey carried out by the mission of the Tohobunka Kenkyusho, 1938-45, by Seiichi Mizuno and Toshio Nagahiro.]

∈ <u>A Study of the Buddhist Cave-temples at Lung-men, Honan</u> [12,17,16, 482,103,28 pp.].

By Seiiti Miduno [Mizuno Seiichi] and Tosio Nagahiro [Nagahiro Toshio]. Tokyo: Zauho Press, 1941.

[Note Appendix I, by Zenryū Tukamoto (Tsukamoto Zenryū): "Buddhism under the Northern Wei dynasty as seen in the cave-temples at Lung-men" (in Japanese and English).]

Nagai Kazumi   永井算巳   Modern Chinese history. Modern Sino-Japanese historical relations.

　　Yen 567, Teng #573.

Nagao Gadjin

　　see Nagao Gajin.

Nagao Gajin   長尾雅人   Buddhist studies.* Indian and Tibetan Buddhism. Mongolian religion.

　　Yen 49, Teng #739.

　　[A book-length English-language study by Nagao of Mādhyamika Buddhism is not listed here.]

Nagao, M.   NC

　　Listed under Mizuno Seiichi and Nagahiro Toshio.

Nagao Masato

　　see Nagao Gajin.

Nagao Mitsuyuki   長尾光之   Chinese language, Six Dynasties, esp. Buddhist texts. Chinese vernacular fiction.

　　Lit 183, Yen 50.

Nagao Sadao   長尾定雄   Chinese poetry, traditional.
　　Yen 50.

Nagasawa Kazutoshi 長沢和俊   Central Asian history. East-West historical
                                              relations.

   Yen 48.

Nagasawa Kikuya   長沢規矩也   Chinese bibliography. Chinese literature,
                                              traditional.

   Lit 184, Yen 47. Teng #708.

   Σ Nagasawa Kikuya chosakushū. No biblio.

      Tokyo: Kyūko Shoin, 1982-89. 10 vols.

   + Nagasawa Kikuya hencho mokuroku.

      Nagasawa Kikuya, ed. & publ. Tokyo, 1978.

   ø Nagasawa sensei koki kinen Toshogaku ronshū [15,639 pp.], 605-635.

   図書学論集

      Nagasawa sensei koki kinenkai, ed. Tokyo: Sanseidō, 1973.

      TRNS #190.

   ∈ Idem, Geschichte der chinesischen Literatur und ihrer gedanklichen
      Grundlage.

      Translated by P. Eugen Feifel. Peking: The Catholic University, 1945
      (12,444 pp.).   2nd ed., Darmstadt: Wissenschaftliche Buchgesell-
      schaft, 1959 (18,432 pp.).   3rd ed., Hirschber: Strauss & Cramer,
      1982 (630 pp.).   4th ed., Hildesheim, Zürich, New York: Georg Olms,
      1982 (1,2,630 pp.); rpt. Taipei: Lucky Book Co., 1984 (630 pp.).
      [Subtitle (1st and 2nd eds.): Nach Nagasawa Kikuya, Shina Gakujutsu
      Bungeishi. Subtitle (3rd and 4th eds.): Mit Berücksichtigung ihres
      geistesgeschichtlichen Hintergrundes. Dargestellt nach Nagasawa
      Kikuya: Shina Gakujutsu Bungeishi.]

Nagase Makoto   長瀬誠   Chinese thought.

   Lit 188, Yen 46.

Nagase Mamoru   長瀬守   Chinese history, Sung and Yuan periods, esp.
                                              water conservancy.

   Yen 46.

Nagashima Eiichirō 永島栄一郎 Chinese language, historical phonology.
  Yen 566.
  + Jimbun gakuhō (Tōkyō Toritsu Daigaku) 98 (March 1974), 4 pp.

Nagasue Yoshitaka 永末嘉孝 Modern Chinese literature.
  Lit 188.

Nagata Hidemasa 永田英正 Chinese history, thru Han period. Chinese
                                        epigraphy.
  Yen 568.

Nagata Toshio 永田敏雄 History of stone rubbings, China and Japan.
  Yen 567.

Nagaya Kenzō 長屋謙三
  see Hayashi Kenzō.

Nagumo Satoru 南雲智 Modern Chinese literature.
  Lit 194.

Naha Toshisada 那波利貞
  see Naba Toshisada.

Naitō Boshin 内藤戊申
  see Naitō Shigenobu.

Naitō Chōhō 内藤潮邦 Mongolian history and society.
  Teng #498.

Naitō Kenkichi 内藤乾吉 Chinese legal history. Chinese art history,
                                        calligraphy.
  Yen 290.
  + Hōgaku zasshi 9.3-4 (March 1953), 500-502.

Naitō Konan   内藤溯南   East Asian history. Chinese historiography.

• <u>Naitō Bunko risuto</u> [205 pp.].

内藤文庫リスト

Kansai Daigaku Toshokan, ed. & publ. Suita, 1989.

[Listing of Naitō's Chinese collection (pp. 1-129), with index (pp. 133-205). Cf. the 1986 entry below published under the same auspices.]

∋ <u>Naitō Konan: Poritikkusu to shinorojii</u> [358,1 pp.]

内藤溯南ーポリティックスとシノロジーーー

By J.A. Fōgeru [Joshua A. Fogel]. Translated by Inoue Hiromasa. Tokyo: Heibonsha, 1989.

[Japanese-language translation of the <u>Politics and Sinology</u> volume listed below.]

•* <u>Naitō Konan nooto</u> [258 pp.], 141-144.

内藤溯南ノート

By Kaga Eiji. Tokyo: Tōhō Shoten, 1987.

• <u>Naitō Bunko Kanseki kokan kosho mokuroku</u> [308 pp.].

内藤文庫漢籍古刊古書目録

Kansai Daigaku Toshokan, ed. & publ. Suita, 1986.

• Bunkyō Daigaku Kyōikugakubu kiyō 19 (Dec. 1985), 1-13.

∈ Joshua A. Fogel, <u>Naitō Konan and the Development of the Conception of Modernity in Chinese History</u>, Armonk, N.Y.: M.E. Sharpe, 1984. 11, 131 pp.

[Translations of essays by Naitō, with an introduction.]

∋ Joshua A. Fogel, <u>Politics and Sinology: The Case of Naitō Konan (1866-1934)</u>, Cambridge, Mass.: Council on East Asian Studies, Harvard University, 1984. 24,420 pp.

[The bibliography (pp. 333-381) includes extensive references to studies of Naitō, to translations of articles by Naitō into Chinese (as well as one into English), and (pp. 335-344) to numerous articles by Naitō <u>not</u> included in his <u>zenshū</u>.]

[Note the Japanese-language translation of the volume, listed above.]

∋ Joshua A. Fogel, "To Reform China: Naitō Konan's Formative Years in the Meiji Press," <u>Modern Asian Studies</u> 16.3 (July 1982), 353-395.

● Konan.

#1	March 1981	2,27 pp.
#2	March 1982	2,36 pp.
#3	Jan. 1983	121 pp.
#4	Dec. 1983	65 pp.

[A journal devoted to the memory of Naitō.]

+ Shoron

[Bibliographical listings and occasional reprinting of works not found in Naitō's <u>zenshu</u>.]

Pt. 1	Shoron 13	Nov. 1978	152-156.
Pt. 2	Shoron 14	May 1979	134-149.
Pt. 3	Shoron 15	Dec. 1979	149-155.
Pt. 4	Shoron 16	Spring 1980	115-121.
Pt. 5	Shoron 17	Autumn 1980	147-149.
Pt. 6	Shoron 18	Spring 1981	199-200.
Pt. 7	Shoron 19	Fall 1981	232-233.
Pt. 8	Shoron 20	Spring and Fall 1982	443.
Pt. 9	Shoron 21	Spring 1983	189-190.

●* Shoron

[Material about Naitō.]

Shoron 10	(Spring 1977), 40.	Shoron 17	78-146 and 150-156.
Shoron 13	73-142 and 157-176.	Shoron 18	193-198.
Shoron 14	80-123 and 150-153.	Shoron 19	134-136.
Shoron 15	132-148.	Shoron 21	148-188.
Shoron 16	104-114 and 122-128.		

● Momoyama rekishi chiri 16-17 (March 1980), 1-15, and 18 (Apr. 1981), 1-22.

∋ Tam Yue-him, "An Intellectual's Response to Western Intrusion: Naitō Konan's View of Republican China," in Iriye Akira, ed., <u>The Chinese and the Japanese: Essays in Political and Cultural Interactions</u> (Princeton: Princeton University Press, 1980), pp. 161-183.

∈ Joshua A. Fogel, "Politics and Sinology: The Case of Naitō Konan (1866-1934)," Columbia University Ph.D. diss., 1980.

[A published revised version is listed above.]

∋ Tilemann Grimm, "Naitō Konan (1866-1934) und sein neues Chinabild," Oriens Extremus 26.1-2 (1979), 27-30.

∋ Okamoto Shumpei, "Japanese Response to Chinese Nationalism: Naitō (Ko'nan) Torajirō's Image of China in the 1920s," in F. Gilbert Chan and Thomas H. Etzold, eds., China in the 1920s: Nationalism and Revolution (New York: New Viewpoints, 1976), pp. 160-175.

●* Tōyōgaku no sōshisha-tachi [320 pp.], 71-118.
東洋学の創始者たち
Yoshikawa Kōjirō, ed. Tokyo: Kōdansha, 1976.
[A reprint of the Tōhōgaku material listed below.]

Σ Naitō Konan zenshū, vol. 14 (1976), 671-750.
Tokyo: Chikuma Shobō, 1969-76. 14 vols.
[Bibliography is supplemented by the Shoron listings cited above.]

* Meiji bungaku zenshū, vol. 78, 455-456.
明治文学全集
Tokyo: Chikuma Shobō, 1976.
[Bibliography mostly of articles and books about Naitō.]

∈ Tam Yue-him, "In Search of the Oriental Past: The Life and Thought of Naitō Konan," Princeton University Ph.D. diss., 1975.

●* Tōhōgaku 47 (Jan. 1974), 146-168.

●* Naitō Konan [2,228 pp.].
By Mitamura Taisuke. Tokyo: Chūō Kōronsha, 1972.
[A short bibliography of studies of Naitō is appended to this biography, p. 227.]

● Ajiabito: Naitō Konan [454 pp.].
アジアびと―内藤湖南―
By Aoe Shunjirō. Tokyo: Jiji Tsūshinsha, 1971.
[A reprint, with altered title, of the book by the same author listed below.]

●* Naitō Konan chosho ten [2,8,1 pp.], 4-8 and 1.
内藤湖南著書店
Osaka: Izumi Shoten, 1969.
[Catalog of an exhibition held at a bookstore in Osaka (Izumi Shoten), Apr. 21-27, 1969.]

- Ryū no seiza: Naitō Konan no Ajia-teki shōgai [456 pp.].

  龍の星座ー内藤湖南のアジア的生涯ー

  By Aoe Shunjirō. Tokyo: Asahi Shimbunsha, 1966.

  [Reprinted, with altered title. See Aoe Shunjirō entry above.]

* Chōsen gakuhō 37-38 (Jan. 1966), 339.

  [Bibliography only of Naitō's contributions to this journal.]

•* Konan hakushi to Goichi taijin [142 pp.].

  湖南博士と伍一大人

  Ishikawa Goichi taijin Naitō Konan hakushi seitan hyakunen kinensai
  jikkō iinkai, ed. & publ. Tokyo, 1965.

  [Note the list of writings about Naitō on p. 142.]

- Tōa jiron 7.11 (Nov. 1965), 2-8.

+ Ko Naitō sensei chojutsu mokuroku [39 pp.], 39 pp.

  Aichi Daigaku Kokusai Mondai Kenkyūjo, ed. & publ. Toyohashi, 1954.

∋ Miyakawa Hisayuki, "An Outline of the Naitō Hypothesis and Its Ef-
  fects on Japanese Studies of China," Far Eastern Quarterly 14.4 (Aug.
  1955), 533-552.

•* Tōyō bijutsu 21 (Apr. 1935), 116-123.

  [Bibliography only of Naitō's writings dealing with the arts.]

+ Shirin 19.4 (Oct. 1934), 197-205.

• Ibid., 193-197.

+ Shinagaku 7.3 (July 1934), 453-473.

• Ibid., 447-452 and 475-542.

ø Naitō hakushi shōju kinen Shigaku ronsō [1,3,1,2,741 pp.], 3 pp.

  史学論叢

  Nishida Naojirō, ed. Tokyo: Kōbundō, 1930.

  TRNS #185, NNO 3:415-416.

ø Naitō hakushi kanreki shukuga Shinagaku ronsō [8,3,1066 pp.], 8 pp.

  支那学論叢

  Haneda Tōru, ed. Kyoto: Kōbundo, 1926.

  TRNS #184, NNO 3:415.

See also the Stefan Tanaka entry under Shiratori Kurakichi.

Naitō Shigenobu   内藤戊申   Chinese history, pre-Han period. Chinese bib-
                                  liography. Chinese bibliography.

Yen 291, Teng #473.

Naitō Shumpo   内藤雋輔   East Asian history, esp. Korean history, Koryo period.

  Yen 290.

Naitō Torajirō   内藤 虎次郎

    see Naitō Konan.

Naka Michiyo   那珂通世   Asian, incl. Mongolian, history.
  *   Meiji bungaku zenshū, vol. 78, 453.
       明治文学全集
       Tokyo: Chikuma Shobō, 1976.
       [Bibliography mostly of works about Naka.]
  +   Idem, Naka Michiyo isho [66,550,149,152,3,70,28,3,17,14,17 pp.], 60-
      65.
       Tokyo: Dai Nippon Tosho Kabushiki Kaisha, 1915.
  See also the Stefan Tanaka entry under Shiratori Kurakichi.

Nakada   中田

    see Nakata.

Nakae Ushikichi   中江丑吉   Traditional Chinese thought and society.
  ∋ Joshua A. Fogel, Nakae Ushikichi in China: The Mourning of Spirit
      (Cambridge, Mass.: Council on East Asian Studies, Harvard University,
      1989). 15,313 pp.
       [Japanese-language translation, by Sakatani Yoshinao, forthcoming
      from Iwanami Shoten.]
  ∋ Joseph P. McDermott, "Uses of Sinology in Modern Japan," Ajia bunka
      kenkyū (Asian Cultural Studies) 25.2 (1987).
       [Article about Nakae.]
  ∋ Joshua Fogel, "Nakae Ushikichi: The Lonely Vision of a Japanese
      Expatriate in China," Illinois Papers in Asian Studies, Volume II:
      Essays in the History of the Chinese Republic (Urbana: Center for
      Asian Studies, University of Illinois, 1983), pp. 5-13.

●* <u>Nakae Ushikichi to iu hito: Sono seikatsu to shisō to gakumon</u> [334,1
  pp.], 291-317.

  中江丑吉という人 ― その生活と思想と学問 ―

  Sakatani Yoshinao, ed. Tokyo: Yamato Shobō, 1979.

  [Includes reminiscences of Nakae and reviews of his work.]

● Chūgoku kenkyū geppō 349 (March 1977), 2-6.

● <u>Nakae Ushikichi no ningenzō</u>.

  中江丑吉の人間像

  Sakatani Yoshinao and Suzuki Tadashi, eds. Nagoya: Fūbaisha, 1970

  (451 pp.); 2nd ed., 1976 (473 pp.); 3rd ed. (476 pp.).

  [A volume of articles and reminiscences about Nakae.]

Nakagawa Kaoru 中川 薫 Chinese literature, late Han period.
  Lit 184, Yen 614.

Nakagawa Manabu 中川 学 Chinese history, T'ang and Five Dynasties
            periods. Economy of overseas Chinese. Mod-
            ern Chinese history.

  Yen 615.

Nakagawa Shigeo 中川 成夫
  Listed under Komai Kazuchika

Nakagawa Toshi 中川 俊 Modern Chinese literature.
  Lit 184, Yen 614.

Nakai Hideki 中川英基 Modern Chinese economic history, esp. indus-
            trialization.

Nakajima Chiaki 中島 千秋 Chinese poetry, pre-T'ang period, esp. <u>fu</u>.
  Lit 186, Yen 617, Teng #597.

Nakajima Chōbun 中嶋長文
  see Nakajima Osafumi.

Nakajima Kanki   中嶋 幹起   Chinese linguistics.

Nakajima Kenzō   中島 健蔵   Modern Japanese author. Sino-Japanese contemporary cultural relations. Music.

    Yen 615.

Nakajima Midori   中嶋 みどり   Modern Chinese literature, Kuo Mo-jo. Chinese
poetry, Shih-ching.

    Lit 187, Yen 619.

Nakajima Mineo   中島 嶺雄   Contemporary Chinese politics.
    Yen 616.
    Also listed under Ishikawa Tadao.

Nakajima Osafumi   中嶋 長文   Modern Chinese literature.
    Lit 186, Yen 619.

Nakajima Ryūzō   中嶋 隆蔵   Chinese thought, Six Dynasties period.
    Lit 187, Yen 617.

Nakajima Satoshi   中嶋 敏   Chinese history, esp. economic history, T'ang
and Sung periods.

    Yen 618.
    ø Nakajima Satoshi sensei koki kinen ronshū, vol. 1 (1980), 7-12.
    Nakajima Satoshi sensei koki kinen jigyōkai, ed. & publ. Tokyo,
    1980-81. 2 vols. 12,1,3,1,3,775,3 pp., and 3,901,3 pp.
    TRNS:oo.

Nakajima Toshio   中島 利郎   Chinese vernacular fiction, Ch'ing period.
    Lit 187.
    Cf. next entry.

Nakajima Toshio   中嶋 敏夫   Chinese literature, traditional.
    Yen 618.
    Cf. preceding entry.

Nakamura Gen

    see Nakamura Hajime.

Nakamura Hajime   中村 元   Buddhist studies.* Indian philosophy. Comparative thought.

    Yen 612, Teng #757.

∈ Idem, <u>A Comparative History of Ideas</u> [20,572 pp.].
Tokyo, 1975. 2nd ed., New York: K.P.I., 1986.

Σ <u>Nakamura Hajime senshū</u>, vol. 23 (1977), 1-52.
Tokyo: Shunjūsha, 1961-77. 23 vols.

ø Nakamura Hajime hakushi kanreki kinen ronshū <u>Indo shisō to Bukkyō</u>
[37,762 pp.], 4-37.

    インド思想と仏教

Nakamura Hajime hakushi kanreki kinenkai, ed. Tokyo: Shunjūsha,
1973.

TRNS:oo.

∈ Idem, <u>Ways of Thinking of Eastern Peoples: India, China, Tibet, Japan</u>
[20,712 pp.].

Revised English translation by Philip P. Wiener. Honolulu: East-West
Center Press, 1964.

[Additional book-length Western-language studies by Nakamura that deal
with India and Japan are not listed here.]

Nakamura Jihee   中村 治兵衛 Chinese economic history, Sung thru modern periods.

    Yen 613, Teng #574.

* Ajia-shi kenkyū (Chūō Daigaku) 10 (1986), 1-5.

ø Nakamura Jihee sensei koki kinen <u>Tōyōshi ronsō</u> [24,1,516 pp.], 9-15.

    東洋史論叢

Nakamura Jihee sensei koki kinen Tōyōshi ronsō henshū iinkai, ed.
Tokyo: Tōsui Shobō, 1986.

TRNS:oo.

Nakamura Keiji   中村圭爾   Chinese history, Six Dynasties.

Nakamura Seiji   中村 清二   Geology and geography of Japan (and China).
  + Kagakushi kenkyū 57 (Jan.-March 1961), 10-13.
  • Ibid., 1-10.

Nakamura Shigeo   中村 茂夫   Chinese art history: painting and art theory.
                                    Chinese law, Ch'ing period.

    Yen 610.
  ∋ M.J. Meijer, Review of Nakamura's study of Ch'ing dynasty law, <u>Shin-
     dai keihō kenkyū</u> 清代刑法研究   (Tokyo: Tōkyō Daigaku Shuppankai,
     1973. 266,4 pp.), in <u>T'oung Pao</u> 66 (1980), 348-353.

Nakamura Shōhachi   中村 璋八   Classical Chinese thought.
    Yen 613.

Nakamura Shun'ya   中村 俊也   Classical Chinese thought.
    Lit 191.

Nakamura Tadashi   中村 義   Modern Chinese history, 1911 Revolution and
                                    Hsi-an Incident.

Nakamura Tadayuki   中村 忠行   Early Japanese literature. Sino-Japanese lit-
                                    erary relations, esp. Ch'ing period. Chi-
                                    nese literature, late Ch'ing and modern
                                    periods.

    Lit 191, Teng #320.

Nakamura Takashi   中村 孝志   Southeast Asian history. Overseas Chinese.
                                    History of Taiwan.

    Yen 611, Teng #147.
    Cf. next entry.

Nakamura Takashi   中村 喬   Chinese literature, T'ang-period fiction.
                                    Chinese works on tea.

    Yen 611.
    Cf. preceding entry.

Nakamura Tetsuo   中村哲夫   Modern Chinese socio-economic history, twen-
                                 tieth century.

Nakamura Yoshihiro 中村嘉弘   Chinese poetry, Chin period, Yuan Hao-wen.
    Lit 192.

Nakane Chie   中根千枝   Social anthropology. Social organization in
                                 India, Tibet, and Japan.
    Yen 620.
    + Tōyō Bunka Kenkyūjo kiyō (Tōkyō Daigaku) 103 (March 1987), 19-30.
    [Book-length Western-language studies by Nakane, none of which deals
    with China, are not listed here.]

Nakanishi Isao   中西功   Social anthropology.
    see Nakanishi Tsutomu.

Nakanishi Kiyoshi   中西清   Kambun studies.
    * Kambun kyōshitsu 103 (July 1972), 13-17.

Nakanishi Kō   中西功
    see Nakanishi Tsutomu.

Nakanishi Susumu   中西進   Japanese literature. Sino-Japanese literary
                                 relations.
    Yen 624.

Nakanishi Tsutomu   中西功   Manchurian and Chinese economy, 1930s. Con-
                                 temporary China.
    + Idem, Chūgoku kakumei no arashi no naka de [5,296 pp.], 288-294.
       中国革命の嵐の中で
       Tokyo: Aoki Shoten, 1974.
    + Rekishi hyōron 282 (Nov. 1973), 98-105.
    • Ibid., 91-97.

Nakano Gishō   中野 義照   Buddhist studies.* Sanskrit language and lit-
                                   erature.

    Yen 626.

    • Hōseishi kenkyū 27 (1978), 366-369.

    ø Nakano kyōju koki kinen rombunshū.

       Nakano kyōju koki kinenkai, ed. & publ. Tokyo?, 1960.

       TRNS #188.

Nakano Miyoko   中野 美代子   Chinese vernacular fiction, esp. Hsi-yu chi.
                                   Modern Chinese literature. Chinese histori-
                                   cal linguistics and literature, Chin and
                                   Yuan periods.

    Lit 190, Yen 625.

    ∈ Idem, A Phonological Study in the 'Phags-pa Script and the Meng-ku
       Tzu-yün [5,172 pp.].

       Canberra: Faculty of Asian Studies in association with Australian
       National University Press, 1971.

       [Note the review by L. Hambis, T'oung Pao 61 (1975), 336-337.]

    ∈ Index to Biographical Material in Chin and Yüan Literary Works.
       First Series [1,1,3,1,4,69 pp.].

       By Igor de Rachewiltz and Nakano Miyoko. Canberra: Faculty of Asian
       Studies in association with Australian National University Press,
       1970.

       [Note the review by Chan Hok-lam, T'oung Pao 58 (1972), 251-256.]

       [Note also the supplemental volumes with the same title, both by Igor
       de Rachewiltz and May Wang: Second Series (1972. 1,1,1,1,96 pp.),
       and Third Series (1979. 19,341 pp.).]

Nakano Tatsu   中野 達   Modern Chinese language.
    Yen 624.

Nakashima   中島

    see Nakajima.

Nakata Katsu   中田 勝   Chinese thought.
    Yen 623.

Nakata Yoshinobu　中田吉信　Chinese Muslims. Chinese bibliography.
　　　Yen 622.

Nakata Yūjirō　　　中田勇次郎　Chinese poetry, tz'u. Chinese art history,
　　　　　　　　　　　　　　　　　　　calligraphy and painting.
　　　Lit 188, Yen 623, Teng #598.
　　ø　Tōyō geirin ronsō　Nakata Yūjirō sensei shōju kinen ronshū　[824
　　　pp.].
　　　東洋芸林論叢
　　　Nakata Yūjirō sensei shōju kinen ronshū kankōkai, ed.　Tokyo: Heibon-
　　　sha, 1985.
　　　TRNS:oo.
　　∈　Chinese Calligraphy [238 pp.].
　　　Nakata Yūjirō, general editor.　Translated and adapted by Jeffrey
　　　Hunter.　New York: Weatherhill/Tankosha, 1983.
　　　[Includes chapters by several Japanese scholars of Chinese calligra-
　　　phy.]

Nakatsuhama Wataru　中津濱渉　Chinese literature, esp. yueh-fu and T'ang-
　　　　　　　　　　　　　　　　　　　period poetry.
　　　Lit 189.

Nakatsuka Akira　　中塚 明　Modern Chinese history, Sino-Japanese War.
　　　Yen 626.

Nakayama Hachirō　中山八郎　Chinese history, incl. economic history, esp.
　　　　　　　　　　　　　　　　　　　Ming and Ch'ing periods.
　　　Lit 193, Yen 621, Teng #575.
　　ø　Nakayama Hachirō kyōju shōju kinen Min Shin shi ronsō [16,381 pp.],
　　　10 pp.
　　　明清史論叢
　　　Nakayama Hachirō kyōju shōju kinen kankōkai, ed.　Tokyo: Ryōgen
　　　Shoten, 1977.
　　　TRNS #189.
　　+　Jimbun kenkyū 23.10 (Sept. 1972), 1-2.

Nakayama Heijirō　中山平次郎　Asian archaeology.

  +　Kodaigaku 8 supplement (Apr. 1959), 119-127.

Nakayama Kyūshirō　中山久四郎　East Asian history. Sino-Japanese cultural
                                          relations.

  +　Tōyō Bunko shohō 6 (1974), 70-98.

  •　Ibid., 44-69.

Nakayama Shigeru　中山茂　　History of science, Japan and China.

  ∈　Idem, Academic and Scientific Traditions in China, Japan, and the
      West [22,251 pp.].
      Translated by Jerry Dusenbury.　Tokyo: University of Tokyo Press,
      1984.

  ∈　Idem, A History of Science in Japan: Chinese Background and Western
      Impact [13,329 pp.].
      Cambridge, Mass.: Harvard Univesity Press, 1969.

  [Additional book-length English-language volumes, one co-edited by
  Nakayama (on Chinese science) and another authored by him (on science in
  Japan), are not listed here.]

Nakayama Tokiko　　中山時子　Chinese language and literature.
      Yen 621.

  +　Chūgoku Bungakkai hō (Ochanomizu Joshi Daigaku) 7 (1988), 3-8.

Nakayama Yoshihiro　中山義弘　Modern Chinese thought and history, esp. Sun
                                        Yat-sen.

      Lit 193, Yen 622.

Nakayashiki Hiroshi　中屋敷宏　Contemporary Chinese thought and literature.
      Lit 192.

Nakazawa Mareo　　中沢希男　Chinese poetry and poetics, Six Dynasties and
                                        T'ang periods.

      Lit 186, Yen 626, Teng #599.

Nakazawa Shinzō   中沢信三   Modern Chinese language and literature.
    Lit 185.

Nakazora Yoshihiko   中空善彦   Contemporary Chinese politics.
    Yen 621.

Nambu Minoru   南部稔   Contemporary Chinese economics, monetary pol-
                                  icy.
    Yen 287.

Namikawa Banri   並河万里   Chinese arts.
    Yen 33.

Nanjō Bun'yū   南條文雄   Buddhist studies.*
    ∋* Hanayama Shinsho, Bibliography on Buddhism, 522-523.
       The Commemoration Committee for Prof. Shinsho Hanayama's Sixty-first
       Birthday, ed. Tokyo: Hokuseido Press, 1961.
       [Bibliography of Nanjō's Western-language writings only.]

Nara Kazuo   奈良和夫   Modern Chinese literature.
    Lit 194.

Naragino Sen
    see Narakino Shimesu.

Narakino Shimesu   楢木野宣   Chinese history, Ch'ing period.
    Yen 663, Teng #559.
    + Gumma Daigaku Kyōiku Gakubu kiyō (Jimbun shakai kagaku hen) 28
       (1978), 307-308.

Nashimoto Yūhei   梨本祐平   Modern Chinese history.
    Yen 241.

Nasu Kiyoshi   那須清   Modern Chinese language.

    Yen 287.

+ Chūgoku bungaku ronshū (Kyūshū Daigaku) 11 (1982), 3-6.

• Ibid., 1-2 and 7-25.

+ Bungaku ronshū (Kyūshū Daigaku) 28 (March 1982), 4 pp.

• Ibid., 2 pp. and 1-12.

Negishi Tadashi   根岸侃   Chinese economy.

+ Hitotsubashi ronsō 32.4 (Oct. 1954), 493-499.

Nemoto Makoto   根本誠   History of Chinese thought, incl. legal
                                 thought. Chinese literature, thru T'ang
                                 period. Japanese literature.

    Lit 202, Yen 143, Teng #474.

+ Tōyō gakujutsu kenkyū 18.3 (June 1979), 200-205.

• Shikan 93 (March 1976), 70.

[A book-length English-language work on the Japanese classics, co-authored by Nemoto, is not listed here.]

Nihei Yasumitsu   NC   Economics.

∈ Technology, Employment Practices and Workers: A Comparative Study of
Ten Cotton Spinning Plants in Five Asian Countries [10,136 pp.].
By Nihei Yasumitsu et al. (incl. Ohtsu Makoto). Hong Kong: Centre of
Asian Studies, University of Hong Kong, 1979.
[The five countries that are compared are Hong Kong, Taiwan, Malaysia, Thailand, and The Philippines.]

Niida Noboru   仁井田陞   Chinese legal and social history.

    Yen 331, Teng #487.

+ Idem, Chūgoku no dentō to kakumei: Niida Noboru shū, vol. 2, 385-416.
中国の伝統と革命 ―仁井田陞集―
Ubukata Naokichi and Fukushima Masao, eds. Tokyo: Heibonsha, 1974.
2 vols. 3,329,7 pp., and 4,416,12 pp.

• Ajia keizai jumpō 738 (Nov. 1968), 4-5 and 3 [sic].

∃* Denis Twitchett, "Niida Noboru and Chinese Legal History," <u>Asia Major</u>
     13 (1967), 218-228.

* Idem, <u>Chūgoku shakai no hō to rinri: Chūgoku hō no genri</u> [2,4,216,1,1
     pp.], 1 p.

中国社会の法と倫理 ― 中国法の原理 ―

Tokyo: Shimizu Kōbundō, 1967.

[Reprint of 1954 edition (Tokyo: Kōbundō), with one page of bibliographical material added.]

ø <u>Niida Noboru hakushi tsuitō rombunshū</u>, vol. 1 (1967), 553-554.

Niida Noboru hakushi tsuitō rombunshū henshū iinkai, ed.   Tokyo:
Keisō Shobō, 1966-70.

   Vol. 1   <u>Zen-kindai Ajia no hō to shakai</u> (1967).   3,554 pp.

前近代アジアの法と社会

   Vol. 2   <u>Gendai Ajia no kakumei to hō</u> (1966).   4,524 pp.

現代アジアの革命と法

   Vol. 3   <u>Nihon hō to Ajia</u> (1970).   3,466 pp.

日本法とアジア

TRNS #193-195.

• Hōseishi kenkyū 17 (1967), 266-268.

∃* Fukushima Masao, "Noboru Niida," <u>The Developing Economies</u> 5.1 (March
     1967), 173-190.

• Tōyō bunka (Tōkyō Daigaku) 42 (March 1967), 1-17.

• Shigaku zasshi 76.1 (Jan. 1967), 91-93.

• Shisō (Iwanami Shoten) 510 (Dec. 1966), 40-57.

• Rekishigaku kenkyū 317 (Oct. 1966), 56-60.

+ Tōyō Bunka Kenkyūjo kiyō (Tōkyō Daigaku) 34 (March 1964), 1-12.

Also listed under Collected Articles #29.

Niijima Atsuyoshi   新島 淳良   Contemporary Chinese education and politics.
                                  Modern Chinese thought, literature, and
                                  language.

Lit 194, Yen 528, Teng #600.

Niimi Yasuhide   新美 保秀   Classical Chinese thought, <u>Lun-yü</u>.
Lit 196.

Nishi Giichi   西 義 一   Chinese poetry, T'ang period.
     Lit 196.

Nishi Giyū   西 義 雄   Buddhist studies.*
     + <u>Nishi Giyū hakushi jūyō chosaku mokuroku.</u>
          Nishi sensei koki shukugakai, ed. & publ. Tokyo?, 1977.

Nishi Junzō   西 順 蔵   Chinese thought and religion.
     Lit 196, Yen 489, Teng #691.
     + Hitotsubashi ronsō 81.3 (March 1979), 112-122.
     + Idem, <u>Chūgoku shisō ronshū</u> [6,639 pp.], 635-639.
     中国思想論集
     Tokyo: Chikuma Shobō, 1969.

Nishi Yoshio   西 義 雄
     see Nishi Giyū.

Nishida Naojirō   西田直二郎
     Listed under Naitō Konan.

Nishida Taichirō   西田太一郎   History of Chinese legal thought. Chinese
                                  socio-economic history. Chinese language,
                                  grammar.
     Yen 491, Teng #642.

Nishida Tatsuo   西田龍雄   Sino-Tibetan languages.
     Yen 490.

Nishijima Sadao   西嶋定生   Chinese economic history, incl. Ming-period
                                  industry. Chinese institutional history,
                                  pre-T'ang period.
     Yen 487, Teng #488.

ø Nishijima Sadao hakushi kanreki kinen   <u>Higashi Ajia shi ni okeru</u>

<u>kokka to nōmin</u> [1,529,4 pp.], 21-55.

東アジア史における国家と農民

Nishijima Sadao hakushi kanreki kinen ronsō henshū iinkai, ed.

Tokyo: Yamakawa Shuppansha, 1984.

TRNS:oo.

Also listed under Collected Articles #17.

Nishijima Shunsei 西嶋篠祇   Chinese economic history, Ming and Ch'ing

periods, tax system.

+ Tōa keizai kenkyū 44.1-2 (Feb. 1975), 107.

Nishikawa Kazumi 西川 一三   Historical geography, northwest and southwest

China.

Yen 485.

Nishikawa Masao 西川 正夫   Chinese history, modern and Five Dynasties

periods.

Nishikawa Nei

see Nishikawa Yasushi.

Nishikawa Yasushi 西川 寧   Japanese artist, calligrapher. Chinese art

history, calligraphy.

Yen 484.

Also listed under Sugimura Yoshihiko.

Nishimoto Iwao 西本 巌   Chinese poetry, T'ang period, Tu Fu.
Lit 199.

Nishimura Akio 西村 晶夫   Contemporary Chinese economy.
Yen 486.

Nishimura Fumiko 西村 富美子   Chinese literature, T'ang period.
Lit 199, Yen 486.

Nishimura Gen'yū　西村元佑　Chinese history, Han thru T'ang periods. Chinese economic history. Chinese bibliography.

   Yen 486, Teng #510.

   +　Ryūkoku shidan 68-69 (Dec. 1974), 193-195.

Nishimura Shigeo　西村茂雄　Modern Chinese history, Manchuria.

   ∋　Ronald Suleski, Review of Nishimura's book on twentieth-century Manchuria, <u>Chūgoku kindai Tōhoku chiiki shi kenkyū</u>　中国近代東北地域史研究　(Kyoto: Hōritsu Bunkasha, 1984. 10,490,7 pp.), in <u>Journal of Asian Studies</u> 45.2 (Feb. 1986), 386-388.

Nishino Teiji　西野貞治　Chinese literature, Six Dynasties and Sung periods. Chinese vernacular fiction.

   Lit 199, Yen 491, Teng #601.

   +　Jimbun Kenkyū (Ōsaka Shiritsu Daigaku) 37.3 (Dec. 1985), 1-2.

Nishioka Haruhiko　西岡晴彦　Chinese literature, T'ang-period fiction.

   Lit 197, Yen 488.

Nishioka Hiroshi　西岡弘　Early Chinese social customs. Chinese literature, thru T'ang period.

   Lit 198, Yen 488.

   +　Kambun Gakkai kaihō (Kokugakuin Daigaku) 31 (Feb. 1986), 1-5.

   +　Ibid. 21 (May 1975), 103-105.

   ●　Ibid., 1.

Nishioka Ichisuke　西岡市祐　Early Chinese thought and religion.

   Lit 197.

Nishisato Kikō　西里喜行

   see Nishizato Yoshiyuki.

Nishitani Keiji　西谷啓治

   Listed under Suzuki Daisetsu.

Nishitani Toshichirō 西谷登七郎   Chinese language, classical stylistics.
     Lit 200, Yen 488, Teng #602.

Nishiya   西谷
     see Nishitani.

Nishizato Kikō
     see Nishzato Yoshiyuki.

Nishizato Yoshiyuki 西里 喜行   Modern Chinese history.

Nitta Daisaku   新田大作   Classical Chinese thought. Chinese histori-
                                  cal texts, Tzu-chih t'ung-chien.
     Lit 200, Yen 530.

Nitta Kōji   新田 幸治   Chinese historical texts, Shih-chi. Chinese
                                  thought.
     Lit 200, Yen 531.

Niwa Taiko   丹羽 克子   Chinese cultural history, Han and Six Dynas-
                                  ties periods.
     Lit 200.

Niwa Tomosaburō   丹羽 友三郎 Chinese history, Yuan period.
     + Mie hōkei 47 (July 1980), 187-196.

Niwa Tomozaburō
     see Niwa Tomosaburō.

Noda Nobuta   野田 允太
     Listed under Hirako Takurei.

Nogami Shunjō   野上 俊静   History of Chinese Buddhism, esp. Liao-Chin-
                                  Yuan period.
     Yen 549, Teng #740.

Nogami Shunsei
    see Nogami Shunjō.

Noguchi Masayuki　野口 正之　Chinese language and cultural history.
    Yen 549.

Noguchi Sadao　野口 定男　Chinese historical texts, Shih-chi.
    Lit 202, Yen 548.

Noguchi Tetsurō　野口 鉄郎　Chinese history, Ming and Ch'ing periods.
                     Sino-Japanese historical relations.

    Yen 549.
    Also listed under Collected Articles #20b.

Nohara Shirō　野原四郎　Modern Chinese history.
    Yen 551.
- Rekishi hyōron 381 (Jan. 1982), 87-91.
+ Chūgoku kenkyū geppō 396 (Feb. 1981), 38-44.
- Ibid., 30-37.
- Senshū shigaku 13 (1981), 80-84.
+ Ibid. 6 (1974).

Noma Kiyoshi　野間 清　Contemporary Chinese politics and agricultur-
                     al economy.

    Yen 547.

Nōmi Tōru　能美 徹　Modern Chinese language.
  * Kita Kyūshū Daigaku Gaikokugo Gakubu kiyō 27 (Dec. 1975), 2 pp.

Nomiyama On　野見山 温　International law. Manchurian history.
  + Fukuoka Daigaku hōgaku ronsō 21.3-4 (#60-61) (March 1977), 4 pp.

Nomura Gakuyō　野村 岳陽　Classical Chinese thought.
  * Kangaku kenkyū (Nihon Daigaku) 3 (March 1965), 13-14.

Nomura Kanetarō
    see Nomura Kentarō.

Nomura Kentarō   野村 兼太郎 (Economic history, Japan and England.)
    ø Nomura hakushi kanreki kinen rombunshū Hōkensei to shihonsei [1,3,
       743 pp.].
       封建制度と資本制
       Takamura Shōhei and Komatsu Yoshitaka, eds. Tokyo: Yūhikaku, 1956.
       TRNS #199, NNO 3:416.

Nomura Kōichi   野村 浩一   Modern Chinese history and thought.
    Yen 545.

Nomura Masayoshi   野村 正良   Altaic languages, esp. Mongolian. Chinese
                                 language.
       Teng #213.
    + Nagoya Daigaku Bungakubu kenkyū ronshū 73 (Bungaku 25) (1978), 1-3.

Nomura Shigeo   野村 茂夫   Classical Chinese thought. Chinese history,
                                 pre-Han period.
    Lit 203, Yen 546.

Nomura Terumasu
    see Nomura Yōshō.

Nomura Yōshō   野村 耀昌   History of Chinese Buddhism.
    Yen 547.

Nomura Zuihō   野村 瑞峯   Chinese language, Sung-period vernacular and
                                 modern period.
    Yen 546.

Nozaki Shumpei   野崎 駿平   Chinese drama and vernacular fiction.
    Lit 203.

Nozawa Toshitaka　野沢俊敬　Modern Chinese literature.
    Lit 203.

Nozawa Yutaka　野沢豊　Modern Chinese history, twentieth century.
    Yen 550.
    +　Jimbun gakuhō (Tōkyō Toritsu Daigaku) 185 (March 1986), 1-11.

Numaguchi Masaru　沼口 勝　Chinese poetry, Six Dynasties period.
    Lit 201, Yen 603.

Numajiri Masataka　沼尻正隆　Classcial Chinese thought.
    Lit 201, Yen 603

Nunome Chōfū　布目 潮渢　Chinese history, esp. Han thru T'ang periods.
                    Chinese works on tea.
    Yen 36, Teng #475.

Ōba Osamu　大庭 脩　Sino-Japanese historical relations. Chinese history, Han period, incl. legal history and wood-strip inscriptions.
    Yen 78, Teng #511.
    ∋ Michel Soymié, Review of Ōba's study of Chinese books imported to Japan in the Edo period, Edo jidai ni okeru karafune mochiwatshisho no kenkyū 江戸時代における唐船持渡書の研究 (Suita: Kansai Daigaku Tōzai Gakujutsu Kenkyūjo, 1967. 2,4,744,60,6 pp. [incl. 6-pp. English summary]), in T'oung Pao 56 (1970), 187-193.

Obata Tatsuo　小畑 龍雄 Chinese history, esp. Ming and Ch'ing periods.
    Yen 518, Teng #476.

Obi Kōichi　小尾 郊一　Chinese literature, Six Dynasties period.
    Lit 79, Yen 518, Teng #603.

ø Obi hakushi koki kinen <u>Chūgokugaku ronshū</u> [26,778 pp.], 15-26.
中国学論集
Obi hakushi koki kinen jigyōkai, ed. Tokyo: Kyūko Shoin, 1983.
TRNS:oo

ø Obi hakushi taikyū kinen <u>Chūgoku bungaku ronshū</u> [36,802 pp.], 27-36.
中国文学論集
Obi hakushi taikyū kinen rombunshū henshū iinkai, ed. Tokyo: Daiichi Gakushūsha, 1976.
[Note the biography of Obi, pp. 779-801.]
TRNS:oo.

Obi Takeo   小尾 孟夫   Chinese history.
     Yen 519.

Ōbuchi Ninji   大淵忍爾   History of Chinese religion, incl. Taoism.
     Lit 59.
+ Okayama Daigaku Hōbun Gakubu gakujutsu kiyō (Shigaku hen) 38 (1977), 2 pp.
Also listed under Collected Articles #20b.

Ochi Shigeaki   越智重明   Chinese history, Six Dynasties period.
     Yen 591, Teng #521.

Ōchō Enichi   横超慧日   History of Chinese Buddhism.
     Yen 177, Teng #741.
• Bukkyōgaku seminaa 37 (May 1983), 61-70 and 43-48 (sic).
∋ Leon Hurvitz, "The Lotus Sutra in East Asia: A Review of <u>Hokke shisō</u>
法華思想   ," <u>Monumenta Serica</u> 29 (1970-71), 697-762.
[Review of Ōchō's study, <u>Hokke shisō</u> (Kyoto: Heirakuji Shoten, 1969. 622,25 pp.).]

Oda Shōgo   小田省吾   (Korean history.)

ø Oda sensei shōju kinen Chōsen ronshū [4,1,2,1074 pp.].

朝鮮論集

Oda sensei shōju kinenkai, ed.   Keijō [Seoul]: Ōsaka Yagō Shoten,

1934.

TRNS #032, NNO 3:408.

Oda Takeo   織田武雄   Chinese natural resources and population.

Human geography. Mongolia.

ø Oda Takeo sensei taikan kinen   Jimbun chirigaku ronsō [11,833,1

pp.], 829-833.

人文地理学論叢

Oda Takeo sensei taikan kinen jigyōkai, ed.   Tokyo: Yanagihara Sho-

ten, 1971.

TRNS:oo.

Cf. next entry.

Oda Takeo   小田武夫   Modern Chinese literature. Chinese vernacular

fiction.

Lit 74, Yen 517.

Cf. preceding entry.

Odake   小竹

see Otake.

Ōfuchi   大淵

see Ōbuchi.

Ogaeri Yoshio   魚返善雄   Chinese literature, esp. vernacular fiction.

Chinese language.

Lit 62, Yen 574, Teng #643.

● Tōhō bungei 3 (Aug. 1951).

Ōgami Masami   大上正美   Chinese literature, Six Dynasties period.

Lit 50.

Ogasawara Hirotoshi 小笠原 博慧 Chinese literature, Six Dynasties period.
    Lit 65.

Ogasawara Senshū   小笠原 宣秀 History of Chinese Buddhism.
        Yen 508, Teng #742.

    ø Ogasawra Senshū hakushi tsuitō rombunshū [363 pp.].
       Ryūkoku Daigaku Tōyōshigaku kenkyūkai, ed. & publ. Kyoto, 1985.
       TRNS:oo

    + Tōyō shien (Ryūkoku Daigaku) 24-25 (1985), 3-10.

    + Ryūkoku shidan 85 (Dec. 1984), 82-89.

    + Ryūkoku shidan 56-57 (Dec. 1966), 545-552.

Ogata Isamu   尾形 勇   Chinese history, esp. Han period.

Ogata Kazuo   緒方 一男   Chinese language.
        Yen 536.

Ogata Korekiyo   緒方 惟精   Early Japanese literature. Sino-Japanese lit-
                                        erary relations.
        Yen 535.

Ogata Sadako   NC   Modern Chinese history. Sino-Japanese rela-
                                        tions. Contemporary China.

    ∈ Idem, Normalization with China: A Comparative Study of U.S. and
       Japanese Processes [12,113 pp.].
       Berkeley: Institute of East Asian Studies, University of California,
       1988.

    ∈ Idem, Defiance in Manchuria: The Making of Japanese Foreign Policy,
       1931-1932 [16,259 pp.].
       Berkeley: University of California Press, 1964.

Ogawa Haruhisa   小川 晴久   Chinese thought, classical and Ch'ing peri-
                                        ods, incl. Wang Fu-chih.
        Lit 71, Yen 502.

Ogawa Heishirō   小川平四郎   Contemporary Chinese politics.
       Yen 501.

Ogawa Kan'ichi   小川貫弌   History of Chinese Buddhism.
       Yen 501.
       + Ryūkoku shidan 66-67 (Dec. 1973), 221-225.
       • Ibid., 208-220.
       + Tōyō shien (Ryūkoku Daigaku) 6 (March 1973), 9-14.

Ogawa Kazusuke   小川和佑
       Listed under Takahashi Kazumi.

Ogawa Shōichi   小川昭一   Chinese poetry, Six Dynasties and T'ang peri-
                                         ods.
       Lit 68, Yen 502.

Ogawa Takuji   小川琢治   Chinese historical geography.
       • Tōhōgaku 54 (July 1977), 153-180.
       * Chirigaku hyōron 44.8 (Aug. 1971), 531.
       + Shirin 27.2 (Apr. 1942), 145-157.
       ø Ogawa hakushi kanreki shukuga Shigaku chirigaku ronsō [18,2,1064
          pp.], 18 pp.
          史学地理学論叢
          Ogawa hakushi kanreki shukuga kinenkai, ed. Kyoto: Kōbundō, 1930.
          TRNS #031, NNO 3:407-408.

Ogawa Tamaki   小川環樹   Chinese language and literature, esp. tradi-
                                         tional poetry and vernacular fiction. Chi-
                                         nese lexicography.
       Lit 69, Yen 499, Teng #604.
       ø Iriya kyōju Ogawa kyōju taikyū kinen Chūgoku bungaku gogaku ronshū
          [4,2,5,23,797,35,4,3 pp.], 7-16.
          中国文学語学論集
          Iriya kyōju Ogawa kyōju taikyū kinenkai, ed. & publ. Kyoto, 1974.
          [Includes a preface in English by Burton Watson, 3 pp.]

Ogawa Yōichi   小川 陽一   Chinese vernacular fiction, Sung and Ming
                                            periods.
        Lit 71, Yen 503.

Ogihara   荻原
        see Ogiwara.

Ogino Minahiko   荻野 三比彦   Japanese history. Sino-Japanese historical
                                            relations.
        Yen 102.

Ogisu Jundō   荻須 純道   History of Zen Buddhism.
        Yen 101.

    +   Hanazono Daigaku kenkyū kiyō 10 (March 1979), 7 pp.

    +   Zengaku kenkyū (Hanazono Daigaku) 57 (1969), 1-7.

Ogiwara Hiroaki   荻原 弘明   Southeast Asian history, incl. Burma. Over-
                                            seas Chinese.
        Yen 102, Teng #148.

    +   Kagoshima Daigaku Kyōyōbu shiroku 20 (1988), 1-16.

    •   Ibid. 19 (1987), 1-4.

    +   Ibid. 14 (1981), 81-88.

Ogiwara Unrai   荻原 雲来   Buddhist studies.
    +   Bukkyō kenkyū 2.2 (March-Apr. 1938), 178-180.

    ø   Ogiwara hakushi kanreki kinen shukuga rombunshū [2,356,1,297,10,3
        pp.]. No. biblo.
        Taishō Daigaku Shuppanbu, ed. Tokyo: Sankibō Busshorin, 1972.
        [Reprint of Ogiwara Unrai kanreki kinen rombunshū, Tokyo: The Taisho
        University, 1930.]
        [Includes several Western-language articles, mostly on Indian Bud-
        dhism, by the following: (in English) R. Davids, L. Poussin,
        Ts. Stcherbatsky, B. Petzold, and R. Kambayashi;   (in German) F.O.
        Schrader, M. Winternitz, O. Strauss, M. Walleser, E. Leumann, and N.
        Fukushima.   Also includes an article by J. Masuda, "Saptaśatika

Prajñāpāramitā Text and the Hsüan-chwang Chinese Version with Notes,"
pp. 185-241.]

TRNS:oo.

∋* Hanayama Shinsho, <u>Bibliography on Buddhism</u>, 819-820.
The Commemoration Committee for Prof. Shinsho Hanayama's Sixty-first
Birthday, ed. Tokyo: Hokuseido Press, 1961.
[Bibliography of Ogiwara's Western-language writings only.]

Oguchi Iichi   小口 偉一   Religion, incl. sociology of religion.
    Yen 507.

Ogura Kinnosuke   小倉金之郎   Mathematics, China and Japan.
    + Kagakushi kenkyū 65 (Jan.-March 1963), 40-47.

Ogura Yoshihiko   小倉芳彦   Classical Chinese thought. Chinese history.
    Yen 498, Teng #672.

Oguri Eiichi   小栗英一   Chinese literature, Chin and Yuan periods.
    Lit 73, Yen 507.

Ōhama Akira   大濱皓   Classical Chinese thought.
    Lit 58, Yen 74.
    + Nagoya Daigaku Bungakubu kenkyū ronshū 48 (Tetsugaku 16) (1968), 1-2.

Ōhara Nobukazu   大原信一   Chinese language.
    Lit 59, Yen 80.
    + Dōshisha gaikoku bungaku kenkyū 33-34 (Sept. 1982), 12-18.
    • Ibid., 1-11 and 19-34.

Ōhara Shin'ichi
    see Ōhara Nobukazu.

Ōhashi Yoichi   大橋与一   Sino-Russian historical relations.
    Yen 83.

Ōhira Zengo   大平善梧   International law, incl. Chinese maritime
                                    law. Japanese law.

    Teng #171.

Ohtsu [Ōtsu] Makoto NC
    Listed under Nihei Yasumitsu.

Ōi Shōjo   NC
    Listed under Yūki Reimon.

Oikawa Tsunetada   及川恒思   Chinese economic history. Chinese political
                                    thought.

    + Hōgaku kenkyū (Keiō Daigaku) 33.2 (Feb. 1960), 604-607.

    • Ibid., 5-7 and 601-603.

Ojima   小島
    see also Kojima.

Ojima Sukema   小島祐馬   Chinese thought.
    Yen 505.

    + Tōhōgaku 60 (July 1980), 199-202.

    + Tōhō gakuhō 39 (March 1968), 321-323.

    • Ibid., 311-321.

    • Tembō 99 (March 1967), 127-131.

    + Shinagaku, vol. 10 special issue [vol. 13 in rpt. ed.] (Apr. 1942),
        821-826.

    Also listed under Takase Takejirō.

Oka Haruo   岡 晴夫   Chinese drama and popular song, Yuan and Ming
                                    periods.

    Lit 62, Yen 125.

Okabe Tatsumi   岡部達味   Contemporary Chinese politics.
    Yen 127.

Okada Hidehiro　岡田英弘　Inner Asian history and philology.
　　Yen 133.

Okada Hideki　岡田英樹　Modern Chinese literature.
　　Lit 65, Yen 133.

Okada Jō　岡田譲　East Asian art history.
　　Yen 131.

Okada Osamu　岡田修　Classical Chinese thought.
　　Yen 132.

Okada Takehiko　岡田武彦　Chinese thought, neo-Confucianism.
　　Lit 65, Yen 132.
　　See Addenda, p. 279.
　　+　Teoriya (Tetsugakuka kiyō) (Kyūshū Daigaku) 16 (1973), 6 pp.

Okada Yoshisaburō
　　see Okada Yoshizaburō.

Okada Yoshizaburō 岡田芳三郎 Chinese epigraphy.
　　Yen 130.

Okai Shingo　岡井慎吾　Chinese language, incl. phonology. <u>Kambun</u>
　　　　　　　　　　　　　　studies.
　　+　Kambungaku 4 (1955), 53-58, and 5 (1956), 28-29.
　　•　Ibid. 4 (1955), 19-53, and 5 (1956), 22-28 and 30-50.

Okamoto Goichi　岡本午一　Chinese history, T'ang period.
　　Teng #531.

Okamoto Keiji　岡本敬二
　　see Okamoto Yoshiji.

Okamoto Ryūzō   岡本 隆三   Modern Chinese literature. Chinese vernacular
                                                fiction. Modern Chinese history, Long
                                                March.

      Lit 68, Yen 126.

Okamoto Shumpei   NC
      Listed under Naitō Konan.

Okamoto Yoshiji   岡本 敬二   Chinese legal history. Inner Asian and Korean
                                                history.

      Yen 125.

      ø Ajia shominzoku ni okeru shakai to bunka   Okamoto Yoshiji sensei
         taikan kinen ronshū [627 pp.], 615-627.
         アジア諸民族における社会と文化
         Okamoto Yoshiji sensei taikan kinen ronshū kankōkai, ed.   Tokyo:
         Kokusho Kankōkai, 1984.
         TRNS:oo.
      • Rekishi jinrui (Tsukuba Daigaku) 12 (1984), 1-10.
      Also listed under Collected Articles #21.

Okamura Sadao   岡村 貞雄   Chinese literature, thru T'ang period, esp.
                                          yueh-fu.
      Lit 66.

Okamura Shigeru   岡村 繁   Chinese literature, thru T'ang period.
      Lit 66, Yen 128.
      + Bungaku kenkyū (Kyūshū Daigaku) 84 (1987), 1-21.
      + Chūgoku bungaku ronshū (Kyūshū Daigaku) 15 (1986), 3-17.

Okatani Motoji   岡谷 元治   East Asian economic history, incl. cotton
                                          industry.
      Yen 129.

Ōkawa Fujio   大川 富士夫   Chinese history, Six Dynasties period.
      Yen 76.

Ōkawa Gansaburō   大川 完三郎   Modern Chinese language.
    Yen 77.

Okazaki Fumio   岡崎 文夫   Chinese history, esp. Six Dynasties period.
    +   Tōhōgaku 70 (July 1985), 220-221.
    •   Ibid., 195-219.
    •   Shūkan Tōyōgaku 4 (Oct. 1960), 1-2.
    +   Tōyōshi kenkyū 11.1 (Sept. 1950), 87-88.
    +   Rekishi 2 (1950), 3 pp.

Okazaki Seirō   岡崎 精郎   Central Asian studies. Tangut language.
    Teng #532.

Okazaki Takashi   岡崎 敬   Chinese archaeology. Chinese history, pre-
                                    T'ang period.
    Yen 129.
    ø   Higashi Ajia no kōko to rekishi   Okazaki Takashi sensei taikan kinen
        ronshū, vol. 1, 5-21.
        東アジアの考古と歴史
        Okazaki Takashi sensei taikan kinen jigyōkai, ed.   Kyoto: Dōhōsha,
        1987.   3 vols.   30,765 pp., 803 pp., and 770 pp.
        TRNS:oo.

Okazaki Toshio   岡崎 俊夫   Modern Chinese literature. Sino-Japanese lit-
                                    erary relations.
    Lit 63.
    +•   Tenjō ningen: Okazaki Toshio bunshū [4,348 pp.], 257-267.
        天上人間一岡崎俊夫文集一
        Okazaki Toshio bunshū kankōkai, ed & publ. n.p., 1961.
        [Note the nempu (pp. 268-269) and in memoriam notices (pp. 271-345)
        for Okazaki.]

Oketani Hideaki   桶谷 秀昭   Fine arts. Modern Japanese (and Chinese) lit-
                                    erature.
    Yen 463.

Ōki Harumoto   大木春基 Chinese poetry, Ch'u-tz'u.
    Lit 50.

Ōkōchi Yasunori   大河内康憲 Modern Chinese language.
    Lit 51, Yen 79.

Ōkubo Takao   大久保隆郎 Classical Chinese thought.
    Lit 50, Yen 80.

Ōkubo Yasushi   大久保泰 Contemporary Chinese political economy.
    Yen 81.

Okuno Shintarō   奥野信太郎 Chinese literature, esp. vernacular fiction,
                                    incl. drama and folktales.
    Lit 72, Teng #630.
    + Geibun kenkyū (Keiō Daigaku) 27 (1969), 433-440.
    • Geinō 10.4 (Apr. 1968), 44-46.

Okuzaki Hiroshi
    see Okuzaki Yūji.

Okuzaki Yūji   奥崎裕司 Chinese socio-economic history and thought,
                                    Ming period.
    Lit 71.

Ōmori Shirō   大森志郎 Early Sino-Japanese historical relations.
                                    Ethnology.
    Yen 84.

Ōmura Masuo   大村益夫 Modern Chinese literature.
    Lit 60, Yen 77.

Ōmura Okimichi   大村興道 Chinese educational history, Ch'ing period.
    Yen 77.

Ōmura Seigai   大村西崖   Chinese art history.

  ∈ <u>Literary Evidence for Early Buddhist Art in China</u> [16,296 pp.].

    By Alexander Coburn Soper. Ascona, Switz.: Artibus Asiae, 1959.

    [Soper draws upon the volume by Ōmura Seigai, <u>Shina bijutsushi: Chōso</u>

    <u>hen</u> 支那美術史—彫塑篇—   (Tokyo: Butsusho Kankōkai Zushōbu,

    1915. 2 vols. 14,6,41,27,461,3 pp., and 434 pp. unbound plates): "I

    have begun in this volume with the earlier half of Ōmura's Buddhist

    history, the art of Han, Chin, and the Six Dynasties, . . ." (p.

    11).]

Ōmuro Mikio   大室 幹雄   Classical Chinese thought.

    Lit 60, Yen 89.

Ono Gemmyō   小野 玄妙   Buddhist studies.* Arts of India.

  Σ <u>Ono Gemmyō Bukkyō geijutsu chosakushū</u>, Suppl. vol., 47-57.

    小野玄妙仏教芸術著作集

    Tokyo: Kaimei Shoin, 1977. 10 vols., and Supplementary volume (<u>Bes</u>-

    <u>satsu</u>).

  + Bukkyō kenkyū 3.5 (1939), 122-128.

Ōno Jitsunosuke   大野 実之助 Chinese literature, esp. T'ang poetry. Early

                                 Chinese thought.

    Lit 57, Yen 85, Teng #605.

  + Chūgoku koten kenkyū 20 (Jan. 1975), 287-293.

  • Ibid., 294-302.

Ōno Katsutoshi   小野 勝年   East Asian history and archaeology. Chinese

                               art history. Sino-Japanese historical rela-

                               tions, T'ang period.

    Yen 521, Teng #10 and #779.

  ø Ono Katsutoshi shōju kinen <u>Tōhōgaku ronshū</u> [2,24,1,574,19 pp.], 5-

    24.

    東方学論集

    Ono Katsutoshi hakushi shōju kinenkai, ed. & publ. Kyoto, 1982.

    TRNS:oo.

  + Tōyō shien (Ryūkoku Daigaku) 4 (1971).

Ono Kazuko   小野和子   Chinese thought, late Ming, Ch'ing, and mod-
                                ern periods. Women's studies.

Lit 75, Yen 520.

∈ Idem, <u>Chinese Women in a Century of Revolution, 1850-1950</u> [26,255
pp.].
Edited by Joshua A. Fogel. Translators: Kathryn Bernhardt, Timothy
Brook, Joshua A. Fogel, Jonathan Lipmann, Susan Mann, and Laurel
Rhodes. Stanford: Stanford University Press, 1989.

Ono Noriaki   小野則秋   Japanese and Chinese bibliography.
Yen 525, Teng #465.

Ono Shihei   小野四平   Chinese vernacular fiction, Yuan and Ming
                                periods. T'ang-period prose.

Lit 76, Yen 520.

Ono Shinji   小野信爾   Modern Chinese history, incl. May Fourth
                                Movement.

Yen 524.

Ono Shinobu   小野 忍   Modern Chinese literature. Chinese vernacular
                                fiction. Modern Chinese educational histo-
                                ry.

Lit 75, Yen 523, Teng #631.
• Tōhōgaku 62 (July 1981), 183-196.
+ Tōkyō Shinaguku hō 13 (1967), 1-8.

Ōno Takashi   大野 峻   Early Chinese thought and literature, <u>Kuo-yü</u>.
Lit 58, Yen 85.
+ Shōnan bungaku (Tōkai Daigaku) 20 (March 1986), 100-102.

Ono Takeo   小野武夫   (Economic history.)
ø <u>Tōyō nōgyō keizai shi kenkyū</u> [2,1,181 pp.].
東洋農業経済史研究
Ono Takeo hakushi kanreki kinen rombunshū kankōkai, ed. Tokyo: Nihon

Hyōronsha, 1948.

TRNS #033, NNO 3:408.

Onoda Kōsaburō   小野田耕三郎 Modern Chinese literature.

Lit 79.

Onodera Ikuo   小野寺郁夫 Chinese history, Sung period.

Onoe Etsuzō   尾上 悦三   Modern and contemporary Chinese economy.

Yen 479.

Onoe Kanehide   尾上兼英   Chinese vernacular fiction. Modern Chinese
                                    literature, Lu Hsun.

Lit 77, Yen 478.

+ Tōyō Bunka Kenkyūjo kiyō (Tōkyō Daigaku) 106 (March 1988), 3-10.

Onogawa Hidemi   小野川秀美 Modern Chinese history and thought. Chinese
                                    bibliography.

Yen 525, Teng #576.

+ Tōhō gakuhō 46 (March 1974), 355.

Also listed under Collected Articles #68.

Onozawa Seiichi   小野沢精一 Classical Chinese thought.

Lit 78, Yen 526.

+ Chūtetsubun Gakkai hō 5 (1980), 39-42.

Ōrui Jun   大類 純   Chinese thought.

Yen 83.

Ōrui Noboru   大類 伸   (Western history. Japanese history. Histori-
                                    ography.)

ø Ōrui Noboru hakushi kiju kinen Shigaku rombunshū [21,346,2 pp.].
   史学論文集
   Nihon Joshi Daigaku shigaku kenkyūkai, ed. Tokyo: Yamakawa Shuppansha, 1962.

   TRNS #037, NNO 3:407.

Ōrui Noburu
    see Ōrui Noboru.

Osabe Kazuo   長部和雄   History of Chinese Buddhism, esp. T'ang and
                                    Sung periods.
    Yen 45, Teng #489.
    + Jimbun ronshū (Kōbe Shōka Daigaku) 9.1-2 (Oct. 1973), 1 p.
    • Ibid., 25-31.

Osada Natsuki   長田夏樹   Altaic and Sino-Tibetan languages. Chinese
                                    literature, T'ang-period fiction. Language
                                    of Chinese vernacular fiction.
    Lit 73, Yen 46.
    + Gaikokugaku kenkyū (Kōbe-shi Gaikokugo Daigaku) 17 (1987), 1-8.
    + Kōbe Gaidai ronsō 37.4 (Oct. 1986), 8-16.

Osaka   尾坂
    see Ozaka.

Ōsaki Fujio   大崎富垞   Chinese economic history, Sung period.
    Teng #545.

Osanai Hiroshi   小山内宏   Contemporary East Asian military affairs.
    Yen 516.

Ōsawa Kazuo   大沢一雄   Classical Chinese thought.
    Yen 87.

Ōsawa Masaaki   大沢正昭   Chinese history, T'ang and Five Dynasties
                                    periods.

Ōsawa Terumichi   大沢陽典   Chinese northern border history, Six Dynas-
                                    ties period.

Ōshiba Takashi　　大芝 孝　　Modern Chinese language and literature. Chinese film.

　　Lit 51, Yen 88.

　　+　Kōbe Gaidai ronsō 37.4 (Oct. 1986), 1-7.

Oshibuchi Hajime　　鴛淵 一　　Asian, esp. Mongolian and Manchurian, history. Chinese history and law, Ch'ing period.

　　Yen 585, Teng #499.

　　+　Jimbun kenkyū 7.8 (Sept. 1956), 1-3.

Ōshima Kiyoshi　　大島 清　　Agricultural economics, incl. China.

　　Yen 75.

Ōshima Shōji　　大島 正二　　Chinese historical linguistics.

　　Lit 52, Yen 76.

Ōshima Riichi　　大島 利一　　Chinese history, pre-Han period. Chinese historical texts, Shih-chi.

　　Lit 52, Yen 74, Teng #512.

Ōshima Toshikazu

　　see Ōshima Riichi.

Ōta Hyōzaburō　　太田兵三郎　　Chinese literary theory, Six Dynasties. Sino-Japanese literary relations.

　　Lit 53, Yen 433.

Ōta Seikyū　　太田青丘

　　see Ōta Hyōzaburō.

Ōta Shōjirō　　太田晶二郎　　Sino-Japanese cultural relations. History of Chinese books in Japan. Chinese bibliography.

　　Teng #709.

Ōta Susumu   太田 進   Modern Chinese literature.
     Lit 53, Yen 432.

Ōta Tatsuo   太田辰夫   Chinese language, history of vernacular. Chi-
                                      nese vernacular fiction. Chinese lexicogra-
                                      phy.
     Lit 54, Yen 433.
     + Kōbe Gaidai ronsō 33.3 (Oct. 1982), 102-114.

Ōta Tsugio   太田 次男   Chinese literature, T'ang period. Sino-Japa-
                                      nese literary relations.
     Lit 55.
     + Shidō Bunko ronshū 21 (1985), 541-545.

Ōta Yukio   太田幸男   Chinese history, esp. pre-Han period.
     Yen 433.

Otagi Hajime   愛宕 元   Chinese history, T'ang and Five Dynasties
                                      periods.

Otagi Matsuo   愛宕 松男   Central Asian history and philology. Chinese
                                      history, Yuan period.
     Yen 4, Teng #500.
     • Bunka 39.3-4 (March 1976), 103-105.
     + Shūkan Tōyōgaku 31 (June 1974), 244-260.

Ōtaka Iwao   大高 巌   Modern Chinese literature.
     + Idem, Kōmei: Aru Chūgoku bungakusha no seishun [150 pp.], 3-7.
        紅迷ーある中国文学者の青春ー
        Ōtaka Iwao tsuitō bunshū kankōkai, ed.   Tokyo: Kyūko Shoin, 1976.

Otake Fumio   小竹 文夫   Modern Chinese history. Chinese economic his-
                                      tory, Ming and Ch'ing periods. Chinese his-
                                      torical texts, Shih-chi and Han shu. Ku
                                      Yen-wu.
     Lit 75, Yen 527, Teng #477.

- Tōa jiron 4.12 (Dec. 1962), 18-19.
- * Shichō 81 (Nov. 1962), 54-55.

Also listed under Collected Articles #21 and #72.

Otake Takeo   小竹 武夫   Chinese historical texts, <u>Shih-chi</u> and <u>Han shu</u>.

Lit 74.
- Tōyō Bunko shohō 14 (1983), 1-18.

Ōtaki Kazuo   大滝 一雄   Classical Chinese thought, incl. <u>Lun-heng</u>.
Lit 56.

Otani Hidejirō   小谷 秀二郎   International relations, incl. China.
Yen 507.

Ōtani Kōshō   大谷 光照   Chinese Buddhism.
Yen 79.

Ōtani Kōtarō   大谷 孝太郎   Modern Chinese thought and economic history.
Teng #577.

Ōtani Toshio   大谷 敏夫   Chinese history and thought, Ch'ing period.
Lit 56.

Ōtsu Makoto   NC
Listed under Nihei Yasumitsu.

Ōtsuka Hirohisa   大塚 博久   Modern Chinese thought.
Yen 89.

Ōtsuka Katsumi   大塚 勝美   Modern Chinese law.
Yen 90.

Ōtsuka Shigeki   大塚繁樹   Sino-Japanese literary relations. Chinese
                                        literature, T'ang-period fiction. Modern
                                        Chinese literature.
    Lit 56.

Ōtsuka Tomoshika   大塚伴鹿   Classical Chinese thought.
    Yen 89.

Ōtsuka Tsuneo   大塚恒雄   Contemporary Chinese economics.
    Yen 90.

Ōtsuka Yūshō   大塚有章   Contemporary Chinese politics.
    Yen 91.

Ōtsuki Nobuyoshi   大槻信良   Chinese thought, incl. neo-Confucianism.
    Lit 57, Yen 91, Teng #692.

Ōtsuki Shinryō
    see Ōtsuki Nobuyoshi.

Ōuchi Tsutomu   大内力   Japanese agricultural economy. Social and
                                        economic theory.

    Yen 81, Teng #97.

Ōuchida Saburō   大内田三郎   Chinese vernacular fiction, Ming period.
    Lit 49, Yen 82.

Ōyabu Masaya   大藪正哉   Chinese history, Yuan period.
    Yen 83.

Oyama   小山
    see also Koyama.

Ōyama Azusa　　　大山 梓　　Modern and contemporary Chinese politics.
　　　　　　　　　　　　　　　　　Asian international relations.

　　Yen 85.

Oyama Masaaki　　小山 正明　　Chinese socio-economic history, Ming and
　　　　　　　　　　　　　　　　　Ch'ing periods.

　　Yen 517.

Ōyama Masaharu　　大山 正春　　Modern Chinese language and literature.
　　Lit 62, Yen 84.

Ōyane Bunjirō　　大矢根 文次郎　Chinese literature, Six Dynasties period.
　　Lit 60, Yen 88.

　　+　Kokubungaku kenkyū (Waseda Daigaku) 50 (June 1973), 102-103.

　　+　Gakujutsu kenkyū (Kokugo, kokubungaku hen) 21 (1972), 1-2.

Ozaka Tokuji　　　尾坂 徳司　　Modern Chinese literature. Chinese vernacular
　　　　　　　　　　　　　　　　　fiction.

　　Lit 73, Yen 475.

Ozaka Tokushi

　　see Ozaka Tokuji.

Ozaki Hotsuki　　　尾崎 秀樹　　Contemporary China.
　　Yen 476.

Ozaki Hotsumi　　　尾崎 秀美　　Modern Chinese economics. Modern Japanese
　　　　　　　　　　　　　　　　　history, Sorge case.

　•+　Ozaki Hotsumi no Chūgoku kenkyū [6,235 pp.], 234-235.

　　　尾崎秀美の中国研究
　　　Imai Seiichi and Fujii Shōzō, eds.　Tokyo: Ajia Keizai Kenkyūjo,
　　　1983.

　　　[The entire volume is devoted to discussion of Ozaki's scholarship.]

　Σ　Ozaki Hotsumi chosakushū, vol. 5 (1979), 409-417.

　　　Tokyo: Keisō Shobō, 1977-79.　5 vols.

∋ Chalmers Johnson, <u>An Instance of Treason: Ozaki Hotsumi and the Sorge Spy Ring</u> (Stanford: Stanford University Press, 1964).   7,278 pp.

Ozaki Hozumi   尾崎秀美
    see Ozaki Hotsumi.

Ozaki Shōtarō   尾崎庄太郎   Contemporary Chinese economy and politics.
    Yen 477, Teng #578.

Ozaki Yūjirō   尾崎雄二郎   History of Chinese language, phonology. Chinese poetics, Six Dynasties period. Chinese poetry, <u>Shih-ching</u>. Early Chinese history.
    Yen 477.

Ozawa Masamoto   小沢正元
    Listed under Uchiyama Kanzō.

P'eng Tse-chou   彭沢周
    see Hō Takushū.

Rai Tsutomu   頼惟勤   Neo-Confucianism, China and Japan. Chinese language, history of phonology. Chinese historical texts, <u>Shih-chi</u> and <u>Tzu-chih t'ung-chien</u>.
    Lit 285, Yen 239, Teng #644.
    + Chūgoku Bungakkai hō (Ochanomizu Daigaku) 6 (1987), 15-23.

Rei Ha   黎波   Chinese literature, esp. vernacular fiction.
    Lit 286.

Rokkaku Tsunehiro   六角恒広   Modern Chinese language.
    Yen 262.

Rokukaku Tsunehiro
    see Rokkaku Tsunehiro.

Ryō Susumu   龍 肅   Japanese history, early and medieval, incl.
                                   history of Mongol invasions.

ø Ishida, Wada, Ryō, Yamanaka yon sensei shōju kinen <u>Shigaku rombunshū</u>
   [41,585 pp.], 27-36.
   石田・和田・龍・山中四先生頌寿記念　史学論文集
   Shōju kinen rombunshū kankōkai iinkai, ed.   Tokyo: Nihon Daigaku
   Shigakkai Shōju Kinen Rombunshū Kankō Iinkai, 1962
   TRNS #015.

Ryū Sampu   劉三富   Chinese literature, T'ang period.
   Lit 286.

Ryūkawa Kiyoshi   龍川 清   Chinese poetry, pre-T'ang period.
   Lit 286.

Saeki Arikiyo   佐伯 有清   Early Japanese institutional history. Sino-
                                   Japanese historical relations.

   Yen 649.

Saeki Tomi   佐伯 富   Chinese history, esp. economic history, Sung
                                   period.

   Yen 647, Teng #546.
   + Shih-yuan (Taipei) 7 (Oct. 1976), 235-255.
   + Tōyōshi kenkyū 32.4 (March 1974), 15 pp.

Saeki Yoshio
   see Saeki Yoshirō

Saeki Yoshirō   佐伯 好郎 History of religion, Christianity in East
                                   Asia, incl. Nestorianism.

   + Hōseishi kenkyū 16 (1967), 241-244.
   • Shikan 72 (Sept. 1965), 98.

Saeki Yūichi   佐伯有一   Modern Chinese history. Chinese socio-econom-
                                    ic history, Ming and Ch'ing periods.
        Yen 649.
        + Tōyō Bunka Kenkyūjo kiyō (Tōkyō Daigaku) 92 (July 1983), 9 pp.

Sagawa Osamu   佐川 修   Classical Chinese thought, esp. Ch'un-ch'iu.
        Lit 120, Yen 650.

Saguchi Tōru   佐口 透   History: Mongolia, China (Yuan period), Rus-
                                    sia in Asia, and Islam in China.
        Yen 650, Teng #150.

Saionji Kazuteru   西園寺一晃   Contemporary China.
        Yen 493.

Saionji Kinkazu   西園寺公一   Contemporary China.
        Yen 492.

Saitō Akio   斎藤 秋男   Chinese educational history. Contemporary
                                    Chinese education. Modern Chinese litera-
                                    ture.
        Lit 116, Yen 601, Teng #114.

Saitō Hishō   斎藤 斐章   (Japanese and European history and politics.)
        ø Saitō sensei koki shukuga kinen rombunshū [99,829 pp.].
           Saitō sensei koki shukugakai, ed. Tokyo: Tōkō Shoin, 1937.
           TRNS #084, NNO 3:411.

Saitō Kiyoko   斎藤 喜代子   Chinese vernacular fiction, esp. Hung-lou
                                    meng.
        Lit 117, Yen 601.

Saitō Michihiko   斎藤 道彦   Modern Chinese thought, May Fourth Movement.
        Lit 118.

Saitō Shō　　　斎藤 晌　　Chinese poetry, T'ang period.

    Lit 118, Yen 600.

Saitō Tadanobu　　斎藤 唯信

    see Saitō Yuishin.

Saitō Tadashi　　斎藤 忠　　East Asian archaeology, esp. Japan and Korea.

    Yen 602.

    +　Saitō Tadashi hakushi nempu chosaku mokuroku.

      Saitō Tadashi hakushi shōju kinenkai, ed. & publ. Tokyo?, 1978.

Saitō Takeshi　　斎藤 毅

    Listed under Hiraoka Teikichi.

Saitō Yoshiaki　　斎藤 斐章

    see Saitō Hishō.

Saitō Yuishin　　斎藤 唯信　　Buddhist studies.*

    •　Ōtani gakuhō 38.1 (June 1958), 59-64.

Sakade Yoshinobu　　坂出 祥伸　　Chinese thought, Ch'ing and modern periods.

    Lit 120.

Sakaguchi Naoki　　阪口 直樹　　Modern Chinese literature.

    Lit 119.

Sakai Ken'ichi　　坂井 健一　　Chinese language, historical phonology.

    Lit 118, Yen 23.

Sakai Tadao　　酒井 忠夫　　History of Chinese religion, incl. Taoism and
                             religious societies. Sino-Japanese cultural
                             relations.

    Yen 230, Teng #490.

ø <u>Rekishi ni okeru minshū to bunka</u> Sakai Tadao sensei koki shukuga
   kinen ronshū [21,1093,30,5 pp.], 7-13.

   歴史における民衆と文化
   Sakai Tadao sensei koki shukuga kinen no kai, ed. Tokyo: Kokusho
   Kankōkai, 1982.
   [Includes English-language articles by Richard Shek, "Elite and
   Popular Reformism in Late Ming: The Traditions of Wang Yang-ming and
   Lo Ch'ing" (pp. 1-21), and Michel Strickmann, "The Tao among the Yao:
   Taoism and the Sinification of South China" (pp. 23-30).]
   TRNS:oo.

Also listed under Collected Articles #20a and #20b.

Sakai Takeo   境 武男   Chinese literature, pre-Han period, esp.
                                 <u>Shih-ching</u>.

   Lit 119.

Sakamoto Ichirō   坂本一郎   Modern Chinese language, incl. Wu dialect.
   + Kōbe Gaidai ronsō 18.3 (Aug. 1967), 103-106.

   • Ibid., 1-2 and 85-101.

   ø Hisae Fukusaburō sensei Sakamoto Ichirō sensei kanreki kinen <u>Chūgoku</u>
      <u>kenkyū</u> [1,196 pp.], 189-193.

      中国研究
      Hisae Fukusaburō sensei Sakamoto Ichirō sensei kanreki kinen gyōji
      jumbi iinkai, ed. & publ. Kobe, 1965.
      [Note the autobiographical outline by Sakamoto, pp. 161-188.]
      TRNS:oo.

Sakamoto Koretada   坂本是忠   Mongolian history. Sino-Soviet border rela-
                                    tions. Minority languages in China.
   Yen 19, Teng #151.

Sakamoto Kusuhiko   阪本楠彦   Agricultural economics, incl. China.
   Yen 23.

Sakamoto Tarō   坂本 太郎   Early Japanese history. Sino-Japanese histor-
                                              ical relations.

   Yen 21, Teng #249.

Sakamoto Tokumatsu   坂本 徳松   Asian politics and society.
   Yen 20.

Sakamoto Yukio   坂本 幸男   Buddhist studies.*
   Teng #743.

   + Ōsaki gakuhō 127 (Oct. 1973), 27-41.

Sakata Shin   坂田 新   Chinese poetry, esp. <u>Shih-ching</u>.
   Lit 119.

Sakatani Yoshinao   阪谷芳直
   Listed twice under Nakae Ushikichi.

Saku Setsu   佐久 節   Chinese poetry, traditional.
   • Shibun 30 (March 1961), 54-57.

Saku Takashi
   see Saku Setsu.

Sakuma Kichiya   佐久間 吉也   Chinese socio-economic history, Six Dynasties
                                              period.

   Teng #523.

Sakuma Shigeo   佐久間 重男   Chinese history, esp. socio-economic history,
                                              Ming period. Chinese ceramics.

   Yen 651, Teng #560.

   ø Sakuma Shigeo kyōju taikyū kinen <u>Chūgokushi tōjishi ronshū</u> [1,23,
   1,631 pp.], 5-9.

     中国史・陶磁史論集
   Sakuma Shigeo kyōju taikyū kinen Chūgokushi tōjishi ronshū henshū
   iinkai, ed. Tokyo: Ryōgen Shoten, 1983.

   TRNS:oo.

Sakurai Akiharu   桜井明治   Chinese language. Overseas Chinese, language
                                  and literature, esp. Malaya.
      Yen 564.

Sambō Masami   三宝政美   Modern Chinese literature and language.
      Lit 128, Yen 339.

Samejima Kunizō   鮫島国三   Modern Chinese language. Contemporary China,
                                  communes.
      Yen 35.
      + Sangyō keizai kenkyū (Kurume) 13.3 (Nov. 1972), 171-174.

Sanaka Sō   佐中壮   Chinese thought and religion, incl. Taoism,
                                  Pao-p'u tzu.
      Lit 124, Yen 661.
      + Kōgakkan Daigaku kiyō 13 (1975), 407-408.

Sanetō Keishū   実藤恵秀   Modern Sino-Japanese historical relations.
                                  Modern Chinese language and literature.
      Lit 124, Yen 386, Teng #579.
      • Shakai kagaku tōkyū (Waseda Daigaku) 33.1 (Sept. 1987), 33-59.
      • Tōyō bungaku kenkyū 16 (March 1968), 29-31.
      + Gakujutsu kenkyū (Jimbun kagaku, shakai kagaku hen) 16 (1967), 209-
         210.
      + Kokubungaku kenkyū (Waseda Daigaku) 36 (Oct. 1967), 129-130.
      • Ibid., 1-15.
      Also listed under Collected Articles #31.

Sano Kōji   佐野公治 Chinese thought, Ming and Ch'ing periods.
      Yen 652.

Sanui Tadahai   讃井唯允 Chinese language.
      Yen 592.

Sasaki Gesshō   佐々木月樵、   Buddhist studies.
    Σ <u>Sasaki Gesshō zenshū</u>, vol. 6 (1929), 943-945.
       Sasaki Gesshō zenshū kankōkai, ed. & publ. Kyoto, 1927-29;   rpt.
       Tokyo: Kokusho Kankōkai, 1973. 6 vols.

Sasaki Heigorō   佐々木平伍郎
    Listed under Hiraoka Teikichi.

Sasaki Kiichi   佐々木基一   Modern Japanese and Chinese literatures.
    Yen 652.

Sasaki Masaya   佐々木正哉   Modern Chinese socio-economic and diplomatic
                                     history.

        Yen 653.

Satake Yasuhiko   佐竹端彦   Chinese history, Han thru Sung periods.

Satō Akira   佐藤昭   Chinese language, history of phonology.
    Yen 661.

Satō Haruo   佐藤春男   Modern Japanese author. Modern Chinese liter-
                                  ature. Chinese vernacular fiction. Chinese
                                  poetry.

    Yen 660.
    Σ <u>Satō Haruo zenshū</u>, vol. 12 (1970), 776-789.
       Tokyo: Kodansha, 1967-70. 12 vols.
       [Note the list of writings about Satō: vol. 12, pp. 790-794.]

Satō Hisashi   佐藤長   Tibetan and Central Asian history.
    Yen 654, Teng #152.
    + Tōyōshi kenkyū 36.4 (March 1978), 8 pp.

Satō Hitoshi   佐藤仁   Chinese thought, Sung period, esp. Chu Hsi.
    Lit 123.

Satō Ichirō   佐藤一郎   Chinese thought, thru Six Dynasties, incl.
                                    Buddhism.

    b. 1920.
    Lit 121, Yen 656.
    Cf. next entry.

Satō Ichirō   佐藤一郎   Chinese literature, esp. Ch'ing and modern
                                    periods.

    b. 1928.
    Lit 122, Yen 659.
    Cf. preceding entry.

Satō Kiyota   佐藤清太   East Asian educational history.
    Yen 655, Teng #115.

Satō Kyōgen   佐藤匡玄   Classical Chinese thought.
    Lit 122, Yen 655.

Satō Masahiko   佐藤雅彦   Chinese art history, ceramics.
    Yen 659.
    ∈ Idem, <u>Chinese Ceramics: A Short History</u> [13,14,255 pp.].
      Translated and adapted by Hanaoka Kiyoko and Susan Barberi. New York
      and Tokyo: Weatherhill/Heibonsha, 1981.
    [Additional book-length English-language studies by Satō on Japanese
    ceramics and on Oriental ceramics in the Iran Basta Museum, Teheran, are
    not listed here.]

Satō Mitsuo   佐藤密雄   Buddhist studies.*
    ø Satō hakushi koki kinen <u>Bukkyō shisō ronsō</u> [12,1118,4,5 pp.], 1-6.
    仏教思想論叢
    Satō Mitsuo hakushi koki kinen rombunshū kankōkai, ed. Tokyo: Sanki-
    bō Busshorin, 1972.
    TRNS #082.

Satō Saburō   佐藤三郎   Modern Sino-Japanese historical relations.
     Yen 657, Teng #306.
        + Yamagata Daigaku kiyō (Jimbun kagaku) 8.4 (Feb. 1977), 4 pp.

Satō Shin'ichirō   佐藤慎一郎   Modern Chinese history, communism. Contempo-
                                     rary China, communes.
        + Takushoku Daigaku ronshū 104-105 (March 1976), 3 pp.

Satō Shinji   佐藤震二   Modern Chinese thought.
     Lit 122, Yen 658, Teng #703.

Satō Shōji   佐藤正二   Japanese diplomat. Contemporary China.
     Yen 657.

Satō Taishun   佐藤泰舜   Chinese Buddhism.
     Yen 656.
        + Idem, Shina Bukkyō shisō ron [5,2,434 pp.], 432-434.
        支那仏教思想論
           Yono (Saitama): Kokeisō, 1960.

Satō Taketoshi   佐藤武敏   Chinese socio-economic history: handicraft
                                     industry, thru T'ang period; water systems,
                                     Sung thru Ch'ing periods.
     Yen 656.
        + Jimbun kenkyū 36.9 (Dec. 1984), 1-5.
        • Chūgokushi kenkyū (Ōsaka Shiritsu Daigaku) 8 (1984), 145-146.

Satō Tamotsu   佐藤保   Chinese poetry, esp. T'ang and Sung periods.
     Lit 123.

Satō Tetsuei   佐藤哲英   Chinese Buddhism.
        + Bukkyōgaku kenkyū 25-26 (May 1968), 1-10.

ø Satō kyōju teinen kinen <u>Bukkyō bunken no kenkyū</u> [10,365,1 pp.],
   1-7.

   仏教文献の研究

   Ryūkoku Daigaku Bukkyō gakkai, ed. Kyoto: Hyakkaen, 1968.

   TRNS:oo

Satō Yūgō   佐藤 祐豪 Japanese and Chinese art history, calligra-
                                phy.

   Yen 660.

Satoi Hikoshichirō 里井彦七郎 Chinese economic history, Ch'ing period. Mod-
                                ern Chinese history.

   Yen 241, Teng #580.

   + Rekishi hyōron 295 (Nov. 1974), 90-91.
   • Ibid. 291 (July 1974), 89-94.
   • Rekishigaku kenkyū 411 (Aug. 1974), 62-63.

Sawada Masahiro   沢田正熙 Chinese poetry, <u>Shih-ching</u>.
   Lit 126.

Sawada Mizuho   沢田瑞穂 Chinese fiction, esp. Six Dynasties. Chinese
                                religion. Chinese legends.

   Lit 126, Yen 594.

   + Chūgoku bungaku kenkyū (Waseda Daigaku) 8 (1982), 1-15.
   + Tenri Daigaku gakuhō (Jimbun, shakai, shizen hen) 85 (March 1973),
      1-10.
   • Ibid., 11-19.

Sawada Takio   沢田多喜男 Classical Chinese thought, esp. <u>Chuang-tzu</u>.
   Lit 125.

Sawaguchi Takeo   沢口剛雄 Chinese poetry, <u>yueh-fu</u>.
   Lit 125.

Sawaya Harutsugu   沢谷昭次   Chinese bibliography. Contemporary China.

Sayama Wataru   佐山済   Early Japanese literature. Sino-Japanese literary relations.

    Yen 662.

Segawa Kōkichi   瀬川孝吉   Ethnography, Taiwan.

    ∈ <u>An Illustrated Ethnography of Formosan Aborigines</u>.   3 vols.

      By Kano Tadao and Segawa Kokichi.

          Vol. 1   <u>The Yami</u> [5,456 pp.].

      Rev. ed., Tokyo: Maruzen Co., 1956. Rev. and enlarged ed., Taipei: Southern Materials Center, 1986.

          Vol. 2   <u>The Tsuo</u>, and Vol. 3   <u>The Bunnu</u>.

      To be published by the Southern Materials Center (Taipei).

Seimiya Tsuyoshi   清宮剛   Chinese thought, Taoism, pre-T'ang period.

    Lit 149.

Seki Akira   関晃   Early Japanese political and social history. Sino-Japanese historical relations.

    Yen 160, Teng #250.

Seki Hiroharu   関寛治   Political science. Asian international relations.

    Yen 159.

    + Tōyō Bunka Kenkyūjo kiyō (Tōkyō Daigaku) 103 (March 1987), 1-18.

Seki Masao   関正郎   Chinese thought, Six Dynasties period, incl. Buddhism.

    Lit 150, Yen 160, Teng #693.

Sekida Katsuki NC   See Addenda, p. 279.

Sekiguchi Shindai   関口真大   Chinese Buddhism, T'ien-t'ai school. Tunhuang Buddhist manuscripts.

    Teng #744.

Sekino Tadashi   関野 真   East Asian architectural and art history.

  * <u>Meiji bungaku zenshū</u>, vol. 78, 456-457.

明治文学全集

    Tokyo: Chikuma Shobō, 1976.

    [Bibliography includes articles about Sekino.]

  + Hōun 16 (March 1936), 18-27.

  • Ibid., 1-17.

  + Tōyōshi kenkyū 1.2 (Dec. 1935), 86-89.

  ∈ <u>Jehol: The Most Glorious and Monumental Relics in Manchoukuo</u>, OR
    <u>Nekka</u> 熱河 . 4 vols., and Supplement.

    By Sekino Tadashi and T. Takeshima. Tokyo: Zauho Press, 1934-37.
    Vols. 1-4: 63, 84, 78, and 74 pp., respectively, with bilingual
    description. Supplement: 1,1,1,9,28 pp. of English text, 1,3,9,229
    pp. of Japanese text, and plates on pp. 231-254.

  ∈ <u>Buddhist Monuments in China</u>, OR <u>Shina Bukkyō shiseki</u> 支那佛教
    史蹟 . 5 vols. (text), and 5 vols. (plates).

    By Tokiwa Daijō and Sekino Tei [Tadashi]. Tokyo: Bukkyo-Shiseki
    Kenkyu-Kwai. Volumes of text, 1925-28: 194, 206, 216, 201, 243 pp.,
    respectively. Volumes of plates, 1931: 150 loose pp. each, with 6-7
    pp. of text per volume. Reprint (partial?), 1937-38.

Sekino Takeshi   関野 雄   East Asian art and archaeology.
    Yen 161, Teng #12.

Sekino Tei   関野 貞
    see Sekino Tadashi.

Senda   千田
    see Chida.

Senō Shigemori   瀬能重衛   Chinese thought, thru Han period.
  + Kangaku kenkyū (Nihon Daigaku) 4 (March 1966), 6-8.

Shiba Rokurō   斯波六郎   Chinese literature, Six Dynasties period,
                         esp. <u>Wen-hsuan</u> and <u>Wen-hsin tiao-lung</u>.
    Lit 131, Teng #606.

•* Tōhōgaku 61 (Jan. 1981), 169-196.

• Shinagaku hō 4 (March 1961), 27-31.

+ Shinagaku kenkyū 24-25 (Oct. 1960), 4 pp.

• Ibid., 1 and 246-252.

Shiba Ryōtarō   司馬遼太郎 Modern Japanese novelist who uses themes from
                                    Chinese history.

Yen 412.

Σ* <u>Shiba Ryōtarō zenshū</u>, vol. 32 (1974), 499-544.
    Tokyo: Bungei Shūnjūsha, 1971-75. 32 vols.

Shiba Yoshinobu   斯波義信 Chinese socio-economic history, Sung period.
    Yen 416.

∈ <u>Commerce and Society in Sung China</u> [4,228 pp.].
    Translated by Mark Elvin. Ann Arbor: Center for Chinese Studies,
    University of Michigan, 1970.

∈ <u>Markets in China during the Sung, Ming, and Ch'ing Periods</u> [2,1,1,2,
    142 pp.].
    By Shiba Yoshinori (sic) and Yamane Yukio. Translated by Wake A.
    Fujioka and Matsuda Mitsugu. Honolulu: East-West Center, University
    of Hawaii (Institute of Advanced Projects, East-West Center, Transla-
    tion Series #23), 1967.

    [The Shiba section in the volume (pp. 1-107) is entitled "Markets and
    Fairs (Temple Markets) in Kiangnan during the Sung Period."]

Shiba Yoshinori
    see Shiba Yoshinobu.

Shibagaki Yoshitarō 柴垣芳太郎 Modern Chinese language.
    Yen 41.

Shibaike Yasuo   芝池靖夫 Contemporary China, esp. economy.
    Yen 605.

Shibata Minoru   芝田 稔   Chinese language: late-Ch'ing Chinese newspa-
                                per vocabulary, Sino-Japanese vocabulary
                                influence.

    Lit 132, Yen 606.

Shibata Takeshi   柴田 武
    Listed under Hattori Shirō.

Shibata Temma   柴田 天馬   Chinese fiction, Ch'ing period, Liao-chai
                                chih-i.

    Lit 132.

Shida Fudōmaro   志田 不動麿   Chinese vernacular fiction, esp. Ming period.
                                Chinese socio-economic history.

    Lit 131, Yen 609, Teng #607.

Shiga Masatoshi   志賀 正年   Modern Chinese language and literature.
    Teng #632.

    + Tenri Daigaku gakuhō (Jimbun, shakai, shizen hen) 96 (March 1975),
       1-19.

Shiga Shūzō   滋賀 秀三   Chinese law, incl. family law.
    Yen 646, Teng #42.

Shigematsu Shunshō 重松 俊章   Chinese history. Chinese popular religion.
    ø Shigematsu sensei koki kinen Kyūshū Daigaku Tōyōshi ronsō [2,3,5,
       363,10 pp.], 3 pp.
       九州大学東洋史論叢
       Hino Kaisaburō, ed.   Fukuoka: Kyūshū Daigaku Bungakubu Tōyōshi Ken-
       kyūshitsu, 1957. {E}
       TRNS #098, NNO 3:412.

Shigematsu Toshiaki 重松 俊章
    see Shigematsu Shunshō.

Shigeta Atsushi   重田　徳   Chinese socio-economic history, Ming and
                              Ch'ing periods.

    Yen 629.

    +　Jimbun kenkyū 25.10 (Dec. 1973), 1-10.

Shigesawa   重沢

    see Shigezawa.

Shigezawa Toshio   重沢俊郎   Classical Chinese thought. Chinese history,
                              esp. thru Han period.

    Teng #673.

Shigezawa Toshirō

    see Shigezawa Toshio.

Shikata Hiroshi   四方　博   Korean economic history. Sino-Korean-Japa-
                              nese historical relations.

    Yen 415.

    • Chōsen gakuhō 68 (July 1973), 73-74.

    • Keizai kagaku (Nagoya Daigaku) 9.3 (March 1962), 1 p.

Shima Kunio   島　邦男   Chinese epigraphy. Early Chinese thought.

    Yen 95, Teng #513.

    +　Kōkotsugaku 12 (Aug. 1980), 12-13.

Shimada Kenji   島田虎次   Chinese thought, Sung thru Ch'ing periods,
                            incl. neo-Confucianism. Modern Chinese
                            thought.

    Lit 133, Yen 92, Teng #694.

    ∈　Idem, <u>Pioneer of the Chinese Revolution: Zhang Binglin and Confucian-</u>
      <u>ism</u> [15,190 pp.].

      Translated by Joshua A. Fogel. Stanford: Stanford University Press,
      1990.

      [Note the translator's "Introduction," pp. v-xv.]

    +　Tōyōshi kenkyū 39.4 (March 1981), 13 pp.

    Also listed under Collected Articles #68.

Shimada Kumiko   島田 久美子
    see Kakei Kumiko.

Shimada Masao   島田 正郎   Chinese history, Liao dynasty. Asian legal
                                                history.

    Yen 94, Teng #43.

    + Shimada Masao sensei roncho mokuroku [40 pp.], 40 pp.

       Meiji Daigaku Hōgakubu Hōshigaku Kenkyūshitsu, ed. & publ.   Tokyo,

       1975.

    + Idem, Ryōsei no kenkyū [4,7,761,12,4,4 pp.], 4 pp.

       遼制之研究

       Ueda (Nagano): Nakazawa Insatsu, 1954;   rpt. Tokyo: Kyūko Shoin,

       1973. {E}

    Cf. next entry.

Shimada Masao   島田 政雄   Modern Chinese literature.
    Lit 133, Yen 93, Teng #633.
    Cf. preceding entry.

Shimada Shūjirō   島田 修二郎 Chinese and Japanese art history, painting.
    Yen 95.

    ∈ Traditions of Japanese Art: Selections from the Kimiko and John
       Powers Collection [393 pp.].

       By John M. Rosenfield and Shimada Shūjirō.   Cambridge: Fogg Art
       Museum, Harvard University, 1970.

    ∈ Painting of the Sung and Yuan Dynasties [47 pp.].

       By Yonezawa Yoshiho and Shimada Shujiro.   Tokyo: Maruyama, 1952.

Shimada Toshihiko   島田 俊彦   Modern Chinese history, esp. World War II.
    Yen 94.

Shimada Yukiko   島田 由紀子 Modern Chinese literature.
    Lit 134.

Shimakura Tamio   島倉民生   Contemporary Chinese economy.
     Yen 97.

Shimasue Kazuyasu   島居一康   Chinese socio-economic history, T'ang and
                                       Sung periods.

Shimazaki Akira   嶋崎昌   Central Asian history.
     Yen 96.
     +   Idem, <u>Zui Tō jidai no Higashi Tōrukisutan kenkyū: Kōshō-koku shi</u>
        <u>kenkyū o chūshin to shite</u> [23,583,36 pp.], 12-17.
        隋唐時代の東トゥルキスタン研究―高昌国史研究を中心として―
        Tokyo: Tōkyō Daigaku Shuppankai, 1977.
     ●   Tōhōgaku 48 (July 1974), 143-144.
     +   Chūō Daigaku Bungakubu kiyō 72 (Shigakuka 19) (March 1974), 193-202.

Shimizu Eikichi   清水栄吉   Chinese literature, traditional fiction,
                                         incl. humor. Modern Chinese literature.
     Lit 134, Yen 325, Teng #634.

Shimizu Kiyoshi   清水潔   Chinese literature and thought, thru T'ang
                                         period.
     Lit 134, Yen 324, Teng #674.

Shimizu Morimitsu   清水盛光   Chinese society and social history, incl.
                                         family. Theory of social groups.
     Teng #124.
     +   Jimbun gakuhō (Kyōto Daigaku) 26 (March 1968), 238-240.

Shimizu Shigeru   清水茂   Chinese literature, esp. T'ang and Sung peri-
                                         ods.
     Lit 135, Yen 324, Teng #608.

Shimizu Taiji   清水泰次   Chinese socio-economic history, esp. Ming
                                         period.
     Yen 326, Teng #561.

ø Shimizu hakushi tsuitō kinen   <u>Mindaishi ronsō</u> [30,692,34,28 pp.],
   11-21.

   明代史論叢

   Shimizu hakushi tsuitō kinen Mindaishi ronsō hensan iinkai, ed.
   Tokyo: Daian, 1962. {E}
   TRNS #097.

+ Shikan 57-58 (March 1960), 254-266.

• Ibid., 245-253.

Shimizu Yasuzō   清水安三   Modern Chinese literature and history.
   Yen 323.

Shimizu Yoshio   清水凱夫   Chinese literature, Six Dynasties period.
   Lit 136.

Shimmura Tōru   新村徹   Modern Chinese literature.
   Lit 141.

   + Chūgoku bungaku ronsō (Ōbirin Daigaku) 10 (March 1985), 1-6.

Shimomi Takao   下見隆雄   Chinese thought, Han and Six Dynasties peri-
                                   ods, incl. Ko Hung.

   Lit 137, Yen 495.

Shimomise Seiichi
   see Shimomise Shizuichi.

Shimomise Shizuichi 下店静市   Chinese and Japanese art history, painting.
   Yen 494, Teng #183.

Shimomura Toratarō 下村寅太郎
   Listed under Suzuki Daisetsu.

Shimotomai Akira   下斗米晟   Classical Chinese thought and neo-Confucian-
                                   ism.

   Lit 136.

Shimura Ryōji   志村 良治   Chinese literature, thru T'ang period.
     Lit 136.

Shimura Takeshi   志村 武
     Listed twice under Suzuki Daisetsu.

Shinjō Shinzō   新城新蔵   Chinese astronomy.
     ∋ S. Elisséef, "Shinjō Shinzō," Harvard Journal of Asiatic Studies 3
          (1938), 430.

Shinkai Hajime   新海 一   Chinese literature, T'ang period, esp. Liu
                                            Tsung-yuan.
     Lit 140, Yen 527.

Chinkai Takaaki   新開 高明   Modern Chinese literature.
     Lit 140.

Shinobu Seizaburō   信夫 清三郎   Modern Japanese history, incl. Sino-Japanese
                                            War.
     Yen 531, Teng #63.

Shinoda Osamu   篠田 統   History of Chinese food.

Shinoda Suburu
     see Shinoda Osamu.

Shinoda Sumeru
     see Shinoda Osamu.

Shinohara Hisao   篠原 寿雄   Chinese Buddhism. Chinese lexicography and
                                            bibliography.
     Yen 527.

Shiomi Atsurō   塩見 敦郎   Chinese poetry, Shih-ching. Chinese Buddhism,
                                            Six Dynasties period.
     Lit 129.

Shiomi Kunihiko   塩見邦彦   Chinese poetry, Six Dynasties period.
    Lit 129.

Shionoya Kan   塩谷 桓   Chinese poetry, traditional. Chinese vernacu-
                                    lar literature, Hsi-hsiang chi.
    Lit 129.

Shionoya On   塩谷 温   Chinese literature, esp. drama and vernacular
                                    fiction. Chinese thought, neo-Confucianism.
    Lit 129.
    + Tōkyō Shinagaku hō 9 (1963), 1-14.
    • Ibid., 15-42.
    + Shibun 36 (March 1963), 104-111.
    • Ibid., 1-104 and 112-115.

Shiraishi Bon   白石 凡
    see Shiraishi Iwao.

Shiraishi Iwao   白石 岩   Journalist. Contemporary Sino-Japanese rela-
                                    tions.
    Yen 18.

Shiraishi Yoshio   白石義夫   Chinese thought, traditional.
    Yen 18.

Shirakawa Shizuka   白川 静   Chinese epigraphy. Early Chinese history,
                                    incl. Shih-chi. Chinese literature, pre-Han
                                    period, esp. Shih-ching.
    Lit 138, Yen 15, Teng #609.
    • Ritsumeikan bungaku 504 (Dec. 1987), 133-141.
    + Ibid. 430-432 (Apr.-June 1981), 10 pp.

Shirakawa Yoshirō   白川義郎   Chinese art history, calligraphic theory, Six
                                    Dynasties period.
    Lit 139.

Shiraki Naoya   白木直也
    see Shiroki Naoya.

Shiranishi Shin'ichirō 白西神郎 Contemporary Asian politics.
    Yen 19.

Shiratori Kiyoshi   白鳥 清   Early Chinese history and religion.
    Yen 17.
    + Idem, <u>Nihon Chūgoku kodaihō no kenkyū</u> [5,262 pp.], 259-260.
       日本・中国古代法の研究
       Tokyo: Kashiwa Shobō, 1972.

Shiratori Kurakichi 白鳥庫吉   Asian, incl. Inner Asian, history.
    ∋ Stefan Tanaka, "Shina: Japan's Representation of China, 1894-1926,"
      University of Chicago Ph.D. diss., 1986.   389 pp.
      [Focuses mostly on Shiratori, but note also the sections on--
          Hattori Unokichi   pp. 222, 227-232, 295-299.
          Hayashi Taisuke   pp. 175-197.
          Inoue Tetsujirō   pp. 71-77, 111-115, 127, 201-204, 222.
          Kume Kunitake   pp. 104-111.
          Miyake Yonekichi   pp. 63-71.
          Naitō Konan   pp. 192-197, 246-251, 286-293, 307-345.
          Naka Michiyo   pp. 61-63.
          Tsuda Sōkichi   pp. 275-280.]
      [University of Chicago, East Asia Library, DS999.T195.]
    ●* <u>Shiratori Kurakichi: Shinwa ron; Torii Ryūzō: Jinruigaku to kōkogaku</u>
       [471 pp.], 11-257, 451-457, and 467-471.
       白鳥庫吉ー神話論ー鳥居龍蔵ー人類学と考古学
       By Shiratori Yoshirō (Shiratori Kurakichi section) and Yawata Ichirō
       (Torii Ryūzō section). Tokyo: Kōdansha, 1978.
       [Note the list of writings about Shiratori, pp. 456-457.]
    ●* <u>Tōyōgaku no sōshisha-tachi</u> [320 pp.], 15-70.
       東洋学の創始者たち
       Yoshikawa Kōjirō, ed. Tokyo: Kōdansha, 1976.
       [A reprint of the <u>Tōhōgaku</u> material listed below.]

- Tōyō Bunko shohō 5 (1973), 1-21, and 6 (1974), 17-43.

•* Tōhōgaku 44 (July 1972), 152-182.

Σ Shiratori Kurakichi zenshū, vol. 10 (1971), 541-569.

   Tokyo: Iwanami Shoten, 1969-71. 10 vols.

• Tōa jiron 6.11 (Nov. 1964), 13-18.

∋+ "The List of Works [by Prof. Shiratori Kurakichi]," Memoirs of the
   Research Department of the Toyo Bunko 15 (1956), 12-30.

∋ [Ishida Mikinosuke,] "A Brief Account of Dr. Shiratori's Life and
   Works," Ibid., 1-11.

   [A translation of the Minzokugaku kenkyū entry listed below.]

ø Shiratori hakushi kinen rombunshū [3,357,4 pp.], 67-82.

   Tōyō Kyōkai Gakujutsu Chōsabu, ed. Tokyo: Tōyō Kyōkai, 1944.

   [The volume is the same as the Tōyō gakuhō issue listed below.]

   [Note the biography of Shiratori, pp. 1-66.]

   TRNS #103.

+ Tōyō gakuhō 29.3-4 (Jan. 1944), 391-406.

• Ibid., 325-390.

• Minzokugaku kenkyū 8.1 (July 1942), 1-12.

+ Shigaku zasshi 53.5 (May 1942), 652-659.

•* Shiratori hakushi kinen tenrankai chinretsu tosho mokuroku [2,2,44
   pp.], 1-5.

   白鳥博士記念展覧会陳列図書目録

   Tōyō Bunko, ed. & publ. Tokyo, 1942.

+ Chin-ling hsueh-pao (Nan-ching) 6.2 (Nov. 1936), 193-199.

• Ibid., 183-193.

ø Shiratori hakushi kanreki kinen   Tōyōshi ronsō   [11,1,1,3,23,904
   pp.], 11 pp.

   東洋史論叢

   Ikeuchi Hiroshi, ed. Tokyo: Iwanami Shoten, 1925.

   TRNS #102, NNO 3:412.

Shiratori Yoshirō 白鳥芳郎 History and ethnology of South China and
                              Southeast Asia.

Yen 17, Teng #153.

Also listed under Shiratori Kurakichi and Torii Ryūzō.

Shiroki Naoya   白木直也   Chinese vernacular fiction, Ming period, esp. Shui-hu chuan. Chinese fiction, T'ang period.

    Lit 139, Yen 16, Teng #610.

Shizutani Masao   静谷正雄   Buddhist studies.*

   + Ryūkoku shidan 78 (March 1980), 1-4.

Shōji Kakuichi   荘司格一   Chinese vernacular fiction. Chinese humor.
    Lit 138, Yen 645.

Shōji Sōichi   庄司荘一   Chinese thought, incl. political thought, Sung period, esp. Wang An-shih.

    Lit 138, Yen 645.

Shūtatsu Sei   周達生   Contemporary Chinese ethnography, Yunnan.

Sōda Hiroshi   相田洋   Chinese religion. History of Chinese popular movements.

    Lit 150.

Sogabe Shizuo   曽我部静雄   Chinese socio-economic history, esp. Tang, Sung, and Chin-period fiscal and monetary matters.

    Yen 599, Teng #491.
   + Shūkan Tōyōgaku 31 (June 1974), 233-243.
   • Ibid. 13 (May 1965), 98-100.
   •* Bunka 29.1 (May 1965), 145-148.

Sōma Takashi   相馬隆   East-West historical relations.
    Yen 495.

Somura Yasunobu   曽村保信   Contemporary Chinese international relations.
    Yen 599.

Sono Toshihiko   曽野 寿彦   Asian archaeology. Sino-Japanese historical
                                                    relations.
        Yen 600.

Sonoie Eishō   園家栄照   Chinese Buddhism.
        Yen 585.

Suda Akiyoshi   須田 昭義   East Asian ethnology.
        Yen 537.

Suda Teiichi   須田 禎一   Modern Chinese literature. Chinese poetry,
                                                    Sung-period tz'u.
        Lit 149, Yen 537.

Sudō   周藤
        see Sutō.

Suematsu Yasukazu   末松 保和   East Asian, esp. Korean, history.
        Yen 276, Teng #718.
        ø Kodai Higashi Ajia shi ronshū, vol. 2, 469-476.
          古代東アジア史論集
          Suematsu hakushi koki kinenkai, ed.   Tokyo: Yoshikawa Kōbundō, 1978.
          2 vols.   12,470 pp., and 5,478 pp.
          TRNS #078.

Suenaga Masao   末永 雅雄   Japanese archaeology and early history. Sino-
                                                    Japanese historical relations.
        Yen 277.
        ø Suenaga sensei beiju kinen kentei rombunshū.
          Suenaga sensei beiju kinenkai, ed.   Nara: Meishinsha, 1985.   2 vols.
          918 pp., and pp. 919-1896.
          TRNS:oo.

ø Suenaga sensei koki kinen <u>Kodaigaku ronsō</u> [3,19,4,1,694,4 pp.], 7-
   19.

   古代学論叢

   Kansai Daigaku nai Suenaga sensei koki kinen Kodaigaku ronsō kankōkai, ed. Suita: Kansai Daigaku Tōzai Gakujutsu Kenkyūjo, 1967.
   TRNS:oo.

Suenobu Yasuo   末延 保雄   Modern Chinese language, phonetics.
   Yen 276.

Suetomi Tōsaku   末富 東作
   see Kaionji Chōgorō.

Suetsuna Joichi   末綱 恕一   Buddhist studies.*
   • Indogaku Bukkyōgaku kenkyū 19.1 (Dec. 1970), 418-420.

Suga Eiichi   菅 栄一   Modern Chinese politics and Sino-Japanese
                                     relations.

   Yen 204.

Sugano Shunsaku   菅野 俊作   Modern Chinese literature, Lu Hsun in Japan.
   Yen 205.

Suganuma Fujio   菅沼 不二男 Contemporary Chinese society and politics.
   Yen 205.

Suganuma Masahisa   菅沼 正久   Contemporary Chinese thought, economy, soci-
                                     ety, and language.

   Yen 205.

Sugaya Gunjirō   菅谷 軍次郎 Chinese literature, T'ang and Sung periods.
   Lit 142.

Sugimori Hisahide   杉森 久英   Contemporary China.
   Yen 374.

Sugimori Masaya   杉森正弥   Modern Chinese literature. Chinese vernacular
                                        fiction. Sino-Japanese literary relations.
    Lit 143, Yen 374.
    + Gogaku bungaku (Hokkaidō Kyōiku Daigaku) 15 (1977), 1 p.
    • Ibid., 69-70.

Sugimoto Kenji   杉本憲司   Chinese archaeology, thru Han period.

Sugimoto Naojirō   杉本直次郎   Southeast Asian history. East-West historical
                                        relations.
    Yen 371, Teng #154.
    • Tōhōgaku 47 (Jan. 1974), 169-170.

Sugimoto Tatsuo   杉本達夫   Modern Chinese literature. Classical Chinese
                                        thought, esp. Hsun-tzu.
    Lit 142, Yen 372.

Sugimoto Yukio   杉本行夫   Early Chinese and Japanese poetry. Sino-Jap-
                                        anese literary relations.
    Lit 143, Teng #611.

Sugimura Kunihiko   杉村邦彦   Chinese calligraphy.
    ∋ P. Demiéville, Review of the reprint of the T'ang edition of the
    Shih-shuo hsin-yü: Tō shōhon "Sesetsu shingo" 唐抄本世説新語
    (vol. 176 of Shoseki meihin sōkan 書跡名品叢刊 . Tokyo:
    Nigensha, 1972. 81,1 pp. Series editors, Nishikawa Yasushi and Kanda
    Kiichirō. Sugimura Kunihiko authored the textual notice in the
    volume, pp. 71-73), in T'oung Pao 59 (1973), 309-310.

Sugimura Yūzō   杉村勇造   Chinese art history.
    Yen 372.
    ∈ Idem, Chinese Sculpture, Bronzes, and Jades in Japanese Collections
    [6,1,46,3,3,3 pp., plus 48,48,48 pl.].
    English adaptation by Burton Watson. Honolulu: East-West Center
    Press, 1966.

Sugino Akio   杉野明夫   Contemporary Chinese economy and politics.
    Yen 374.

Sugiura Toyoji   杉浦豊治   Classical Chinese thought.
    Lit 142.

Sugiyama Nobuzō   杉山信三   Japanese and Chinese art and architectural
                                  history.

    Yen 373.

Sumida Masakazu   澄田正一   Archaeology, incl. China.
    Teng #13.
    + Nagoya Daigaku Bungakubu kenkyū ronshū 74 (Shigaku 25) (1978), 1-3.

Sumida Shōichi

    see Sumida Masakazu.

Sumita Teruo   住田照夫   Modern Chinese language. Chinese lexicography.
    Yen 644.

Sutō Yōichi   須藤洋一   Chinese literature, Ch'ing and modern peri-
                                  ods.

    Lit 149.

Sutō Yoshiyuki   周藤吉之   Chinese socio-economic history, T'ang thru
                                  Sung periods and Ch'ing period. Korean his-
                                  tory.
    Yen 630, Teng #492.
    ∋* Denis C. Twitchett, "Recent Work on Medieval Chinese Social History
        by Sudo Yoshiyuki," Journal of the Economic and Social History of the
        Orient 1.1 (Aug. 1957), 145-148.

Suwa Gijō   諏訪義讓   Buddhist studies.* Buddhism in Central Asia.
    Yen 647.

Suwa Suiga   須羽水雅   Chinese art history, calligraphy.
   • Shoron 6 (May 1975), 32-43.

Suyama Takashi   須山 卓   Overseas Chinese, esp. economics.
      Yen 536.
      + Keiei to keizai (Nagasaki Daigaku) 56.3 (#144) (Jan. 1977), 251-252.

Suzue Gen'ichi   鈴江言一   Modern Chinese history, incl. Sun Yat-sen,
                                  labor history, and communist revolution.

   +• Suzue Gen'ichi den: Chūgoku kakumei ni kaketa ichi Nihonjin [1,4,14,
      265,15,1 pp.], 261-265.
      鈴江言一伝 ― 中国革命にかけた日本人 ―
      By Etō Shinkichi and Kyo Shukushin (Hsu Shu-chen).   Tokyo: Tōkyō
      Daigaku Shuppankai, 1984.
   • Ajia kenkyū 8.4 (Dec. 1961), 67-86.

Suzuki Akira   鈴木明   Modern Chinese history. Taiwan, night life.
      Yen 255.

Suzuki Chūsei   鈴木中正   Chinese history, Ch'ing and modern periods.
                                  Chinese relations with South and Southwest
                                  Asia. Chinese religious history, esp. mil-
                                  lenary movements, Ch'ing period.
      Yen 259, Teng #493.
      + Aichi Daigaku bungaku ronsō 73 (July 1983), 143-149.

Suzuki Daisetsu   鈴木大拙   Buddhist thought.*
         [Daisetz T. Suzuki]
   [The numerous books in Western languages by Suzuki Daisetsu are not
   listed here individually. For references, see the relevant bibliograph-
   ical entries below, especially the ones in Suzuki Daisetsu zenshū and
   Suzuki Daisetsu no hito to gakumon.]
   ∋ A Zen Life: D.T. Suzuki Remembered [19,250 pp.]
      Abe Masao, ed. Photographs by Francis Haar. New York: Weatherhill,
      1986.
      [A volume devoted to Suzuki.]

+ Gendai no esupuri 133 (1978).

•* Kaisō Suzuki Daisetsu [10,452 pp.], 429-450.

回想鈴木大拙

Nishitani Keiji, ed. Tokyo: Shunjūsha, 1975.

[Includes dozens of reminiscences of Suzuki, including many by Westerners translated into Japanese, with the original source cited at
the end of each piece. Also, 32 pp. of photos.]

* Suzuki Daisetsu shū [400 pp.], 391-398.

Furuta Shōkin, ed. Tokyo: Chikuma Shobō, 1974.

• Seishun no Suzuki Daisetsu [310,6 pp.].

青春の鈴木大拙

By Shimura Takeshi. Tokyo: Kōsei Shuppansha, 1973.

[The opening chapter (pp. 13-59) is a study of Suzuki's early years.
The two other chapters are anthologizes of Suzuki's early work.]

•* Suzuki Daisetsu: Hito to shisō [7,542 pp.], 527-539.

鈴木大拙 ── 人と思想 ──

Hisamatsu Shin'ichi, Yamaguchi Susumu, and Furuta Shōkin, eds.
Tokyo: Iwanami Shoten, 1971.

Σ Suzuki Daisetsu zenshū, vol. 30 (1970), 649-666.

Tokyo: Iwanami Shoten, 1968-71. 32 vols.

[Suzuki's Western-language works are listed separately: vol. 30,
661-666.]

•* Kiyozawa Manshi, Suzuki Daisetsu [509 pp.], 499-503.

清沢満之・鈴木大拙

Hashimoto Mineo, ed. Tokyo: Chūō Kōronsha, 1970.

∃+ The Eastern Buddhist N.S. 2.1 (Aug. 1967), 216-229.

[The entire issue (232 pp.) is devoted to in memoriam notices, articles, and reminiscences about Suzuki.]

∃ Furuta Shōkin, "Daisetz T. Suzuki," in Ibid., 116-123.

The same English-language memoir also appears in the following:

    Japan Quarterly 14.1 (Jan.-March 1967), 82-86.

    Suzuki Gakujutsu Zaidan kenkyū nempō 3 (March 1966), 9-16.

•* Suzuki Daisetsu zuibunki [273 pp.], 270-273.

鈴木大拙随聞記

By Shimura Takeshi. Tokyo: Nihon Hōsō Shuppan Kyōkai, 1967.

●* <u>Suzuki Daisetsu no kotoba to shisō</u> [223 pp.], 220-223.

鈴木大拙の言葉と思想

By Akizuki Ryōmin. Tokyo: Kōdansha, 1967.

[A short outline of Suzuki's thought, including a biography (pp. 1-46).]

∋ Miyamoto Shoson, "In Memoriam Dr. Daisetz T. Suzuki," <u>Indogaku Bukkyōgaku kenkyū</u> 15.2 (March 1967), 987-994.

∋ Joseph M. Kitagawa, "Appreciation of Daisetz Suzuki," <u>Ibid</u>., 9-15.

●* Ōtani gakuhō 46.2 (Sept. 1966), 73-82.

[Bibliography of Suzuki's works appearing in this journal only or having a connection with Ōtani University.]

● Suzuki Gakujutsu Zaidan kenkyū nempō 3 (March 1966), 1-9.

∋* Hanayama Shinsho, <u>Bibliography on Buddhism</u>, 729-731.

The Commemoration Committee for Prof. Shinsho Hanayama's Sixty-first Birthday, ed. Tokyo: Hokuseido Press, 1961.

[Bibliography of Suzuki's Western-language writings only.]

●* <u>Suzuki Daisetsu no hito to gakumon</u> [198 pp.], 189-196.

鈴木大拙の人と学問

Shimomura Toratarō et al., eds. Tokyo: Shunjūsha, 1961; rpt. 1975 and 1981.

[Includes reminiscences of Suzuki by twelve scholars, including one by R.H. Blyth translated into Japanese. There are two bibliographies of Suzuki's works, one of his writings in Japanese and Chinese (pp. 189-192), the other of his writings in English (pp. 193-196).]

ø* Suzuki Daisetsu hakushi shōju kinen rombunshū <u>Bukkyō to bunka</u> [17, 263,266,6 pp.], 6 pp.

仏教と文化

Yamaguchi Susumu, ed. Tokyo: Suzuki Gakujutsu Zaidan, 1960.

[Half of the work is comprised of articles in English by such luminaries as Charles Morris, Erich Fromm, Paul Tillich, Arnold Toynbee, and Walter Gropius. Note the English-language contributions concerning Buddhism by Edward Conze, Christmas Humphreys, and Hu Shih.]

TRNS:oo.

Suzuki Kei   鈴木 敬   Chinese art history, esp. painting.

   Yen 253.

∈ <u>Comprehensive Illustrated Catalog of Chinese Paintings</u>, or <u>Chūgoku</u>

   <u>kaiga sōgō zuroku</u>.

中国絵画総合図録

Compiled by Suzuki Kei. Tokyo: University of Tokyo Press, 1982-83.

5 vols.

     Vol. 1   American and Canadian Collections. 11,484 pp.

     Vol. 2   Southeast Asian and European Collections. 8,377 pp.

     Vol. 3   Japanese Collections: Museums. 6,421 pp.

     Vol. 4   Japanese Collections: Temples and Individuals. 12,654

               pp.

     Vol. 5   Indexes. 2,1,551 pp.

   [English and Japanese texts. Chiefly illustrations.]

ø Suzuki Kei sensei kanreki kinen <u>Chūgoku kaigashi ronshū</u> [7,362,168,

   9,3 pp.]. No biblio.

中国絵画史論集

Suzuki Kei sensei kanreki kinenkai, ed. Tokyo: Yoshikawa Kōbunkan,

1981.

   [Includes English-language articles (168 pp.) by Richard Vinograd,

   Lothar Ledderose, David Sensabaugh, Richard Stanley-Baker, Jon

   Bourassa, and Joan Stanley-Baker. Also includes Chinese-language

   summaries (9 pp.) of all articles.]

   TRNS:oo.

+ Tōyō Bunka Kenkyūjo kiyō (Tōkyō Daigaku) 85 (March 1981), 8 pp.

Suzuki Kiichi   鈴木喜一   Classical Chinese thought and neo-Confucian-
                                                                ism.

   Lit 148.

Suzuki Masao   鈴木正夫   Modern Chinese literature.

   Lit 147, Yen 257.

Suzuki Naoji   鈴木直治   Chinese language, historical grammar, esp. vernacular fiction.

   Lit 147, Yen 258.

  + Kanazawa Daigaku Kyōyōbu ronshū (Jimbun kagaku hen) 13 (1975), 4 pp.

Suzuki Osamu   鈴木 治   East-West historical relations. Asian art history.

   Yen 257.

  + Idem, Yūrashia Tōzai kōshō shi ronkō [6,417,3 pp.], 414-416.
ユーラシア東西交渉史論攷
   Tokyo: Kokusho Kankōkai, 1974.

Suzuki Shūji   鈴木修次   Chinese literature, esp. traditional poetry.
   Lit 144, Yen 255, Teng #612.

Suzuki Shun   鈴木 俊   Chinese institutional history, Six Dynasties and T'ang periods.

   Yen 254, Teng #155.

  • Hōseishi kenkyū 26 (1977), 317-319.

  • Tōhōgaku 51 (Jan. 1976), 157-169.

  ø Suzuki Shun sensei koki kinen Tōyōshi ronsō [27,432 pp.], 10-19.
東洋史論叢
   Suzuki Shun sensei koki kinen Tōyōshi ronsō hensan iinkai, ed.
   Tokyo: Yamakawa Shuppansha, 1975.
   [Note Suzuki's discussion of his fifty years in the field, pp. 415-432.]
   TRNS #109.

  * Chūō Daigaku Bungakubu kiyō 76 (Shigakuka 20) (March 1975), 9-18.

  • Ibid., 1-9.

  ø Suzuki Shun kyōju kanreki kinen Tōyōshi ronsō [14,9,4,782 pp.], 9-14.
東洋史論叢
   Suzuki Shun kyōju kanreki kinenkai, ed. & publ. Tokyo, 1964.
   TRNS #108.

  Also listed under Collected Articles #17.

Suzuki Tadashi   鈴木正   Chinese history, Ming and Ch'ing periods.
    Teng #562.
    Also listed under Nakae Ushikichi.

Suzuki Takeju   鈴木武樹   Early Japanese history. Sino-Japanese histor-
                                              ical relations.
    Yen 256.

Suzuki Takeshi   鈴木健之   Chinese popular literature.
    Lit 146, Yen 258.

Suzuki Takurō   鈴木択郎   Modern Chinese language and literature.
    Yen 257.
- Aichi Daigaku Kokusai Mondai Kenkyūjo kiyō 69 (Aug. 1981), 1-56, and
  70 (Dec. 1981), 139-180.

Suzuki Tomoo   鈴木智夫   Modern Chinese economic history.

Suzuki Torao   鈴木虎雄   Chinese poetry and poetics, traditional.
    Lit 146, Yen 252.
+ Tōhōgaku 52 (July 1976), 162-165.
- Ibid., 143-161.
+ Hyōken Suzuki Torao sensei chojutsu mokuroku.

豹軒鈴木虎雄先生著述目録
    Yoshida-machi kyōiku iinkai, ed.   Yoshida-machi, Nishi Kambara-gun
    (Niigata), 1968.
●* Hyōken Suzuki Torao sensei [4,4,2,1,1,160 pp.], 1 p.

豹軒鈴木虎雄先生
    Yoshida-machi kyōiku iinkai, ed.   Yoshida-machi, Nishi Kambara-gun
    (Niigata), 1968.
    [A volume of reminiscences about Suzuki.]
    Also listed under Kano Naoki.

Suzuki Yoshijirō   鈴木由次郎   Classical Chinese thought, esp. I ching. Neo-
                                              Confucianism.
    Lit 148, Yen 259, Teng #675.

ø Suzuki hakushi koki kinen <u>Tōyōgaku ronsō</u> [698,26 pp.]. No biblio.
東洋学論叢
Suzuki hakushi koki kinen shukugakai, ed. Tokyo: Meitoku Shuppansha,
1972.
[Includes (in the 26-pp. section at the back) one article in English
by L.H. Kwan on the <u>I ching</u> and one in French by Max Kaltenmark on
Taoism.]
TRNS:oo.

Suzuki Yoshikazu 鈴木喜一
    see Suzuki Kiichi.

Tabobashi Kiyoshi 田保橋潔 Korean history. History of Japanese foreign
                                relations. Sino-Japanese relations, Ch'ing
                                period.
  + Tōhōgaku 65 (Jan. 1983), 192-194.
  • Ibid., 168-192.
  Also listed under Collected Articles #7.

Tabohashi Kiyoshi
    see Tabobashi Kiyoshi.

Tachibana Shiraki 橘　樸 Modern Chinese society and economy.
  • Tōa 163 (Jan. 1981), 12-22.
  +• <u>Tachibana Shiraki</u> [406 pp.], 394 (cf. 397-403).
      By Yamamoto Hideo. Tokyo: Chūō Kōronsha, 1977.
      [Note the list of works about Tachibana, pp. 395-396.]
  ∋* Yamamoto Hideo, "Shiraki Tachibana," <u>The Developing Economies</u> 4.3
      (Sept. 1966), 381-403.

Tada Yūkei 多田 裕計 Modern Chinese literature.
    Lit 167.

Tada Kensuke 多田 狷介 Chinese history, thru Six Dynasties period.
    Yen 109.

Tadokoro Gikō
     see Tadokoro Yoshiyuki.

Tadokoro Yoshiyuki 田所 義行   Classical Chinese thought, also neo-Confu-
                                   cianism. Chinese poetry, T'ang period.
                                   Sino-Japanese cultural relations.
     Lit 168, Yen 452, Teng #613.
     + Nihon bungaku (Tōkyō Joshi Daigaku) 22 (March 1964), 99-100.

Taga Akigorō   多賀 秋五郎 Chinese educational history. Chinese genealo-
                                   gy.
     Yen 109, Teng #116.
     ∈ Idem, The History of Education in T'ang China.
         Translated by P.A. Herbert. Osaka: Osaka University Press, 1986.
     ø Taga Akigorō hakushi koki kinen rombunshū Ajia no kyōiku to shakai
         [516 pp.], 5-7.
         アジアの教育と社会
         Isobe Takeo, ed. Tokyo: Fumaidō Shoten, 1983.
         TRNS:oo.
     Also listed under Collected Articles #26 and #32.

Tagawa Seiichi   田川 誠一   Japanese Diet member. Contemporary China.
                                   Sino-Japanese relations.
     Yen 452.

Taguchi Nobuo   田口 暢穂 Chinese poetry, T'ang period.
     Lit 159.

Tai Kokki   戴 国輝   Modern Chinese history, esp. Taiwan. Overseas
                                   Chinese.

Tai Kuo-hui
     see Tai Kokki.

Takabatake   高畠
    see also Takahata.

Takabatake Jō   高畠穣   Modern Chinese literature.
    Lit 158.

Takada Atsushi   高田淳   Chinese thought: classical, Ch'ing, and mod-
                                                 ern periods.

    Lit 153, Yen 141.

Takada Osamu   高田修   Buddhist art history, esp. India.
    Yen 141.
    + Idem, <u>Bukkyō bijutsushi ronkō</u> [493,8,3,1 pp.], 490-493.
       仏教美術史論考
       Tokyo: Chūō Kōron Bijutsu Shuppan, 1969.
    •* Bunka 35.1-2 (Dec. 1971), 77-79.

Takada Shinji   高田真治   Classical Chinese thought.
    Lit 154, Yen 452.
    •* Shibun 80 (Aug. 1976), 1-8.
    ø <u>Takada hakushi koki kinen ronsō</u> [1,4,162 pp.], 2 pp.
       Daitō Bunka Daigaku Kangakkai, ed. & publ. Tokyo, 1963.
       [<u>Daitō Bunka Kangakkai shi</u> #6 (Dec. 1963).]
       TRNS:oo.

Takada Shōji   高田昭二   Modern Chinese literature.
    Lit 154, Yen 143, Teng #635.

Takagi Masakazu   高木正一   Chinese poetry, Six Dynasties and T'ang peri-
                                       ods. Chinese poetics, Six Dynasties period.

    Lit 151, Yen 135, Teng #614.

Takagi Shigetoshi   高木重俊   Chinese poetry, T'ang period.
    Lit 150.

Takagi Takeo   高木健夫   Modern Chinese history.
      Yen 134.

Takagi Tomonosuke   高木友之助   Chinese thought, thru Han period.
      Yen 136.

Takahashi Hitoshi   高橋 均   Chinese language. Classical Chinese thought.
      Yen 138.

Takahashi Kazumi   高橋和巳   Modern Japanese novelist. Chinese literature,
                                    esp. Six Dynasties period.

      Lit 155, Yen 136.

      Σ Takahashi Kazumi zenshū, vol. 20 (1980), 423-425.

         Tokyo: Kawade Shobō Shinsha, 1977-80.   20 vols.

         [Note the list of books and articles on Takahashi, including reviews

         of his works: vol. 20, 426-454.]

      +• Takahashi Kazumi [247 pp.], 240-247.

         No ed.   Tokyo: Kawade Shobō Shinsha, 1980.

         [Consists of articles on Takahashi.]

      * Kokubungaku: Kaishaku to kyōzai no kenkyū 23.1 (Jan. 1978), 93-118.

      • Ibid., 9-92.

      •* Takahashi Kazumi kenkyū [253 pp.], 243-251.

         高橋和巳研究
         Ogawa Kazusuke, ed.   Tokyo: Kyōiku Shuppan Sentaa, 1976.

         [Note the list of books and articles about Takahashi, pp. 219-242.]

      +• Fukashi no ummei, aruiwa Takahashi Kazumi ni tsuite no dampenteki na

         kōsatsu [6,276 pp.], 236-267.

         不果志の運命 あるいは高橋和巳についての断片的な考察
         By Kawanishi Masaaki.   Tokyo: Kōdansha, 1974.

         [Takahashi's works, including his essays, are listed especially

         clearly in bold-face type in this bibliography.   Note also the list-

         ing of additional items related to the writer-scholar, pp. 268-275.]

      Σ Takahashi Kazumi sakuhinshū, vol. 10 (1972), 329-343.

         Tokyo: Kawade Shobō Shinsha, 1969-74.   10 vols.

[Vol. 10, a separate volume (bekkan) entitled Shijin no ummei 詩人の
運命 , is about the late T'ang poet Li Shang-yin.]

+● Takahashi Kazumi ron [352 pp.], 317-352.
高橋和己論
Haniya Yutaka, ed. Tokyo: Kawade Shobō Shinsha, 1972.

●* Takahashi Kazumi o dō toraeru ka [382 pp.], 363-371.
高橋和己をどうとらえるか
Kōchi Sō et al., eds. Tokyo: Haga Shoten, 1972.
[Note the listing of contents of those periodicals having issues
devoted to Takahashi since his death the preceding year, pp. 371-
374.]

* Idem, Ankoku e no shuppatsu [248 pp.], 244-248.
暗黒への出発
Tokyo: Tokuma Shoten, 1971.

● Tateishi Haku volume on Takahashi Kazumi (see Addenda, p. 279).

●* Bungei 10.8 (Aug. 1971), 190-193.
[The entire issue (208 pp.) is devoted to articles on Takahashi.]

●* Ningen to shite 6 (June 1971), 363-382.
[The entire issue (383 pp.) is devoted to articles on Takahashi.
Note the ones on his scholarship, pp. 217-262.]

●* Waseda 7 (Apr. 1968), 57-69.

Takahashi Kiyoshi   高橋清   Chinese literature, Six Dynasties.
    Yen 138.

Takahashi Kumpei   高橋君平   Chinese language and literature.
    Lit 156, Yen 137.

Takahashi Minoru   高橋稔   Chinese literature, Six Dynasties and T'ang-
                                    period fiction.
    Lit 157.

Takahashi Moritaka   高橋盛孝   East Asian ethnology. Paleosiberian (incl.
                                    Gilyak) and Tibetan languages. Chinese leg-
                                    ends.
    Lit 157, Yen 139, Teng #24.

ø Takahashi sensei kanreki kinen <u>Tōyōgaku ronshū</u> [10,2,251,46 pp.],
   6-10.

東洋学論集

Kansai Daigaku Tōzai Gakujutsu Kenkyūjo, ed. & publ. Suita, 1967.

TRNS #119.

Takahashi Shigeki 高橋繁樹 Chinese vernacular fiction and drama, incl.
                                    Yuan-period drama.

   Lit 156.

Takahashi Susumu 高橋進 Classical Chinese thought and neo-Confucian-
                                    ism.

   Lit 156.

Takahashi Yūji 高橋勇治 Modern Chinese history, Sun Yat-sen. Modern
                                    Chinese (constitutional) law. Contemporary
                                    Chinese thought and politics.

   Yen 140, Teng #64.

   + Chiba Daigaku hōkei kenkyū 3 (1974), 163-166.

   + Shakai kagaku kenkyū (Tōkyō Daigaku) 20.5-6 (March 1969), 266-268.

   • Ibid., 247-266.

Takahashi Zentarō 高橋善太郎 Early Sino-Japanese relations. Chinese histo-
                                    ry, T'ang period.

   Yen 139.

   + Aichi Kenritsu Daigaku Bungakubu ronshū (Ippan kyōiku gakuka hen) 30
      (1980), 69-72.

Takahata 高畠
   see also Takabatake.

Takahata Kanga 高畠寛我 Buddhist studies.* Indian Buddhism.

   ø Konishi, Takahata, Maeda san kyōju shōju kinen <u>Tōyōgaku ronsō</u>.

東洋学論叢

Bukkyō Daigaku, ed. Kyoto: Heirakuji Shoten, 1952.

TRNS:oo.

Takahata Tsunenobu 高畑常信 Chinese thought, Sung period, esp. Sung-peri-
                                    od study of Lun-yü.

    Lit 157.

Takakura Katsumi   高倉克巳   Modern Chinese literature.
    Lit 151.

Takakura Shin'ichirō 高倉新一郎 Modern Japanese history, esp. of Hokkaido.
                                    Sino-Japanese historical relations.

    Yen 133.

Takakusu Junjirō   高楠順次郎 Buddhist studies.*

    +• Setchō Takakusu Junjirō no kenkyū: Sono shōgai to jiseki [3,261 pp.],
       165-224.

       雪頂・高楠順次郎の研究 ― その生涯と事蹟 ―
       Musashino Joshi Daigaku Bukkyō Bunka Kenkyūjo, ed.   Tokyo: Daitō
       Shuppansha, 1979.

    Σ Takakusu Junjirō zenshū. No biblio.
       Tokyo: Kyōiku Shinchōsha, 1977-79. 9 vols.

    ∋* Hanayama Shinsho, Bibliography on Buddhism, 735-738.
       The Commemoration Committee for Prof. Shinsho Hanayama's Sixty-first
       Birthday, ed. Tokyo: Hokuseido Press, 1961.

       [Bibliography of Takakusu's Western-language writings only.]

    ∈ Idem, The Essentials of Buddhist Philosophy [221 pp.].
       Edited by Wing-tsit Chan and Charles A. Moore. Honolulu: University
       of Hawaii Press, 3rd ed., 1956;   rpt. Westport, Conn.: Greenwood
       Press, 1973.

    [Additional book-length Western-language works by Takakusu that do not
    deal with China are not listed here.]

Takamatsu Kōmei
    see Takamatsu Takaaki.

Takamatsu Takaaki   高松亨明 Chinese literary theory, Six Dynasties and
                                    T'ang periods.

    Lit 158.

Takamine Ryōshū　　高峯了州　　Buddhist studies.

+　Bukkyōgaku kenkyū 16-17 (Oct. 1959), 2-5.

Takamine Ryūshū

　　see Takamine Ryōshū.

Takamura Shōhei　　高村象平

　　Listed under Nomura Kentarō.

Takao Giken　　　高雄義堅　　Chinese Buddhism.

+　Idem, Sōdai Bukkyōshi no kenkyū [7,1,206,25 pp.], 200-203.

　　宋代仏教史の研究

　　Kyoto: Hyakkaen, 1975.

●　Ryūkoku shidan 66-67 (Dec. 1973), 202-207.

Takase Seiken　　高瀬惺軒

　　see Takase Takejirō.

Takase Takejirō　　高瀬武次郎　Chinese thought.

ø　Takase hakushi kanreki kinen Shinagaku ronsō [3,3,3,853 pp.], 3 pp.

　　支那学論叢

　　Ojima Sukema and Takase hakushi kanreki kinenkai, eds.　Kyoto: Kōbun-

　　dō, 1928.

　　TRNS #117, NNO 3:412-413.

Takashi Masao　　高志真夫　　Chinese literature, Six Dynasties.

　　Lit 151.

Takashima Toshio　　高島俊男　　Chinese vernacular fiction, Ming period. Mod-
　　　　　　　　　　　　　　　　　　　ern Chinese literature.

　　Lit 152, Yen 134.

Takata　　　高田

　　see also Takada.

Takata Shōjirō   NC
     Listed under Ishihara Akira.

Takebe Toshio   武部利男   Chinese poetry, T'ang period, esp. Li Po.
     Lit 166, Yen 481.

Takebe Yoshiaki   武部良明   Modern Chinese language.
     Yen 481.

Takeda Akira   竹田晃   Chinese literature, Six Dynasties period,
                                esp. fiction.
     Lit 166, Yen 642.
     See also Addenda, p. 279.

Takeda Ryōji
     see Takeda Ryūji.

Takeda Ryūji   竹田龍兒   Chinese history, T'ang period. History of
                                South China. Sino-Vietnamese historical
                                relations.
     Yen 642, Teng #533.
     + Shigaku 46.3 (Feb. 1975), 126-128.

Takeda Sakae   竹田復   Chinese literature, pre-T'ang period. Chi-
                                nese lexicography.
     Lit 166, Yen 641.
     • Tōhōgaku 37 (March 1969), 169-192.
     + Kangaku kenkyū (Nihon Daigaku) 2 (March 1964), 4-7.

Takeda Taijun   武田泰淳   Chinese historical texts, Shih-chi. Modern
                                Japanese author who uses Chinese themes.
     Yen 482.

Takeda Yukio   武田幸男   East Asian, esp. Korean, history.
     Yen 483.

Takeji Sadao   竹治 貞夫   Chinese poetry, esp. Ch'u-tz'u. Chinese bib-
                                                liography.

    Lit 165.

Takekoshi Yosaburō 竹越与三郎   Taiwanese history.
    ∈ Idem, Japanese Rule in Formosa [15,342 pp.].
        Translated by George Braithwaite. London: Longmans, Green, and Co.,
        1907; rpt. Taipei: Southern Materials Center, 1978.

Takemura Shōhō   武邑 尚邦   Buddhist studies.*
    + Bukkyōgaku kenkyū 39-40 (Nov. 1984), 3-11.

Takemura Takuichi   竹村 卓一   Contemporary Chinese anthropology, Southern
                                                China.

Takeoka Yatsuo   竹岡 八雄   Classical Chinese thought.
    Yen 635.

Takeshima Takuichi 竹島 卓一   East Asian architectural history.
    Yen 634, Teng #195.
    ∈ Jehol: The Most Glorious and Monumental Relics in Manchoukuo, OR
       Nekka 熱河 . 4 vols., and Supplement.
       By Sekino Tadashi and T. Takeshima. Tokyo: Zauho Press, 1934-37.
       Vols. 1-4: 63, 84, 78, and 74 pp., respectively, with bilingual
       description. Supplement: 1,1,1,9,28 pp. of English text, 1,3,9,229
       pp. of Japanese text, and plates on pp. 231-254.

Takeuchi Hiroyuki   竹内 弘行   Chinese thought, late Ch'ing period. Chinese
                                                historical texts, Shih-chi.

    Lit 160, Yen 637.

Takeuchi Minoru   竹内 実   Modern Chinese history and literature. Chi-
                                                nese vernacular fiction. Contemporary Chi-
                                                na.

    Lit 161, Yen 640.
    + Tōhō gakuhō 60 (March 1988), 733-750.

Takeuchi Rizō   竹内理三   Japanese history, early and medieval periods.
                                       Sino-Japanese historical relations.

   Yen 638, Teng #251.

Takeuchi Teruo   竹内照夫   Classical Chinese thought. Chinese historical
                                       texts, <u>Shih-chi</u> and <u>Tzu-chih t'ung-chien</u>.

   Lit 160, Yen 638, Teng #676.

Takeuchi Yoshimi   竹内 好   Modern Japanese author. Modern Chinese liter-
                                       ature, esp. Lu Hsun.

   Lit 163, Yen 636, Teng #636.

Σ   <u>Takeuchi Yoshimi zenshū</u>, vol. 17 (1982), 175-279.

     Tokyo: Chikuma Shobō, 1980-82.   17 vols.

•   <u>Tsuitō Takeuchi Yoshimi</u> [5,291 pp.].

     Ro Jin tomo no kai, ed. & publ.   Sagamihara (Kanagawa), 1978.

•   Bungaku 45.5 (May 1977), 539-547.

•   Gendai no me 18.5 (May 1977), 146-159.

•   Tembō 221 (May 1977), 14-65.

•* <u>Takeuchi Yoshimi ron</u> [273 pp.], 272.

     竹内好論
     Tokyo: San'ichi Shobō, 1976.

     [Note the bibliography of material about Takeuchi, p. 273.]

+   <u>Gendai Nihon bungaku taikei</u>, vol. 78, 467-470.

     現代日本文学大系
     Tokyo: Chikuma Shobō, 1971.

*   <u>Nihon gendai bungaku zenshū</u>, vol. 93, 437-441.

     日本現代文学全集
     Tokyo: Kōdansha, 1968.

•   Shin Nihon bungaku 22.2 (#235) (Feb. 1967), 85-91.

+• <u>Takeuchi Yoshimi chosaku nōto</u> [197 pp.], 21-191.

     竹内好著作ノート
     Tatsuma Shōsuke, ed.   Tokyo: Tosho Shimbunsha, 1965.

     [Note the list of articles about Takeuchi, pp. 18-19.]

Takeuchi Yoshio   武内義雄   Classical Chinese thought and textual criti-
                                          cism.

    Lit 163, Yen 481.

  Σ Takeuchi Yoshio zenshū, vol. 10 (1979), 479-483.

    Tokyo: Kadokawa Shoten, 1978-79. 10 vols.

  ●* Tōhōgaku 58 (July 1979), 184-206.

  ●* Bunka 30.4 (March 1967), 126-127.

  ● Ibid. 24.4 (Dec. 1960), 128-134.

  + Ibid. 20.6 (Nov. 1956), 107-115.

  ● Kaitoku 37 (Oct. 1966), 73-84.

  ● Shisō (Iwanami Shoten) 375 (Sept. 1955), 86-97.

Takeuchi Yoshirō   竹内芳郎   Modern Chinese literature.
    Yen 635.

Taki Ryōichi   滝 遼一   History of East Asian music.
    Teng #201.

Taki Shigeru   田木 繁   Chinese poetry, T'ang period, Tu Fu.
    Lit 158.

Takigawa Masajirō
    see Takikawa Masajirō.

Takikawa Masajirō 滝川政次郎 Japanese and Chinese legal history.
    Yen 381.

  + Takikawa Masajirō roncho mokuroku.
    Mimeographed. Tokyo?, 1974.

  + Kokugakuin hōgaku 5.2 (Oct. 1967), 222-225.

  ø Takikawa hakushi kanreki kinen rombunshū, vol. 1 [2,13,4,2,255 pp.],
    5-13.

    Ueda (Nagano): Nakazawa Insatsu, 1957. 2 vols.
        Vol. 1   Tōyōshi hen   東洋史篇   2,13,4,2,255 pp.
        Vol. 2   Nihonshi hen   日本史篇   pp. 257-930.
    TRNS #120, NNO 3:413 (vol. 1 only).

Takisawa   滝沢

    see Takizawa.

Takizawa Seiichirō 滝沢 精一郎 Chinese literature, Six Dynasties, incl. T'ao
                                            Ch'ien.

    Lit 158.

Takizawa Toshiaki 滝沢 俊亮 Chinese ethnology. Chinese legends.
    Lit 159.

Takizawa Toshisuke

    see Takizawa Toshiaki.

Tamada Tsuguo   玉田 継雄 Chinese epigraphy.
    Yen 584.

Tamai Korehiro

    see Tamai Zehaku.

Tamai Zehaku   玉井是博 Chinese socio-economic history, esp. T'ang
                                 and Sung periods.

+ Idem, Shina shakai keizai shi kenkyū [1,4,3,618,3 pp.], 4 pp.
    支那社会経済史研究
    Tokyo: Iwanami Shoten, 1942.

* Keijō Teidai Shigakkai shi 18 (March 1942), 1-3.

Tamaki Kōshirō   玉城康四郎 Chinese Buddhism.

    Yen 583.

• Bunka 42.3-4 (March 1979), 76-80.

• Ronshū (Tōhoku Indogaku Shūkyō Gakkai) 5 (Dec. 1978), 1-2.

ø Tamaki hakushi kanreki kinen ronshū Hotoke no kenkyū [21,697 pp.],
    4-17.
    仏の研究
    Tamaki Kōshirō hakushi kanreki kinenkai, ed. Tokyo: Shunjūsha, 1977.

    NNO:oo

Tamori Noboru   田森襄   Chinese poetry, esp. Sung-period tz'u and Yuan-period ch'ü. Chinese vernacular fiction.

    Lit 172, Yen 453.

Tamura Jitsuzō   田村実造   Chinese history, esp. Sung thru Ch'ing periods. Liao dynasty: history, society, language. Manchurian and Mongolian history.

    Yen 450, Teng #547.

    ø   Tamura hakushi shōju   Tōyōshi ronsō   [2,1,716,62 pp.], 4-12.

東洋史論叢

    Tamura hakushi taikan kinen jigyōkai, ed. & publ. Tokyo, 1968.

    [Includes articles in German by W. Fuchs, in French by Haneda Akira and L. Ligetti, and in English by P. Ratchnevsky.]

    TRNS #112.

    Also listed under Collected Articles #39 and #41.

Tamura Shunsuke   田村俊介   Historical geography. East-West historical relations.

    Yen 451.

Tan Kyōji   丹喬二   Chinese history, esp. Sung period.

Tanabe Hisao   田辺尚雄   History of East Asian music.

    Yen 449.

    ø   Tanabe sensei kanreki kinen   Tōa ongaku ronsō   [4,2,1,6,5,1,867,8 pp.], 5 pp.

東亜音楽論叢

    Tanabe sensei kanreki kinenkai, ed. Tokyo: Yamaichi Shobō, 1943.

    TRNS #111, NNO 3:413.

    +   Tōyō ongaku kenkyū 26-29 (July 1971), 121-128.

Tanaka Ari   田中有   History of Chinese language, esp. wood-strip inscriptions, Han period.

    Yen 460.

Tanaka Hakashi   田中佩刀   Classical Chinese thought.
   Lit 171.

Tanaka Hiroshi   田中宏   Overseas Chinese. Modern Chinese language.
                                        Taiwan, Japanese rule.
   Yen 454.

Tanaka Ichimatsu   田中一松   Chinese and Japanese art history, esp. paint-
                                        ing.
   Yen 459, Teng #185.

Tanaka Issei   田仲一成   Chinese drama, Ming and Ch'ing periods. Mod-
                                        ern Chinese thought and literature.
   Lit 169, Yen 460.

Tanaka Junshō   田中順照   Buddhist thought.
   • Mikkyō bunka 64-65 (Oct. 1963), 141-143.

Tanaka Katsumi   田中克巳   Manchurian and Korean history. Chinese histo-
                                        ry, Ch'ing period. Chinese poetry, T'ang
                                        period.
   Lit 169, Yen 455, Teng #156.
   * <u>Nihon no shika</u>, vol. 24, 423-425.
   日本の詩歌
   Tokyo: Chūō Kōronsha, 1976.

Tanaka Kazuo   田中和夫   Chinese literature and language.
   Yen 453.

Tanaka Kenji   田中謙二   Chinese literature, esp. Yuan-period drama
                                        and <u>ch'ü</u>. Chinese historical texts, <u>Shih-
                                        chi</u> and <u>Tzu-chih t'ung-chien</u>.
   Lit 170, Yen 456, Teng #615.
   + Tōhō gakuhō 49 (Feb. 1977), 403-405.

Tanaka Masami   田中正美   Modern Chinese history.

    Yen 457, Teng #581.

ø Chūgoku kin-gendaishi no shomondai Tanaka Masami sensei taikan kinen

    ronshū [17,489 pp.], 1-8.

    中国近現代史の諸問題

    Tanaka Masami sensei taikan kinen ronshū kankōkai, ed. Tokyo: Koku-

    sho Kankōkai, 1984.

    TRNS:oo.

 • Rekishi jinrui (Tsukuba Daigaku) 11 (1983), 1-8.

    Cf. next entry.

Tanaka Masami   田中麻紗巳   Classical Chinese thought.

    Lit 171.

    Cf. preceding entry.

Tanaka Masatoshi   田中正俊   Chinese history, Ming and Ch'ing periods.

                             Chinese economic history.

    Yen 458.

Tanaka Masumi   田仲益見   Modern Chinese language.

    Yen 461.

 + Yokohama Shiritsu Daigaku ronsō (Jimbun kagaku keiretsu) 27.3 (1976),

    155-158.

Tanaka Naokichi   田中直吉   Contemporary international relations, incl.

                             China.

    Yen 459.

Tanaka Suiichirō 田中萃一郎 Chinese history.

 • Shigaku 45.4 (Oct. 1973), 49-61.

 + Ibid. 2.4 (Nov. 1923), 109-128.

 + Idem, Tanaka Suiichirō shigaku rombunshū [4,28,3,685,3 pp.], 28 pp.

    田中萃一郎 史学論文集

    Mita shigakkai, ed. & publ. Tokyo, 1932.

Tanaka Takeo   田中健夫   Korean-Japanese and Sino-Japanese historical
                                      relations, esp. Muromachi period.
    Yen 454.

Tanaka Tamotsu   田中有
    see Tanaka Ari.

Tanaka Toshiaki 田中利明   Chinese literature and thought, traditional.
    Yen 456.
    + Gakudai kokubun (Ōsaka Kyōiku Daigaku) 30 (1987), 7-12.

Tanaka Yoshinosuke 田中克巳
    see Tanaka Katsumi.

Tani Mitsutaka   谷光隆   Chinese history, Ming period.
    Yen 157.
    + Neiraku shien (Nara Joshi Daigaku) 29 (March 1984), 3-4.

Tani Shin'ichi   谷信一   Japanese art history. Chinese art history,
                                      Sung and Yuan periods.
    Yen 158, Teng #186.

Tanida Etsuji   谷田閲次   Chinese art history.
    Yen 159.

Tanigawa Michio 谷川道雄   Chinese history, Six Dynasties and T'ang pe-
                                      riods.
    Yen 158.
    ∈ Idem, <u>Medieval Chinese Society and the Local "Community"</u> [39,141
    pp.].
    Translated, with an introduction, by Joshua A. Fogel. Berkeley:
    University of California Press, 1985.
    ∋ Joshua A. Fogel, "A New Direction in Japanese Sinology," <u>Harvard
    Journal of Asiatic Studies</u> 44.1 (June 1984), 225-247.

[Review article of a volume edited by Tanigawa: <u>Chūgoku shitaifu kaikyū to chiiki shakai to no kankei ni tsuite no sōgōteki kenkyū</u> 中国士大夫階級と地域社会との関係についての総合的研究 ([Kyoto: Kyōto Daigaku Bungakubu] 1983. 141 pp.).]

Taniguchi Kikuo   谷口 規矩雄 Chinese socio-economic history, Ming period.

Taniguchi Tetsuo   谷口 鉄雄 Buddhist art history.
  + Tetsugaku nempō 33 (1974), 4 pp.

Tarumoto Teruo   樽本照雄 Chinese vernacular fiction, Ch'ing period.
    Lit 173.

Tarunaga Hidehiko   垂永英彦 Chinese poetry, T'ang period, esp. Li Shang-
                                                    yin.
    Lit 172.

Tasaka Kōdō   田坂興道 History of Islam in China.
    + Idem, <u>Chūgoku ni okeru Kaikyō no denrai to sono guzū</u>, vol. 1, 9-16.
    中国における回教の伝来とその弘通
       Tokyo: Tōyō Bunko, 1964. 2 vols. 852 pp.; 3 pp., pp. 853-1726, 6
       pp.
       [Note the extensive bibliography on Islam in China: vol. 2, 1688-
       1726, including Western-language works (pp. 1710-1726).]
    + Chūō Daigaku Bungakubu kiyō 14 (Shigakuka 4) (Dec. 1958), 115-121.

Tasaka Okimichi
    see Tasaka Kōdō.

Tateishi Haku   立石 伯   see Addenda, p. 279 (under Takahashi Kazumi).

Tateishi Hiroo   立石 広男   Chinese language, esp. Six Dynasties period.
    Yen 242.

Tatsuma Shōsuke   立間 祥介 Chinese vernacular fiction. Modern Chinese
                                                    literature.
    Lit 167, Yen 242.
    Also listed under Takeuchi Yoshimi.

Tayama Shigeru   田山茂   Mongolian history.
  • Shigaku kenkyū (Hiroshima) 111 (June 1971), 95-97.

Tazaka   田坂
    see Tasaka.

Tazawa Yutaka   田沢坦   Asian art history and archaeology, esp. Ja-
                                        pan.
        Yen 461.

Terada Gō   寺田剛   Chinese history, Sung period, incl. educa-
                                        tional history.
        Yen 414.

Terada Takanobu   寺田隆信   Chinese socio-economic history, esp. Ming
                                        period, incl. trade.
        Yen 415.

Teraji Jun   寺地遵   Chinese history and thought, esp. Ming peri-
                                        od.
        Yen 413.

Teraoka Ryūgan   寺岡龍含   Chinese thought, esp. Chuang-tzu. Tun-huang
                                        texts.
        Yen 414, Teng #677.

Tetsui Yoshinori   鉄井慶紀   Chinese myth and legend.
        Lit 177.

Tezuka Takayoshi   手塚隆義   Chinese and North Asian history.
        Yen 408.

Tezuka Yoshimichi   手塚良道   Classical Chinese thought.
  • Tetsugaku (Hiroshima) 13 (Oct. 1961), 130-134.

Tochio Takeshi   栃尾 武   Chinese bibliography, lei-shu. Chinese legends.

    Lit 180.

Toda Hiroaki   戸田 浩曉

    see Toda Kōgyō.

Toda Kenji   NC   Chinese calligraphy.

    ∈ Chinese Calligraphy [7,70,1 pp.].

       By Lucy Driscoll and Kenji Toda.   Chicago: University of Chicago
       Press, 1935.   2nd ed. (rpt.), New York: Paragon, 1964.

Toda Kōgyō   戸田 浩曉   Chinese poetics, Six Dynasties period, Wen-
hsin tiao-lung.

    Lit 179.

    + Jōnan Kangaku (Risshō Daigaku) 12 (Oct. 1970), 2-4.

Toda Teijō   戸田 貞三   (Sociology.)

    ø Toda Teijō hakushi kanreki shukuga kinen rombunshū Gendai shakaigaku
    no shomondai [2,2,552 pp.].

    現代社会学の諸問題

    Tōkyō Daigaku shakai gakkai, ed.   Tokyo: Kōbundō, 1949.

    TRNS #146, NNO 3:415.

Toda Teisuke   戸田 禎佑   Chinese art history, esp. Sung and Yuan periods.

    Yen 180.

Toda Toyosaburō   戸田 豊三郎   Classical Chinese thought, incl. I-ching.

    Lit 180, Yen 180, Teng #678.

    + Tetsugaku (Hiroshima) 21 (March 1970), 2 pp.

Tōdō Akiyasu   藤堂 明保   History of Chinese language: phonology, grammar, etymology. Chinese lexicography.

    Lit 178, Yen 437, Teng #645.

Togawa Yoshio   戸川芳郎   Chinese literature and thought, esp. Han pe-
                                                          riod.
        Lit 178, Yen 179.

Togawa Yoshirō
        see Togawa Yoshio.

Tōhata Seiichi   東畑精一   Modern and contemporary Chinese political
                                                          economy.
        Yen 105.

Toki Zenmaro   土岐善麿   Japanese literature, poetry. Chinese poetry,
                                                          esp. T'ang period. Sino-Japanese literary
                                                          relations. Chinese lexicography.
        Yen 466.

Tokiwa Daijō   常盤大定   Chinese Buddhism. Buddhist monuments in China.
   • Bukkyōgaku seminaa 8 (Oct. 1968), 62-74.
   ø Tokiwa hakushi kanreki kinen Bukkyō ronsō [5,10,649 pp.], 10 pp.
        仏教論叢
        Tokiwa hakushi kanreki kinenkai, ed. Tokyo: Kōbundō, 1933.
        TRNS #179.
   ∈ Buddhist Monuments in China, OR Shina Bukkyō shiseki 支那佛教
        史蹟   . 5 vols. (text), and 5 vols. (plates).
        By Tokiwa Daijō and Sekino Tei. Tokyo: Bukkyo-Shiseki Kenkyu-Kwai.
        Volumes of text, 1925-28: 194, 206, 216, 201, 243 pp., respectively.
        Volumes of plates, 1931: 150 loose pp. each, with 6-7 pp. of text
        per volume. Reprint (partial?), 1937-38.

Tokiwai Kenjū   常盤井賢十 Classical Chinese thought.
        Teng #679.

Tokuda Noriyuki   德田教之 Comtemporary Chinese politics and political
                                                          thought.
        Yen 100.

Tokuda Takeshi   徳田 武   Sino-Japanese literary relations.
    Yen 101.

Tokunaga Kiyoyuki   徳永 清行   Chinese economics, esp. finance and trade.
    Teng #101.
    + Dōshisha shōgaku 25.4-6 (March 1974), 651-658.

Tominaga Kazutaka   富永 一登   Chinese literature, Six Dynasties and T'ang
                                         periods.
    Lit 181.

Tominaga Makita   富永 牧太   Chinese bibliography.
    Yen 124.

Tomita Kōjirō   NC   Chinese art history.
    ∈ <u>Portfolio of Chinese Paintings in the Museum (Yuan to Ch'ing Peri-</u>
      <u>ods)</u>.
    By Tomita Kojiro and Tseng Hsien-chi. Boston: Museum of Fine Arts,
    1961. 2 bound booklets. 7,30,2 pp. (English text), and 45 pp.
    (Chinese text); and 178 unbound plates.
    ∈ <u>Portfolio of Chinese Paintings in the Museum (Han to Sung Periods)</u>.
    By Tomita Kojiro. Cambridge: Harvard University Press (for the
    Museum of Fine Arts), 1933. 10,21 pp. (English text, bound); 5 pp.
    (Chinese text, unbound); and 143 unbound plates.

Tomoeda Ryūtarō   友枝 龍太郎   Chinese thought, neo-Confucianism.
    Lit 181, Yen 572.
    + Seinan Gakuin Daigaku kokusai bunka ronshū 1.1 (July 1986), 3-10.

Tonami Mamoru   礪波 護   Chinese history, T'ang period.
    Yen 240.

Toppata Shigenao   鳥羽田 重直   Chinese literature, Six Dynasties, esp. fic-
                                           tion.
    Lit 180.

Torii Hisayasu   鳥居久靖   Chinese vernacular fiction. Chinese language.
     Lit 182, Yen 297, Teng #646.

   ø Torii Hisayasu sensei kakō kinen ronshū Chūgoku no gengo to bungaku
      [7,429,251 pp.], 235-251.

      Torii Hisayasu kyōju kakō kinenkai, ed. Nara: Tenri Jihōsha, 1972.
      TRNS #181.

   + Tenri Daigaku gakuhō (Jimbun, shakai, shizen hen) 78 (March 1972), 1-
      18.

Torii Katsuyuki   鳥井克之   Modern Chinese language.
     Yen 298.

Torii Ryūzō   鳥居龍蔵   Asian archaeology and anthropology.

   •* Shiratori Kurakichi: Shinwa ron; Torii Ryūzō: Jinruigaku to kōkogaku
       [471 pp.], 259-450 and 458-466.
       白鳥庫吉ー神話論ー鳥居龍蔵ー人類学と考古学
       By Shiratori Yoshirō (Shiratori Kurakichi section) and Yawata Ichirō
       (Torii Ryūzō section). Tokyo: Kōdansha, 1978.

   Σ Torii Ryūzō zenshū, vol. 13 (1977), 177-222.
      Tokyo: Asahi Shimbunsha, 1975-77. 13 vols.
      [Volume 13 (bekkan) has a general index (pp. 5-176) for the preceding
      12 volumes.]

   + Torii Ryūzō shū, vol. 2, 204-214.
      Tokyo: Tsukiji Shokan, 1974. 2 vols. 4,218 pp., and 4,215 pp.

   • Torii Ryūzō hakushi no omoide [7,196,3 pp.].
      鳥居龍蔵博士の思い出
      Tokushima Kenritsu Torii Ryūzō Hakubutsukan, ed. & publ. Tokushima,
      1970.
      [Torii Kinen Hakubutsukan kiyō #4.]

   + Jinruigaku zasshi 63.3 (Feb. 1954), 103-112.

   ∋* Harada Yoshito, "Torii Ryūzō," Artibus Asiae 16.1-2 (1953), 123.

   ∈ Idem, Sculptured Stone Tombs of the Liao Dynasty [14,134 pp.].
      Peking: Harvard-Yenching Institute (Poplar Island Press), 1942.

∈ Note the following China-related monographs by Torii Ryūzō, published in French in the 1910s by the Journal of the College of Science, Imperial University, University of Tokyo. They are held by Harvard-Yenching Library, where they are cataloged as separate titles. (Original journal issue is given in parentheses.)

> Populations préhistoriques de la manchourie méridionale [80,50 pp.]. 1915 (Vol. 30, article 8).
>
> Les Mandchoux [35,27 pp.]. 1914 (Vol. 36, article 6).
>
> Les Aborigènes de Formose [17,66 pp.]. 1910 (Vol. 28, article 6).

[A book by Torii on the Ainu (in French) and a pamphlet by him on the anthropology of ancient Japan (in English) are not listed here.]

Toriyama Kiichi   鳥山喜一   East Asian history.

+ Idem, Bokkai shijō no shomondai [2,3,352,11 pp.], 345-350.
  渤海史上の諸問題
  Funaki Katsuma, ed. Tokyo: Kazama Shobō, 1968.

+ Hakusan shigaku 4 (1959), 53-58.

+ Chūō Daigaku Bungakubu kiyō 9 (Shigakuka 3) (Sept. 1957), 179-182.

+ Toriyama Kiichi sensei ryaku nempu chosaku mokuroku [1,12 pp.], 7-12.
  Toriyama Matsumoto ryō sensei koki shukuga kinenkai, ed. & publ.
  n.p., 1956.

Toyama Gunji   外山軍治   Chinese history: T'ang, Sung, and esp. Chin periods. Chinese calligraphy and art collecting.

Yen 468, Teng #478.

+ Hyōrin 14 (March 1975), 5-20.

• Ibid., 1-4.

Tōyama Shigeki   遠山茂樹   Japanese history, Meiji period. Modern Chinese history, Sino-Japanese War and World War II.

Yen 589, Teng #308.

Also listed under Collected Articles #52.

Toyofuku Kenji   豊福 健二   Chinese literature, Six Dynasties period.
    Lit 182.

Toyoshima Mutsumi   豊嶋 睦   Classical Chinese thought.
    Lit 182.

Tsuboi Yoshimasa   壺井 義正   Chinese bibliography. Confucianism in Japan.
    Yen 178.

Tsuchiya Shin'ichi   土屋 伸一   Chinese language.
    + Bōei Daigakkō kiyō 26 (March 1973), 13-14.

Tsuda Sōkichi   津田 左右吉 Japanese   history   and   thought.   Chinese
                                            thought.
    Yen 221.
    ∈ Idem, <u>An Inquiry into the Japanese Mind As Mirrored in Literature:</u>
       <u>The Flowering of the Common People Literature</u> [7,332 pp.].
       Translated by Fukumatsu Matsuda. Tokyo: Japan Society for the Promo-
       tion of Science, 1970.
       [Note the prefatory section: Naomi Kurita, "Dr. Sōkichi Tsuda: His
       Life and Work," pp. 1-28.]
    Σ <u>Tsuda Sōkichi zenshū</u>, vol. 28 (1966), 566-590.
       Tokyo: Iwanami Shoten, 1963-66. 28 vols., plus 5 vols. (<u>bekkan</u>).
    • Shikan 63-64 (March 1962), 131-138.
    See also the Stefan Tanaka entry under Shiratori Kurakichi.

Tsuda Yoshirō   津田 芳郎   Chinese socio-economic history, Sung period.

Tsueshita Ryūshi
    see Tsueshita Takayuki.

Tsueshita Takayuki   杖下 隆之   Classical Chinese thought.
    Yen 603, Teng #680.

Tsuge Hideomi   柘植 秀臣   Chinese science and medicine.
    Yen 604.

Tsuge Masanobu   津下 正章   Chinese poetry, Six Dynasties period, T'ao
                                   Ch'ien.
    Lit 175.

Tsujimoto Haruhiko 辻本春彦   Chinese language, phonology.
    Yen 663.
    ø Idachi Yoshitsugu, Tsujimoto Haruhiko ryō kyōju taikan kinen Chūgoku
       gogaku bungaku ronshū [9,4,513,1 pp.]. No biblio.
       中国語学文学論集
       Idachi Yoshitsugu, Tsujimoto Haruhiko ryō kyōju taikan kinen ronshū
       kankōkai, ed.   Tokyo: Tōhō Shoten, 1983.
       TRNS:oo.

Tsukamoto Shunkō   塚本 俊孝   History of Chinese Buddhism.
    Teng #746.

Tsukamoto Terukazu   塚本 照和   Chinese vernacular fiction, Ch'ing period.
                                 Taiwan, literature under Japanese rule.
    Lit 174.

Tsukamoto Zenryū   塚本 善隆   History of Chinese Buddhism.
    Teng #747.
    ∈ Idem, A History of Early Chinese Buddhism: From Its Introduction to
       the Death of Hui-yüan.
       Translated by Leon Hurvitz. Tokyo: Kodansha, 1985. 2 vols. 17,652
       pp., and pp. 657-1305.
    •* Bongu-shō: Tsukamoto Zenryū ibunshū [5,2,2,1,224 pp.], 1 p.
       凡愚抄ー 塚本善隆遺文集ー
       Konishi Teruo, ed. Kyoto: Tsukamoto Kazuko 塚本和子, 1982.
       [Note the material on Tsukamoto, pp. 204-224.]
    + Sankō Bunka Kenkyūjo johō 15 (March 1979), 13-17.
    Σ Tsukamoto Zenryū chosakushū, vol. 7 (1975), 487-498.
       Tokyo: Daitō Shuppansha, 1974-75. 7 vols.

ø   Tsukamoto hakushi shōju kinen <u>Bukkyō shigaku ronshū</u> [13,969,9,96
    pp.], 5-8.

    仏教史学論集

    Tsukamoto hakushi shōju kinenkai, ed. & publ. Tokyo, 1961.

    [Includes one article in French (by P. Demiéville) and two in English
    (by L. Hurwitz and W. Liebenthal).]

    TRNS #143, NNO 3:413-415.

∈   <u>Wei Shou. Treatise on Buddhism and Taoism</u> [1 p. and pp. 25-103].

    Translated by Leon Hurvitz. Kyoto: Jimbunkagaku Kenkyusho, Kyoto
    University, 1956.

    [Subtitle: An English Translation of the Original Chinese Text of
    Wei-shu CXIV and the Japanese Annotation of Tsukamoto Zenryū.]

    [Text in Chinese and English; annotation in English.]

    [Reprinted from Mizuno Seiichi and Nagahiro Toshio (qq.v.), <u>Yün-kang:</u>
    <u>The Buddhist Cave-temples of the Fifth Century A.D. in North China.</u>
    Vol. 16 Supplement.]

Also listed under Mizuno Seiichi and Nagahiro Toshio.

Tsukinowa Tokifusa 月輪 時房 East Asian history and archaeology.
    Yen 592.

Tsukiyama Jisaburō 筑山 治三郎 Chinese history, T'ang period.
    Yen 643.

Tsuneishi Shigeru 常石 茂 Chinese literature, thru Han period. Chinese
                                       vernacular fiction, Ch'ing period.

    Lit 176.

Tsunoda Bun'ei
    see Tsunoda Fumie.

Tsunoda Fumie 角田 文衛 Asian archaeology and anthropology.
    Yen 237, Teng #25.

ø Tsunoda Fumie hakushi koki kinenkai   <u>Kodaigaku sōron</u> [11,2,750

pp.], 739-749.

古代学叢論

Heian Hakubutsukan Kenkyūkai, ed.   Kyoto: Tsunoda Fumie sensei koki

kinen jigyōkai, 1983.

TRNS:oo

Tsuru Haruo   都留春雄   Chinese poetry, Six Dynasties (T'ao Ch'ien)

and T'ang (Wang Wei) periods. Chinese

prose, Ming and Ch'ing periods.

Lit 176, Yen 107.

Tsurumi Naohiro   鶴見 尚弘   Chinese social history, Ming period.

Tsutagawa Yoshihisa 蔦川芳久 Classical Chinese thought.

Lit 175.

Tsutakawa Yoshihisa

see Tsutagawa Yoshihisa.

Tsutsumi Tomekichi 堤 留吉   Chinese poetry, T'ang period, Po Chü-i.

* Kokubungaku kenkyū (Waseda Daigaku) 36 (Oct. 1967), 126-129.

Ubukata Naokichi   幼方直吉   Contemporary China. Contemporary Chinese law.

Yen 572.

Also listed under Niida Noboru.

Uchida Gimpū   内田 吟風   Central Asian history. Chinese history, Six

Dynasties period.

Yen 292, Teng #524.

ø Uchida Gimpū hakushi shōju kinen <u>Tōyōshi ronshū</u> [16,558,2 pp.], 3-

16.

東洋史論集

Uchida Gimpū hakushi shōju kinenkai, ed.   Kyoto: Dōhōsha, 1978.

TRNS:oo.

+● <u>Uchida Gimpū sensei chosaku mokuroku, fu kinen bunshū</u>.
ed.? publ.?, 1971.

Uchida Michio   内田道夫   Chinese fiction. Chinese language, grammar.
                                    Chinese lexicography.
Lit 43, Yen 292, Teng #616.
+ Jimbun gakuhō (Tōkyō Toritsu Daigaku) 140 (March 1980), 5-10.
+ Shūkan Tōyōgaku 29 (June 1973), 1-9.

Uchida Naosaku   内田直作   East Asian economic history. Overseas Chi-
                                    nese, economy and society.
Yen 295, Teng #103.
+ Keizai kenkyū (Seijō Daigaku) 55-56 (1976).

Uchida Ryū   内田龍   Classical Chinese thought.
Lit 45.

Uchida Sennosuke   内田泉之助   Chinese literature, traditional poetry and
                                    T'ang-period fiction.
Lit 43, Yen 293.

Uchida Tomoo   内田智雄   Chinese legal history. Chinese society, fami-
                                    ly system. Chinese religion.
Yen 294, Teng #494.
+ Dōshisha hōgaku 30.1 (#152) (May 1978), 177-182.
Also listed under Hiroike Senkurō.

Uchino Kumaichirō 内野熊一郎 Classical Chinese thought. Chinese stone and
                                    wooden tablets, Han period.
Lit 45, Yen 296, Teng #617.
+ Kangaku kenkyū (Nihon Daigaku) 13-14 (Nov. 1975), 9 pp.
ø Uchino hakushi kanreki kinen <u>Tōyōgaku ronshū</u> [16,487,17 pp.], 1-13.
  東洋学論集
  Kan Gi bunka kenkyūkai, ed. & publ. Tokyo, 1964. {E}

Uchino Tairei   内野台嶺   East Asian thought.

ø Uchino Tairei sensei tsuitō rombunshū [2,166 pp.], 22-28.
   Ko Uchino Tairei sensei tsuitō rombunshū kankōkai, ed. & publ.
   Tokyo, 1954.
   TRNS #027, NNO #:407.

Uchiyama Chinari   内山知也   Chinese literature, T'ang-period fiction.
   Lit 45, Yen 289.

Uchiyama Kanzō   内山完造   Bookstore proprietor in China. Conduit of
                             political-literary information to China.
                             Author of books on Chinese everyday life.

∍ Paul Scott, "Uchiyama Kanzō: A Case Study in Sino-Japanese Interac-
   tion," Sino-Japanese Studies 2.2 (May 1990), 47-56.

•* Uchiyama Kanzō den: Nit-Chū yūkō ni tsukushita idai na shomin [280
   pp.], 279-280.
   内山完造伝 ─ 日中友好につくした偉大な庶民 ─
   By Ozawa Masamoto. Tokyo: Banchō Shobō, 1972.

Uchiyama Masao   内山雅生   Chinese rural society, twentieth century.

Uchiyama Tomoya   内山知也
   see Uchiyama Chinari.

Uchiyama Toshihiko 内山俊彦   Classical Chinese thought.
   Lit 47, Yen 289.

Uda Rei   宇田礼   Modern Chinese literature.
   Lit 43.

Ueda Atsuo   植田渥雄   Modern Chinese literature.
   Lit 41, Yen 608.

Ueda Masaaki   上田正昭   Japanese and Korean history, early period.
                            Sino-Japanese historical relations.

   Yen 377.

Ueda Sanae   上田早苗   Chinese history, Han period.

Ueda Toshio   植田 捷雄   Modern Chinese history, external relations,
                                        incl. Sino-Japanese historical relations.
     Yen 607, Teng #173.

     + Waseda shakai kagaku kenkyū 14 (Feb. 1975), 211-230.

     + Tōyō Bunka Kenkyūjo kiyō (Tōkyō Daigaku) 37 (March 1965), 1-13.

Ueda Yoshibumi
     see Ueda Yoshifumi.

Ueda Yoshifumi   上田 義文   Buddhist studies.*
     Teng #748.

     ●* Nagoya Daigaku Bungakubu kenkyū ronshū 48 (Tetsugaku 16) (March
        1968), 1-4.

Uehara Tadamichi   上原 淳道   Early Chinese history and thought.
     Yen 380.

     Σ Uehara Tadamichi chosakusen. No biblio.
        Uehara Tadamichi o yomu kai, ed. Tokyo: Kenkyū Shuppan, 1980-82. 2
        vols.

     + Jimbun kagakuka kiyō 75 (Tōkyō Daigaku Kyōyō Gakubu) Rekishi to bunka
        14 (Rekishigaku kenkyū hōkoku 18) (March 1982), 191-196.

     ● Ibid., 184-190.

     Also listed under Kaizuka Shigeki.

Ueki Hisayuki   植木久行   Chinese literature, Six Dynasties period.
     Lit 40.

Uemura Kōji   上村 幸次   Chinese literature, Sung and Ming periods,
                                        esp. humor. Chinese language. Chinese bib-
                                        liography.
     Lit 42, Yen 375, Teng #618.

Uemura Rokurō   上村 六郎   East Asian art history: dyeing, weaving, paper making, painting.

     Teng #187.

Uemura Seiji   植村 清二   Central Asian, Mongolian, and Chinese history. Great Wall of China.

     Yen 607, Teng #548.

Ueno Hideo   上野 秀夫   Contemporary Chinese economy.
     Yen 379.

Ueno Hideto   上野 日出刀   Chinese literature, Sung period.
     Lit 42.

Ueno Keiji   上野 惠司   Chinese drama and vernacular fiction. Modern Chinese thought and language.

     Lit 41.

Ueno Kenchi   上野 賢知   Classical Chinese thought, <u>Tso chuan</u>.
     Lit 41.

Ueno Kōshi   上野 昂志   Modern Chinese literature.
     Lit 42.

Ueno Masatomo   上野 賢知
     see Ueno Kenchi.

Ueno Teruo   上野 照夫   Indian and Chinese art history.
     Yen 378, Teng #761.
      +   Bukkyō geijutsu 106 (March 1976), 58-63.

Ueyama Shumpei   上山 春平   East Asian thought. Modern Asian history.
     Yen 377.

Ui Hakuju   宇井 伯寿   Buddhist studies.

    Yen 577.

+ Idem, <u>Indo tetsugaku kara Bukkyō e</u> [3,566 pp.], 517-544.

インド哲学から仏教へ

Tokyo: Iwanami Shoten, 1976.

[Note the short biography of Ui on pp. 505-511, the <u>in memoriam</u>
pieces for him on pp. 545-560, and the assessment of his work on pp.
560-564.]

Σ <u>Ui Hakuju chosaku senshū</u>. No biblio.

Tokyo: Daitō, 1966-68. 8 vols.

+ Shindō (Nagoya) 24.11 (1968).

• Indogaku Bukkyōgaku kenkyū 16.2 (March 1968), 412-416.

+• Ajia Afurika bunken chōsa hōkoku 86 (Gengo shūkyō 13) (1964), 2,39
pp.

ø Ui Hakuju hakushi kanreki kinen rombunshū <u>Indo tetsugaku to Bukkyō
no shomondai</u> [563 pp.]. No biblio.

印度哲学と仏教の諸問題

Miyamoto Shōson et al., eds. Tokyo: Iwanami Shoten, 1951.

TRNS #022, NNO 3:406-407.

Ukita Kazutami   浮田和民   (Western history.)

ø Ukita Kazutami hakushi kinen <u>Shigaku rombunshū</u> [4,4,2,649 pp.].

史学論文集

Waseda Daigaku shigakkai, ed. Tokyo: Rokkō Shobo, 1943.

TRNS #026, NNO 3:407.

Umebara   梅原

    see Umehara.

Umehara Kaoru   梅原 郁   Chinese history, Sung and Yuan periods, ad-
                                     ministration and society. Chinese bibliog-
                                     raphy.

    Yen 271.

∋ Patricia Ebrey, Review article, "The Dynamics of Elite Domination in
Sung China," <u>Harvard Journal of Asiatic Studies</u> 48.2 (Dec. 1988, 493-
519.

[Umehara's <u>Sōdai kanryō seido kenkyū</u> 宋代官僚制度研究 (Kyoto:
Dōhōsha, 1985. 24,643 pp.) is one of five works reviewed.]

Umehara Sueji   梅原 末治 Asian archaeology.
  Yen 270, Teng #14.

• Nihon rekishi 311 (Apr. 1974), 52-53.

+• Idem, <u>Kōkogaku rokujūnen</u> [3,2,342 pp.], 237-342.
      考古学六十年
    Tokyo: Heibonsha, 1973.

•* Tōhōgaku 38 (Aug. 1969), 135-161.

+ <u>Umehara Sueji chosaku mokuroku tsuiho</u> [7,1 pp.], 7 pp.
    Kyōto Daigaku Kōkogaku Kenkyūshitsu, ed. & publ. Kyoto, 1963.
    [A supplement to the following entry.]

+ <u>Umehara Sueji chosaku mokuroku</u> [4,74,13 pp.], 74 pp.
    Kyōto Daigaku Kōkogaku Kenkyūshitsu, ed. & publ. Kyoto, 1956.
    [Note the subject index at the back. China is pp. 9-10, but addi-
    tional China entries are found under subject headings: e.g. under
    "mirrors" on pp. 11-12.]

∋* Charles C.S. Gardner and Ching-ying Lee Mei (Mrs. Kuang-ti Mei),
    "Umehara Sueji," <u>Bibliographies of Fourteen Non-American Specialists</u>
    <u>on the Far East</u>. Mimeographed. Cambridge, Mass., 1960 [separate
    pagination for each entry], 2 pp.

Umehara Takeshi   梅原 猛   Buddhist studies.* Japanese thought. Sino-
                                Japanese historical relations.
  Yen 269.

Umemoto Katsumi   梅本 克巳 Chinese thought and politics.
  Yen 268.

Umemoto Sutezō   楳本 捨三 Modern Chinese history, incl. Manchuria.
  Yen 272.

Umene Satoru   梅根 悟   East Asian educational history.
        Yen 268.

Unno Kazutaka   海野一隆   Chinese historical geography.
        + Kenkyū shūroku (Jimbun, shakai kagaku) (Ōsaka Daigaku) 33 (Jan.
           1985), 83-89.

Unno Taitetsu   NC
        Listed under Yūki Reimon.

Uno Seiichi   宇野 精一   Classical Chinese thought.
        Lit 47, Yen 578, Teng #681.
        Σ <u>Uno Seiichi chosakushū</u>, vol. 1 (1986), 474-510.
           Tokyo: Meiji Shoin, 1986-90. 6 vols.
        + Tōkyō Shinagaku hō 16 (1971), 16-30.

Uno Shigeaki   宇野重昭   Contemporary Chinese politics and history,
                                          the military.
        Yen 581.

Uno Tetsujin
        see Uno Tetsuto.

Uno Tetsuto   宇野哲人   Classical Chinese thought and neo-Confucian-
                                          ism.
        Lit 48, Yen 580.
        ∋ Joshua A. Fogel, "Confucian Pilgrim: Uno Tetsuto's Travels in China,
           1906," in Joshua A. Fogel and Irene Bloom, eds., <u>Varieties of Neo-</u>
           <u>Confucian Experience: Essays in Honor of Professors Wm. Theodore</u>
           <u>de Bary and Wing-tsit Chan</u>, forthcoming.
        ⌀ Uno Tetsuto sensei hakuju shukuga kinen <u>Tōyōgaku ronsō</u> [21,2,8,
           1339,3,2,4 pp.], 21 pp.
           東洋学論叢
           Uno Tetsuto sensei hakuju shukuga kinenkai, ed. & publ. Tokyo, 1974.
           TRNS #025.

+ Idem, <u>Hitosuji no michi hyakunen</u> [316,3 pp.], 307-316.

一筋の道百年

Tokyo: Shūeisha, 1974.

• Chūtetsubun Gakkai hō 1 (Oct. 1974), 1-4.

• Tōyō bunka (Nagoya) 19 (Oct. 1974), 7-23.

* Shibun 77 (Sept. 1974), 2-4

• Ibid. 34 (Sept. 1962), 51-72.

• **Tōhōgaku 48 (July 1974), 145-163.**

+ Ibid. 24 (Sept. 1962), 139-145.

• Ibid. 24 (Sept. 1962), 115-138.

ø Uno Tetsuto hakushi beiju kinen ronshū <u>Chūgoku no shisōka</u>, vol. 2

(1965), 849-860.

中国の思想家

Tōkyō Daigaku Bungakubu Chūgoku Tetsugaku Kenkyūshitsu, ed. Tokyo:

Keisō Shobō. 2 vols. Vol. 1 (1963), 435 pp.; vol. 2 (1965), pp.

437-864.

[Consists of short chapters outlining the thought of many famous

Chinese "thinkers" from the pre-Han period until the early twentieth

century: e.g., Yang Hsiung (53 B.C.-A.D. 18), Cheng Hsuan (127-200),

Liu Tsung-yuan (773-819), Lu Chiu-yuan (1139-1192), and Ch'en Tu-hsiu

(1879-1942).]

TRNS:oo.

Ura Ren'ichi   浦 廉一   Sino-Japanese relations, Ch'ing period.

  + Shigaku kenkyū (Hiroshima) 72 (Apr. 1959), 1-3.

  • Ibid., 82-85.

Ushijima Tokuji   牛島 徳次   Chinese language, grammar.

    Lit 42, Yen 299.

Ushioda Fukizō   潮田富貴蔵 Chinese historical geography, Han period.

    Teng #514.

Usui Katsumi   臼井 勝美   Modern Sino-Japanese historical relations.

    Yen 231.

Utsugi Akira   宇都木章   Chinese history, pre-Han period.
     Yen 577.

Utsunomiya Kiyokichi
     see Utsunomiya Kiyoyoshi.

Utsunomiya Kiyoyoshi 宇都宮清吉 Chinese history, esp. socio-economic history,
                              Han and Six Dynasties periods.
     Lit 47, Yen 576, Teng #515 and #785.
     ∅ Nagoya Daigaku Bungakubu nijisshūnen kinen ronshū [2,2,6,808,2 pp.],
        1-4.
        名古屋大学文学部二十周年記念論集
        Nagoya Daigaku Bungakubu, ed. & publ. Nagoya, 1969.
        TRNS #183.

Utsunomiya Tokuma   宇都宮徳馬 Japanese Diet member. Contemporary China.
                              Contemporary Sino-Japanese relations.
     Yen 575.

Utsuo Masanobu   撫尾正信   History of Chinese Buddhism, esp. Six Dynas-
                              ties period.
     Teng #749.

Wada Hironori   和田博徳   Chinese historical relations with Manchuria,
                              Japan, and Southeast Asia, incl. Vietnam.
     Yen 168, Teng #157.

Wada Hisanori   和田久徳   Southeast Asian history. Overseas Chinese.
                              Indian history, medieval period.
     Yen 168, Teng #158.
     + Ochanomizu shigaku 26-27 (1983), 6-12.

Wada Sei   和田清   Chinese, Mongolian, and Manchurian history.
     Yen 169, Teng #159.
     • Tōhōgaku 56 (July 1978), 144-171.
     • Ibid. 27 (Feb. 1964), 137-154.

- Shigaku zasshi 72.10 (Oct. 1963), 113-115.

- Tōyō gakuhō 46.1 (June 1963), 143-149.

ø Ishida, Wada, Ryō, Yamanaka yon sensei shōju kinen Shigaku rombunshū
   [41,585 pp.], 13-26.

   石田・和田・龍・山中四先生頌寿記念　史学論文集

   Shōju kinen rombunshū kankō iinkai, ed. Tokyo: Nihon Daigaku Shigakkai Shōju Kinen Rombunshū Kankō Iinkai, 1962.

   TRNS #015

ø Wada hakushi koki kinen Tōyōshi ronsō [48,1076,54 pp.], 19-34.

   東洋史論叢

   Wada hakushi koki kinen Tōyōshi ronsō hensan iinkai, ed.   Tokyo:
   Kōdansha, 1961. {E}

   TRNS #254, NNO 3:421-422.

∋+ Enoki Kazuo, "Writings of Dr. Sei WADA," Memoirs of the Research
   Department of the Toyo Bunko 19 (1960), 3-19.

∋ Enoki Kazuo, "Dr. Sei WADA," Ibid., 1-2.

ø Wada hakushi kanreki kinen Tōyōshi ronsō [45,806,71 pp.], 18-30.

   東洋史論叢

   Wada hakushi kanreki kinen Tōyōshi ronsō hensan iinkai, ed.   Tokyo:
   Kōdansha, 1951.

   TRNS #253, NNO 3:420-421.

Also listed under Iwasa Seiichirō and Collected Articles #30.

Wada Toshio   和田利男   Chinese literature, T'ang period.
   Lit 287, Teng #619.

Wakamori Tarō   和歌森太郎   Ethnology and social history, esp. Japan.
   Yen 167, Teng #231.

Wakatsuki Toshihide 若槻　俊秀   Chinese thought, incl. Buddhism, Six Dynas-
                                         ties period.
   Lit 287.

Watanabe Hiroshi   渡辺 浩   Japanese thought, incl. neo-Confucianism.
                                    East Asian political thought.

  ∋ Bob Tadashi Wakabayashi, "Early-Modern Japanese Confucianism: The
    Gyōza-Manjū Controversy," Sino-Japanese Studies Newsletter 1.1 (Nov.
    1988), 10-23.

    [Review article on Watanabe's study, Kinsei Nihon shakai to Sōgaku
    近世日本社会と宋学   (Tokyo: Tōkyō Daigaku Shuppankai, 1985.
    8,252 pp.]

Watanabe Hiroyoshi 渡辺 紘良 Chinese history, Sung period.

Watanabe Kaigyoku   渡辺 海旭 Buddhist studies.*

  ∋* Hanayama Shinsho, Bibliography on Buddhism, 795.
    The Commemoration Committee for Prof. Shinsho Hanayama's Sixty-first
    Birthday, ed. Tokyo: Hokuseido Press, 1961.
    [Bibliography of Watanabe's Western-language writings only.]

  Σ* Kogetsu zenshū, vol. 1, 753-754.
    壺月全集
    Kogetsu zenshū kankōkai, ed. & publ. Tokyo, 1933. 2 vols.
    [Bibliography of Watanabe's Western-language writings only.]

Watanabe Kaikyoku
    see Watanabe Kaigyoku.

Watanabe Kogetsu.
    see Watanabe Kaigyoku.

Watanabe Kuntarō   渡辺 薫太郎
    see Watanabe Shigetarō.

Watanabe Mitsuo   渡辺 三郎 Japanese and Chinese language.

  ø* Watanabe Mitsuo hakushi koki kinen Nit-Chū gobun kōshōshi ronsō
    [899 pp.], 885-896.
    日本語文交渉史論叢
    Watanabe Mitsuo hakushi koki kinen rombunshū kankōkai, ed. Tokyo:

Ōfūsha, 1979.

TRNS:oo.

Watanabe Ryūsaku 渡辺 龍策 Chinese law. Modern Chinese history, incl. 1911 Revolution. Sino-Japanese historical relations. Japanese constitution.

Yen 108.

+ Chūkyō Daigaku kyōiku ronsō 16.1 (1975).

Watanabe Shigetarō 渡辺薫太郎 Manchurian and Mongolian languages.

+ Tōyōshi kenkyū 2.1 (Sept.-Oct. 1936), 92-94.

Watanabe Shōkō 渡辺 照宏 Buddhist studies.* Indian Buddhism.

Yen 108.

Watanabe Suguru

see Watanabe Takashi.

Watanabe Takashi 渡辺 卓 Classical Chinese thought.

Lit 288, Yen 107, Teng #682.

+ Idem, <u>Kodai Chūgoku shisō no kenkyū</u> [7,839,20,4 pp.], 837-839.

古代中国思想の研究
Tokyo: Sōbunsha, 1973.

Yabuki Keiki 矢吹慶輝 Buddhist studies.

+ Taishō Daigaku gakuhō 30-31 (March 1940), 574-581.

• Ibid., 1-5 and 569-573.

+ Shūkyō kenkyū 1.2 (#100) (Sept. 1939), 416-421.

• Ibid., 393-416.

+ Bukkyō kenkyū 3.5 (1939), 114-116.

Yabuki Susumu 矢吹 晋 Contemporary Chinese politics and economy.

Yen 401.

Yabuuchi Kiyoshi 藪内 清   History of science in Asia, esp. China.
    Yen 431, Teng #203.

* Chung-kuo k'o-chi shih liao (Peking) 3 (Aug. 1983), 26-30.

* K'o-hsueh-shih i-ts'ung (Hu-ho-hao-t'e, Inner Mongolia) 8 (March
    1983), 22.
    [Bibliography of Yabuuchi's works published in the 1970s.]

ø Tōyō no kagaku to gijutsu Yabuuchi Kiyoshi sensei shōju kinen rom-
    bunshū [20,449 pp.], 5-16.
    東洋の科学と技術
    Yabuuchi Kiyoshi sensei shōju kinen rombunshū shuppan iinkai, ed.
    Kyoto: Dōhōsha, 1982.
    TRNS:oo.

∋ Anon., "The 1972 George Sarton Medal Awarded to Kiyosi Yabuuti," Isis
    64.1 (#221) (March 1973), 103-104.

+ Tōhō gakuhō 41 (March 1970), 763-765.
    Also listed under Collected Articles #69 and #71.

Yagi Sōsaburō
    see Yagi Sōzaburō.

Yagi Sōzaburō   八木奘三郎 Archaeology: general, Japan, and China.
    + Shokō (Mantetsu) 78 (Dec. 1935), 1-2.

Yagimoto Minoru   柳本 実   Classical Chinese thought.
    Lit 265, Yen 261.

Yagisawa Hajime   八木沢 元   Chinese fiction, Six Dynasties and T'ang pe-
                                riods. Chinese drama, esp. Ming period.
    Lit 264, Yen 14.

Yahagi Take   矢作 武   Sino-Japanese literary relations. Chinese
                                literature, Six Dynasties period. Shih-shuo
                                hsin-yü.
    Yen 402.

Yahata   八幡
    see Yawata.

Yajima Genryō   矢島 玄亮   Chinese thought. Chinese and Japanese bibli-
                                          ography.

   + <u>Yajima Genryō jokyōju chosaku mokuroku</u>.
     Tōhoku Daigaku Kinen Shiryōshitsu, ed.? & publ. Sendai, 1967.

Yajima Suketoshi 矢島祐利
    Listed under Mikami Yoshio.

Yajima Tetsusuke 矢嶋 徹輔   Chinese literature, Six Dynasties period.
    Lit 265.

Yamada Hideo   山田 英雄   Chinese poetry, Six Dynasties period.
    Lit 272.

Yamada Katsuhisa 山田 勝久   Chinese literature, Six Dynasties and T'ang
                                        periods.
    Lit 269.

Yamada Katsumi   山田 勝美   Classical Chinese thought. Han-period writ-
                                 ings: <u>Yen-t'ieh lun</u> and <u>Lun-heng</u>. Chinese
                                 language, etymology.
    Lit 270, Yen 367.
   + Kokubungaku ronshū (Jōchi Daigaku) 12 (1979).

Yamada Keiji   山田 慶児   History of Chinese science. Modern and con-
                                 temporary Chinese history.
    Yen 366.

Yamada Keizō   山田 敬三   Modern Chinese literature.
    Lit 270, Yen 365.

Yamada Kentarō   山田憲太郎 History of spices and perfumes. East-West
                                historical relations, incl. trade via
                                Southeast Asia.

  ∋ Lin Tien Wai, Review of Yamada's study of the history of perfumery
     and spices in East Asia: <u>Tōa kōryō shi kenkyū</u> 東亜香料史研究
     (Tokyo: Chūō Kōron Bijutsu Shuppan, 1976. 497,11,1,4,1 pp. [incl. 4-
     pp. English summary], in <u>T'oung Pao</u> 64 (1978), 268-277.

  + Nagoya Gakuin Daigaku ronshū (Sangyō Kagaku Kenkyūjo) 11 (1967), 9
     pp.

  ∋ Edward H. Schafer, Review of Yamada's history of aromatics East and
     West, <u>Tōzai kōyaku shi</u> 東西香薬史 (Tokyo: Fukumura Shoten,
     1956. 21,513 pp. [2nd ed., 1957?]), in <u>Journal of the American Orien-
     tal Society</u> 77.4 (Oct.-Dec. 1957), 288.

Yamada Kiyoto   山田清人 Education, incl. China.
     Yen 366.

Yamada Nakaba   NC   Japanese history, Mongol invasions.
  ∈ Idem, <u>Ghenkō: The Mongol Invasion of Japan</u> [22,1,277 pp.].
     Introduction by Lord Armstrong. London: Smith, Elder & Co., 1916.

Yamada Nobuo   山田信夫 Central Asian, Mongolian, and Chinese histo-
                                ry.
     Yen 369, Teng #160.

  + <u>Yamada Nobuo sensei ryaku nempu roncho kōen nado mokuroku</u> [28 pp.],
     6-26.
     Yamada Nobuo kyōju taikan kinen jigyōkai, ed. & publ. Osaka, 1983.

Yamada Norio   山田野理夫 Modern Chinese literature.
     Lit 272.

Yamada Ryōken   山田亮賢 Chinese Buddhism.
     Teng #750.

Yamada Ryūjō   山田 龍城   Buddhist studies.* Indian Buddhism.

    Teng #762.

    +   Bunka 20.4 (July 1956), 724-727.

Yamada Sumeru   山田 統   Classical Chinese thought.

    Lit 271, Yen 368.

    Σ   Yamada Sumeru chosakushū.

        Tokyo: Meiji Shoin, 1981-82. 4 vols.

        [Note the bibliographies of Yamada's work: vol. 1, 415-418; vol. 2,
        473-476;   vol. 3, 411-414;   and vol. 4, 433-436.   Note also the
        supplementary material on Yamada: vol. 1, 14 pp., and vol. 4, 417-
        431.]

Yamada Taku   山田 琢   Classical Chinese thought.

    Lit 271, Yen 369, Teng #683.

    +   Kanazawa Daigaku Kyōyōbu ronshū (Jimbun kagaku hen) 13 (1975), 4 pp.

Yamada Toshiaki   山田 利明   Chinese thought, Taoism, Six Dynasties and
                                              T'ang periods.

    Lit 272.

Yamagishi Tokuhei   山岸 德平   Japanese literature, medieval period. Sino-
                                      Japanese literary relations. Chinese lan-
                                      guage.

    Yen 350.

Yamagiwa Akira   山極 晃   Contemporary China. International relations,
                                        China.

    Yen 359.

Yamaguchi Ichirō   山口 一郎   Modern Chinese thought. Modern Sino-Japanese
                                      relations.

    Lit 267, Yen 362, Teng #704.

Yamaguchi Kakutaka　山口角鷹   Sino-Japanese literary relations. History of
                                       the Chinese language.
       Yen 360, Teng #647.

Yamaguchi Kazuko　　山口和子   Modern Chinese language.
       Yen 360.

Yamaguchi Kōsaku　　山口光朔   Japanese history. East Asian thought.
       Yen 359.

Yamaguchi Osamu　　山口修   Manchurian and Mongolian history.
       Teng #549.

Yamaguchi Susumu　　山口益   Buddhist studies.*
       Yen 361, Teng #751.

       ∋ Paul Demiéville, "Yamaguchi Susumu (1895-1976), Nécrologie," Journal
          asiatique 265 (1977), 15-16.

       + Suzuki Gakujutsu Zaidan kenkyū nempō 14 (Oct. 1977), 119-125.

       • Tōhōgaku 54 (July 1977), 181-182.

       + Ōtani gakuhō 57.1 (June 1977), 80-88.

       • Bukkyōgaku seminaa 24 (Oct. 1976), 95.

       ø Yamaguchi hakushi kanreki kinen Indogaku Bukkyōgaku ronsō [290,164
          pp.], 11-14.

          印度学仏教学論叢
          Yamaguchi hakushi kanreki kinenkai, ed. Kyoto: Hōzōkan, 1955.

          TRNS #238.

       Also listed twice under Suzuki Daisetsu.

Yamaguchi Tamehiro 山口為広   Chinese literature, Six Dynasties period.
       Lit 267.

Yamaguchi Yoshio　　山口義男   Classical Chinese thought, also neo-Confuc-
                                       ianism. Chinese bibliography.
       Yen 363, Teng #684.

Yamaguchi Zuihō　　山口 瑞鳳　　Tibetan studies. Sino-Tibetan languages.
　　Yen 361.

　　　• Hsi-tsang yen-chiu (Ch'eng-tu) 1986.1 (#17), 100-103.

Yamamoto Hideo　　山本 秀夫　　Modern Chinese agrarian economy and society.
　　Yen 354.
　　Also listed twice under Tachibana Shiraki.

Yamamoto Iwao　　山本 嚴　　Classical Chinese thought.

Yamamoto Kazuyoshi　山本 和義　　Chinese poetry, esp. Sung period, Su Shih.
　　Lit 275.

Yamamoto Kengo　　山本 謙吾　　Linguistics. Manchurian language.
　　Yen 353.

Yamamoto Kenkichi　山本 健吉　　Sino-Japanese literary relations.
　　Yen 352.

Yamamoto Mamoru　　山本 守　　Manchurian and Mongolian history.
　　Teng #501.

Yamamoto Noboru　　山本 登　　Asian economy.
　　Yen 354.

Yamamoto Noritsuna　山本 紀綱　Modern Japanese, Chinese, and Korean history.
　　Yen 352.

Yamamoto Sumiko　　山本 澄子　Modern Chinese history. Religion in China,
　　　　　　　　　　　　　　　　　Christianity.
　　Yen 355.
　　Also listed under Intro., Footnote 4.

Yamamoto Takayoshi　山本 隆義　Chinese history, T'ang thru Ming periods.
　　Teng #479.

Yamamoto Tatsurō   山本 達郎   Sino-Vietnamese historical relations. South-
                                east Asian history. Tun-huang manuscripts.
    Yen 351, Teng #161.

    • Ajia bunka kenkyū (Asian Cultural Studies) 13 (Nov. 1981), 3-32.

    ø Yamamoto Tatsurō hakushi koki kinen <u>Tōnan Ajia Indo no shakai to</u>
       <u>bunka</u>, vol. 1, 28-51.

       東南アジア・インドの社会と文化

       Yamamoto Tatsurō hakushi koki kinen ronsō henshū iinkai, ed. Tokyo:
       Yamakawa Shuppansha, 1980. 2 vols. 65,1,508,5 pp., and 5,1,510,4
       pp.

       [Note the roundtable discussion with Yamamoto about his scholarship:
       vol. 2, 459-510.]

       TRNS:oo.

    ø Yamamoto hakushi kanreki kinen <u>Tōyōshi ronsō</u> [21,526,5 pp.]. No
       biblio.

       東洋史論叢

       Yamamoto hakushi kanreki kinen Tōyōshi ronsō hensan iinkai, ed.
       Tokyo: Yamakawa Shuppansha, 1972.

       TRNS #241.

    Also listed under Collected Articles #6.

Yamamoto Tetsuya   山本 哲也   Chinese vernacular fiction.
    Yen 356.

Yamamuro Mitsuyoshi
    see Yamamuro Saburō.

Yamamuro Saburō   山室三良   Classical Chinese thought and neo-Confucian-
                              ism.
    Lit 274, Teng #685.

    + Tetsugaku nempō 28 (1969), 4 pp.

Yamana Masataka   山名正孝   Contemporary Chinese economics and politics.
    Yen 363.

    + Shōdai ronshū (Kōbe Shōka Daigaku) 24.1-3 (June 1972), 1-4.

    • Ibid., 270-280.

Yamane Mitsuyoshi　山根三芳　Chinese thought, neo-Confucianism.
    Lit 273, Yen 357.

Yamane Miyoshi
    see Yamane Mitsuyoshi.

Yamane Yukio　　　山根幸夫　Chinese socio-economic history, esp. Ming and
                             Ch'ing periods, incl. tax system. Chinese
                             bibliography.　Modern　Sino-Japanese　rela-
                             tions.

    Yen 356, Teng #563.

    ∈　Markets in China during the Sung, Ming, and Ch'ing Periods [2,1,1,2,
       142 pp.].

       By Shiba Yoshinori (sic) and Yamane Yukio.　Translated by Wake A.
       Fujioka and Matsuda Mitsugu.　Honolulu: East-West Center, University
       of Hawaii (Institute of Advanced Projects, East-West Center, Transla-
       tions Series #23), 1967.

       [The Yamane section in the volume (pp. 109-142) is entitled "Periodic
       Markets in North China during the Ming and Ch'ing Periods."]

Yamanoi Yū　　　　山ノ井　山井湧　Chinese thought, Sung thru early Ch'ing peri-
                               ods.

    Lit 273, Yen 358.

    +　Chūtetsubun Gakkai hō 6 (1981), 45-50.

Yamanouchi　　　　山内
    see also Yamauchi.

Yamanouchi Kazuo　山内一男　Contemporary Chinese economy.
    Yen 364.
    +　Keizai shirin (Hōsei Daigaku) 33.3-4 (March 1986), 87-97.

Yamanouchi Masahiko 山之内正彦　Chinese poetry, T'ang period.
    Lit 274.

Yamaoka Riichi   山岡利一   Classical Chinese thought. Chinese litera-
                                      ture, Ch'ing period.
     Lit 267.

Yamashita Minoru   山下実   Classical Chinese thought.
     Lit 268.

Yamashita Ryūji   山下龍二   Chinese thought, esp. Ming period.
     Lit 269, Yen 370.
     + Nagoya Daigaku Bungakubu kenkyū ronshū 102 (1988), 1-5.

Yamashita Ryūzō   山下龍三   Contemporary Chinese politics and economy.
                                      Modern Chinese history, 1930s and 1940s.
     Yen 371.

Yamashita Toraji   山下寅次   Asian history.
     ∅ Yamashita sensei kanreki kinen Tōyōshi rombunshū [3,12,8,4,2,18,824
       pp.], 12 pp.
       東洋史論文集
       Kikeikai, ed. Tokyo: Rokumeikan, 1938.
       TRNS #240, NNO 3:420.

Yamauchi   山内
     see also Yamanouchi.

Yamauchi Haruo   山内春夫   Chinese poetry, T'ang period.
     Lit 266.

Yamauchi Masahiro   山内正博   Chinese history, Sung period. Chinese bibli-
                                      ography.

Yamazaki Hiroshi   山崎宏   History of Chinese Buddhism. East Asian his-
                                      tory.
     Yen 365, Teng #534.
     • Risshō Daigaku Bungakubu ronsō 56 (Sept. 1976), 15-18.

ø   Yamazaki sensei taikan kinen Tōyōshigaku ronshū [18,3,4,541 pp.],
     9-18.

     東洋史学論集

     Yamazaki sensei taikan kinenkai, ed. & publ. Tokyo, 1967.

        TRNS #106.

     Also listed twice under Collected Articles #82.

Yamazaki Jun'ichi   山崎 純一   Traditional Chinese books of instruction for
                                   women. Chinese literature, T'ang period.

     Lit 268.

Yamazaki Michio   山崎 道夫   East Asian thought, neo-Confucianism.
        Yen 364.

Yamazaki Shu   NC
     ∈ Idem, The Earth of China [160 pp.].
        Kyoto: Kyoto Shoin, 1988.

Yamazaki Tadashi   山崎 忠   Mongolian language.
     * Tōyōshi kenkyū 15.1 (July 1956), 88-90.

Yanagida Seizan   柳田 聖山   Buddhist studies, Zen.
     + Tōhō gakuhō 59 (March 1987), 591-599.
     + Hanazono Daigaku kenkyū kiyō 8 (March 1977), 1-8.
     ∋ P. Demiéville, Review of Yanagida's translation of the Lin-chi lu,
        Rinzai roku 臨済録 (Tokyo: Daizō Shuppan, 1972. 406 pp.), in
        T'oung Pao 59 (1973), 306-308.
        [Note also in the same issue of T'oung Pao (pp. 302-306) Demiéville's
        review of a related article by Yanagida. The review includes a find-
        ing list collating passages of the Lin-chi lu treated in different
        studies by Yanagida.]

Yanagida Setsuko   柳田 節子   Chinese socio-economic history, esp. Sung and
                                   Yuan periods.

Yanagita Setsuko
    see Yanagida Setsuko.

Yanagimachi Tatsuya 柳町達也 Chinese thought.
    Lit 266, Yen 261.

Yanai Kenji   箭内健次 Japanese international relations, Edo period.
                                    East Asian history.
    Yen 203, Teng #174.

Yanai Watari
    see Yanai Wataru.

Yanai Wataru   箭内亘 Manchurian and Mongolian history. Chinese
                                   history, esp. Yuan period.
- • Tōhōgaku 59 (Jan. 1980), 147-169.
- + <u>Mōkoshi kenkyū</u> [45,989,30,117,50,3 pp.], 5-10.
      蒙古史研究
      Yanai Wataru and Iwai Hirosato, eds. Tokyo: Tōkō Shoin, 1930; rpt.
      1966.
      NNO 3:439-440.
- +• Yen-ching hsueh-pao (Peking) 8 (Dec. 1930), 1645-1649.

Yanase Kiyoshi   柳瀬喜代志 Classical Chinese thought. Chinese fiction,
                                  Six Dynasties and T'ang periods.
     Lit 266.

Yano Chikara   矢野主税 Chinese history, Six Dynasties and T'ang pe-
                                riods.
    Yen 402, Teng #535.
- + Shakai kagaku ronsō (Nagasaki Daigaku) 25 (1976), 2 pp.

Yano Jin'ichi   矢野仁一 Modern Chinese history. East-West and Sino-
                                Japanese historical relations.
- + Tōyōshi kenkyū 28.4 (March 1970), 45-56.

• Ibid., 1-44.

• Tōhōgaku 28 (July 1964), 131-147.

Yano Mitsuji   矢野光治   Chinese linguistics.

Yano Niichi   矢野仁一
   see Yano Jin'ichi.

Yashiro Yukio   矢代幸雄   Art history, incl. East Asia.
      Yen 400, Teng #189.

Yasuda Kiyoshi   保田清   Chinese thought, neo-Confucianism, Wang Yang-
                                       ming.

      Teng #695.

Yasui Kōzan   安居香山   Early Chinese thought and religion.
      Yen 10, Teng #686.

Yasumoto Hiroshi   安本博   Classical Chinese thought.
      Yen 5.

Yasuno Shōzō   安野省三   Chinese socio-economic history, Ming and
                                       Ch'ing periods.

      Yen 11.

Yawata Ichirō   小幡一郎   Archaeology.
      Yen 14, Teng #15.
      + Yūrashia 7 (Dec. 1972), 3-19.
      Also listed under Shiratori Kurakichi and Torii Ryūzō.

Yazawa Toshihiko   矢沢利彦   East-West historical relations. Religion in
                                       China, Christianity, Ming and Ch'ing peri-
                                       ods.

      Yen 400, Teng #564.

Yoda Yoshiie   依田憙家   Contemporary China. Modern Chinese history.
    Yen 561.

Yoda Yoshikata   依田義賢   Modern Japanese playwright. Contemporary
                                   Sino-Japanese relations.
    Yen 561.

Yokemura Ichigaku 除村一学
    Listed under Collected Articles #62.

Yokogawa Jirō   横川次郎   Chinese economy, incl. communes. Sino-Soviet
                                   relations.
    ∋ Joshua A. Fogel, "Obituary," <u>Sino-Japanese Studies</u> 2.2 (May 1990), 2.
    • Chūgoku kenkyū geppō 495 (May 1989), 41.

Yokomatsu Takashi   横松宗   Chinese thought, esp. modern period. Chinese
                                   educational history.
    Lit 276, Yen 176.

Yokota Terutoshi   横田輝俊   Chinese literature, Ming period, incl. poet-
                                   ics.
    Lit 276, Yen 177, Teng #620.

Yokoyama Eizō   横山永三   Modern Chinese literature. Chinese poetry,
                                   traditional.
    Lit 278.

Yokoyama Hiroshi   横山宏   Chinese language. Contemporary Chinese eco-
                                   nomics.
    Yen 175.
    Cf. next entry.

Yokoyama Hiroshi   横山 弘   Chinese literature, esp. Six Dynasties peri-
                                      od.

    Lit 278, Yen 175.

    Cf. preceding entry.

Yokoyama Iseo   横山伊勢雄   Chinese poetry, Sung period, esp. Su Shih.

    Lit 277, Yen 176.

Yokoyama Suguru   横山 英   Chinese socio-economic history, esp. modern
                                      period. Modern Chinese political history.

    Yen 176, Teng #480.

Yoneda Kenjirō   米田 賢次郎   Chinese history, esp. Han period. Chinese
                                      farm economy, Han thru Six Dynasties peri-
                                      ods. Chinese calligraphy, Han thru Six Dy-
                                      nasties periods.

    Yen 273, Teng #516.

Yoneyama Toratarō   米山 寅太郎   Chinese lexicography.

    Yen 273.

Yonezawa Hideo   米沢 秀夫   Contemporary Chinese economics. Overseas Chi-
                                      nese.

    Yen 274.

Yonezawa Yoshiho   米沢 嘉圃   Chinese and Japanese art history, painting.

    Yen 273, Teng #190.

    ∈ Japanese Painting in the Literati Style [190 pp.].

      By Yonezawa Yoshiho and Yoshizawa Chu. Translated and adapted by
      Betsy Iverson Monroe. New York and Tokyo: Weatherhill/Heibonsha,
      1974.

    + Tōyō Bunka Kenkyūjo kiyō (Tōkyō Daigaku) 43 (March 1967), 45-49.

    ∈ Idem, Painting in the Ming Dynasty [9,118 pp.].

      Tokyo: Maruyama, 1956.

∈ Idem, <u>Flower and Bird Painting of the Sung Dynasty</u> [24 pp.].
   Translated by Miyamoto Shozaburo. London: Faber and Faber, 1961.
∈ <u>Painting of Sung and Yuan Dynasties</u> [8,47,39 pp.].
   By Yonezawa Yoshiho and Shimada Shujiro. Tokyo: Maruyama, 1952.
Also listed under Akiyama Terukazu.

Yoshida Kenkō   吉田贄抗   Classical Chinese thought. Chinese historical
                                    texts, <u>Shih-chi</u>.
     Lit 283, Yen 196, Teng #652.

Yoshida Kin'ichi   吉田金一   Sino-Russian historical relations.
     Yen 195.

Yoshida Kōhei   吉田公平   Chinese thought, esp. Ming and Ch'ing periods.
     Yen 195.

Yoshida Megumu   吉田恵   History of Chinese language. Chinese poetry,
                                    <u>Shih-ching</u>. Modern Chinese language and
                                    literature.
     Lit 284.

Yoshida Mitsukuni   吉田光邦   History of Chinese and Japanese science.
     Yen 194, Teng #204.

Yoshida Sachio   吉田幸夫   Modern Chinese literature and language.
     Lit 284, Yen 196.

Yoshida Tomio   吉田富夫   Modern Chinese literature and politics.
     Lit 284, Yen 193.

Yoshida Tora   吉田寅   Chinese history, esp. Sung and Yuan periods,
                                    salt monopoly.

Yoshihara Fumiaki   吉原文昭   Classical Chinese thought.
     Lit 285.

Yoshii Taijun   吉井 泰順   Early Chinese thought. Sino-Japanese cultural
                                        relations.

    Yen 193.

Yoshikawa Kōjirō   吉川 幸次郎   Chinese literature, incl. Yuan drama and
                                        T'ang poetry. East Asian thought.

    Lit 279, Yen 190, Teng #621.

∈   Idem, <u>Five Hundred Years of Chinese Poetry, 1150-1650: The Chin,
    Yuan, and Ming Dynasties</u> [19,215 pp.].

    Translated with a Preface by John Timothy Wixted.   Including an
    Afterword by William S. Atwell.   Princeton: Princeton University
    Press, 1989.

    [Note the discussion of Yoshikawa's scholarship and literary style in
    the "Translator's Preface" (pp. xi-xix) and of his scholarship in the
    "Afterword" (pp. 191-196).]

Σ   <u>Yoshikawa Kōjirō zenshū</u> (<u>Kettei ban</u> 決定版).

    Tokyo: Chikuma Shobō, 1984-88.   28 vols.

    [This is a reprint of the next entry, with 4 volumes added, and with
    the addition of ca. 10-30 pages to each of the earlier volumes.]

Σ   <u>Yoshikawa Kōjirō zenshū</u>, vol. 24 (1975), 403-461.

    Tokyo: Chikuma Shobō, 1973-75.   24 vols.

    [Note the subject indexes in vol. 24, pp. 463-478.]

    [This is a reprint of the next entry, with 4 volumes added.]

Σ   <u>Yoshikawa Kōjirō zenshū</u>.   No biblio.

    Tokyo: Chikuma Shobō, 1968-70; rpt. Taipei, ca. 1980.   20 vols.

    [Cf. the preceding entries, for added material and volumes.]

•   Ssu-ch'uan Ta-hsueh hsueh-pao ts'ung-k'an (Ch'eng-tu) 21 (Nov. 1983),
    12.

∈   Idem, <u>Jinsai, Sorai, Norinaga: Three Classical Philologists of Mid-
    Tokugawa Japan</u> [4,1,299 pp.].

    Translated by Kikuchi Yūji.   Tokyo: The Tōhō Gakkai, 1983.

•   <u>Yoshikawa Kōjirō</u> [7,293 pp.].

    Kuwabara Takeo, Fuji Masaharu, and Kōzen Hiroshi, eds.   Tokyo:
    Chikuma Shobō, 1982.

[Comprised solely of reminiscences of Yoshikawa by his students and colleagues. In addition to numerous pieces originally in Japanese, includes Japanese-language translations of the contributions in the In Memoriam pamphlet listed below, as well as of additional memorial notes by Ho P'ei-chung and J.-P. Diény.]

∋ J.P.Diény, "Yoshikawa Kōjirō (1904-1980)," T'oung Pao 67 (1981), 4-9.

● Tōhōgaku 61 (Jan. 1981), 197-209.

● Hsueh-lin man-lu (Peking) 4 (1981), 164-172.

● Wen-hsueh i-ch'an (Peking) Jan. 1981, 139-146.

∋ In Memoriam: Tributes to Kōjirō Yoshikawa, 1904-1980 [2,33 pp.].
No ed. Mimeographed. New York: Columbia University, May 8, 1980.
[Includes tributes to Yoshikawa in English by W.T. deBary, C.T. Hsia, Donald Keene, Hakeda Yoshito, Kano Gunkatsu, Glen W. Baxter, Burton Watson, and J. Mason Gentzler. All appear in Japanese translation, together with other contributions, in the volume noted above edited by Kuwabara Takeo et al.]

● Biburia 74 (Apr. 1980), 94-95.

∅ Yoshikawa hakushi taikyū kinen Chūgoku bungaku ronshū [4,2,4,1,28, 910,13 pp.], 4-28.
中国文学論集
Yoshikawa kyōju taikan kinen jigyōkai, ed. Tokyo: Chikuma Shobō, 1968.
[Includes the English-language article by Burton Watson, "Literary Theory in the Eastern Han," 13 pp.]
[Note also the French-language review of this volume, which includes synopses of the articles it contains, by Jean-Pierre Diény, "Vues japonaises sur la littérature chinoise," T'oung Pao 57 (1971), pp. 1-30.]
TRNS #246.

∈ Idem, An Introduction to Sung Poetry [12,191 pp.].
Translated by Burton Watson. Cambridge: Harvard University Press, 1967.

∋ Burton Watson, "Some New Japanese Translations of Chinese Literature," Far Eastern Quarterly 14.2 (Feb. 1955), 245-249.
[Mostly about Yoshikawa's scholarship, with discussion of four of his works.]

Also listed under Aoki Masaru, Hattori Unokichi et al. (Ikeuchi Hiroshi, Kano Naoki, Kuwabara Jitsuzō, Naitō Konan, Shiratori Kurakichi), and Collected Articles #8.

Yoshikawa Tadao   吉川 忠夫   Chinese history and thought, esp. Six Dynasties period.

Yen 189.

Yoshimura Gorō   吉村 五郎   Modern Chinese language. Chinese vernacular fiction.

Yen 192.

Yoshimura Hisako   吉村 尚子   Chinese vernacular fiction, Ch'ing period. Modern Chinese literature.

Lit 285.

Yoshinami Takashi   好並 隆司   Chinese history: Han, Wei, and Chin periods.
Yen 167.

Yoshino Sakuzō   吉野 作造   Early twentieth-century Japanese political scientist and liberal leader. Commentator on contemporary China.

  + Kokubungaku (Kansai Daigaku) 44 (Aug. 1970), 43-75.
  ∋* Matsuo Takayoshi, "Sakuzō Yoshino," <u>The Developing Economies</u> 5.2 (June 1967), 388-404.

Yoshioka Gihō
  see Yoshioka Yoshitoyo.

Yoshioka Yoshitoyo 吉岡 義豊 Chinese religion, Taoism.
  Teng #653.
  + <u>Ko Yoshioka Yoshitoyo hakushi etsureki oyobi chojutsu</u>.
     Yoshioka hakushi honsōgi shikkō iinkai, ed. & publ. Tokyo?, 1979.
  • Tōhō shūkyō 54 (Nov. 1979), 79-88.

ø Yoshioka hakushi kanreki kinen <u>Dōkyō kenkyū ronshū: Dōkyō no shisō</u>
   <u>to bunka</u> [26,803,21,4 pp.], 11-22.

   道教研究論集 一 道教の思想と文化 一

   Yoshioka Yoshitoyo hakushi kanreki kinen ronshū kankōkai, ed. Tokyo:
   Kokusho Kankōkai, 1977.

   [Includes a French-language article by M. Soymié, "Les dix jours de
   jeûne du taoïsme," 21 pp.]

   TRNS #245.

Also listed under Collected Articles #19 and #20b.

Yoshizawa Chū   吉沢 忠   Japanese and Chinese art history, painting.
    Yen 197.

∈ <u>Japanese Painting in the Literati Style</u> [190 pp.].

   By Yonezawa Yoshiho and Yoshizawa Chu. Translated and adapted by
   Betsy Iverson Monroe. New York and Tokyo: Weatherhill/Heibonsha,
   1974.

Yū Chūkun   游 仲勲   Contemporary Chinese economy. Economy of
                                      overseas Chinese.

    Yen 568.

Yu Chung-hsun

    see Yū Chūkun.

Yuasa Kōson

    see Yuasa Yukihiko.

Yuasa Yukihiko   湯浅 幸孫   Chinese thought: classical, neo-Confucian,
                                      and Ch'ing-period. Ch'ing-period discus-
                                      sions of emancipation of women.

    Lit 275, Yen 435.

+ Chūgoku shisōshi kenkyū (Kyōto Daigaku) 4 (1981), 309-312.

Yūki Reimon   結城令聞   Chinese Buddhism.
    Yen 209.

ø Yūki kyōju shōju kinen <u>Bukkyō shisōshi ronshū</u> [19,811,2,133,4 pp.],
   4-11.

仏教思想史論集

   Yūki kyōju shōju kinen rombunshū kankōkai, ed. Tokyo: Daizō Shuppan,
   1964.

   [Includes English-language articles by Miyamoto Shōson, Kenneth
   Inada, Stanley Weinstein, Unno Taitetsu, Miyuki Mokusen, and Ōi
   Shōjo. The last article outlines some of Yūki's major research.]

   TRNS:oo.

+ Tōyō Bunka Kenkyūjo kiyō (Tōkyō Daigaku) 31 (March 1963), 1-8.

ADDENDA

Katō Shūichi   加藤周一   Continued.

∈ Idem, <u>The Japan-China Phenomenon: Conflict or Compatibility?</u> [103
   pp.].

   With an introduction by Arnold Toynbee. Translated from the Japanese
   by David Chibbett. London: Paul Norbury Publications, 1974; Tokyo,
   New York and San Francisco: Kodansha International Ltd., 1975.

Kiyose, Gisaburo N. NC   Historical linguistics, Jurchen language.

∈ Idem, <u>A Study of the Jurchen Language and Script</u> [260 pp.].

   Kyoto: Hōritsubunka-sha, 1977.

Kudō Naotarō   工藤直太郎   Chinese literature and art, esp. T'ang-period
                                poetry.

∈ Idem, <u>The Life and Thoughts of Li Ho: The T'ang Poet</u> [106,2 pp.].

   Tokyo: Waseda University Press, 1969.

∈ Idem, <u>Chinese Landscape Painting and Nature Poetry</u> [70,5 pp.].

   Tokyo: Waseda University Law Association, 196-?.

Okada Takehiko   岡田武彦   Continued.

∋* Rodney L. Taylor, <u>The Confucian Way of Contemplation: Okada Takehiko</u>
   <u>and the Tradition of Quiet-Sitting</u> (Columbia, S.C.: University of
   South Carolina Press, 1988). 5,2,230 pp.

   [Note the selected bibliography of Okada's works, pp. 222-223.]

Sekida Katsuki   NC   Ch'an Buddhism, China and Japan.

∈ Idem, <u>Two Zen Classics: Mumonkan and Hekiganroku</u> [413 pp.].
   Edited and introduced by A.V. Grimstone. New York: Weatherhill,
   1977.

Takahashi Kazumi   高橋和巳   Continued.

• <u>Takahashi Kazumi no sekai</u> [224 pp.].
   高橋和己の世界
   By Tateishi Haku. Tokyo: Kōdansha, 1972.

Takeda Akira   竹田晃   Continued.

ø Takeda Akira sensei taikan kinen <u>Higashi Ajia bunka ronsō</u> [1,1,7,
   22,556,1 pp.] 7-22.
   東アジア文化論叢
   Takeda Akira sensei taikan kinen gakujutsu rombunshū henshū iinkai,
   ed. Tokyo: Kyūko Shoin, 1991.

APPENDIX

Additional Volumes of Collected Articles concerning China

For discussion of the "Appendix," see the "Introduction," Section VI: "Festschriften and Collected Articles concerning China."

Although entries are listed alphabetically in the "Appendix," many volumes have two-part titles. To cite two examples:

#49 Sōritsu hyakushūnen kinen Nishō Gakusha Daigaku ronshū

#83 Shigakkai sōritsu gojūnen kinen Tōzai kōshōshi ron

Volumes with the name of a university as part of their title are alphabetized under the name of the university. Thus, entry #49 is listed under "Nishō Gakusha Daigaku." Otherwise, volumes are alphabetized by their subject title (which generally gives a better suggestion as to the contents of the work). Hence, entry #83 is listed under "Tōzai kōshōshi ron." Alternate titles are crosslisted alphabetically wherever potentially helpful.

Chinese characters for phrases making up editing entities cited (if unclear in context) appear in Index C. Characters for publishers appear in Index F.

Note that in the body of the Handbook, "Collected Articles" refers to the "Appendix."

1 Ajia bōeki no tembō.

アジア貿易の展望

Chūgoku Kenkyūjo Bōeki Iinkai, ed. Tokyo: Tōyō Keizai Shimbunsha, 1948. 5,13,272 pp.

TRNS #004, NNO 3:426-427.

2 Ajia bunka no saininshiki Ajia Bunka Toshokan kaikan kinen rombunshū.

アジア文化の再認識　アジア文化図書館開館記念論文集

Ajia Bunka Toshokan, ed. Tokyo: Asahi Shimbunsha, 1957. 2,327 pp.

TRNS #003, NNO 3:422.

Ajia Bunka Toshokan kaikan kinen rombunshū.

see entry #2.

3   Ajia bunkashi ronsō 1.
     アジア文化史論叢 1
     Ryūsha Kaisei Shōgakkai, ed. Tokyo: Yamakawa Shuppansha, 1978. 11,1,
     425,2 pp.
     [Includes an English-language article by Hayashi Kensaku, "The Fukui
     Microblade Technology and Its Relationships in Northeast Asia and
     North America," pp. 313-420.]
     TRNS #002.

4   Ajia: Kako to genzai Konoe Kazan Kō gojūnen-sai kinen ronshū.
     アジア 過去と現在 近衛霞山公五十年祭記念論集
     Konoe Kazan Kō Gojūnen-sai Kinen Ronshū Henshū Iinkai, ed.   Tokyo:
     Kazan Kurabu, 1955. 2,2,306,1,11,1 pp.
     TRNS #081.

5   Amerika no shin Ajia-kan.
     アメリカの新アジア観
     Chūgoku Kenkyūjo, ed. Tokyo: Chōryūsha, 1948. 4,1,208 pp.
     TRNS #005, NNO 3:427.

6   Betonamu Chūgoku kankeishi Kyoku-shi no taitō kara Shin-Futsu sensō
     made.
     ベトナム中国関係史 曲氏の抬頭から清仏戦争まで
     Yamamoto Tatsurō, ed. Tokyo: Yamakawa Shuppansha, 1975. 13,722,50
     pp.
     TRNS #220.

7   Chōsen Shina bunka no kenkyū.
     朝鮮支那文化の研究
     Tabobashi Kiyoshi, ed. Tokyo: Tōkō Shoin, 1929. 2,1,603,2 pp.
     TRNS #140.

     Chūgoku bungaku.
         see entry #50.

8   Chūgoku bungaku ronshū.

中国文学論集

Yoshikawa Kōjirō, ed.   Tokyo: Shinchōsha, 1966.   328 pp.

TRNS #136.

9   Chūgoku chūseishi kenkyū   Rikuchō Zui Tō no shakai to bunka.

中国中世史研究 六朝隋唐の社会と文化

Chūgoku Chūseishi Kenkyūkai, ed.   Tokyo: Tōkai Daigaku Shuppankai,

1970.   10,500 pp.

TRNS #131.

10   Chūgoku keizai hatten no tōkei-teki kenkyū.

中国経済発展の統計的研究

Ajia Keizai Kenkyūjo, ed. & publ.   Tokyo, 1960-62.   3 vols.

          Vol. 1   Nov. 1960   5,269 pp.

          Vol. 2   March 1962   11,326 pp.

          Vol. 3   Nov. 1962   10,306,2 pp.

[These volumes appear in the Ajia Keizai Kenkyūjo chōsa kenkyū hōkoku

sōshō series as #7, #20, and #34.]

[Vol. 1 includes an English summary.]

TRNS #126.

Chūgoku kindaika no shakai kōzō.

     see entry #82.

11   Chūgoku kodai no shakai to bunka   Sono chiiki-betsu kenkyū.

中国古代の社会と文化 その地域別研究

Chūgoku Kodaishi Kenkyūkai, ed.   Tokyo: Tōkyō Daigaku Shuppankai,

1957.   4,3,347,2 pp.

TRNS #129, NNO 3:434.

12   Chūgoku kodaishi kenkyū.

中国古代史研究

Chūgoku Kodaishi Kenkyūkai, ed.   5 vols.   Tokyo: Yoshikawa Kōbunkan

(vols. 1-3), Yūzankaku Shuppan (vol. 4-5).

Vol. 1	1960	3,3,398 pp.
Vol. 2	1965	4,3,376 pp.
Vol. 3	1969	10,500 pp.
Vol. 4	1976	373,1 pp.
Vol. 5	1982	293 pp.

TRNS #127 (vols. 1-4), NNO 3:434-435 (vol. 1).

13 Chūgoku kodaishi no shomondai.

中国古代史の諸問題

Mikami Tsugio and Kurihara Tomonobu, eds. Tokyo: Tōkyō Daigaku Shuppankai, 1954. 4,3,271,13 pp.

TRNS #128, NNO 3:434.

14 Chūgoku minshū hanran no sekai, and Zoku Chūgoku minshū hanran no
sekai.

中国民衆反乱の世界 続中国民衆反乱の世界

Seinen Chūgoku Kenkyūsha Kaigi, ed. Tokyo: Kyūko Shoin, 1974 and
1983. 3,1,394 pp., and 5,1,590 pp.

TRNS #137 (1974 vol.).

15 Chūgoku no gendai bunka.

中国の現代文化

Chūgoku Kenkyūjo, ed. Tokyo: Hakujitsu Shoin, 1948. 2,6,320 pp.

TRNS #133, NNO 3:435.

16 Chūgoku no Nihon ron.

中国の日本論

Chūgoku Kenkyūjo, ed. Tokyo: Chōryūsha, 1948. 218 pp.

TRNS #135, NNO 3:435.

Chūgoku no shakai to shūkyō.

   see entry #82.

Chūgoku no shūkyō to shakai.

   see entry #82.

17   Chūgokushi no jidai kubun.

中国史の時代区分

Suzuki Shun and Nishijima Sadao, eds.   Tokyo: Tōkyō Daigaku Shuppankai, 1957.   6,373 pp.

TRNS #130, NNO 3:435.

18   Daidō Gakuin ronsō.

大同学院論叢

Daidō Gakuin, ed.   Shinkyō [Manchuria]: Manshū Gyōsei Gakkai.

          Vol. 1   Oct. 1939   1,1,1,321 pp.
          Vol. 2   March 1940   2,1,1,273 pp.
          Vol. 3   Dec. 1940   2,1,1,297 pp.
          Vol. 4   Nov. 1941
          Vol. 5   Nov. 1942   2,1,1,248 pp.

TRNS #116 (vols. 1-4).

19   Dōkyō kenkyū.

道教研究

Yoshioka Yoshitoyo and Michel Soymié, eds. {E}

          Vol. 1   Dec. 1965   Tokyo: Shōshinsha   294,14 pp.
          Vol. 2   March 1967   Tokyo: Shoshinsha   292,6 pp.
          Vol. 3   Nov. 1968   Tokyo: Shoshinsha   318,6 pp.
          Vol. 4   Feb. 1971   Tokyo: Henkyōsha   2,290,8 pp.

[Note "Bibliographie du Taoïsme: études dans les langues occiden-
tales": Part 1, by M. Soymié and F. Litsch, in vol. 3, 247-318; Part
2, by M. Soymié, in vol. 4, 237-290.]
[All 4 volumes have article summaries in French.]
TRNS #177.

20a   Dōkyō no sōgō-teki kenkyū.

道教の総合的研究

Sakai Tadao, ed.   Tokyo: Kokusho Kankōkai, 1977.   455,16 pp.
[Japanese-language edition of the papers presented at the 2nd Interna-
tional Conference on Taoist Studies, Tateshina (Nagano), Japan, 1972.
Includes translations of papers originally presented in English (by

J. Needham, J.L. Dull, M. Porkert, K.M. Schipper, and N. Sivin) that
do not appear in the English-language volume for the conference. Cf.
entry #20b.]
TRNS #178.

20b Facets of Taoism: Essays in Chinese Religion.
Holmes Welch and Anna Seidel, eds. New Haven and London: Yale Univer-
sity Press, 1979. 1,302 pp.
[Includes five papers presented at the 2nd International Conference on
Taoist Studies, Tateshina (Nagano), Japan, 1972 (including one by
Miyakawa Hisayuki), as well as additional articles in English by
Michel Strickmann, Yoshioka Yoshitoyo, Ōfuchi Ninji, and a biblio-
graphic survey entitled "Taoist Studies in Japan," by Sakai Tadao and
Noguchi Tetsurō, pp. 269-287. Cf. entry #20a.]
TRNS:oo.

21   Genshi keihōshi no kenkyū yakuchū.
元史刑法志の研究譯註
Otake Fumio and Okamoto Yoshiji, eds. Tokyo: Kyōiku Shoseki, 1962.
4,359 pp.
[Note the bibliography of materials for research on the Yuan dynasty,
pp. 329-359.]
TRNS #070.

22   Hatten tojō-koku kenkyū Chiiki hen.
発展途上国研究 地域篇
Ajia Keizai Kenkyūjo, ed. Tokyo: Ajia Keizai Shuppankai, 1978. 4,1,
130,1,279,1,19 pp.
TRNS #202.

23   Indai seidō bunka no kenkyū.
殷代青銅文化の研究
Kyōto Daigaku Jimbun Kagaku Kenkyūjo, ed. & publ. Kyoto, 1954.
1,261,11 pp.
[A separate issue of Tōhō gakuhō: vol. 23 (March 1953).]
TRNS #023.

24   <u>Jimbun kagaku no shomondai</u>.

人文科学の諸問題

Hachi Gakkai Rengō, ed.   Kyoto: Seki Shoin, 1949.   3,230 pp.

TRNS #107, NNO 3:443.

25   <u>Keijō Teikoku Daigaku sōritsu jisshūnen kinen rombunshū</u>.

京城帝国大学創立十周年記念論文集

Tokyo: Ōsaka Yagō Shoten, 1936.

Keijō Teikoku Daigaku Hōgaku Bungakkai ronsan   Vol. 4

2,273,31,1,4 pp.

Keijō Teikoku Daigaku Bungakkai ronsan   Vol. 5

2,317,4 pp.

Keijō Teikoku Daigaku Bungakkai ronsan   Vol. 6

2,400,4 pp.

[See <u>Shigaku ronsō</u> (entry #60 below) for Vol. 7.]

TRNS #065.

<u>Kigen nisen roppyaku-nen kinen</u>.

see entry #59.

26   <u>Kindai Ajia kyōikushi kenkyū</u>.

近代アジア教育史研究

Taga Akigorō, ed.   Tokyo: Iwasaki Gakujutsu Shuppansha.

Vol. 1   1969   5,5,645,4 pp.
Vol. 2   1975   3,6,792,4,2,1 pp.

[Not to be confused with entries #32 & #33.]

TRNS #057 (vol. 1 only).

27   <u>Kindai Chūgoku kenkyū</u>.

近代中国研究

Gakujutsu Kenkyū Kaigi Gendai Chūgoku Kenkyū Tokubetsu Iinkai, ed.

Tokyo: Kōgakusha, 1948.   5,361 pp.

TRNS #060, NNO 3:428.

28   Kindai Chūgoku kenkyū.

近代中国研究

Kindai Chūgoku Kenkyū Iinkai, ed. & publ. Tokyo.

      Vol. 1   Sept. 1958   1,347,6,26 pp.

      Vol. 2   Dec. 1958   1,390,22 pp.

      Vol. 3   Aug. 1959   1,347,21,1 pp.

      Vol. 4   July 1960   1,254,136,8 pp.

      Vol. 5   May 1963   1,340 pp.

      Vol. 6   May 1964   1,359 pp.

      Vol. 7   Dec. 1966   1,483 pp.

[Vols. 1-4 have English summaries.]

TRNS #061 (vols. 1-7), NNO 3:428 (vols. 1-4).

29   Kindai Chūgoku no shakai to keizai.

近代中国の社会と経済

Niida Noboru, ed. Tokyo: Tōkō Shoin, 1951. 1,2,2,350 pp.

TRNS #062, NNO 3:428-429.

Kindai Chūgoku nōson shakai shi kenkyū.

    see entry #82.

30   Kindai Shina bunka.

近代支那文化

Wada Sei et al., eds. Tokyo: Kōfūkan, 1943. 7,294 pp.

TRNS #059, NNO 3:427-428.

31   Kindai Shina shisō.

近代支那思想、

Sanetō Keishū, ed. Tokyo: Kōfūkan, 1942. 4,8,366 pp.

TRNS #058, NNO 3:427.

32   Kinsei Ajia kyōikushi kenkyū.

近世アジア教育史研究

Taga Akigorō, ed. Tokyo: Bunri Shoin, 1966. 10,1,967 pp.

[Not to be confused with entries #26 & #33.]

[Note the bibliography of Japanese-language studies on the history of education in Asia, pp. 905-929, and the bibliography of Chinese-language studies on the history of Chinese education, pp. 930-967.]
TRNS:oo.

33   Kinsei Chūgoku kyōikushi kenkyū Sono bunkyō seisaku to shomin kyōiku.
近世中国教育史研究 その文教政策と庶民教育
Hayashi Tomoharu, ed.   Tokyo: Kokudosha, 1958.   3,2,541,13 pp.
[Not to be confused with entries #26 & #32.]
TRNS #056, NNO 3:427.

34   Kita Shina no nōgyō to keizai.
北支那の農業と経済
Minami Manshū Tetsudō Kabushiki Kaisha Chōsabu, ed.   Tokyo: Nihon Hyōronsha, 1942.   2 vols.   2,2,6,326,5 pp.;   and 8 pp., pp. 329-903, and 6,7,14 pp.
TRNS #050.

Konoe Kazan Kō gojūnen-sai kinen ronshū.
     see entry #4.

35   Kyōto Daigaku Bungakubu   Gojisshūnen kinen ronshū.
京都大学文学部 五十周年記念論集
Kyōto Daigaku Bungakubu, ed. & publ. Kyoto, 1956. 3,4,1,1082,38 pp.
{E}
[Kyōto Daigaku Bungakubu kenkyū kiyō #4.]
TRNS #054.

36   Kyūshū Daigaku Bungakubu   Sōritsu gojisshūnen kinen rombunshū.
九州大学文学部 創立五十周年記念論文集
Kyūshū Daigaku Bungakubu, ed. & publ. Fukuoka, 1975.   8,1144 pp.
TRNS #053.

37 Kyūshū Daigaku Bungakubu   <u>Sōritsu yonjisshūnen kinen rombunshū</u>.

九州大学文学部 創立四十周年記念 論文集

Kyūshū Daigaku Bungakubu, ed. & publ. Fukuoka, 1966. 2,3,1063,392,3

pp.

TRNS #052.

38 Kyūshū Teikoku Daigaku Hōbun Gakubu jisshūnen kinen <u>Tetsugaku shigaku</u>

<u>bungaku rombunshū</u>.

九州帝国大学法文学部十周年記念

哲学史学文学論文集

Kyūshū Teikoku Daigaku Hōbun Gakubu, ed. Tokyo: Iwanami Shoten, 1937.

4,2,1063,13 pp.

TRNS #051, NNO 3:423

39 <u>Man Mō shi ronsō</u>.

満蒙史論叢

Tamura Jitsuzō, ed.   Shinkyō (Manchuria): Nichi-Man Bunka Kyōkai.

          Vol. 1   Aug. 1938   2,1,321,1 pp.

          Vol. 2   Dec. 1939   1,484,2 pp.

          Vol. 3   Dec. 1940   1,391,2 pp.

          Vol. 4   July 1943

TRNS #227.

40 <u>Man Sen chiri rekishi kenkyū hōkoku</u>.

満鮮地理歴史研究報告

Tōkyō Teikoku Daigaku Bunka Daigaku, ed. & publ. Tokyo, 1915-41; rpt.

Seoul, 1978.   16 vols.

TRNS #226.

41 <u>Mindai Man Mō shi kenkyū</u>.

明代満蒙史研究

Tamura Jitsuzō, ed.   Kyoto: Kyōto Daigaku Bungakubu, 1963.   3,2,662,

15,23,2 pp. {E}

TRNS #231.

Monumenta Serindica.

    see entry #57.

42   Nagoya Daigaku Bungakubu   Jisshūnen kinen ronshū.

名古屋大学文学部　十周年記念論集
Nagoya Daigaku Bungakubu, ed. & publ. Nagoya, 1959. 2,2,950,2 pp.

TRNS #182, NNO 3:426.

43   Nagoya Daigaku Bungakubu   Nijisshūnen kinen ronshū.

名古屋大学文学部　二十周年記念論集
Listed under Utsunomiya Kiyoyoshi as a Festschrift entry.

44   Nairiku Ajia no kenkyū.

内陸アジアの研究
Yūrashia Gakkai, ed. & publ. Tokyo, 1955. 8,4,377 pp. {E}

[A Festschrift dedicated to Sven Hedin. Includes Western-language
articles by Iwao Kobori, John Maringer, and Yves Hervouet.]

[Yūrashia Gakkai kenkyū hōkoku #3. Cf. entries #84 & #85.]

TRNS #186, NNO 3:440-441.

45   Nairiku Ajia shi ronshū.

内陸アジア史論集
Nairiku Ajia-shi Gakkai, ed.

    Vol. 1   Tokyo: Daian, 1964; rpt. Kokusho Kankōkai,
                1979. 7,369,1 pp.

    Vol. 2   Tokyo: Kokusho Kankōkai, 1979. 2,4,349,1 pp.

TRNS #187 (vol. 1 only).

46   Nihon bunkashi ronsan Zaidan Hōnin Meiji Shōtoku Kinen Gakkai setsu-
ritsu nijūgo shūnen kinen rombun.

日本文化史論纂
財団法人 明治聖徳記念学会設立二十五周年記念論文

Katō Genchi, ed. Tokyo: Chūbunkan, 1937. 2,4,702,14 pp.

TRNS #085, NNO 3:424.

47   Nihon Daigaku Shigakuka gojisshūnen kinen   <u>Rekishigaku rombunshū</u>.
      日本大学史学科五十周年記念 歴史学論文集
      Shigakuka Sōritsu Gojisshūnen Kinen Jigyō Jikkō Iinkai, ed. & publ.
      Tokyo, 1978.   5,681,4 pp.
      TRNS #196.

48   <u>Nihon Daigaku sōritsu shichijūnen kinen rombunshū</u> Dai-ikkan Jimbun
      kagaku hen.
      日本大学創立七十年記念論文集 第一巻 人文科学篇
      Nihon Daigaku, ed. & publ. Tokyo, 1960.   2,8,1126 pp.
      TRNS #197, NNO 3:426.

49   Sōritsu hyakushūnen kinen   <u>Nishō Gakusha Daigaku ronshū</u>   Chūgoku
      bungaku hen.
      創立百周年記念 二松学舎大学論集 中国文学篇
      Nishō Gakusha Daigaku, ed. & publ. Tokyo, 1977.   3,474 pp.
      TRNS #192.

50   <u>Nishō Gakusha Daigaku sōritsu hachijisshūnen kinen ronshū</u>.
      二松学舎大学創立八十周年記念論集
      Nishō Gakusha Daigaku, ed. and publ. Tokyo, 1957.   263,8 pp.
      TRNS #191, NNO 3:426.

51   Ōsaka Daigaku Bungakubu   <u>Sōritsu jisshūnen kinen ronsō</u>.
      大阪大学文学部 創立十周年記念論叢
      Ōsaka Daigaku Bungakubu, ed. & publ. Toyonaka, 1959.   7,789,154,4 pp.
      TRNS #036, NNO 3:423.

      <u>Rekishigaku rombunshū</u>.
          see entry #47.

52   <u>Rekishigaku ronshū</u>: Daigaku seminaa sōsho.
      歴史学論集 大学セミナー双書
      Tōyama Shigeki and Nagahara Keiji, eds. Tokyo: Kawade Shobō Shinsha,

1961.   5,399 pp.

TRNS #250.

53   Risshō Daigaku Shigakkai sōritsu gojisshūnen kinen   <u>Shūkyō shakai shi</u>
<u>kenkyū</u>.

立正大学史学会創立五十周年記念　宗教社会史研究

Risshō Daigaku Shigakkai, ed.   Tokyo: Yūzankaku Shuppan, 1977.   753,
3,1 pp.

TRNS #101.

54   Risshō Daigaku Shigakkai sōritsu sanjūgo shūnen kinen   <u>Shigaku rombun-</u>
<u>shū</u>.

立正大学史学会創立三十五周年記念　史学論文集

Risshō Daigaku Shigakkai, ed. & publ.   Tokyo, 1960.   6,514 pp.

TRNS #247.

55   <u>Ritsumeikan sanjūgo shūnen kinen rombunshū</u>   Bungaku hen.

立命館三十五周年記念論文集　文学篇

Ritsumeikan Shuppanbu, ed. & publ.   Kyoto, 1935.   11,1,3,401 pp.

TRNS #248.

56   <u>Ritsumeikan sōritsu gojisshūnen kinen rombunshū</u>   Bungaku hen.

立命館創立五十周年記念論文集　文学篇

Ritsumeikan Daigaku Jimbun Kagaku Kenkyūjo, ed. & publ.   Kyoto, 1951.
9,2,544 pp.

TRNS #249, NNO 3:426.

57   <u>Seiiki bunka kenkyū</u>.

西域文化研究

Seiiki Bunka Kenkyūkai, ed.   Kyoto: Hōzōkan.   6 vols. {E}

    Vol. 1   1958   Chinese Buddhist Texts from Tunhuang in Eastern
                Turkestan   293,87,10 pp.

    Vol. 2   1959   Chinese Fragmentary Manuscripts on Social and Eco-
                nomic System in the T'ang Era Unearthed from Tun-
                huang and Turfan, Facs. 1.   463,27,2,55,5 pp.

Vol. 3   1960   Ibid., Facs. 2.   488,26,6 pp.

Vol. 4   1961   Buddhist Manuscripts and Secular Documents of the Ancient Languages in Central Asia.   51,316,1,2,47,3 pp.   (Vol. 4, Bessatsu.   2 pp. plus pp. 314-462.)

Vol. 5   1962   The Ancient Buddhist Arts in Central Asia and Tun-huang.   20,25,22,357,27,6 pp.

Vol. 6   1963   Miscellaneous Essays on the Art and History of Central Asia and Tun-huang.   3,22,271,62,5 pp.

[English title: Monumenta Serindica.]

TRNS #083, NNO 3:430-432.

Shigakkai sōritsu gojūnen kinen.

see entry #83.

58   Shigaku kenkyū kinen ronsō.

史学研究記念論叢

Hiroshima Bunrika Daigaku Shigakuka Kyōshitsu, ed.   Kyoto: Yanagihara Shoten, 1950.   8,602,16 pp.

TRNS #091, NNO 3:424-425.

Shigaku rombunshū.

see entries #54 and #59.

59   Shigaku rombunshū   Kigen nisen roppyakunen kinen.

史学論文集 紀元二千六百年記念

Kyōto Teikoku Daigaku Bungakubu, ed.   Kyoto: Naigai Shuppan, 1941.   3,5,2, 1195 pp.

TRNS #049, NNO 3:423.

60   Shigaku ronsō.

史学論叢

Tokyo: Iwanami Shoten, 1938.   1,521,5 pp.

[Keijō Teikoku Daigaku Bungakkai ronsan, vol. 7.   Cf. entry #25 above.]

TRNS #093.

61   Shin Shina kensetsu no seiji keizai mondai.

新支那建設の政治経済問題

Kokusai Keizai Gakkai, ed.   Tokyo: Tōkō Shoin, 1939.   211 pp.

TRNS #105.

62   Shina bunka dansō.

支那文化談叢

Yokemura Ichigaku, ed.   Tokyo: Natori Shoten, 1942.   4,258 pp.

TRNS #088, NNO 3:433.

63a   Shina bunka ronsō.

支那文化論叢

Ch'en Heng-che, ed.   Translated by Ishida Mikinosuke.   Tokyo: Seikatsusha, 1942.   15,454 pp.

[Translation of entry #63b.]

TRNS #089.

63b   Symposium on Chinese Culture.

Sophia H. Chen Zen [Ch'en Heng-che], ed.   Shanghai: Institute of
Pacific Relations, 1931.   7,373 pp.

[Prepared for the Fourth Biennial Conference of the Institute of
Pacific Relations, Hangchow, Oct. 21-Nov. 4, 1931.]

[English-language articles, mostly by well-known Chinese of the time,
on aspects of Chinese culture and society, including ones, for example, on Chinese music (Y.R. Chao), geology (W.H. Wong), and agriculture (R. Feng).]

[For Japanese-language translation, see entry #63a.]

64   Shina keizai jijō kenkyū.

支那経済事情研究

Matsuo Takeji and Fukukawa Shōzō, eds.   Tokyo: Keiō Gijuku Daigaku Tōa
Jijō Kenkyūkai, 1935.   5,2,481,2 pp.

TRNS #086.

65   Shina kenkyū.
      支那研究
      Kyōiku Gakujutsu Kenkyūkai, ed. Tokyo: Dōbunkan, 1916. 4,16,464 pp.
      [Cf. entry #66.]
      TRNS:oo, NNO 3:432-433.

66   Shina kenkyū.
      支那研究
      Mochizuki Shina Kenkyū Kikin, ed.   Tokyo: Iwanami Shoten, 1930.
      1,2,441 pp.
      [Cf. entry #65.]
      TRNS #087.

67   Shinchō no henkyō tōji seisaku.
      清朝の辺疆統治政策
      Tōa Kenkyūjo, ed. Tokyo: Shibundō, 1944. 2,10,398 pp.
      TRNS #106.

68   Shingai kakumei no kenkyū.
      辛亥革命の研究
      Onogawa Hidemi and Shimada Kenji, eds. Tokyo: Chikuma Shobō, 1978.
      6,4, 450,27 pp.
      TRNS #104.

      Shūkyō shakai shi kenkyū.
          see entry #53.

69   Sō Gen jidai no kagaku gijutsu shi.
      宋元時代の科学技術史
      Yabuuchi Kiyoshi, ed.   Kyoto: Kyōto Daigaku Jimbun Kagaku Kenkyūjo,
      1967. 7,468 pp.
      TRNS #110.

      Sōdai shakai keizai shi kenkyū.
          see entry #82.

Sōritsu hyakushūnen kinen   <u>Nishō Gakusha Daigaku ronshū</u>   Chūgoku
bungaku hen.
    see entry #49.

70   <u>Tairiku bunka kenkyū</u>, and <u>Zoku Tairiku bunka kenkyū</u>.

大陸文化研究 続大陸文化研究

Keijō Teikoku Daigaku Tairiku Bunka Kenkyūkai, ed.   Tokyo: Iwanami
Shoten, 1940 and 1943.   5,2,546 pp., and 3,2,492 pp.
TRNS #114-115, NNO 3:433-434.

71   <u>Tenkō kaibutsu no kenkyu</u>.

天工開物の研究

Yabuuchi Kiyoshi, ed.   Tokyo: Kōseisha Kōseikaku, 1953.   4,483,15 pp.
[Subtitled <u>Kyōtō Daigaku Jimbun Kagaku Kenkyūjo kenkyū hōkoku</u>.]
TRNS #144, NNO 3:435-436.

<u>Tetsugaku shigaku bungaku rombunshū</u>.
    see entry #38.

72   Tōa Dōbun Shoin Daigaku   <u>Tōa Chōsa hōkoku-sho</u>   (Shōwa jūroku nendo).

東亜同文書院大学 東亜調査報告書（昭和十六年度）

Otake Fumio, ed.   Shanghai: Tōa Dōbun Shoin Daigaku, 1942.   2,2,870
pp.
TRNS #149.

73   <u>Tochi shoyū no shiteki kenkyū</u>.

土地所有の史的研究

Tōkyō Daigaku Tōyō Bunka Kenkyūjo, ed.   Tokyo: Tōkyō Daigaku Shuppankai, 1956.   2,614,13,1 pp. {E}
TRNS #145.

<u>Tōhō Gakkai sōritsu jūgo shūnen kinen</u>.
    see entry #74.

Tōhō Gakkai sōritsu nijūgo shūnen kinen.

    see entry #75.

74   Tōhōgaku ronshū Tōhō Gakkai sōritsu jūgo shūnen kinen.

東方学論集　東方学会創立十五周年記念

Tōhō Gakkai, ed. & publ. Tokyo, 1962. 7,403,42 pp. {E}

[Cf. entry #75.]

TRNS #158, NNO 3:425.

75   Tōhōgaku ronshū Tōhō Gakkai sōritsu nijūgo shūnen kinen.

東方学論集　東方学会創立二十五周年記念

Tōhō Gakkai, ed. & publ. Tokyo, 1972. 9,867,49 pp. {E}

[Cf. entry #74.]

TRNS #159.

Tōyō Bunka Kenkyūjo sōsetsu sanjisshūnen kinen ronshū.

    see entry #76.

76   Tōyō bunka to asu Tōyō Bunka Kenkyūjo sōsetsu sanjisshūnen kinen
ronshū.

東洋文化と明日　東洋文化研究所創設三十周年記念論集

Tōyō Bunka Kenkyūjo sōsetsu sanjisshūnen kinen jigyō iinkai, ed.

Machita: Mukyūkai, 1970. 11,450 pp.

TRNS #176.

77   Tōyō Kyōkai Chōsabu gakujutsu hōkoku Dai-issatsu.

東洋協会調査部　学術報告　第一冊

Tōyō Kyōkai, ed. & publ. Tokyo, 1909. 3,2,1,275 pp.

TRNS #163.

78   Tōyō no bunka to shakai Dai-isshū.

東洋の文化と社会　第一輯

Kyōto Daigaku bungakubu Shina Tetsugakushi Kenkyūshitsu, ed. Kyoto:

Kyōiku Taimusu-sha, 1950. 2,3,203,4 pp.

TRNS #175.

79   <u>Tōyō no ie to kanryō</u>.

東洋の家と官僚

Tōyō Bunka Kenkyū Kaigi, ed.   Tokyo: Seikatsusha, 1948.   5,1,2,296 pp.

TRNS #173, NNO 3:438.

80   <u>Tōyō no shakai</u>.

東洋の社会

Hiroshima Bunri-dai Tōyōshi Kenkyūshitsu, ed.   Tokyo: Meguro Shoten,

1948.   2,1,397 pp.

TRNS #174, NNO 3:438.

81   <u>Tōyōgaku sōhen</u>.

東洋学叢編

Ishida Mikinosuke and Ishihama Juntarō, eds.   Tokyo: Tōkō Shoin, 1934.

2,2,236,84,2 pp.

[Volume dedicated to Wang Kuo-wei.   Includes an English-language

article by B. Asai on the Sedik language of Formosa, 84 pp.]

TRNS #162, NNO 3:436.

82   <u>Tōyōshigaku ronshū</u>.

東洋史学論集

8 vols.

     Vol. 1   No subtitle.

                Tōkyō Kyōiku Daigaku Tōyōshigaku Kenkyūshitsu, ed.   To-

                kyo: Shimizu Shoin, 1953.   3,2,340 pp.

     Vol. 2   <u>Chūgoku no shakai to shūkyō</u>.

                中国の社会と宗教

                Yamazaki Hiroshi, ed.   Tokyo: Fumaidō Shoten, 1954.

                2,1,452,2 pp.

     Vol. 3   No subtitle.

                Tōkyō Kyōiku Daigaku Tōyōshigaku Kenkyūshitsu, ed.   To-

                kyo: Fumaidō Shoten, 1954.   2,3,422,3 pp.

     Vol. 4   No subtitle.

                Yamazaki Hiroshi, ed.   Tokyo: Fumaidō Shoten, 1955.

                2,2,546,2,15 pp. {E}

Vol. 5   <u>Sōdai shakai keizai shi kenkyū</u> (Jō).

宋代社会経済史研究 (上)

Tōkyō Kyōiku Daigaku Ajiashi Kenkyūkai Sōdaishi Kenkyūbu,
ed.   Tokyo: Fumaidō Shoten, 1960.   2,1,196 pp.

Vol. 6   <u>Chūgoku kindaika no shakai kōzō</u>.

中国近代化の社会構造

Tōkyō Kyōiku Daigaku Bungakubu Tōyōshigaku Kenkyūkai
Ajiashi Kenkyūkai and Chūgoku Kindaishibu-kai, eds.
Tokyo: Daian, 1960.   2,225,2 pp.

Vol. 7   <u>Chūgoku no shūkyō to shakai</u>.

中国の宗教と社会

Tōkyō Kyōiku Daigaku Tōyōshigaku Kenkyūshitsu and Chūgoku
Shisō-Shūkyō-shi Kenkyūkai, eds.   Tokyo: Fumaidō Shoten,
1965.   3,245,2 pp.

Vol. 8   <u>Kindai Chūgoku nōson shakai shi kenkyū</u>.

近代中国農村社会史研究

Tōkyō Kyōiku Daigaku Tōyōshigaku Kenkyūshitsu and Ajiashi
Kenkyūkai Chūgoku Kindaishi Kenkyūkai, eds.   Tokyo: Daian, 1967.   2,2,363 pp.

TRNS #164-171.

83   <u>Tōzai kōshōshi ron</u>   Shigakkai sōritsu gojūnen kinen.

東西交渉史論　史学会創立五十年記念

Shigakkai (Tokyo), ed.   Tokyo: Fuzambō, 1939.   2 vols.   6,2,3,3,766
pp., and 23,3 pp. plus pp. 767-1410.

TRNS #155, NNO 3:424.

84   <u>Yūboku minzoku no kenkyū</u>.

遊牧民族の研究

Yūrashia Gakkai, ed. & publ.   Tokyo, 1955.   6,368 pp.

[<u>Yūrashia Gakkai kenkyū hōkoku</u> #2.   Cf. entries #44 & #85.]

TRNS #243, NNO 3:440.

85   <u>Yūboku minzoku no shakai to bunka</u>.

遊牧民族の社会と文化

Yūrashi Gakkai, ed.   Kyoto: Shizen Shigakkai, 1952.   6,219 pp. {E}

[<u>Yūrashia Gakkai kenkyū hōkoku</u> #1.   Cf. entries #44 & #84.]

TRNS #244, NNO 3:440.

<u>Zaidan Hōnin Meiji Shōtoku Kinen Gakkai setsuritsu nijūgo shūnen kinen</u>
<u>rombun</u>.

see entry #46.

<u>Zoku Chūgoku minshū hanran no sekai</u>.

see entry #14.

<u>Zoku Tairiku bunka kenkyū</u>.

see entry #70.

Japanese Surnames in the <u>Handbook</u>, Listed by Chinese Reading

Note: <u>Kokuji</u> (i.e. "Chinese" characters originating in Japan) are romanized and alphabetized as "X." Japanese <u>kana</u> (and ケ) are listed as "XX."

CHINESE READING	KANJI (and KANA)	JAPANESE READING
A-lai-yeh	阿頼耶	Araya
A-nan	阿南	Anami
A-pu	阿部	Abe
Ai-chia	愛甲	Aiko
Ai-tang	愛宕	Otagi
An-chü	安居	Yasui
An-pen	岸本	Kishimoto
An-pen	安本	Yasumoto
An-pien	岸辺	Kishibe
An-pu	安部	Abe
An-ta	安達	Adachi
An-t'eng	安藤	Andō
An-tung	安東	Andō
An-yeh	安野	Yasuno
Ao-ch'i	奥崎	Okuzaki
Ao-yeh	奥野	Okuno
Chai-t'eng	斎藤	Saitō
Ch'ai-t'ien	柴田	Shibata
Ch'ai-yuan	柴垣	Shibagaki

Chang-hsia	杖下	Tsueshita
Ch'ang-ku-ch'uan	長谷川	Hasegawa
Ch'ang-ku-pu	長谷部	Hasebe
Ch'ang-kuang	長広	Nagahiro
Ch'ang-lai	長瀬	Nagase
Ch'ang-p'an	常盤	Tokiwa
Ch'ang-p'an-ching	常盤井	Tokiwai
Ch'ang-pu	長部	Osabe
Ch'ang-shih	常石	Tsuneishi
Ch'ang-t'ien	長田	Osada
Ch'ang-tse	長沢	Nagasawa
Ch'ang-wei	長尾	Nagao
Ch'ang-wu	長屋	Nagaya
Chao	朝	see Ch'ao
Chao-k'ao	沼尻	Numajiri
Chao-k'ou	沼口	Numaguchi
Ch'ao-t'ien	潮田	Ushioda
Ch'ao-ts'ang	朝倉	Asakura
Che-chih	柘植	Tsuge
Chen-nei	陣内	Jinnouchi
Chen-XX-nei	陣ノ内	Jinnouchi
Chen-wu	真武	Matake
Ch'eng-t'ien	澄田	Sumida
Chi-ching	吉井	Yoshii
Chi-ch'uan	及川	Oikawa
Chi-ch'uan	吉川	Yoshikawa

Chi-kang	吉岡	Yoshioka
Chi-pien	磯辺	Isobe
Chi-t'ien	姫田	Himeda
Chi-t'ien	紀田	Kida
Chi-t'ien	吉田	Yoshida
Chi-tse	吉沢	Yoshizawa
Chi-ts'un	吉村	Yoshimura
Chi-yeh	吉野	Yoshino
Chi-yuan	吉原	Yoshihara
Ch'i-ho-tse	気賀沢	Kegasawa
Ch'i-t'ien	旗田	Hatada
Chia	榎	Enoki
Chia-ching	家井	Inoi
Chia-fei-yuan	甲斐原	Kaihara
Chia-ho	加賀	Kaga
Chia-mao	加茂	Kamo
Chia-t'eng	加藤	Katō
Chia-ti	加地	Kaji
Chiang-fan	江幡	Ebata
Chiang-fu	江副	Ezoe
Chiang-k'ou	江口	Eguchi
Chiang-lien	江連	Ezure
Chiang-shang	江上	Egami
Chiang-tao	江嶋	Ejima
Chiang-t'ou	江頭	Egashira
Chiao-tao	鮫島	Samejima

Chiao-t'ien	角田	Tsunoda
Ch'iao-ch'uan	橋川	Hashikawa
Ch'iao-pen	橋本	Hashimoto
Chieh-ch'eng	結城	Yūki
Chieh-t'ien	櫛田	Kushida
Chien	筧	Kakei
Chien-nei	箭内	Yanai
Chien-yeh	間野	Mano
Ch'ien	乾	Inui
Ch'ien-ching	浅井	Asai
Ch'ien-ch'uan	浅川	Asakawa
Ch'ien-ch'uan	前川	Maegawa
Ch'ien-hai	浅海	Asami
Ch'ien-tao	前嶋	Maejima
Ch'ien-t'ien	千田	Chida
Ch'ien-t'ien	前田	Maeda
Ch'ien-yeh	浅野	Asano
Ch'ien-yeh	前野	Maeno
Ch'ien-yuan	千原	Chihara
Chih-chi	枝吉	Edayoshi
Chih-ch'ih	芝池	Shibaike
Chih-ho	志賀	Shiga
Chih-ku	埴谷	Haniya
Chih-mu	植木	Ueki
Chih-t'ien	織田	Oda
Chih-t'ien	芝田	Shibata

Chih-t'ien	志田	Shida
Chih-t'ien	植田	Ueda
Chih-ts'un	志村	Shimura
Chih-ts'un	植村	Uemura
Ch'ih-chung	赤塚	Akatsuka
Ch'ih-nei	池内	Ikeuchi
Ch'ih-pan	赤坂	Akasaka
Ch'ih-shang	池上	Ikegami
Ch'ih-sung	赤松	Akamatsu
Ch'ih-t'ien	池田	Ikeda
Ch'ih-wei	赤尾	Akao
Chin-chih	今枝	Imaeda
Chin-ching	今井	Imai
Chin-ch'üan	今泉	Imaizumi
Chin-chung	近重	Chikashige
Chin-fu	今富	Imatomi
Chin-hsi	今西	Imanishi
Chin-hsia	津下	Tsuge
Chin-hu	金戸	Kaneto
Chin-kang	金岡	Kanaoka
Chin-ku	金谷	Kanaya
Chin-k'u	今堀	Imahori
Chin-kuan	今関	Imazeki
Chin-pin	今浜	Imahama
Chin-t'eng	近藤	Kondō
Chin-t'ien	金田	Kaneda

Chin-t'ien	津田	Tsuda
Chin-t'ien-i	金田一	Kindaichi
Chin-ts'ang	金倉	Kanakura
Chin-tse	金沢	Kanazawa
Chin-ts'un	今村	Imamura
Chin-tzu	金子	Kaneko
Chin-wan	金丸	Kanamaru
Chin-ying	今鷹	Imataka
Chin-yung	今永	Imanaga
Ch'in	秦	Hata
Ching	境	Sakai
Ching-ch'i	井崎	Inosaki
Ching-k'ou	井口	Inokuchi
Ching-k'ou	京口	Kyōguchi
Ching-ku	静谷	Shizutani
Ching-kuan	井貫	Inuki
Ching-nei	井内	Iuchi
Ching-po	井波	Inami
Ching-shang	井上	Inoue
Ching-shou	井手	Ide
Ching-t'ung	井筒	Izutsu
Ching-XX-ch'i	井ノ崎	Inosaki
Ch'ing-chiang	青江	Aoe
Ch'ing-kung	清宮	Seimiya
Ch'ing-mu	青木	Aoki
Ch'ing-mu-t'ing	清木庭	Kiyokoba

Ch'ing-pu	軽部	Karube
Ch'ing-shan	青山	Aoyama
Ch'ing-shui	清水	Shimizu
Ch'ing-sung	慶松	Keimatsu
Ch'ing-ti	青地	Aochi
Ch'ing-tse	清沢	Kiyozawa
Chiu-ching	酒井	Sakai
Chiu-ching	臼井	Usui
Chiu-chung	久重	Hisae
Chiu-mi	久米	Kume
Chiu-pao-t'ien	久保田	Kubota
Chiu-sung	久松	Hisamatsu
Ch'iu-chen	秋貞	Akisada
Ch'iu-chi	秋吉	Akiyoshi
Ch'iu-kang	秋岡	Akioka
Ch'iu-shan	秋山	Akiyama
Ch'iu-t'ien	秋田	Akita
Ch'iu-wei	萩尾	Hagio
Ch'iu-yeh	秋葉	Akiba
Ch'iu-yuan	萩原	Hagiwara
Ch'iu-yueh	秋月	Akizuki
Chou-ta	周達	Shūtatsu
Chou-t'eng	周藤	Sutō
Chu-ch'iao	諸橋	Morohashi
Chu-chih	竹治	Takeji
Chu-ching	諸井	Moroi

Chu-hsiung	猪熊	Inokuma
Chu-hu	諸戸	Moroto
Chu-kang	竹岡	Takeoka
Chu-k'ou	猪口	Inoguchi
Chu-nei	竹内	Takeuchi
Chu-sha	竺沙	Chikusa
Chu-shan	筑山	Tsukiyama
Chu-tao	竹島	Takeshima
Chu-t'ien	住田	Sumita
Chu-t'ien	竹田	Takeda
Chu-ts'un	竹村	Takemura
Chu-X	猪俣	Inomata
Chu-yueh	竹越	Takekoshi
Chü	橘	Tachibana
Chü-ch'ih	菊池	Kikuchi
Chü-ching	駒井	Komai
Chü-tao	具島	Gushima
Chü-ti	菊地	Kikuchi
Chü-t'ien	菊田	Kikuta
Chü-t'ien	駒田	Komada
Ch'u-shih	出石	Izushi
Ch'u-ts'un	除村	Yokemura
Ch'uan-ch'i	川崎	Kawasaki
Ch'uan-chin	船津	Funatsu
Ch'uan-chiu-pao	川久保	Kawakubo
Ch'uan-ho	川合	Kawai

Ch'uan-hsi	川西	Kawanishi
Ch'uan-k'ou	川口	Kawaguchi
Ch'uan-lai	川瀬	Kawase
Ch'uan-mu	船木	Funaki
Ch'uan-pei	川北	Kawakita
Ch'uan-pen	川本	Kawamoto
Ch'uan-shang	川上	Kawakami
Ch'uan-sheng	川勝	Kawakatsu
Ch'uan-t'ien	傳田	Denda
Ch'uan-t'ien	川田	Kawada
Ch'uan-t'ien	川添	Kawazoe
Ch'uan-yeh	川野	Kawano
Ch'uan-yueh	船越	Funakoshi
Ch'uan-yueh	川越	Kawagoe
Ch'üan	泉	Izumi
Chuang-ssu	荘司／庄司	Shōji
Ch'ui-yeh	吹野	Fukino
Ch'ui-yung	垂永	Tarunaga
Chün-tao	君島	Kimishima
Chung-chiang	中江	Nakae
Chung-chin-pin	中津濱	Nakatsuhama
Chung-ching	中井	Nakai
Chung-ch'uan	中川	Nakagawa
Chung-chung	中塚	Nakatsuka
Chung-hsi	中西	Nakanishi
Chung-ken	中根	Nakane

Chung-k'ung	中空	Nakazora
Chung-pen	塚本	Tsukamoto
Chung-po	中鉢	Chūbachi
Chung-shan	中山	Nakayama
Chung-tao	中嶋	Nakajima
Chung-tao	中島	Nakajima
Chung-t'ien	中田	Nakata
Chung-tse	中沢	Nakazawa
Chung-ts'un	中村	Nakamura
Chung-wu-fu	中屋敷	Nakayashiki
Chung-XX-chiang	鐘ヶ江	Kanegae
Chung-yeh	中野	Nakano
Ch'ung-sung	重松	Shigematsu
Ch'ung-t'ien	重田	Shigeta
Ch'ung-tse	重澤	Shigezawa
Erh-yü	児玉	Kodama
Fan-chung	飯塚	Iizuka
Fan-tao	飯島	Iijima
Fan-t'ien	飯田	Iida
Fan-ts'ang	飯倉	Iikura
Fang-ho	芳賀	Haga
Fei-hou	肥後	Higo
Feng-fu	豊福	Toyofuku
Feng-tao	豊嶋	Toyoshima
Feng-wu	蜂屋	Hachiya
Fu-ching	福井	Fukui

Fu-ch'uan	福川	Fukukawa
Fu-kuei-yuan	富貴原	Fukihara
Fu-ma	夫馬	Fuma
Fu-pen	福本	Fukumoto
Fu-pu	服部	Hattori
Fu-shan	福山	Fukuyama
Fu-shih	富士	Fuji
Fu-tao	福島	Fukushima
Fu-t'ien	福田	Fukuda
Fu-t'ien	浮田	Ukita
Fu-tse	福沢	Fukuzawa
Fu-wei	撫尾	Utsuo
Fu-wu	福武	Fukutake
Fu-wu	釜屋	Kamaya
Fu-yuan	福原	Fukuhara
Fu-yung	福永	Fukunaga
Fu-yung	富永	Tominaga
Hai-lao-tse	海老沢	Ebisawa
Hai-yeh	海野	Unno
Hai-yin-ssu	海音寺	Kaionji
Hao-ping	好並	Yoshinami
Hei-ch'uan	黒川	Kurokawa
Hei-pan	黒坂	Kurosaka
Hei-t'ien	黒田	Kuroda
Hei-yen	黒岩	Kuroiwa
Heng-ch'ao	横超	Ōchō

Heng-ch'uan	横川	Yokogawa
Heng-shan	横山	Yokoyama
Heng-sung	横松	Yokomatsu
Heng-t'ien	横田	Yokota
Ho-ch'i	河鰭	Kawabata
Ho-chien	鶴見	Tsurumi
Ho-ch'üan	和泉	Izumi
Ho-ko-sen	和歌森	Wakamori
Ho-nei	河内	Kawachi
Ho-pu	河部	Kawabe
Ho-shan	合山	Gōyama
Ho-shang	河上	Kawakami
Ho-ti	河地	Kawachi
Ho-t'ien	河田	Kawata
Ho-t'ien	和田	Wada
Ho-yeh	河野	Kōno
Ho-yuan	河原	Kawahara
Ho-yuan	河源	Kawahara
Ho-yuan-ch'i	河原崎	Kawarazaki
Hou-t'eng	後藤	Gotō
Hsi	西	Nishi
Hsi-ch'uan	細川	Hosokawa
Hsi-ch'uan	西川	Nishikawa
Hsi-kang	西岡	Nishioka
Hsi-ku	細谷	Hosoya
Hsi-ku	西谷	Nishitani

Hsi-li	西里	Nishizato
Hsi-pen	西本	Nishimoto
Hsi-tao	西嶋	Nishijima
Hsi-t'ien	細田	Hosoda
Hsi-t'ien	西田	Nishida
Hsi-ts'un	西村	Nishimura
Hsi-yeh	西野	Nishino
Hsi-yuan-ssu	西圓寺	Saionji
Hsia-chien	狭間	Hazama
Hsia-chien	下見	Shimomi
Hsia-tien	下店	Shimomise
Hsia-tou-mi	下斗米	Shimotomai
Hsia-ts'un	下村	Shimomura
Hsiang-ching	向井	Mukai
Hsiang-ch'uan	香川	Kagawa
Hsiang-ma	相馬	Sōma
Hsiang-pan	香坂	Kōsaka
Hsiang-p'u	相浦	Aiura
Hsiang-shan	向山	Mukōyama
Hsiang-tao	向嶋	Mukōjima
Hsiang-t'ien	相田	Sōda
Hsiang-yuan	相原	Aihara
Hsiao-chu	小竹	Otake
Hsiao-ch'uan	小川	Ogawa
Hsiao-ch'üan	小泉	Koizumi
Hsiao-feng	小峰	Komine

Hsiao-hsi	小西	Konishi
Hsiao-k'ou	小口	Oguchi
Hsiao-ku	小谷	Otani
Hsiao-li	小栗	Oguri
Hsiao-li-yuan	小笠原	Ogasawara
Hsiao-lin	小林	Kobayashi
Hsiao-nan	小南	Kominami
Hsiao-shan	小杉	Kosugi
Hsiao-shan	小山	Koyama / Oyama
Hsiao-shan-nei	小山内	Osanai
Hsiao-shou	小守	Komori
Hsiao-sung	小松	Komatsu
Hsiao-tao	小島	Kojima / Ojima
Hsiao-tao	小嶋	Kojima
Hsiao-t'ien	小田	Oda
Hsiao-t'ien	篠田	Shinoda
Hsiao-ts'ang	小倉	Ogura
Hsiao-tse	小沢	Ozawa
Hsiao-wei	小尾	Obi
Hsiao-X	小畑	Obata
Hsiao-yeh	小野	Ono
Hsiao-yeh-ch'uan	小野川	Onogawa
Hsiao-yeh-ssu	小野寺	Onodera
Hsiao-yeh-t'ien	小葉田	Kobata
Hsiao-yeh-t'ien	小野田	Onoda
Hsiao-yeh-tse	小野沢	Onozawa

Hsiao-yü	小玉	Kodama
Hsiao-yuan	篠原	Shinohara
Hsin-ch'eng	新城	Shinjō
Hsin-fu	信夫	Shinobu
Hsin-hai	新海	Shinkai
Hsin-k'ai	新開	Shinkai
Hsin-mei	新美	Niimi
Hsin-tao	辛島	Karashima
Hsin-tao	新島	Niijima
Hsin-t'ien	新田	Nitta
Hsin-ts'un	新村	Shimmura
Hsing	星	Hoshi
Hsing-ch'uan	星川	Hoshikawa
Hsing-shan	興膳	Kōzen
Hsiung-ku	熊谷	Kumagai
Hsiung-tai	熊代	Kumashiro
Hsiung-yeh	熊野	Kumano
Hsu-fang	緒方	Ogata
Hsu-shan	須山	Suyama
Hsu-shih	許勢	Konose
Hsu-t'eng	須藤	Sutō
Hsu-t'ien	須田	Suda
Hsu-yü	須羽	Suwa
Hsueh-tse	穴沢	Anazawa
Hu	護	Mori
Hu-ching	壺井	Tsuboi

Hu-ch'uan	戸川	Togawa
Hu-t'ien	戸田	Toda
Hua-ch'i	花崎	Hanazaki
Hua-ching	花井	Hanai
Hua-fang	花房	Hanabusa
Hua-shan	花山	Hanayama
Huang	荒	Ara
Huang-ching	荒井	Arai
Huang-mu	荒木	Araki
Huang-wei	荒尾	Arao
Hui-ku	恵谷	Etani
I-chien	逸見	Hemmi
I-ch'uan	衣川	Kinugawa
I-hai	一海	Ikkai
I-lai	伊瀬	Ise
I-t'eng	伊藤	Itō
I-ti-chih	伊地智	Idachi
I-t'ien	依田	Yoda
I-tung	伊東	Itō
I-wo	儀我	Giga
I-yuan	一円	Ichien
I-yuan	伊原	Ihara
Jen-ching-t'ien	仁井田	Niida
Jih-hsia-pu	日下部	Kusakabe
Jih-kao	日高	Hidaka
Jih-pi-yeh	日比野	Hibino

Jih-yeh	日野	Hino
Jih-yuan	日原	Hihara
Jo-kuei	若槻	Wakatsuki
Ju-chiang	入江	Irie / Iriye
Ju-ku	入谷	Iritani
Ju-shih	入矢	Iriya
Kan	乾	Inui
Kang	岡	Oka
Kang-ch'i	岡崎	Okazaki
Kang-ching	岡井	Okai
Kang-ku	岡谷	Okatani
Kang-pen	岡本	Okamoto
Kang-pu	岡部	Okabe
Kang-t'ien	岡田	Okada
Kang-ts'un	岡村	Okamura
Kao-ch'iao	高橋	Takahashi
Kao-chih	高知	Kōchi
Kao-chih	高志	Takashi
Kao-feng	高峯	Takamine
Kao-hsiung	高雄	Takao
Kao-lai	高瀬	Takase
Kao-ma	高馬	Kōma
Kao-mu	高水	Takagi
Kao-nan	高楠	Takakusu
Kao-sung	高松	Takamatsu
Kao-tao	高島	Takashima

Kao-t'ien	高田	Takada
Kao-ts'ang	高倉	Takakura
Kao-ts'un	高村	Takamura
Kao-X	高畠	Takabatake / Takahata
Kao-X	高畑	Takahata
Ken-an	根岸	Negishi
Ken-pen	根本	Nemoto
K'o-erh	可児	Kani
Kou-k'ou	溝口	Mizoguchi
Ku	谷	Tani
Ku-chiu	古厩	Furumaya
Ku-ch'uan	谷川	Tanigawa
Ku-ho	古賀	Koga
Ku-k'ou	谷口	Taniguchi
Ku-tao	古島	Furushima
Ku-t'ien	古田	Furuta
Ku-t'ien	谷田	Tanida
Ku-tse	古沢	Furusawa
Ku-wu	古屋	Furuya
Ku-yeh	古野	Furuno
K'u	堀	Hori
K'u-chiang	堀江	Horie
K'u-ch'ih	堀池	Horiike
K'u-ch'uan	堀川	Horikawa
K'uai-shan	檜山	Hiyama
Kuan	関	Seki

Kuan	菅	Suga
Kuan-chao	菅沼	Suganuma
Kuan-k'ou	関口	Sekiguchi
Kuan-ku	菅谷	Sugaya
Kuan-yeh	関野	Sekino
Kuan-yeh	菅野	Sugano
Kuang-ch'ang	広常	Hirotsune
Kuang-ch'ih	広池	Hiroike
Kuang-kang	光岡	Mitsuoka
Kuei-ching	亀井	Kamei
Kuei-t'ou	鬼頭	Kitō
Kung-ch'i	宮崎	Miyazaki
Kung-ch'uan	宮川	Miyagawa / Miyakawa
Kung-hsia	宮下	Miyashita
Kung-nei	宮内	Miyauchi
Kung-pan	宮坂	Miyasaka
Kung-pen	宮本	Miyamoto
Kung-t'eng	工藤	Kudō
Kung-t'ien	宮田	Miyata
Kung-tse	宮沢	Miyazawa
Kuo-chih	国枝	Kunieda
Lai	頼	Rai
Lai-ch'uan	瀬川	Segawa
Lai-neng	瀬熊	Senō
Li	黎	Rei
Li-chien	立間	Tatsuma

Li-ching	里井	Satoi
Li-lin	栗林	Kuribayashi
Li-pen	梨本	Nashimoto
Li-po	礪波	Tonami
Li-shih	立石	Tateishi
Li-t'ien	栗田	Kurita
Li-yuan	笠原	Kasahara
Li-yuan	栗原	Kurihara
Lien-shih	蓮実	Hasumi
Lien-t'ien	鎌田	Kamata
Lin	林	Hayashi
Lin-t'ien	林田	Hayashida
Lin-wu	林屋	Hayashiya
Ling-chao	菱沼	Hishinuma
Ling-chiang	鈴江	Suzue
Ling-mu	鈴木	Suzuki
Ling-pu	綾部	Ayabe
Liu	劉	Ryū
Liu-chiao	六角	Rokkaku
Liu-lai	柳瀬	Yanase
Liu-pen	柳本	Yagimoto
Liu-t'ien	柳田	Yanagida
Liu-ting	柳町	Yanagimachi
Lu	麓	Fumoto
Lu-li	芦立	Ashidate
Lu-tao	鹿島	Kajima

Lu-ti	鹿地	Kaji
Lu-t'ien	芦田	Ashida
Lu-tse	芦沢	Ashizawa
Lu-tzu-mu	鹿子林	Kanokogi
Lu-yeh	鹿野	Kano
Lung	龍	Ryō
Lung	滝	Taki
Lung-ch'uan	龍川	Ryūkawa
Lung-ch'uan	滝川	Takikawa
Lung-tse	滝沢	Takizawa
Ma-ch'ang	馬場	Baba / Bamba
Ma-sheng	麻生	Asō
Ma-yuan	馬淵	Mabuchi
Mai-sheng	麦生	Mugifu
Mao-chung	毛塚	Kezuka
Mei-ken	梅根	Umene
Mei-pen	梅本	Umemoto
Mei-t'ien	毎田	Maida
Mei-yuan	梅原	Umehara
Mi-ku	米谷	Maiya
Mi-shan	米山	Yoneyama
Mi-t'ien	米田	Yoneda
Mi-tse	米沢	Yonezawa
Ming-yeh	明野	Akeno
Mo-fu	末富	Suetomi
Mo-kang	末網	Suetsuna

Mo-sung	末松	Suematsu
Mo-yen	末延	Suenobu
Mo-yung	末永	Suenaga
Mu-chia-t'ien	目加田	Mekada
Mu-ch'üan	木全	Kimata
Mu-hu	牧戸	Makito
Mu-nan	木南	Kinami
Mu-shan	木山	Kiyama
Mu-t'ien	木田	Kida
Mu-t'ien	牧田	Makita
Mu-ts'un	木村	Kimura
Mu-wei	牧尾	Makio
Mu-yeh	牧野	Makino
Na-hsu	那須	Nasu
Na-k'o	那珂	Naka
Na-po	那波	Naba
Nai-liang	奈良	Nara
Nan-pen	楠本	Kusumoto
Nan-pu	南部	Nambu
Nan-shan	楠山	Kusuyama
Nan-t'iao	南條	Nanjō
Nan-yun	南雲	Nagumo
Nei-shan	内山	Uchiyama
Nei-t'eng	内藤	Naitō
Nei-t'ien	内田	Uchida
Nei-yeh	内野	Uchino

Neng-mei	能美	Nōmi
Niao-ching	鳥井	Torii
Niao-chü	鳥居	Torii
Niao-ch'uan	蔦川	Tsutagawa
Niao-shan	鳥山	Toriyama
Niao-yü-t'ien	鳥羽田	Toppata
Niu-tao	牛島	Ushijima
Pa-fan	八幡	Yawata
Pa-mu	八木	Yagi
Pa-mu-tse	八木沢	Yagisawa
Pai	柏	Kashiwa
Pai-ch'uan	白川	Shirakawa
Pai-hsi	白西	Shiranishi
Pai-lai	百瀬	Momose
Pai-mu	白木	Shiroki
Pai-niao	白鳥	Shiratori
Pai-shih	白石	Shiraishi
Pan-ching	坂井	Sakai
Pan-ch'u	坂出	Sakade
Pan-k'ou	阪口	Sakaguchi
Pan-ku	阪谷	Sakatani
Pan-pen	坂本	Sakamoto
Pan-pen	阪本	Sakamoto
Pan-t'ien	坂田	Sakata
Pan-yeh	坂野	Banno
Pan-yeh	板野	Itano

Pao-t'ien	保田	Yasuda
Pei-ch'uan	北川	Kitagawa
Pei-chung	貝塚	Kaizuka
Pei-kang	北岡	Kitaoka
Pei-shan	北山	Kitayama
Pei-ts'un	北村	Kitamura
Pen-t'ien	本田	Honda
Pen-to	本多	Honda
Pieh-chih	別枝	Bekki
P'ien-kang	片岡	Kataoka
P'ien-shan	片山	Katayama
Pin	濱	Hama
Pin-hsia	濱下	Hamashita
Pin-k'ou	濱口	Hamaguchi
Pin-tao	濱島	Hamashima
Pin-t'ien	濱田	Hamada
Ping-ho	並河	Namikawa
P'ing-ching	平井	Hirai
P'ing-ch'uan	平川	Hirakawa
P'ing-chung	平中	Hiranaka
P'ing-chung	平塚	Hiratsuka
P'ing-kang	平岡	Hiraoka
P'ing-lai	平瀬	Hirase
P'ing-mu	平木	Hiraki
P'ing-shan	平山	Hirayama
P'ing-t'ien	平田	Hirata

P'ing-tzu	平子	Hirako
P'ing-yeh	平野	Hirano
Po-to-yeh	波多野	Hatano
Pu-mu	布目	Nunome
P'u	浦	Ura
P'u-ch'ih	蒲池	Kamachi
San-chai	三宅	Miyake
San-ch'i	三崎	Misaki
San-hao	三好	Miyoshi
San-ku	三谷	Mitani
San-pao	三宝	Sambō
San-p'in	三品	Mishina
San-p'u	三浦	Miura
San-sen	三森	Mitsumori
San-shang	三上	Mikami
San-tao	三島	Mishima
San-t'ien-ts'un	三田村	Mitamura
San-tse	三沢	Misawa
Sang-shan	桑山	Kuwayama
Sang-t'ien	桑田	Kuwata
Sang-yuan	桑原	Kuwabara
Sen	森	Mori
Sen-an	森安	Moriyasu
Sen-ch'uan	森川	Morikawa
Sen-ku	森谷	Moritani
Sen-t'ien	森田	Morita

Sen-yeh	森野	Morino
Shan-an	山岸	Yamagishi
Shan-chi	山極	Yamagiwa
Shan-ch'i	山崎	Yamazaki
Shan-chih-nei	山之内	Yamanouchi
Shan-ching	山井	Yamanoi
Shan-hsia	山下	Yamashita
Shan-kang	山岡	Yamaoka
Shan-ken	山根	Yamane
Shan-k'ou	山口	Yamaguchi
Shan-ming	山名	Yamana
Shan-nei	山内	Yamanouchi / Yamauchi
Shan-pen	杉本	Sugimoto
Shan-pen	山本	Yamamoto
Shan-p'u	杉浦	Sugiura
Shan-sen	杉森	Sugimori
Shan-shan	杉山	Sugiyama
Shan-shih	山室	Yamamuro
Shan-t'ien	山田	Yamada
Shan-ts'un	杉村	Sugimura
Shan-XX-ching	山ノ井	Yamanoi
Shan-yeh	杉野	Sugino
Shang-ch'i	上妻	Kōzuma
Shang-kang	上岡	Kamioka
Shang-pan	上坂	Kōsaka
Shang-shan	上山	Ueyama

Shang-t'ien	上田	Ueda
Shang-ts'un	上村	Uemura
Shang-wei	上尾	Kamio
Shang-yeh	上野	Ueno
Shang-yuan	上原	Uehara
Shen-chin	深津	Fukatsu
Shen-hu	神戸	Kambe
Shen-ku	神谷	Kamiya
Shen-lin	神林	Kambayashi
Shen-p'u	深浦	Fukaura
Shen-t'ien	深田	Fukada
Shen-t'ien	神田	Kanda
Sheng-ts'un	勝村	Katsumura
Shih-ch'iao	石橋	Ishibashi
Shih-ching	石井	Ishii
Shih-ch'uan	市川	Ichikawa
Shih-ch'uan	石川	Ishikawa
Shih-ch'ui	矢吹	Yabuki
Shih-hei	石黒	Ishiguro
Shih-ku	市古	Ichiko
Shih-pin	石濱	Ishihama
Shih-tai	矢代	Yashiro
Shih-tao	石島	Ishijima
Shih-tao	矢島	Yajima
Shih-tao	矢嶋	Yajima
Shih-t'eng	実藤	Sanetō

Shih-t'ien	石田	Ishida
Shih-tse	矢沢	Yazawa
Shih-tso	矢作	Yahagi
Shih-ts'un	市村	Ichimura
Shih-yeh	矢野	Yano
Shih-yeh-tse	市野沢	Ichinosawa
Shih-yuan	市原	Ichihara
Shih-yuan	石原	Ishihara
Shih-yung	是永	Korenaga
Shou-chung	手塚	Tezuka
Shou-pen	守本	Morimoto
Shou-wu	守屋	Moriya
Shou-yeh	狩野	Kano
Shui-ku	水谷	Mizutani
Shui-shang	水上	Mizukami
Shui-tse	水沢	Mizusawa
Shui-yeh	水野	Mizuno
Shui-yuan	水原	Mizuhara
Sou-nei	藪内	Yabuuchi
Ssu-fang	泗方	Shikata
Ssu-kang	寺岡	Teraoka
Ssu-ma	司馬	Shiba
Ssu-po	斯波	Shiba
Ssu-ti	寺地	Teraji
Ssu-t'ien	寺田	Terada
Sui-chi	穂積	Hozumi

Sung-ch'i	松崎	Matsuzaki
Sung-chih	松枝	Matsueda
Sung-ching	松井	Matsui
Sung-hsia	松下	Matsushita
Sung-kang	松岡	Matsuoka
Sung-pen	松本	Matsumoto
Sung-p'u	松浦	Matsuura
Sung-tao	松島	Matsushima
Sung-t'ien	松田	Matsuda
Sung-ts'un	松村	Matsumura
Sung-wan	松丸	Matsumaru
Sung-wei	松尾	Matsuo
Sung-yeh	松野	Matsuno
Sung-yuan	松原	Matsubara
Sung-yung	松永	Matsunaga
Ta-ch'i	大崎	Ōsaki
Ta-ch'iao	大橋	Ōhashi
Ta-chih	大芝	Ōshiba
Ta-chiu-pao	大久保	Ōkubo
Ta-ch'uan	大川	Ōkawa
Ta-chung	大塚	Ōtsuka
Ta-ho-nei	大河内	Ōkōchi
Ta-kao	大高	Ōtaka
Ta-ku	大谷	Ōtani
Ta-kuei	大槻	Ōtsuki
Ta-lei	大類	Ōrui

Ta-lung	大滝	Ōtaki
Ta-mu	大木	Ōki
Ta-nei	大内	Ōuchi
Ta-nei-t'ien	大内田	Ōuchida
Ta-pin	大濱	Ōhama
Ta-p'ing	大平	Ōhira
Ta-sen	大森	Ōmori
Ta-shan	大山	Ōyama
Ta-shang	大上	Ōgami
Ta-shih	大室	Ōmuro
Ta-shih-ken	大矢根	Ōyane
Ta-sou	大藪	Ōyabu
Ta-tao	大島	Ōshima
Ta-t'ing	大庭	Ōba
Ta-tse	大沢	Ōsawa
Ta-ts'un	大村	Ōmura
Ta-yeh	大野	Ōno
Ta-yuan	大淵	Ōbuchi
Ta-yuan	大原	Ōhara
T'ai-t'ien	太田	Ōta
Tan	丹	Tan
Tan-yü	丹羽	Niwa
T'ang-ch'ien	湯浅	Yuasa
Tao	島	Shima
Tao-ch'i	嶋崎	Shimazaki
Tao-chü	島居	Shimasue

Tao-t'ien	稲田	Inada
Tao-t'ien	島田	Shimada
Tao-ts'ang	島倉	Shimakura
Tao-tuan	道端	Michibata
Tao-X	稲畑	Inahata
Tao-yeh	稲葉	Inaba
Te-t'ien	徳田	Tokuda
Te-yung	徳永	Tokunaga
T'eng-chi	藤吉	Fujiyoshi
T'eng-chia	藤家	Fujiie
T'eng-chih	藤枝	Fujieda
T'eng-ching	藤井	Fujii
T'eng-ch'uan	藤川	Fujikawa
T'eng-chung	藤塚	Fujizuka
T'eng-kang	藤岡	Fujioka
T'eng-pen	藤本	Fujimoto
T'eng-shan	藤善	Fujiyoshi
T'eng-t'ang	藤堂	Tōdō
T'eng-t'ien	藤田	Fujita
T'eng-tse	藤沢	Fujisawa
T'eng-ts'un	藤村	Fujimura
T'eng-yeh	藤野	Fujino
T'eng-yuan	藤原	Fujiwara
Ti-hsu	荻須	Ogisu
Ti-yeh	荻野	Ogino
Ti-yuan	荻原	Ogiwara

T'i	堤	Tsutsumi
T'ieh-ching	鉄井	Tetsui
T'ien-ch'uan	田川	Tagawa
T'ien-chung	田中	Tanaka
T'ien-chung	田仲	Tanaka
T'ien-hai	天海	Amagai
T'ien-k'ou	田口	Taguchi
T'ien-mu	田木	Taki
T'ien-pan	田坂	Tazaka
T'ien-pao-ch'iao	田保橋	Tabobashi
T'ien-pien	田辺	Tanabe
T'ien-sen	田森	Tamori
T'ien-shan	田山	Tayama
T'ien-suo	田所	Tadokoro
T'ien-tse	田沢	Tazawa
T'ien-ts'un	田村	Tamura
T'ien-yeh	天野	Amano
Ting-t'ien	町田	Machida
To-ho	多賀	Taga
To-t'ien	多田	Tada
Tsan-ching	讚井	Sanui
Ts'ang-chü	蔵居	Kurai
Ts'ang-kuang	倉光	Kuramitsu
Ts'ang-shih	倉石	Kuraishi
Ts'ang-t'ien	倉田	Kurata
Tsao-ch'uan	早川	Hayakawa

Ts'ao-sen	草森	Kusamori
Ts'ao-yeh	草野	Kusano
Tse-k'ou	沢口	Sawaguchi
Tse-ku	沢谷	Sawaya
Tse-t'ien	沢田	Sawada
Tseng-ching	増井	Masui
Tseng-t'ien	増田	Masuda
Tseng-ts'un	増村	Masumura
Tseng-ts'un	曽村	Somura
Tseng-wo-pu	曽我部	Sogabe
Tseng-yeh	曽野	Sono
Tseng-yuan	増淵	Masubuchi
Tseng-yung	増永	Masunaga
Tso-chiu	佐久	Saku
Tso-chiu-chien	佐久間	Sakuma
Tso-chu	佐竹	Satake
Tso-ch'uan	佐川	Sagawa
Tso-chung	佐中	Sanaka
Tso-k'ou	佐口	Saguchi
Tso-po	佐伯	Saeki
Tso-shan	佐山	Sayama
Tso-t'eng	佐藤	Satō
Tso-XX-mu	佐々木	Sasaki
Tso-yeh	佐野	Sano
Tsou-fang	諏訪	Suwa
Tsu-li	足立	Adachi

Tsu-li	足利	Ashikaga
Tsu-li-yuan	足立原	Adachibara
Tsun-pen	樽本	Tarumoto
Ts'un-shan	村山	Murayama
Ts'un-shang	村上	Murakami
Ts'un-sung	村松	Muramatsu
Ts'un-t'ien	村田	Murata
Tu-liu	都留	Tsuru
Tu-pien	渡辺	Watanabe
T'u-ch'i	土岐	Toki
T'u-ching	土井	Doi
T'u-chü	土居	Doi
T'u-fang	土方	Hijikata
T'u-fei	土肥	Dohi
T'u-wu	土屋	Tsuchiya
Tung	東	Higashi
Tung	洞	Hora
Tung-en-na	東恩納	Higaonna
Tung-shan	東山	Higashiyama
Tung-X	東畑	Tōhata
T'ung-k'ou	樋口	Higuchi
T'ung-ku	桶谷	Oketani
Tzu-ho	滋賀	Shiga
Wa	窪	Kubo
Wa-t'ien	窪添	Kubozue
Wai-shan	外山	Toyama

Wan-shan	丸山	Maruyama
Wan-wei	丸尾	Maruo
Wang	網	Ami
Wang-yueh	望月	Mochizuki
Wei-ch'i	尾崎	Ozaki
Wei-hsing	尾形	Ogata
Wei-pan	尾坂	Ozaka
Wei-shang	尾上	Onoe
Wei-t'eng	尾藤	Bitō
Wei-t'eng	衛藤	Etō
Wu	呉	Kure
Wu-ching	五井	Goi
Wu-i	武邑	Takemura
Wu-nei	武内	Takeuchi
Wu-pu	武部	Takebe
Wu-shih-lan	五十嵐	Igarashi
Wu-t'eng	武藤	Mutō
Wu-t'ien	武田	Takeda
X-pen	辻本	Tsujimoto
X-ti	畑地	Hatachi
X-wei	栃尾	Tochio
X-yeh	俣野	Matano
Yeh-ch'i	野崎	Nozaki
Yeh-chien	野間	Noma
Yeh-chien-shan	野見山	Nomiyama
Yeh-k'ou	野口	Noguchi

Yeh-shang	野上	Nogami
Yeh-t'ien	野田	Noda
Yeh-tse	野沢	Nozawa
Yeh-ts'un	野村	Nomura
Yeh-yuan	野原	Nohara
Yen-ch'eng	岩城	Iwaki
Yen-ch'i	岩崎	Iwasaki
Yen-chien	岩見	Iwami
Yen-chien	塩見	Shiomi
Yen-ching	岩井	Iwai
Yen-ch'ung	岩重	Iwashige
Yen-ku	塩谷	Shionoya
Yen-sheng	岩生	Iwao
Yen-tso	岩佐	Iwasa
Yen-ts'un	岩村	Iwamura
Yi		see I
Ying	英	Hanabusa
Ying-ching	桜井	Sakurai
Ying-shan	影山	Kageyama
Yu-chih	友枝	Tomoeda
Yu-fang	幼方	Ubukata
Yu-kao	有高	Aritaka
Yu-kuang	有光	Arimitsu
Yu-mu-yeh	楢木野	Narakino
Yu-pu	遊部	Asobe
Yu-t'ien	有田	Arita

Yü-ch'eng	玉城	Tamaki
Yü-ching	玉井	Tamai
Yü-ching	宇井	Ui
Yü-fan	魚返	Ogaeri
Yü-hsi	羽溪	Hatani
Yü-kung	雨宮	Amenomiya
Yü-mao-t'ien	羽毛田	Hakeda
Yü-shou-hsi	御手洗	Mitarai
Yü-shui	輿水	Koshimizu
Yü-t'ien	羽田	Haneda
Yü-t'ien	玉田	Tamada
Yü-t'ien	宇田	Uda
Yü-t'ien-yeh	羽田野	Hadano
Yü-tu-kung	宇都宮	Utsunomiya
Yü-tu-mu	宇都木	Utsugi
Yü-yeh	宇野	Uno
Yuan	原	Hara
Yuan-chia	園家	Sonoie
Yuan-shan	遠山	Tōyama
Yuan-t'eng	遠藤	Tōyama
Yuan-t'ien	原田	Harada
Yuan-yuan	鴛淵	Oshibuchi
Yueh-chih	越智	Ochi
Yueh-lun	月輪	Tsukinowa
Yung-ching	永井	Nagai
Yung-mo	永末	Nagasue

Yung-tao   永島   Nagashima

Yung-t'ien   永田   Nagata

Yung-yuan   永原   Nagahara

Non-Japanese Cited in the **Handbook**

For discussion of Index B, see the "Introduction," Section VIII, Part 5: "Indexes: Japanese / Non-Japanese Cited."

NAME	SEE **ENTRY** OR **ENTRIES** UNDER
Araki, James T.	Inoue Yasushi (3)
Atwell, William S.	Yoshikawa Kōjirō
Barberi, Susan	Satō Masahiko
Bastid, Marianne	Muramatsu Yuji
Baxter, Glen W.	Yoshikawa Kōjirō
Bernhardt, Kathryn	Ono Kazuko
Bester, John	Inoue Yasushi
Birnbaum, Alfred T.	Miyakawa Torao
Blyth, R.H.	Suzuki Daisetsu
Bourassa, Jon	Suzuki Kei
Braithwaite, George	Takekoshi Yosaburō
Brook, Timothy	Ono Kazuko
Cartier, Michel	Muramatsu Yūji
Chan, F. Gilbert	Naitō Konan
Chan Hok-lam	Nakano Miyoko
Chao, Y.R.	Collected Articles #63b
Ch'en Heng-che	Collected Articles #63a & 63b
Ch'en Hsin-ming =	Izumi Kiyoshi
Ch'en Shun-ch'en =	Chin Shunshin
Chibbett, David	Katō Shūichi
Conze, Edward	Suzuki Daisetsu
Daniels, Christian	Intro. #17

Davids, R.   Ogiwara Unrai

Davidson, Jeremy   Intro., Footnote 15

de Bary, Wm. T.   Yoshikawa Kōjirō

Demiéville, P.   Akizuki, Ryōmin, Kano Naoki, Sugi-
                                    mura Kunihiko, Tsukamoto Zen-
                                    ryū, Yamaguchi Susumu, Yana-
                                    gida Seizan (2), Yoshikawa
                                    Kōjirō

Diény, Jean-Pierre   Yoshikawa Kōjirō (3)

Driscoll, Lucy   Toda Kenji

Dull, J.L.   Collected Articles #20a

Dusenbury, Jerry   Nakayama Shigeru

Ebrey, Patricia   Umehara Kaoru

Elisséef, Serge   Hamada Kōsaku (2), Shinjō Shinzō

Elman, Benjamin A.   Hihara Toshikuni

Elvin, Mark   Hoshi Ayao, Shiba Yoshinobu

Etzold, Thomas H.   Naitō Konan

Fairbank, John K.   Intro., Footnote 4 (2)

Feifel, P. Eugen   Nagasawa Kikuya

Feng, R.   Collected Articles #63b

Fernström-Flygare, W.   Mizuno Seiichi, Nagahiro Toshio

Figgess, John   Koyama Fujio (2)

Fogel, Joshua A.   Chin Shunshin (2), Goi Naohiro,
                                    Itō Chūta, Itō Takeo, Naitō
                                    Konan (5), Masuda Wataru,
                                    Nakae Ushikichi (2), Ono
                                    Kazuko, Shimada Kenji, Tani-
                                    gawa Michio (2), Uno Tetsuto,
                                    Yokogawa Jirō

Franke, Herbert   Mikami Tsugio (3)

Fraser, Dana R.   Iriya Yoshitaka

Fromm, Erich   Suzuki Daisetsu

Fuchs, W.   Tamura Jitsuzō

Seidensticker, E.G.   Inoue Yasushi

Sensabaugh, David   Suzuki Kei

Shek, Richard   Sakai Tadao

Sivin, N.   Collected Articles #20a

Soper, Alexander C.   Akiyama Terukazu, Ōmura Seigai

Soymié, Michel   Ikeda On, Ōba Osamu, Collected
                                           Articles #19

Stanley-Baker, Joan   Suzuki Kei

Stanley-Baker, Richard   Suzuki Kei

Stcherbatsky, Ts.   Ogiwara Unrai

Stein, R.A.   Fukui Kōjun

Strauss, O.   Ogiwara Unrai

Strickmann, Michel   Sakai Tadao, Collected Articles #20b

Suleski, Ronald   Nishimura Shigeo

Swann, P.C.   Mizuno Seiichi, Nagahiro Toshio

Tam Yue-him   Naitō Konan (2)

Tanaka, Stefan   Shiratori Kurakichi

Taylor, Rodney L.   Okada Takehiko

Teng Ssu-yü   Intro. #5

Tillich, Paul   Suzuki Daisetsu

Toynbee, Arnold   Katō Shūichi, Suzuki Daisetsu

Tregear, M.   Akiyama Terukazu

Tseng Hsien-chi   Tomita Kōjirō

Tsiang, Katherine S.   Mino Yutaka (2)

Twitchett, Denis   Niida Noboru, Sudō Yoshiyuki

van Gulik, R.   Mutō Chōzō

Vandermeersch. L.   Ikeda Suetoshi

Vinograd, Richard   Suzuki Kei

Wakabayashi, Bod Tadashi   Watanabe Hiroshi

Walleser, M.   Ogiwara Unrai

Wang Kuo-wei   Collected Articles #81

Wang, May   Nakano Miyoko

Japanese Phrases Cited in the <u>Handbook</u>,
with Chinese Characters and English Equivalents

Chinese characters for phrases commonly repeated in book titles in the <u>Handbook</u>, as well as in names of group or institutional editors cited, can generally be determined by consulting the following list of phrases. Note that Index F, "Publishers of East Asian-Language Books Cited, with Chinese Characters," lists those "ed. & publ." (i.e., editor and publisher) entities that cannot be readily determined from the following list or from other information supplied where the phrasing originally appears.

PHRASE	KANJI (or KANA)	ENGLISH EQUIVALENT
Ajia	アジア	Asia
Ajia-shi	アジア史	Asian history
beiju	米寿	88th-birthday celebration
bekkan	別巻	supplementary volume
bessatsu	別冊	supplementary volume
bōeki	貿易	trade
Bukkyō	仏教	Buddhism
bungakubu	文学部	literature department
bunshū	文集	collection of articles
chojutsu	著述	writings
chōsabu	調査部	research section
chosaku	著作	writings
chosakusen	著作選	selection of writings
chosakushū	著作集	collection of writings
chosho	著書	writings

Chūgoku	中国	China
dōkōkai	同好会	friends' association
etsureki	閲歴	curriculum vitae
fu	附	appended
gakujutsu	学術	scholarship
gendai	現代	contemporary
gyōji	行事	event, function, observance
gyōseki	業績	achievements
hakkōsho	発行所	issuing agency
hakuju	白寿	99th-birthday celebration
hakushi	博士	Dr., Ph.D.
hatsubaisho	発売所	distributor
hencho	編著	edited and authored works
henshū	編集	editing
honsōgi	本葬儀	funeral service
hyakunen	百年	100 years
ichiran	一覧	summary
iinkai	委員会	committee
ikō	遺稿	posthumous manuscripts
ikōshū	遺稿集	collection of posthumous manu-scripts
insatsujo	印刷所	printer
isō	遺草	posthumous writings
isho	遺書	posthumous volume
jigyō	事業	task, affair, undertaking
jigyōkai	事業界	committee doing an undertaking

jikkō	実行	carrying out, execution
jimbun kagaku	人文科学	humanistic sciences
jokyōju	助教授	assistant or associate professor
jumbikai	準備会	committee making arrangements
jūyō	重要	important
kaigi	会議	conference
kakō	華甲	61st-birthday celebration
Kambun	漢文	Classical Chinese writing, incl. that by Japanese
kana	かな	Japanese syllabic writing
Kanji	漢字	Chinese characters
kankō	刊行	publishing
kankōkai	刊行会	publication committee
kanreki	還暦	60th-birthday celebration
keishuku	慶祝	congratulation, celebration
keizai	経済	economics
kenkyūjo	研究所	research institute
kenkyūkai	研究会	research society
kenkyūshitsu	研究室	seminar or research office
kentei	献呈	presentation
kiju	喜寿	77th-birthday celebration
kindaishi	近代史	modern history
kinen	記念	commemoration
kinenkai	記念会	commemoration committee
ko	故	the former or deceased

kodaishi	古代史	ancient history
kōen	講演	lectures
koki	古稀	70th-birthday celebration
kōkogaku	考古学	archaeology
kokusai	国際	international
kyōiku	教育	education
kyōju	教授	professor
mokuroku	目録	catalog
nai	内	within
nempu	年譜	chronological biography
ombin	音便	sound change
oyobi	及び	and
rekishi	歴史	history
roku	録	record
rokujūsan-sai	六十三歳	63 years
rombun	論文	article
rombunshū	論文集	collection of articles
roncho	論著	writings
ronshū	論集	collection of articles
ronsō	論叢	collection of articles
ryaku	略	abbreviated
sakuhinshū	作品集	collection of writings
sakusei	作成	drafting
sanjūnen	三十年	30 years
seitan	生誕	birth
seminaaru	セミナール	seminar

sensei	先生	professor
senshū	選集	anthology
shakai	社会	society, social
shigakkai	史学会	history society
shigaku	史学	history
shigakuka	史学科	faculty of history
shikkō	執行	carrying out, performance
Shina	支那	China
shisō	思想	thought
shōju	頌寿	congratulations on long life
shosatsu	小冊	booklet
shū	集	collection
shukuga	祝賀	celebration, felicitations
shukugakai	祝賀会	celebration committee
shuppan	出版	publishing
shuppanbu	出版部	publishing department
shuppankai	出版会	publishing group or committee
shūshū seiribu	収集整理部	acquisitions department
taikan	退官	retirement
taikyū	退休	retirement
teinen	停年	retirement year
tetsugakushi	哲学史	history of philosophy
Tōa	東亜	East Asia
tokubetsu	特別	special
Tōyōshi	東洋史	Oriental history
Tōyōshigaku	東洋史学	study of Oriental history

Tōzai	東西	East-West
tsuiho	追補	supplement
tsuitō	追悼	<u>in memoriam</u>
tsuiokushū	追憶集	collection of reminiscences
(... o) yomu kai	(…を)読む会	group reading or studying (...)
zaishoku	在職	period of service
zenshū	全集	complete works
zonkō	存稿	extant manuscripts
zuihitsushū	随筆集	collection of miscellaneous writings

East Asian-Language Journals Cited, with Chinese Characters

For discussion of conventions followed in capitalizing journal titles, see the "Introduction," Section VIII, Part 2: "Capitalization: Journal and Book Titles."

JOURNAL TITLE	KANJI (and KANA)
Aichi Daigaku bungaku ronsō	愛知大学文学論叢
Aichi Daigaku Kokusai Mondai Kenkyūjo kiyō	愛知大学国際問題研究所紀要
Aichi Kenritsu Daigaku Bungakubu ronshū (Ippan kyōiku gakuka hen)	愛知県立大学文学部論集（一般教育学科編）
Ajia Afurika bunken chōsa hōkoku (Gengo shūkyō)	アジア・アフリカ文献調査報告（言語宗教）
Ajia Afurika gengo bunka kenkyū	アジア・アフリカ言語文化研究
Ajia Afurika Gengo Bunka Kenkyūjo tsūshin	アジア・アフリカ言語文化研究所通信
Ajia bunka kenkyū (Asian Cultural Studies)	アジア文化研究
Ajia keizai jumpō	アジア経済旬報
Ajia kenkyū	アジア研究
Ajia-shi kenkyū (Chūō Daigaku)	アジア史研究（中央大学）
Biburia	ビブリア
Bijutsushi kenkyū (Waseda Daigaku)	美術史研究（早稲田大学）
Bōei Daigakkō kiyō	防衛大学校紀要
Bukkyō Daigaku Daigakuin kenkyū kiyō	仏教大学大学院研究紀要
Bukkyō geijutsu	仏教芸術

Bukkyō kenkyū	仏教研究
Bukkyōgaku kenkyū	仏教学研究
Bukkyōgaku seminaa	仏教学セミナー
Bungaku (Iwanami Shoten)	文学（岩波書店）
Bungaku kenkyū (Kyūshū Daigaku)	文学研究（九州大学）
Bungaku ronshū (Kyūshū Daigaku)	文学論輯（九州大学）
Bungei	文芸
Bunka	文化
Bunkyō Daigaku Kyōiku Gakubu kiyō	文教大学教育学部紀要
Chiba Daigaku hōkei kenkyū	千葉大学法経研究
Chikaki ni arite	近きに在りて
Chin-ling hsueh-pao (Nan-ching)	金陵学級（南京）
Chirigaku hyōron	地理学評論
Chōsen gakuhō	朝鮮学報
Chōsenshi Kenkyūkai rombunshū	朝鮮史研究会論文集
Chūgoku Bungakkai hō (Ochanomizu Joshi Daigaku)	中国文学会報（お茶の水女子大学）
Chūgoku bungaku kenkyū (Waseda Daigaku)	中国文学研究（早稲田大学）
Chūgoku bungaku ronshū (Kyūshū Daigaku)	中国文学論集（九州大学）
Chūgoku bungaku ronsō (Ōbirin Daigaku)	中国文学論叢（桜美林大学）
Chūgoku kenkyū geppō	中国研究月報
Chūgoku koten kenkyū	中国古典研究
Chūgoku shisōshi kenkyū (Kyōto Daigaku)	中国思想史研究（京都大学）
Chūgokugo-gaku	中国語学
Chūgokushi kenkyū (Ōsaka Shiritsu Daigaku)	中国史研究（大阪市立大学）

Chūkyō Daigaku kyōiku ronsō	中京大学教育論叢
Chung-kuo k'o-chi shih liao (Peking)	中国科技史料（北京）
Chūō Daigaku Bungakubu kiyō (Shigakuka)	中央大学文学部紀要（史学科）
Chūō keizai	中央経済
Chūtetsubun Gakkai hō	中哲文学会報
Daitō Bunka Daigaku Kangakkai shi	大東文化大学漢学会誌
Dōshisha gaikoku bungaku kenkyū	同志社外国文学研究
Dōshisha hōgaku	同志社法学
Dōshisha shōgaku	同志社商学
Firosofia	see Philosophia
Fukuoka Daigaku hōgaku ronsō	福岡大学法学論叢
Fukuoka Daigaku keizaigaku ronsō	福岡大学経済学論叢
Gaikokugo kenkyū (Kōbe-shi Gaikokugo Daigaku)	外国語研究（神戸市外国語大学）
Gaikokugo-ka kenkyū kiyō (Tōkyō Daigaku)	外国語科研究紀要（東京大学）
Gakudai kokubun (Ōsaka Kyōiku Daigaku)	学大国文（大阪教育大学）
Gakuen ronshū (Hokkai Gakuen Daigaku)	学園論集（北海学園大学）
Gakujutsu kenkyū	学術研究
Chirigaku, rekishigaku, shakai kagaku hen	地理学・歴史学・社会科学篇
Kokugo, kokubungaku hen	国語・国文学篇
Kyōiku, shakai kyōiku, kyōiku shinri, taiiku hen	教育・社会教育・教育心理・体育篇
Jimbun kagaku, shakai kagaku hen	人文科学・社会科学篇
Geibun kenkyū (Keiō Daigaku)	芸文研究（慶応大学）
Geinō	芸能

Gekkan kōkogaku jaanaru	月刊考古学ジャーナル
Gendai no esupuri	現代のエスプリ
Gendai no me	現代の眼
Gogaku bungaku (Hokkaidō Kyōiku Daigaku)	語学文学（北海道教育大学）
Gumma Daigaku Kyōiku Gakubu kiyō (Jimbun shakai kagaku hen)	群馬大学教育学部紀要（人文社会科学編）
Hakuen (Kansai Daigaku)	泊園（関西大学）
Han	韓
Hanazono Daigaku kenkyū kiyō	花園大学研究紀要
Hikone ronsō (Jimbun kagaku tokushū)	彦根論叢（人文科学）
Hikone ronsō (Shiga Daigaku)	彦根論叢（滋賀大学）
Hitotsubashi ronsō	一橋論叢
Hōbun ronsō (Kumamoto Daigaku) (Shigaku hen)	法文論叢（熊本大学）（史学篇）
Hōgaku kenkyū (Keiō Daigaku)	法学研究（慶応大学）
Hōgaku zasshi	法学雑誌
Hokkaidō Daigaku Bungakubu kiyō	北海道大学文学部紀要
Hōkō	方向
Hokuritsu shigaku (Kanazawa Daigaku)	北陸史学（金沢大学）
Hōsei shigaku	法政史学
Hōseishi kenkyū	法政史研究
Hōun	宝雲
Hsi-tsang yen-chiu (Ch'eng-tu)	西蔵研究（成都）
Hsueh-lin man-lu (Peking)	学林漫録（北京）
Hyōrin	評林
Ia	咿啞

Indogaku Bukkyōgaku kenkyū	印度学仏教学研究
Indogaku shiron shū	インド学試論集
Jen-wen yueh-k'an (Shanghai)	人文月刊（上海）
Jimbun gakuhō (Kyōto Daigaku)	人文学報（京都大学）
Jimbun gakuhō (Tōkyō Toritsu Daigaku)	人文学報（東京都立大学）
Jimbun kagaku kenkyū hōkoku (Nagasaki Daigaku Kyōiku Gakubu)	人文科学研究報告（長崎大学教育学部）
Jimbun Kagakuka kiyō (Tōkyō Daigaku Kyōyō Gakubu) (Rekishi to bunka, Rekishigaku kenkyū hōkoku)	人文科学科紀要（東京大学教養学部）（歴史と文化、歴史学研究報告）
Jimbun kenkyū	人文研究
Jimbun ronshū (Kōbe Shōka Daigaku)	人文論集（神戸商科大学）
Jinruigaku zasshi	人類学雑誌
Jishin (Daini-shū)	地震（第二輯）
Jissen kokubungaku	実践国文学
Jōchi shigaku	上智史学
Jōnan Kangaku (Risshō Daigaku)	城南漢学（立正大学）
Kagakushi kenkyū	科学史研究
Kagoshima Daigaku Kyōyōbu shiroku	鹿児島大学教養部史録
Kainan shigaku	海南史学
Kaitoku	懐徳
Kambun Gakkai kaihō (Kokugakuin Daigaku)	漢文学会会報（国学院大学）
Kambun kyōshitsu	漢文教室
Kambungaku	漢文学
Kanazawa Daigaku Kyōyōbu ronshū (Jimbun kagaku hen)	金沢大学教養部論集（人文科学篇）

Kangaku kenkyū (Nihon Daigaku)	漢学研究（日本大学）
Kansai Daigaku Chūgoku Bungakkai kiyō	関西大学中国文学会紀要
Kansai Gakuin shigaku	関西学院史学
Keiei kenkyū (Ōsaka Shiritsu Daigaku)	経営研究（大阪市立大学）
Keiei to keizai (Nagasaki Daigaku)	経営と経済（長崎大学）
Keijō Teidai Shigakkai shi	京城帝大史学会誌
Keizai kagaku (Nagoya Daigaku)	経済科学（名古屋大学）
Keizai kenkyū (Seijō Daigaku)	経済研究（成城大学）
Keizai ronsō (Kyōto Daigaku)	経済論叢（京都大学）
Keizai shirin (Hōsei Daigaku)	経済志林（法政大学）
Keizaigaku zasshi (Ōsaka Shiritsu Dai- gaku)	経済学雑誌（大阪市立大学）
Keizaikei (Kantō Gakuin Daigaku)	経済系（関東学院大学）
Kenkyū (Kōbe Daigaku)	研究（神戸大学）
Kenkyū shūroku (Jimbun, shakai kagaku) (Ōsaka Daigaku)	研究集録（人文・社会科学） （大阪大学）
Kindai (Kōbe Daigaku)	近代（神戸大学）
Kita Kyūshū Daigaku Gaikokugo Gakubu kiyō	北九州大学大学外国語学部紀要
Kōbe Gaidai ronsō	神戸外大論叢
Kodai bunka	古代文化
Kodai Oriento Hakubutsukan kiyō (Bulletin of The Ancient Orient Museum)	古代オリエント博物館紀要
Kodaigaku	古代学
Kōgakkan Daigaku kiyō	皇学館大学紀要
K'o-hsueh-shih i-ts'ung (Hu-ho-hao-t'e, Inner Mongolia)	科学史譯叢（呼和浩特・内蒙古）

Kōkogaku ronsō	考古学論叢
Kōkotsugaku	甲骨学
Kokubungaku: Kaishaku to kyōzai no kenkyū	国文学 ― 解釈と教材の研究 ―
Kokubungaku (Kansai Daigaku)	国文学（関西大学）
Kokubungaku kenkyū (Waseda Daigaku)	国文学研究（早稲田大学）
Kokubungaku ronshū (Jōchi Daigaku)	国文学論集（上智大学）
Kokugakuin hōgaku	国学院法学
Kokugakuin zasshi	国学院雑誌
Kokumin keizai zasshi	国民経済雑誌
Kokushigaku	国史学
Konan	湖南
Kyōto Daigaku Bungakubu kenkyū kiyō	京都大学文学部研究紀要
Li-shih chiao-hsueh (T'ien-chin)	歴史教学（天津）
Li-shih hsueh-pao (Taipei) (Kuo-li T'ai-wan Shih-fan Ta-hsueh)	歴史学報（台北）（国立台湾師範大学）
Mie hōkei	三重法経
Mikkyō bunka	密教文化
Minzokugaku kenkyū	民族学研究
Momoyama rekishi chiri	桃山歴史・地理
Morarojii kenkyū	モラロジー研究
Musashi Daigaku ronshū	武蔵大学論集
Nagoya Daigaku Tōyōshi kenkyū hōkoku	名古屋大学東洋史研究報告
Nagoya Daigaku hōsei ronshū	名古屋大学法政論集
Nagoya Daigaku Bungakubu kenkyū ronshū	名古屋大学文学部研究論集
(Shigaku)	（史学）
(Bungaku)	（文学）
(Tetsugaku)	（哲学）

Nagoya Gakuin Daigaku ronshū (Sangyō Ka-gaku Kenkyūjo)	名古屋学院大学論集（産業科学研究所）
Nagoya Gakuin Daigaku ronshū (Shakai ka-gaku hen)	名古屋学院大学論集（社会科学篇）
Neiraku shien (Nara Joshi Daigaku)	寧楽史苑（奈良女子大学）
Nihon bungaku (Tōkyō Joshi Daigaku)	日本文学（東京女子大学）
Nihon Bunka Kenkyūjo kenkyū hōkoku (Tō-hoku Daigaku)	日本文化研究所研究報告（東北大学）
Nihon Gakushiin kiyō	日本学士院紀要
Nihon kosho tsūshin	日本古書通信
Nihon rekishi	日本歴史
Ningen to shite	人間として
Nung-shih yen-chiu (Peking)	農史研究（北京）
Ochanomizu shigaku	お茶の水史学
Okayama Daigaku Hōbun Gakubu gakujutsu kiyō (Shigaku hen)	岡山大学法文学部学術紀要（史学篇）
Ōryō shigaku	鷹陵史学
Ōsaka Daigaku Indo Tōnan-Ajia Kenkyū Sen-taa ihō	大阪大学インド東南アジア研究センター彙報
Ōsaka Daigaku keizaigaku	大阪大学経済学
Ōsaki gakuhō	大崎学報
Ōtani gakuhō	大谷学報
Otaru Shōka Daigaku jimbun kenkyū	小樽商科大学人文研究
Philosophia (Firosofia) (Waseda Daigaku)	Philosophia（フィロソフィア）（早稲田大学）
Rekishi	歴史

Rekishi hyōron	歴史評論
Rekishi jinrui (Tsukuba Daigaku)	歴史人類（筑波大学）
Rekishi kenkyū (Ōsaka Kyōiku Daigaku)	歴史研究（大阪教育大学）
Rekishi kyōiku	歴史教育
Rekishi to bunka	see Jimbun Kagakuka kiyō
Rekishigaku chirigaku nempō	歴史学地理学年報
Rekishigaku kenkyū	歴史学研究
Rekishigaku kenkyū hōkoku	see Jimbun Kagakuka kiyō
Risshō Daigaku Bungakubu ronsō	立正大学文学部論叢
Risshō shigaku	立正史学
Ritsumeikan bungaku	立命館文学
Ronshū (Tōhoku Indogaku Shūkyō Gakkai)	論集（東北印度学宗教学会）
Ryūkoku shidan	竜谷史壇
Saga Daigaku Kyōyōbu kenkyū kiyō	佐賀大学教養部研究紀要
SAMBHĀṢĀ (Nagoya Daigaku)	SAMBHĀṢĀ（名古屋大学）
Sangyō keizai kenkyū (Kurume)	産業経済研究（久留米）
Sankō Bunka Kenkyūjo johō	三康文化研究所所報
Seinan Ajia kenkyū (Kyōto Daigaku)	西南アジア研究（京都大学）
Seinan Gakuin Daigaku bunri ronshū	西南学院大学文理論集
Seinan Gakuin Daigaku kokusai bunka ron-shū	西南学院大学国際文化論集
Senshū shigaku	専修史学
Setsurin	説林
Shakai kagaku kenkyū (Tōkyō Daigaku)	社会科学研究（東京大学）
Shakai kagaku kiyō (Tōkyō Daigaku)	社会科学紀要（東京大学）

Shakai kagaku ronsō (Nagasaki Daigaku)	社会科学論叢 (長崎大学)
Shakai kagaku tōkyū (Waseda Daigaku)	社会科学討究 (早稲田大学)
Shakaigaku ronsō (Nihon Daigaku)	社会学論叢 (日本大学)
Shibun	斯文
Shichō	史潮
Shidō bunko ronshū	斯道文庫論集
Shien (Kyūshū Daigaku)	史淵 (九州大学)
Shien (Rikkyō Daigaku)	史苑 (立教大学)
Shigaku	史学
Shigaku kenkyū (Hiroshima)	史学研究 (広島)
Shigaku zasshi	史学雑誌
Shih-chieh hua-hsueh chi-k'an (Taipei)	世界華学季刊 (台北)
Shih-huo yueh-k'an (fu-k'an) (Taipei)	食貨月刊 (復刊) (台北)
Shih-yuan (Taipei)	史原 (台北)
Shikai (Tōkyō Gakugei Daigaku)	史海 (東京学芸大学)
Shikan	史観
Shin Nihon bungaku	新日本文学
Shinagaku	支那学
Shinagaku hō	支那学報
Shinagaku kenkyū	支那学研究
Shindō (Nagoya)	信道 (名古屋)
Shirayuri Joshi Daigaku kenkyū kiyō	白百合女子大学研究紀要
Shirin	史林
Shisen (Kansai Daigaku)	史泉 (関西大学)
Shisō (Iwanami Shoten)	思想 (岩波書店)
Shisō (Kyōto Joshi Daigaku)	思窗 (京都女子大学)

Shisō (Nihon Daigaku)	史叢（日本大学）
Shōdai ronshū (Kōbe Shōka Daigaku)	商大論集（神戸商科大学）
Shōgaku ronsan (Chūō Daigaku)	商学論纂（中央大学）
Shokō (Mantetsu)	書香（満鉄）
Shōnan bungaku (Tōkai Daigaku)	湘南文学（東海大学）
Shoron	書論
Shoshigaku	書誌学
Shūkan Tōyōgaku	集刊東洋学
Shūkyō kenkyū	宗教研究
Shundai shigaku (Meiji Daigaku)	駿台史学（明治大学）
Shūsho geppō	収書月報
Ssu-ch'uan Ta-hsueh hsueh-pao ts'ung-k'an (Ch'eng-tu)	四川大学学報叢刊（成都）
Suzuki Gakujutsu Zaidan kenkyū nempō	鈴水学術賎団研究年報
Taishō Daigaku gakuhō	大正大学学報
Takushoku Daigaku ronshū	拓殖大学論集
Tembō	展望
Tenri Daigaku gakuhō (Gakujutsu Kenkyūkai shi)	天理大学学報（学術研究会誌）
Tenri Daigaku gakuhō (Jimbun, shakai, shizen hen)	天理大学学報（人文・社会・自然篇）
Teoriya (Tetsugakuka kiyō) (Kyūshū Daigaku)	テオリヤ（哲学科紀要）（九州大学）
Tetsugaku (Hiroshima)	哲学（広島）
Tetsugaku nempō	哲学年報
Tōa	東亜

Tōa jiron   東亜時論

Tōa keizai kenkyū   東亜経済研究

Tōhō bungei   東方文芸

Tōhō gakuhō [Kyōto]   東方学報〔京都〕

Tōhō shūkyō   東方宗教

Tōhōgaku   東方学

Tōkai shigaku   東海史学

Tōkō   東光

Tōkyō Shinagaku hō   東京支那学報

Toshokan zasshi   図書館雑誌

Tōyō bijutsu   東洋美術

Tōyō bungaku kenkyū   東洋文学研究

Tōyō bunka (Mukyūkai)   東洋文化（無窮会）

Tōyō bunka (Nagoya)   東洋文化（名古屋）

Tōyō bunka (Tōkyō Daigaku)   東洋文化（東京大学）

Tōyō Bunka Kenkyūjo kiyō (Mukyūkai)   東洋文化研究所紀要（無窮会）

Toyō Bunka Kenkyūjo kiyō (Tōkyō Daigaku)   東洋文化研究所紀要（東京大学）

Tōyō Bunko shohō   東洋文庫書報

Tōyō gakuhō   東洋学報

Tōyō gakujutsu kenkyū   東洋学術研究

Tōyō kodai chūsei shi kenkyū (Tōkyō Gaku-   東洋古代中世史研究（東京
    gei Daigaku)   学芸大学）

Tōyō no shisō to shūkyō (Waseda Daigaku)   東洋の思想と宗教（早稲田大学）

Tōyō ongaku kenkyū   東洋音楽研究

Tōyō shien (Ryūkoku Daigaku)   東洋史苑（竜谷大学）

Tōyōgaku kenkyū   東洋学研究

Tōyōshi kenkyū	東洋史研究
Tōyōshi ronshū (Tōhoku Daigaku)	東洋史論集（東北大学）
Tu shu (Peking)	読書（北京）
UP (Tōkyō Daigaku)	UP（東京大学）
Waseda	ワセダ
Waseda shakai kagaku kenkyū	早稲田社会科学研究
Wen-hsueh i-ch'an (Peking)	文学遺産（北京）
Yamagata Daigaku kiyō (Jimbun kagaku)	山形大学紀要（人文科学）
Yamanashi Daigaku Gakugei Gakubu kenkyū hōkoku	山梨大学学芸学部研究報告
Yen-ching hsueh-pao (Peking)	燕京学報（北京）
Yokohama Shiritsu Daigaku ronsō (Jimbun kagaku keiretsu)	横浜市立大学論叢（人文科学系列）
Yūrashia	ユーラシア
Yūrashia Gakkai kenkyū hōkoku	ユーラシア学会研究報告
Zen Bunka Kenkyūjo kiyō (Nagoya)	禅文化研究所紀要（名古屋）
Zengaku kenkyū (Hanazono Daigaku)	禅学研究（花園大学）

China-Related Western-Language Books and Monographs

by Japanese Scholars of China

Western-language titles in Index E are book-length China-related works **BY** Japanese scholars of China. Several of the volumes are co-authored, and a few are edited works. (Full bibliographic information on each can be found in the body of the <u>Handbook</u> under the author's name, where each entry is preceded by the symbol ∈.)

Separate titles in English **ABOUT** scholar-entrants also appear in the <u>Handbook</u>, but are not listed in Index E. They can be found in the body of the <u>Handbook</u> under the following names: Arao Sei, Naitō Konan, Nakae Ushikichi, Okada Takehiko, Ozaki Hotsumi, Shiratori Kurakichi, Suzuki Daisetsu, and Yoshikawa Kōjirō. (Like other Western-language items about entrants and their work, such entries are preceded by the symbol ∍.)

In Index E, multiple titles by the same author appear in the same reverse-chronological order that they do in the body of the <u>Handbook</u>.

Western-language volumes by Suzuki Daisetsu are not included. (See the main entry under Suzuki's name for references to comprehensive listings of his Western-language books and articles.) Bibliographies cited in Footnote 4 of the "Introduction" are also not listed here.

AUTHOR	**TITLE**
Akiyama Terukazu	Arts of China. Vol. 1: Neolithic Cultures to the T'ang Dynasty: Recent Discoveries.
----------	Arts of China. Vol. 2: Buddhist Cave Temples: New Researches.
Andō Hikotarō	Peking.
Bamba Nobuya	Japanese Diplomacy in a Dilemna: New Light on Japan's China Policy, 1924-1929.
Banno Masataka	China and the West, 1858-1861: The Origins of the Tsungli Yamen.

Chikashige Masumi   Alchemy and Other Chemical Achievements of the
                             Ancient Orient: The Civilization of Japan
                             and China in Early Times as Seen from the
                             Chemical Point of View.

Chin Shunshin   Murder in a Peking Studio (Pekin Yūyūkan).

Harada Kinjirō   The Pageant of Chinese Painting.

Hasebe Rakuji   Chinese Ceramics.

Hashimoto Keizō   Hsü Kuang-ch'i and Astronomical Reform: The Pro-
                             cess of the Chinese Acceptance of Western
                             Astronomy, 1629-1635.

Hashimoto Mantarō   The Hakka Dialect: A Linguistic Study of Its Pho-
                             nology, Syntax and Lexicon.

Hayashiya Seizō   Chinese Ceramics.

Hoshi Ayao   The Ming Tribute Grain System.

Ikeda Daisaku   The Flower of Chinese Buddhism.

Inoue Yasushi   Wind and Waves.

----------   Tun-huang.

----------   The Roof Tile of Tempyo.

----------   Journey beyond Samarkand.

----------   Flood.

----------   Lou-lan.

Iriya Yoshitaka   The Recorded Sayings of Layman P'ang: A Ninth-
                             Century Zen Classic.

Ishihara Akira   The Tao of Sex.

Itō Takeo   Life along the South Manchurian Railway: The Mem-
                             oirs of Itō Takeo.

Izutsu Toshihiko   Sufism and Taoism: A Comparative Study of Key
                             Philosphical Concepts

Kaizuka Shigeki   Confucius.

Kamachi Noriko   Reform in China: Huang Tsun-hsien and the Japa-
                             nese Model.

Kano Tadao   An Illustrated Ethnography of Formosan Aborigi-
                             nies. 3 vols.

Kataoka Tetsuya   Resistance and Revolution in China: The Commu-
                             nists and the Second United Front.

Miyagawa Torao   Chinese Painting.

Miyashita Tadao   The Currency and Financial System of Mainland
                           China.

Miyazaki Ichisada   China's Examination Hell: The Civil Service Exam-
                           inations of Imperial China.

Miyazaki Tōten   My Thirty-three Years' Dream: The Autobiography
                           of Miyazaki Tōten

Mizuno Seiichi   Yün-kang: The Buddhist Cave-temples of the Fifth
                           Century A.D. in North China.

----------   A Study of the Buddhist Cave-temples at Lung-men,
                           Honan.

Munakata Kiyohiko   Ching Hao's "Pi-fa-chi": A Note on the Art of the
                           Brush.

Nagahiro Toshio   Yün-kang: The Buddhist Cave-temples of the Fifth
                           Century A.D. in North China.

----------   A Study of the Buddhist Cave-temples at Lung-men,
                           Honan.

Nagasawa Kikuya   Geschichte der chinesischen Literatur und ihrer
                           gedanklichen Grundlage.

Naitō Konan   Naitō Konan and the Development of the Conception
                           of Modernity in Chinese History.

Nakamura Hajime   A Comparative History of Ideas.

----------   Ways of Thinking of Eastern Peoples: India, Chi-
                           na, Tibet, Japan.

Nakano Miyoko   A Phonological Study in the 'Phags-pa Script and
                           the Meng-ku Tzu-yün.

----------   Index to Biographical Material in Chin and Yüan
                           Literary Works.

Nakata Yūjirō   Chinese Calligraphy.

Nakayama Shigeru   Academic and Scientific Traditions in China, Ja-
                           pan, and the West.

----------   A History of Science in Japan: Chinese Background
                           and Western Impact.

Tanigawa Michio	Medieval Chinese Society and the Local "Community."
Tokiwa Daijō	Buddhist Monuments in China. 5 vols.
Toda Kenji	Chinese Calligraphy.
Tomita Kōjirō	Portfolio of Chinese Paintings in the Museum (Yüan to Ch'ing Periods).
----------	Portfolio of Chinese Paintings in the Museum (Han to Sung Periods).
Torii Ryūzō	Sculptured Stone Tombs of the Liao Dynasty.
----------	Populations préhistoriques de la manchourie méridionale.
----------	Les Mandchoux.
----------	Les Aborigènes de Formose.
Tsuda Sōkichi	An Inquiry into the Japanese Mind As Mirrored in Literature: The Flowering of the Common People Literature
Tsukamoto Zenryū	A History of Early Chinese Buddhism: From Its Introduction to the Death of Hui-yüan. 2 vols.
----------	Wei Shou. Treatise on Buddhism and Taoism.
Yamada Nakaba	Ghenkō: The Mongol Invasion of Japan.
Yamane Yukio	Markets in China during the Sung, Ming, and Ch'ing Periods.
Yamazaki Shu	The Earth of China.
Yonezawa Yoshiho	Japanese Painting in the Literati Style.
----------	Painting in the Ming Dynasty.
----------	Flower and Bird Painting of the Sung Dynasty.
----------	Painting of Sung and Yuan Dynasties.
----------	Arts of China. Vol. 3: Paintings in Chinese Museums: New Collections.
Yoshikawa Kōjirō	Five Hundred Years of Chinese Poetry, 1150-1650: The Chin, Yuan, and Ming Dynasties.
----------	Jinsai, Sorai, Norinaga: Three Classical Philologists of Mid-Tokugawa Japan.
----------	An Introduction to Sung Poetry.
Yoshizawa Chū	Japanese Painting in the Literati Style.

Publishers of East Asian-Language Books Cited, with Chinese Characters

Index F supplies Chinese characters for the names of publishers cited in the
Handbook. The index also includes several group or institutional editors, as
well as "ed. & publ." (i.e., editor and publisher) entities, not easily treated
in Index C.

PUBLISHER	KANJI (and KANA)
Aichi Daigaku Kokusai Mondai Kenkyūjo	愛知大学国際問題研究所
Ajia Keizai Kenkyūjo	アジア経済研究所
Ajia Keizai Shuppankai	アジア経済出版会
Aoki Shoten	青木書店
Asahi Shimbunsha	朝日新聞社
Ashi Shobō	葦書房
Banchō Shobō	畬町書房
Bungei Shunjūsha	文芸春秋社
Bunri Shoin	文理書院
Butsusho Kankōkai Zushōbu	佛書刊行会図像部
Chikuma Shobō	筑摩書房
Chōryūsha	潮流社
Chūbunkan	沖文館
Chūgoku Shoten	中国書店
Chung-kuo She-hui K'o-hsueh Ch'u-pan-she	中国社会科学出版社
Chūō Keizai Kenkyūjo	中央経済研究所
Chūō Kōron Bijutsu Shuppan	中央公論美術出版
Chūō Kōron Jigyō Shuppan	中央公論事業出版

Chūō Kōronsha	中央公論社
Chūsekisha	神積舎
Dai Nippon Tosho Kabushiki Kaisha	大日本図書株式会社
Daian	大安
Daihōrin-kaku	大法輪閣
Daiichi Gakushūsha	第一学習社
Daitō Bunka Daigaku Kangakkai	大東文化大学漢学会
Daitō Shuppansha	大東出版社
Daizō Shuppan	大蔵出版
Dōbunkan	同文館
Dōhōsha	同朋舎
Fūbaisha	風媒社
Fujii Shoten	藤井書店
Fukumura Shoten	福村書店
Fumaidō Shoten	不昧堂書店
Fuzambō	富山房
Fuzankai	富山会
Gendai Jaanarizumu Shuppankai	現代ジャーナリズム出版会
Hachi Gakkai Rengō	八学会連合
Haga Shoten	芳賀書店
Hakujitsu Shoin	白日書院
Hanawa Shobō	塙書房
Hasshūkai	発丑会
Heian Hakubutsukan Kenkyūkai	平安博物館研究会
Heibonsha	平凡社
Heirakuji Shoten	平楽寺書店

Henkyōsha	辺境社
Hiroike Gakuen Shuppanbu	広池学園出版部
Hiroshima Bunrika Daigaku Shigakuka Kyōshitsu	広島文理大学史学科教室
Hōritsu Bunkasha	法律文化社
Hōyū Shoten	朋友書店
Hōzōkan	法蔵館
Hyakkaen	百華苑
Iwanami Shoten	岩波書店
Iwasaki Gakujutsu Shuppansha	岩崎学術出版社
Izumi Shoten	いづみ書店
Jiji Tsūshinsha	時事通信社
Kadokawa Shoten	角川書店
Kaimei Shoin	開明書院
Kan-Gi Bunka Kenkyūkai	漢魏文化研究会
Kansai Daigaku Toshokan	関西大学図書館
Kansai Daigaku Tōzai Gakujutsu Kenkyūjo	関西大学東西学術研究所
Kashiwa Shobō	柏書房
Kawade Shobō	河出書房
Kawade Shobō Shinsha	河出書房新社
Kazama Shobō	風間書房
Kazan Kurabu	霞山倶楽部
Keiō Gijuku Daigaku Tōa Jijō Kenkyūkai	慶應義塾大学東亜事情研究所
Keiō Tsūshin	慶應通信
Keijō Teikoku Daigaku Tairiku Bunka Kenkyūkai	京城帝国大学大陸文化研究会

Keisō Shobō	勁草書房
Kembun Shuppan	研文出版
Kenkyū Shuppan	研究出版
Kikeikai	棋溪会
Kindai Chūgoku Kenkyū Iinkai	近代中国研究委員会
Kinokuniya	紀国屋
Kōbundō	弘文堂
Kōdansha	講談社
Kōfūkan	光風館
Kōgakusha	好学社
Kokeisō	古径荘
Kokudosha	国土社
Kokuritsu Kokkai Toshokan	国立国会図書館
Kokusho Kankōkai	国書刊行会
Kōseisha Kōseikaku	恒生社厚生閣
Kōsei Shuppansha	交成出版社
Kyōiku Shinchōsha	教育新潮社
Kyōiku Shoseki	教育書籍
Kyōiku Shuppan Sentaa	教育出版センター
Kyōiku Taimusu-sha	教育タイムス社
Kyōto Daigaku Bungakubu	京都大学文学部
Kyūto Daigaku Bungakubu Tōyōshi Kenkyūkai	京都大学文学部東洋史研究会
Kyōto Daigaku Jimbun Kagaku Kenkyūjo	京都大学人文科学研究所
Kyōto Daigaku Kōkogaku Kenkyūshitsu	京都大学考古学研究室
Kyōto Hōgakkai	京都法学会

Kyōto Teikoku Daigaku Bungakubu Kōkogaku Kenkyūshitsu	京都帝国大学文学部考古学研究室
Kyūko Shoin	汲古書院
Kyūshū Daigaku Bungakubu	九州大学文学部
Kyūshū Daigaku Bungakubu Tōyōshi Kenkyūshitsu	九州大学文学部東洋史研究室
Manshū Gyōsei Gakkai	満州行政学会
Meguro Shoten	目黒書店
Meiji Daigaku Hōgakubu Hōshigaku Kenkyūshitsu	明治大学法学部法史学研究室
Meiji Shoin	明治書院
Meitoku Shuppansha	明徳出版社
Minami Manshū Tetsudō Kabushiki Kaisha Chōsabu	南満州鉄道株式会社調査部
Mita Shigakkai	三田史学会
Mochizuki Shina Kenkyū Kikin	望月支那研究基金
Mombushō Daigaku Gakujutsu-kyoku	文部省大学学術局
Mombushō Gakujutsu Kokusai-kyoku	文部省学術国際局
Mukyūkai	無窮会
Nagasaki Kōtō Shōgyō Gakkō Kenkyūkan	長崎高等商業学校研究館
Nagata Bunshōdō	永田文昌堂
Naigai Shuppan	内外出版
Nakazawa Insatsu	中沢印刷
Nara Meishinsha	奈良明新社
Natori Shoten	名取書店

Nichi-Man Bunka Kyōkai   日満文化協会

Nigensha   二玄社

Nihon Daigaku   日本大学

Nihon Gakujutsu Shinkōkai   日本学術振興会

Nihon Hōsō Shuppan Kyōkai   日本放送出版協会

Nihon Hyōronsha   日本評論社

Nihon Joshi Daigaku Shigaku Kenkyūkai   日本女子大学史学研究会

Nishō Gakusha Daigaku   二松学舎大学

Ōbirin   Daigaku   Bungakubu   Chūgokugo   桜美林大学文学部中国語
     Chūgoku Bungakuka   中国文学科

Ochanomizu Shobō   御茶の水書房

Ōfūsha   櫻楓社

Ogihara Seibunkan   荻原星文館

Oka Shoin   岡書院

Ōkiku Shoin   桜菊書院

Ōsaka Daigaku Bungakubu   大阪大学文学部

Ōsaka Yagō Shoten   大阪屋号書店

Rikkyō   Daigaku   Hakubutsukan-gaku   立教大学博物館学
     Kenkyūshitsu   研究室

Rikkyō Daigaku Shigakkai   立教大学史学会

Risshō Daigaku Shigakkai   立正大学史学会

Ritsumeikan Daigaku Jimbun Gakkai   立命館大学人文学会

Ritsumeikan   Daigaku   Jimbun   Kagaku   立命館大学人文科学
     Kenkyūjo   研究所

Ritsumeikan Shuppanbu   立命館出版部

Ro Jin Tomo no Kai   魯迅友の会

Rokkō Shobō	六甲書房
Rokumeikan	六盟館
Ryōgen Shoten	燎原書店
Ryūkei Shosha	竜溪書舎
Ryūkoku Daigaku Bukkyō Gakkai	竜谷大学仏教学会
Ryūkoku Daigaku Tōyōshigaku Kenkyūkai	竜谷大学東洋史学研究会
Ryūsha Kaisei Shōgakkai	流沙海西奨学会
Sangai Kakumei Kenkyūkai	辛亥革命研究会
San'ichi Shobō	三一書房
Sankibō Busshorin	山喜房仏書林
Sanseidō	三省堂
Sanseisha	三省社
Seibundō	清文堂
Seikatsusha	生活社
Seinen Chūgoku Kenkyūsha Kaigi	青年中国研究者会議
Seishin Shobō	省心書房
Sekai Seiten Kankō Kyōkai	世界聖典刊行協会
Seki Shoin	関書院
Shibundō	至文堂
Shimizu Kōbundō	清水弘文堂
Shimizu Shoin	清水書院
Shin Hyōron	新評論
Shinchōsha	新潮社
Shōshinsha	昭森社
Shūeisha	集英社
Shunjūsha	春秋社

Sōbunsha	創文社
Suzuki Gakujutsu Zaidan	鈴木学術財団
Taishūkan Shoten	大修館書店
Tankōsha	淡交社
Tenri Daigaku Shuppanbu	天理大学出版部
Tenri Jihōsha	天理時報社
Tōa Dōbun Shoin Daigaku	東亜同文書院大学
Tōhō Gakkai	東方学会
Tōhō Shoten	東方書店
Tōhoku Daigaku Kinen Shiryōshitsu	東北大学記念資料室
Tōkai Daigaku Shuppankai	東海大学出版会
Tōkō Shoin	刀江書院
Tokuma Shoten	徳間書店
Tōkyō Daigaku Shuppankai	東京大学出版会
Tōkyō Daigaku Tōyō Bunka Kenkyūjo	東京大学東洋文化研究所
Tōkyō Kyōiku Daigaku Tōyōshigaku Kenkyūshitsu	東京教育大学東洋史学研究室
Tōkyō Teikoku Daigaku Bunka Daigaku	東京帝国大学文科大学
Toriyama Matsumoto Ryō Sensei Koki Kinenkai	鳥山松本両先生古稀記念会
Tosho Shimbunsha	図書新聞社
Tōsui Shobō	刀水書房
Tōyō Bunko	東洋文庫
Tōyō Keizai Shimbunsha	東洋経済新聞社
Tōyō Kyōkai	東洋協会
Tōyōshi Kenkyūkai	東洋史研究会

Tsukiji Shokan	築地書館
Waseda Daigaku Shuppanbu	早稲田大学出版部
Yamaichi Shobō	山一書房
Yamakawa Shuppansha	山川出版社
Yamato Shobō	大和書房
Yanagihara Shoten	柳原書店
Yoshikawa Kōbunkan	古川弘文館
Yūhikaku	有斐閣
Yoshida-machi Kyōiku Iinkai	吉田町教育委員会
Yūrashia Gakkai	ユーラシア学会
Yūzankaku Shuppan	雄山閣出版
Zayūhō Kankōkai	座右宝刊行会

Places of Publication Cited, with Chinese Characters

Cited as places of publication, Japanese place names are listed as they normally appear in English (namely, as Tokyo, Kyoto, etc., rather than Tōkyō, Kyōto, and so on).

PLACE NAME	KANJI
Fukuoka	福岡
Hiroshima	広島
Kashiwa (Chiba)	柏(千葉)
Keijō	京城
Kobe	神戸
Kyoto	京都
Machita	町田
Nagano	長野
Nagasaki	長崎
Nagoya	名古屋
Nan-ching	南京
Nara	奈良
Okayama	岡山
Osaka	大阪
Peking	北京
Sagamihara (Kanagawa)	相摸原(神奈川)
Sendai	仙台
Shanghai	上海

Shinkyō (Manchuria)   新京（満州）

Suita   吹田

Tenri   天理

Tokushima   徳島

Tokyo   東京

Toyohashi   豊橋

Toyonaka   豊中

Ueda (Nagano)   上田（長野）

Yamagata   山形

Yono (Saitama)   与野（埼玉）

Yoshida-machi, Nishi Kambara-gun   吉田町, 西蒲原郡

   (Niigata)   （新潟）

Index H

Scholars in the <u>Handbook</u>, Listed by Field of Study

Explanation

Index H lists scholars in the <u>Handbook</u> according to their fields of study. The index is arranged first by "MAIN HEADINGS," capitalized and listed alphabetically, that give major areas of study. These are generally followed by "key headings," "subheadings," and occasionally "sub-subheadings," which further define these broad categories. Thus, the index is in the form of an outline or "right-branching tree." As an outline, the sections appear as follows:

MAIN HEADING

    Key heading

        Subheading

           Sub-subheading

Scholars' names are listed alphabetically under appropriate sections.

There are two important practical pieces of advice to give users of the <u>Handbook</u>. The first is to look through the "Outline and Contents" of Index H that immediately follows this explanatory section. The second is to start with the <u>furthest indented subsection</u> relevant to a research area, and having checked names in it, <u>to work up through</u> the sections under which it is "branched": i.e., to go from the more specific to the more general.

Indented subsections are assumed to include references to <u>all sections under which they are indented</u>--i.e., to the same field more generally defined-- to the extent relevant to one's research topic--and to <u>all sections indented under them</u>--again, to the extent relevant.

Cross-references are assumed to refer not only to the sections indicated but also to relevant subsections beneath them.

Note that in cross-references to other sections in the index, "**below**" and "**above**" usually point to **coordinate** subsections <u>under the same main heading</u>. For example, under the main heading "ART," one finds the key heading "Art History - China" followed by "See also 'Buddhist Art History' below." And under the same main heading of "ART," one finds the key heading "Buddhist Art History" followed by "See also 'Art History: Asia' above." In other words, "below" and

"above" normally refer to equally indented subsections under the same main heading.

Names often appear <u>both</u> under a key heading <u>and</u> under a subsection below
it. This happens when the terms "especially" or "including" are used to charac-
terize the subsection. For example, when a scholar's field is characterized as
"Chinese thought, esp. (or incl.) neo-Confucianism," the person's name is listed
<u>both</u> under the key heading "Thought - China" <u>and</u> under the sub-subheading "Neo-
Confucianism" (both of which appear under the same main heading of "THOUGHT").
By contrast, a scholar whose work is said to be on "Chinese thought, Sung
period" will be listed only under the section "Sung Thought - China."

Note the discussion of problems involved in characterizing scholars' fields
of study, as outlined in Section IV of the "Introduction" ("Personal Names and
Fields of Study of Japanese Scholars of China"), where one also finds clarifica-
tion of the time periods covered by the terms "Classical Chinese thought,"
"Modern Chinese history," Chinese vernacular fiction," and "Modern Chinese
literature." The use of the term "Buddhist studies*" (with an asterisk) is
explained in Section VIII, Part 1, of the "Introduction."

Index H Fields of Study

OUTLINE AND CONTENTS

Scholars in the <u>Handbook</u>, Listed by Fields of Study

AGRICULTURE

See "ECONOMICS: Agriculture-China"

ANTHROPOLOGY / ETHNOLOGY

Furuno Kiyoto
Ishida Eiichirō
Kindaichi Kyōsuke
Nakane Chie
Ōmori Shirō

Anthropology / Ethnology - Asia

See also "Anthropology/Ethnology" under "INDIA," "JAPAN," "KOREA,"
  "OKINAWA," "MANCHURIA," "OKINAWA," "SOUTHEAST ASIA," and "TAIWAN"
Akiba Takashi
Egami Namio
Hattori Takeshi
Inoue Hideo
Ishida Eiichirō
Kawachi Yoshihiro
Mabuchi Tōichi
Matsumoto Nobuhiro
Mishina Shōhei
Nakane Chie
Suda Akiyoshi
Takahashi Moritaka
Torii Ryūzō
Tsunoda Fumie
Wakamori Tarō

Anthropology / Ethnology - China

See also "TAIWAN: Anthropology/Ethnology"
Akita Shigeaki
Fujisawa Yoshimi
Itō Seiji
Makino Tatsumi
Shiratori Yoshirō
Shūtatsu Sei
Takemura Takuichi
Takizawa Toshiaki

ARCHAEOLOGY

Sumida Masakazu
Yagi Sōzaburō
Yawata Ichirō

Archaeology - Asia

See also "Archaeology" under "JAPAN," "KOREA," and "MANCHURIA"
Andō Kōsei
Arimitsu Kyōichi
Egami Namio
Harada Yoshito
Higuchi Takayasu
Kawachi Yoshihiro
Komai Kazuchika
Miyagawa Torao
Nakayama Heijirō
Ono Katsutoshi
Saitō Tadashi
Sekino Takeshi
Sono Toshihiko
Tazawa Yutaka
Torii Ryūzō
Tsukinowa Tokifusa
Tsunoda Fumie
Umehara Sueji

Archaeology - China

See also "EPIGRAPHY: China" and "HISTORY: Ancient-China"
Fujita Kunio
Fujita Motoharu
Hamada Kōsaku
Hayashi Minao
Karube Jion
Matsuzaki Hisakazu
Mikami Tsugio
Mitsumori Sadao
Mizuno Seiichi
Okazaki Takashi
Sugimoto Kenji
Sumida Masakazu
Yagi Sōzaburō

ARCHITECTURE

Architectural History - Asia

See also "ART: Asia" and "ART: Buddhist Art History"
Fukuyama Toshio
Itō Chūta
Murata Jirō
Sugiyama Nobuzō
Takeshima Takuichi

Architectural History - China

Iida Sugashi
Sekino Tadashi
Tokiwa Daijō

AROMATICS / SPICES

   See "MISCELLANEOUS: Aromatics"

ART

   Art History - Asia

      See also "Buddhist Art History" below;   also, "ARCHITECTURE: Asia,"
         "INDIA: Art," and "JAPAN: Art"
      Akiyama Terukazu
      Etō Shun
      Fukuyama Toshio
      Hemmi Baiei
      Iijima Shunkei
      Kitagawa Momoo
      Machida Kōichi
      Matsubara Saburō
      Miyagawa Torao
      Okada Jō
      Oketani Hideaki
      Sekino Takeshi
      Suzuki Osamu
      Tazawa Yutaka
      Uemura Rokurō
      Yashiro Yukio

      Art History - China (including Painting)

         See also "Buddhist Art History" below, and "ARCHITECTURE: China"
         Akiyama Terukazu
         Aoki Masaru
         Etō Shun
         Fujita Kunio
         Fukumoto Masakazu
         Hamada Kōsaku
         Harada Kinjirō
         Hasumi Shigeyasu
         Hayashiya Seizō
         Higuchi Takayasu
         Hijikata Teiichi
         Iida Sugashi
         Ishida Mosaku
         Itō Seiji
         Kanda Kiichirō
         Kawakami Kei
         Kobayashi Taichirō
         Kosugi Kazuo
         Koyama Fujio
         Kudō Naotarō
         Kumagai Nobuo
         Matsubara Saburō
         Matsumoto Eiichi
         Matsushita Takaaki
         Mino Yutaka
         Mizuhara Ikō

Mizuno Seiichi
Munakata Kiyohiko
Nagahiro Toshio
Nakamura Shigeo
Nakata Yūjirō
Namikawa Banri
Ōmura Seigai
Ono Katsutoshi
Sekino Tadashi
Shimada Shūjirō
Shimomise Shizuichi
Sugimura Yūzō
Sugiyama Nobuzō
Suzuki Kei
Tanaka Ichimatsu
Tani Shin'ichi
Tanida Etsuji
Toda Teisuke
Tomita Kōjirō
Toyama Gunji
Ueno Teruo
Yonezawa Yoshiho
Yoshizawa Chū

Art Theory - China

Aoki Masaru
Munakata Kiyohiko
Nakamura Shigeo
Shirakawa Yoshirō

Calligraphy - China

Fujiwara Sosui
Fukumoto Masakazu
Iijima Shunkei
Ishibashi Keijūrō
Kanda Kiichirō
Mizuhara Ikō
Munakata Kiyohiko
Naitō Kenkichi
Nakata Yūjirō
Nishikawa Yasushi
Satō Yūgō
Shirakawa Yoshirō
Sugimura Kunihiko
Suwa Suiga
Toda Kenji
Toyama Gunji
Yoneda Kenjirō

Ceramics - China

Hasebe Gakuji
Hayashiya Seizō

Koyama Fujio
Mino Yutaka
Sakuma Shigeo
Satō Masahiko

Buddhist Art History

See also "Art History: Asia" above; also, "ARCHITECTURE: Asia," "BUD-
    DHISM," "INDIA: Art," and "JAPAN: Art"
Hirako Takurei
Matsubara Saburō
Matsumoto Eiichi
Mizuno Seiichi
Nagahiro Toshio
Sekino Tadashi
Takada Osamu
Taniguchi Tetsuo
Tokiwa Daijō

ASTRONOMY

See "SCIENCE"

BIBLIOGRAPHY - China / Japan

Abe Ryūichi
Araki Toshikazu
Arita Kazuo
Banno Masataka
Enoki Kazuo
Fujita Masanori
Gotō Kimpei
Ichiko Chūzō
Ikeda Makoto
Ishida Mikinosuke
Iwashige Hidemaru
Izumi Kiyoshi
Kamachi Noriko
Kanda Kiichirō
Katsumura Tetsuya
Kawagoe Yasuhiro
Kawase Kazuma
Kinugawa Tsuyoshi
Kuraishi Takeshirō
Kurata Junnosuke
Mizukami Shizuo
Nagasawa Kikuya
Naitō Shigenobu
Nakata Yoshinobu
Nishimura Gen'yū
Ono Noriaki
Onogawa Hidemi
Ōta Shōjirō
Sawaya Harutsugu
Shinohara Hisao

Takeji Sadao
Tochio Takeshi
Tominaga Makita
Tsuboi Yoshimasa
Uemura Kōji
Umehara Kaoru
Yajima Genryō
Yamaguchi Yoshio
Yamane Yukio
Yamauchi Masahiro

BOTANY

See "SCIENCE"

BUDDHISM

Buddhist Studies - including China-related

See also "ARCHITECTURE: Asia," "ART: Asia," "ART: Buddhist Art History," "RELIGION: East Asia," and "TUN-HUANG TEXTS"
Fukaura Shōbun
Fukuhara Ryōgon
Furuta Shōkin
Matsumoto Bunzaburō
Misaki Ryōshū
Mochizuki Shinkō
Ogiwara Unrai
Sasaki Gesshō
Takamine Ryōshū
Tanaka Junshō
Ui Hakuju
Yabuki Keiki

Buddhism - China

See also "Ch'an/Zen Buddhism" below; also, "ARCHITECTURE: China," "LITERATURE: Buddhist Literature," and "RELIGION: China"
Andō Tomonobu
Andō Toshio
Chikusa Masaaki
Kaji Tetsujō
Kamata Shigeo
Kimura Kiyotaka
Makita Tairyō
Michibata Ryōshū
Moroto Tatsuo
Nagao Mitsuyuki
Nogami Shunjō
Nomura Yōshō
Ōchō Enichi
Ogasawara Senshū
Ogawa Kan'ichi
Osabe Kazuo
Ōtani Kōshō

Ch'an / Zen Buddhism

Buddhist Studies* - mostly non-China-related

Nagao Gajin
Nakamura Hajime
Nakano Gishō
Nanjō Bun'yū
Nishi Giyū
Ono Gemmyō
Saitō Yuishin
Sakamoto Yukio
Satō Mitsuo
Shizutani Masao
Suetsuna Joichi
Suwa Gijō
Suzuki Daisetsu
Takahata Kanga
Takakusu Junjirō
Takemura Shōhō
Ueda Yoshifumi
Umehara Takeshi
Watanabe Kaigyoku
Watanabe Shōkō
Yamada Ryūjō
Yamaguchi Susumu

CENTRAL / INNER ASIAN STUDIES

See also "HISTORY: Asia" and "TUN-HUANG TEXTS"
Abe Takeo
Dohi Yoshikazu
Enoki Kazuo
Etani Toshiyuki
Fujieda Akira
Fukada Kyūya
Haneda Akira
Haneda Tōru
Hatani Ryōtai
Ikeuchi Hiroshi
Inaba Iwakichi
Inoue Yasushi
Ise Sentarō
Ishihama Juntarō
Iwasa Seiichirō
Kodama Shinjirō
Kuwabara Jitsuzō
Maeda Masana
Maejima Shinji
Mano Eiji
Matsuda Hisao
Matsumura Jun
Mori Masao
Nagasawa Kazutoshi
Okada Hidehiro
Okamoto Yoshiji
Okazaki Seirō

Otagi Matsuo
Satō Hisashi
Shiratori Kurakichi
Suwa Gijō
Uchida Gimpū
Uemura Seiji
Yamada Nobuo

CHILDREN'S LITERATURE

See "MISCELLANEOUS: Children's Literature"

CLOTHING - History of

See "MISCELLANEOUS: Clothing"

CONTEMPORARY CHINA

See also "ECONOMICS: Modern/Contemporary-China," "HISTORY: Contemporary-China," "INTERNATIONAL RELATIONS: China/Asia," "THOUGHT: Modern-China," "MISCELLANEOUS: Film," and "MISCELLANEOUS: Popular Culture"
Akioka Ieshige
Fukushima Yutaka
Hidaka Rokurō
Higashiyama Kaii
Ichiko Chūzō
Kawasaki Hideji
Kimura Ihee
Maiya Ken'ichirō
Matsuoka Yōko
Miyakawa Kiyoshi
Nakanishi Tsutomu
Nakayashiki Hiroshi
Ogata Sadako
Ozaki Hotsuki
Saionji Kazuteru
Saionji Kinkazu
Sakamoto Tokumatsu
Samejima Kunizō
Satō Shin'ichirō
Satō Shōji
Sawaya Haratsugu
Shibaike Yasuo
Shiraishi Iwao
Suganuma Fujio
Suganuma Masahisa
Tagawa Seiichi
Takeuchi Minoru
Ubukata Naokichi
Utsunomiya Tokuma
Yamagiwa Akira
Yoda Yoshiie

Contemporary Politics - China

Akao Yoshinori
Akasaka Mitsuo
Amenomiya Yōzō
Arai Takeo
Asami Kazuo
Baba Akio
Doi Akio
Etō Shinkichi
Fujii Shōzō
Hidaka Rokurō
Hirano Yoshitarō
Ikeda Makoto
Ikegami Teiichi
Ishida Moriaki
Ishida Seiichi
Ishikawa Tadao
Itō Takeo
Kitamura Minoru
Kobayashi Hideo
Kobayashi Kōji
Kojima Reiitsu
Kurai Ryōzō
Kuroda Hisao
Kusano Fumio
Matsumura Kazuto
Matsuoka Yōko
Mitsuoka Gen
Miyazaki Seryū
Mukōyama Hiroo
Nakajima Mineo
Nakazora Yoshihiko
Niijima Atsuyoshi
Noma Kiyoshi
Ogawa Heishirō
Okabe Tatsumi
Ōtsuka Yūshō
Ōyama Azusa
Ozaki Shōtarō
Suga Eiichi
Suganuma Fujio
Sugimori Hisahide
Sugino Akio
Takahashi Yūji
Tōhata Seiichi
Tokuda Noriyuki
Umemoto Katsumi
Uno Shigeaki
Yabuki Susumu
Yamashita Ryūzō

CUSTOMS - China

    Akita Shigeaki
    Fujikawa Masakazu
    Harada Yoshito
    Kageyama Seiichi
    Nishioka Hiroshi
    Uchiyama Kanzō

ECONOMICS

    General / Miscellaneous

        Asobe Kyūzō
        Furushima Toshio
        Hisae Fukusaburō
        Kamioka Kazuyoshi
        Miyake Takeo
        Mutō Chōzō
        Nomura Kentarō
        Ono Takeo
        Ōshima Kiyoshi
        Ōuchi Tsutomu
        Sakamoto Kusuhiko

    Economics / Economic History - Asia

        See also "Economic History-China" below; also, "HISTORY: Asia" and
           "OVERSEAS CHINESE"; and the economics-related sections under "HONG
           KONG," "INDIA," "JAPAN," "MANCHURIA," "SOUTHEAST ASIA," and "TAIWAN"
        Hara Kakuten
        Iizuka Kōji
        Kanokogi Noboru
        Kashiwa Sukekata
        Kawano Shigetō
        Kojima Reiitsu
        Nihei Yasumitsu
        Okatani Motoji
        Uchida Naosaku
        Yamamoto Noboru

        **Economy / Economic History / Economic Thought - Modern and Contem-
           porary - China**

           See also "Economic History: China" below; also, "GEOGRAPHY:
           Economic Geography-China," "HISTORY: Modern-China," and
           "OVERSEAS CHINESE"; and the economics-related sections under
           "HONG KONG," "MANCHURIA," and "TAIWAN"
           Adachi Ikutsune
           Adachi Keiji
           Adachi Toshio
           Aiko Katsuya
           Akeno Yoshio
           Amano Motonosuke
           Andō Hikotarō
           Asobe Kyūzō
           Baba Akio

Doi Akira
Ezoe Toshio
Fujimoto Akira
Fukushima Yutaka
Furushima Kazuo
Giga Sōichirō
Hamashita Takeshi
Hatano Yoshihiro
Hirano Yoshitarō
Hiraoka Kentarō
Hirase Minokichi
Hisae Fukusaburō
Horie Eiichi
Inoue Kiyoshi
Ishida Kōhei
Ishikawa Shigeru
Itō Takeo
Iuchi Hirobumi
Izumi Takayuki
Kagawa Shun'ichirō
Kamioka Kazuyoshi
Kawachi Jūzō
Kimura Masutarō
Kitamura Hironao
Kobata Atsushi
Kobayashi Fumio
Kobayashi Hideo
Kobayashi Susumu
Kojima Masami
Kojima Reiitsu
Kojima Shinji
Kōsaka Torizō
Kōzuma Takae
Kusano Fumio
Matsuno Shōji
Mitsuoka Gen
Miyashita Tadao
Miyazaki Seryū
Mukai Akira
Muramatsu Yūji
Nakagawa Manabu
Nakai Hideki
Nakamura Jihee
Nakamura Tetsuo
Nakanishi Tsutomu
Nambu Minoru
Negishi Tadashi
Nishimura Akio
Ōkubo Yasushi
Onoe Etsuzō
Ōtani Kōtarō
Ōtsuka Tsuneo

Ozaki Hotsumi
Ozaki Shōtarō
Sasaki Masaya
Shibaike Yasuo
Shimakura Tamio
Suganuma Masahisa
Sugino Akio
Suyama Takashi
Suzuki Tomoo
Tachibana Shiraki
Tōhata Seiichi
Tokunaga Kiyoyuki
Uchida Naosaku
Ueno Hideo
Yabuki Susumu
Yamamoto Hideo
Yamana Masataka
Yamanouchi Kazuo
Yamashita Ryūzō
Yokoyama Hiroshi
Yokoyama Suguru
Yonezawa Hideo
Yū Chūkun

Agriculture / Agricultural Society - China

See also "Economic History-China" below, and "CONTEMPORARY
    CHINA"
Adachi Ikutsune
Aiko Katsuya
Amano Motonosuke
Furushima Toshio
Hatada Takashi
Hayashi Megumi
Hisae Fukusaburō
Imanaga Seiji
Kashiwa Sukekata
Kondō Yasuo
Kumashiro Yukio
Noma Kiyoshi
Ōshima Kiyoshi
Sakamoto Kusuhiko
Yamamoto Hideo

Economic History - China

See also "Economic History: Modern/Contemporary-China" above; also,
    "GEOGRAPHY: Historical Geography-China" and "HISTORY"
Amagai Kenzaburō
Amano Motonosuke
Edayoshi Isamu
Fukuzawa Yokurō
Hozumi Fumio
Inaba Ichirō

Kageyama Seiichi
Katō Shigeru
Kimura Masao
Kitamura Hironao
Nakayama Hachirō
Nishida Taichirō
Nishijima Sadao
Nishimura Gen'yū
Oikawa Tsunetada
Shida Fudōmaro
Shimizu Taiji
Sogabe Shizuo
Tamai Zehaku
Tanaka Masatoshi
Terada Takanobu
Yamada Kentarō
Yamane Yukio
Yokoyama Suguru

Economic History - Han / Six Dynasties

Kageyama Tsuyoshi
Sakuma Kichiya
Satō Taketoshi
Utsunomiya Kiyoyoshi
Yoneda Kenjirō

Economic History - T'ang / Sung

Fukuzawa Sōkichi
Fukuzawa Yokurō
Kawahara Yoshirō
Mishima Hajime
Nakajima Satoshi
Nakamura Jihee
Ōsaki Fujio
Satō Taketoshi
Shiba Yoshinobu
Shimasue Kazuyasu
Sogabe Shizuo
Sutō Yoshiyuki
Tamai Zehaku
Tsuda Yoshirō
Yanagida Setsuko

Economic History - Ming / Ch'ing

Hamashita Takeshi
Ichiko Shōzō
Iwami Hiroshi
Kishimoto Mio
Murakami Naojirō
Nakamura Jihee
Nakayama Hachirō
Nishijima Sadao

Nishijima Shunsei
Okuzaki Yūji
Otake Fumio
Oyama Masaaki
Sakuma Shigeo
Satoi Hikoshichirō
Shigeta Atsushi
Shimizu Taiji
Sutō Yoshiyuki
Taniguchi Kikuo
Terada Takanobu
Yamane Yukio
Yasuno Shōzō

EDUCATION

Hidaka Rokurō
Yamada Kiyoto

Education - Asia

Fukuzawa Sōkichi
Hayashi Tomoharu
Hiratsuka Masunori
Satō Kiyota

Education - China

Abe Hiroshi
Igarashi Masakazu
Niijima Atsuyoshi
Ōmura Okimichi
Ono Shinobu
Saitō Akio
Taga Akigorō
Terada Gō
Umene Satoru
Yamada Kiyoto
Yamazaki Jun'ichi
Yokomatsu Takashi

EPIGRAPHY - China

See also "ARCHAEOLOGY: China" and "HISTORY: Ancient-China"
Akatsuka Kiyoshi
Hayashi Minao
Itō Michiharu
Kaizuka Shigeki
Katō Jōken
Matsumaru Michio
Nagata Hidemasa
Nagata Toshio
Okada Yoshizaburō
Shima Kunio
Shirakawa Shizuka
Tamada Tsuguo

ETHNOLOGY

   See "ANTHROPOLOGY"

FILM

   See "MISCELLANEOUS: Film"

FOLKTALES

   See "MYTHOLOGY"

FOOD - History of

   See "MISCELLANEOUS: Food"

GENEALOGY

   See "MISCELLANEOUS: Genealogy"

GEOLOGY

   See "SCIENCE"

GEOGRAPHY

   See also "JAPAN: Geography," "MONGOLIA: Geography," and "SOUTHEAST ASIA:
     Historical Geography"
   Iizuka Kōji
   Matsuda Hisao
   Mikami Masatoshi
   Mochizuki Katsumi
   Oda Takeo
   Tamura Shunsuke

     Geography / Economic Geography - China

       Asakawa Kenji
       Imai Seiichi
       Nakamura Seiji
       Oda Takeo

     Historical Geography - China

       Akiyama Motohide
       Aoyama Sadao
       Bekki Atsuhiko
       Fujiyoshi Masumi
       Hibino Takeo
       Keimatsu Mitsuo
       Maeda Masana
       Mori Shikazō
       Nishikawa Kazumi
       Ogawa Takuji
       Unno Kazutaka
       Ushioda Fukizō

GREAT WALL

   See "MISCELLANEOUS: Great Wall"

HISTORY

Kamo Giichi
Kobayashi Hideo

History - Asia

See also "History-East Asia," "History-China," and the key headings
beginning with "Sino-Japanese Cultural Relations" below; also,
"CENTRAL/INNER ASIAN STUDIES" and "MISCELLANEOUS: History-Western
Asia"; and the "History" sections under "INDIA," "JAPAN," "KOREA,"
"MANCHURIA," "MONGOLIA," "OKINAWA," "SOUTHEAST ASIA," "TAIWAN,"
"TIBET," and "U.S.S.R."
Abe Takeo
Aoki Tomitarō
Fujieda Akira
Inaba Iwakichi
Iwai Hirosato
Karashima Noboru
Miyake Yonekichi
Naka Michiyo
Oshibuchi Hajime
Shiratori Kurakichi
Suematsu Yasukazu
Ueyama Shumpei
Yamashita Toraji

History - East Asia

See also "History-Asia" above, and "History-China" below
Aritaka Iwao
Hashimoto Masukichi
Ishida Mikinosuke
Itō Takao
Izushi Yoshihiko
Kanda Kiichirō
Kuwabara Jitsuzō
Matsuo Takayoshi
Mishina Shōhei
Naitō Konan
Naitō Shumpo
Nakayama Kyūshirō
Ono Katsutoshi
Takeda Yukio
Toriyama Kiichi
Tsukinowa Tokifusa
Yamazaki Hiroshi
Yanai Kenji

History - China

See also "History-Asia" and "History-East Asia" above; also, "WOMEN'S
STUDIES"
Aoyama Kōryō
Aritaka Iwao

Dohi Yoshikazu
Enoki Kazuo
Fujieda Akira
Fujimoto Kōzō
Fujita Motoharu
Fujita Toyohachi
Fujiyoshi Masumi
Fukuzawa Yokurō
Gotō Kimpei
Gotō Sueo
Hatada Takashi
Hibino Takeo
Ichimura Sanjirō
Inoue Yasushi
Ishibashi Ushio
Ishihama Juntarō
Itō Tokuo
Kamata Shigeo
Kawahara Masahiro
Kawakatsu Yoshio
Kimura Masao
Koga Noboru
Kurihara Tomonobu
Matsui Shūichi
Matsumoto Yoshimi
Miyakawa Hisayuki
Mori Shikazō
Morita Akira
Moriya Mitsuo
Nakae Ushikichi
Nakayama Hachirō
Niida Noboru
Nishida Taichirō
Nishijima Sadao
Noguchi Masayuki
Nunome Chōfū
Obata Tatsuo
Obi Takeo
Ogata Isamu
Ogura Yoshihiko
Okazaki Fumio
Ōta Yukio
Saeki Tomi
Shiba Ryōtarō
Shida Fudōmaro
Shigematsu Shunshō
Shimizu Morimitsu
Shimizu Taiji
Shiratori Yoshirō
Sōda Hiroshi
Takeda Ryūji
Tamura Jitsuzō

Tan Kyōji
Tanaka Suiichirō
Tezuka Takayoshi
Uemura Seiji
Wada Hironori
Wada Sei
Yamada Nobuo
Yamamoto Noritsuna
Yoneda Kenjirō
Yoshida Tora
Yoshikawa Tadao

History - China - Ancient (thru Han)

See also "ARCHAEOLOGY: China" and "EPIGRAPHY"
Ebata Shin'ichirō
Ikeda Yūichi
Itō Seiji
Izushi Yoshihiko
Kageyama Tsuyoshi
Kaizuka Shigeki
Kubota Takeshi
Kumagai Osamu
Masubuchi Tatsuo
Matsumaru Michio
Mori Yasutarō
Nagata Hidemasa
Nishijima Sadao
Nishioka Hiroshi
Okazaki Takashi
Ōshima Riichi
Ōta Yukio
Shigezawa Toshio
Shirakawa Shizuka
Shiratori Kiyoshi
Sugimoto Kenji
Tada Kensuke
Uehara Tadamichi

History - China - pre-Han

Aihara Shunji
Egashira Hiroshi
Hayashi Taisuke
Itō Michiharu
Naitō Shigenobu
Nomura Shigeo
Ozaki Yūjirō
Utsugi Akira

History - China - Ch'in / Han

Fujiie Reinosuke
Fujikawa Masakazu
Goi Naohiro

Hamaguchi Shigekuni
Hiranaka Reiji
Hori Toshikazu
Itō Tokuo
Kageyama Tsuyoshi
Kamata Shigeo
Kawachi Jūzō
Koga Noboru
Kurihara Tomonobu
Mori Shikazō
Nishimura Gen'yū
Niwa Taiko
Nunome Chōfū
Ōba Osamu
Ogata Isamu
Satake Yasuhiko
Tanaka Ari
Uchino Kumaichirō
Ueda Sanae
Ushioda Fukizō
Utsunomiya Kiyoyoshi
Yamada Katsumi
Yoneda Kenjirō
Yoshinami Takashi

History - China - Six Dynasties

Fujiie Reinosuke
Fujikawa Masakazu
Funaki Katsuma
Hamaguchi Shigekuni
Hori Toshikazu
Kano Naosada
Katsumura Tetsuya
Kawachi Jūzō
Kawakatsu Yoshio
Kikuchi Hideo
Kobayashi Noboru
Kubozoe Yoshifumi
Masumura Hiroshi
Miyakawa Hisayuki
Miyazaki Ichisada
Mori Shikazō
Moriya Mitsuo
Nakamura Keiji
Nishijima Sadao
Nishimura Gen'yū
Niwa Taiko
Nunome Chōfū
Ochi Shigeaki
Ōkawa Fujio
Okazaki Fumio
Okazaki Takashi

Ōsawa Terumichi
Sakuma Kichiya
Satake Yasuhiko
Satō Taketoshi
Suzuki Shun
Tada Kensuke
Tanigawa Michio
Uchida Gimpū
Utsunomiya Kiyoyoshi
Yano Chikara
Yoshikawa Tadao
Yoshinami Takashi

History - China - T'ang / Sung

Aoyama Sadao
Chikusa Masaaki
Fujiyoshi Masumi
Fukuzawa Yokurō
Hino Kaisaburō
Ikeda Makoto
Kurihara Masuo
Miyazaki Ichisada
Mori Katsumi
Nakajima Satoshi
Satake Yasuhiko
Satō Taketoshi
Shimasue Kazuyasu
Sogabe Shizuo
Sutō Yoshiyuki
Tamai Zehaku
Toyama Gunji
Yamamoto Takayoshi

History - China - T'ang

Aritaka Iwao
Dohi Yoshikazu
Fujisawa Yoshimi
Fukuzawa Sōkichi
Funakoshi Taiji
Hamaguchi Shigekuni
Hiraoka Takeo
Hori Toshikazu
Ikeda On
Ishida Mikinosuke
Kaneko Shūichi
Kegasawa Yasunori
Kikuchi Hideo
Koga Noboru
Kubozoe Yoshifumi
Matsui Shūichi
Matsumoto Akira
Matsunaga Masao

Mishima Hajime
Naba Toshisada
Nakagawa Manabu
Nishimura Gen'yū
Nunome Chōfū
Okamoto Goichi
Ono Katsutoshi
Ōsawa Masaaki
Otagi Hajime
Suzuki Shun
Takahashi Zentarō
Takeda Ryūji
Tanigawa Michio
Tonami Mamoru
Tsukiyama Jisaburō
Yano Chikara

History - China - Five Dynasties

Hatachi Masanori
Kikuchi Hideo
Nakagawa Manabu
Nishikawa Masao
Ōsawa Masaaki
Otagi Hajime

History - China - Sung

Araki Toshikazu
Chikusa Masaaki
Hatachi Masanori
Higashi Kazuo
Honda Osamu
Ide Tatsurō
Ihara Hiroshi
Imahori Seiji
Kawahara Masahiro
Kawahara Yoshirō
Kawakami Kōichi
Kida Tomoo
Kinugawa Tsuyoshi
Kiyokoba Azama
Kusano Yasushi
Nagase Mamoru
Nakamura Jihee
Onodera Ikuo
Ōsaki Fujio
Saeki Tomi
Satō Taketoshi
Shiba Yoshinobu
Tamura Jitsuzō
Tan Kyōji
Terada Gō
Tsuda Yoshirō

Umehara Kaoru
Watanabe Hiroyoshi
Yamauchi Masahiro
Yanagida Setsuko
Yoshida Tora

History - China - Liao / Chin / Yuan

See also "MONGOLIA: History"
Abe Takeo
Aoyama Kōryō
Aritaka Iwao
Ebisawa Tetsuo
Hagiwara Jumpei
Honda Osamu
Inosaki Takaoki
Iwamura Shinobu
Kawachi Yoshihiro
Kawazoe Shōji
Kinugawa Tsuyoshi
Kobayashi Takashirō
Maeda Naonori
Mikami Tsugio
Miyazaki Ichisada
Mori Katsumi
Murakami Masatsugu
Nagase Mamoru
Nakamura Jihee
Niwa Tomosaburō
Otagi Matsuo
Ōyabu Masaya
Ryō Susumu
Saguchi Tōru
Shimada Masao
Sogabe Shizuo
Tamura Jitsuzō
Toyama Gunji
Umehara Kaoru
Yamada Nakaba
Yamamoto Takayoshi
Yanagida Setsuko
Yanai Wataru
Yoshida Tora

History - China - Ming / Ch'ing

See also "MANCHURIA: History"
Asai Motoi
Fujii Hiroshi
Fuma Susumu
Hamashima Atsutoshi
Hamashita Takeshi
Hoshi Ayao
Imanishi Shunjū

Iwami Hiroshi
Kanda Nobuo
Kataoka Shibako
Kawakatsu Mamoru
Kishimoto Mio
Kuribayashi Nobuo
Mitamura Taisuke
Momose Hiromu
Mori Masao
Nakamura Jihee
Nakayama Hachirō
Nishijima Shunsei
Noguchi Tetsurō
Obata Tatsuo
Otake Fumio
Oyama Masaaki
Saeki Yūichi
Satō Taketoshi
Shigeta Atsushi
Suzuki Tadashi
Tamura Jitsuzō
Tanaka Masatoshi
Yamane Yukio
Yasuno Shōzō

History - China - Ming

Ejima Hisao
Hagiwara Jumpei
Matsuura Akira
Mori Katsumi
Nishijima Sadao
Okuzaki Yūji
Sakuma Shigeo
Shimizu Taiji
Tani Mitsutaka
Taniguchi Kikuo
Terada Takanobu
Teraji Jun
Tsurumi Naohiro
Yamamoto Takayoshi

History - China - Ch'ing

See also "HISTORY: China-Modern" below, and "MANCHURIA:
   History"
Fujizuka Chikashi
Gotō Sueo
Haga Noboru
Hattori Unokichi
Hosoya Yoshio
Ichiko Shōzō
Ihara Kōsuke
Imahori Seiji

Inaba Seiichi
Ishibashi Hideo
Kageyama Seiichi
Kambe Teruo
Kawakubo Teirō
Kitamura Hironao
Kondō Hideki
Matsumura Jun
Murakami Naojirō
Narakino Shimesu
Oshibuchi Hajime
Ōtani Toshio
Satoi Hikoshichirō
Sutō Yoshiyuki
Suzuki Chūsei
Tabobashi Kiyoshi
Tanaka Katsumi
Ura Ren'ichi

History - China - Modern

See also "ECONOMICS: Modern/Contemporary-China," "THOUGHT: Modern-China," "THOUGHT: Political-China," "WOMEN'S STUDIES," "MISCELLANEOUS: Labor History," and "MISCELLANEOUS: Popular Culture"
Abe Hiroshi
Adachi Keiji
Akiyama Yoshiteru
Asakawa Kenji
Banno Masataka
Chin Shunshin
Endō Saburō
Etō Shinkichi
Fujii Matsuichi
Fujimura Michio
Fujita Masanori
Furumaya Tadao
Haga Noboru
Hanabusa Nagamichi
Hara Kakuten
Hata Ikuhiko
Hatano Yoshihiro
Hazama Naoki
Himeda Mitsuyoshi
Hirano Ken'ichirō
Hō Takushū
Hora Tomio
Horikawa Takeo
Horikawa Tetsuo
Ichiko Chūzō
Ikeda Makoto
Imahori Seiji
Imanaga Seiji

Inaba Shōju
Inoue Hiromasa
Irie Keishirō
Ishida Yoneko
Ishikawa Tadao
Iwamura Michio
Iwasaki Fukuo
Kaihara Fumio
Kamachi Noriko
Kasahara Tokushi
Kataoka Tetsuya
Katō Yūzō
Kawabata Genji
Kawachi Jūzō
Kawai Teikichi
Kikuchi Takaharu
Kitamura Hironao
Kitamura Minoru
Kitayama Yasuo
Kobayashi Kazumi
Kobayashi Takashi
Kojima Shinji
Kojima Yoshio
Kubota Bunji
Makita Eiji
Masui Tsuneo
Matsuno Shōji
Mikami Taichō
Mitani Takashi
Mitsuoka Gen
Miyazaki Tōten
Momose Hiromu
Muramatsu Yūji
Nagai Kazumi
Nakagawa Manabu
Nakamura Jihee
Nakamura Tadashi
Nakamura Tetsuo
Nakatsuka Akira
Nakayama Yoshihiro
Nashimoto Yūhei
Nishikawa Masao
Nishimura Shigeo
Nishizato Yoshiyuki
Nohara Shirō
Nomura Kōichi
Nozawa Yutaka
Ogata Sadako
Okamoto Ryūzō
Ono Shinji
Onogawa Hidemi
Otake Fumio

Ōyama Azusa
Saeki Yūichi
Sasaki Masaya
Satō Shin'ichirō
Satoi Hikoshichirō
Shimada Toshihiko
Shimizu Yasuzō
Suzue Gen'ichi
Suzuki Akira
Suzuki Chūsei
Tachibana Shiraki
Tai Kokki
Takagi Takeo
Takahashi Yūji
Takeuchi Minoru
Tanaka Masami
Tōyama Shigeki
Uchiyama Kanzō
Uchiyama Masao
Ueda Toshio
Umemoto Sutezō
Watanabe Ryūsaku
Yamada Keiji
Yamamoto Hideo
Yamamoto Noritsuna
Yamamoto Sumiko
Yamashita Ryūzō
Yano Jin'ichi
Yoda Yoshiie
Yokoyama Suguru
Yoshida Tomio
Yoshino Sakuzō

Republican Period - China

Adachi Keiji
Fujii Shōzō
Hamashita Takeshi
Hashikawa Tokio
Hirano Tadashi
Ishijima Noriyuki
Kimura Masutarō
Kojima Yoshio

World War II - China

Akiyama Yoshiteru
Arai Shin'ichi
Endō Saburō
Hiraoka Masaaki
Ishikawa Tatsuzō
Shimada Toshihiko
Tōyama Shigeki

Contemporary History - China

See also "CONTEMPORARY CHINA," "ECONOMICS: Modern/Contem-
   porary-China," "THOUGHT: Political-China," and "MISCEL-
   LANEOUS: Film"
Akiyama Yoshiteru
Ishida Moriaki
Ishida Yoneko
Kitamura Minoru
Uno Shigeaki
Yamada Keiji

Historical Texts - China - <u>Shih-chi</u>, <u>Tzu-chih t'ung-chien</u>, etc.

Fukushima Yoshihiko
Harada Taneshige
Ikkai Tomoyoshi
Imataka Makoto
Kaji Nobuyuki
Kusamori Shin'ichi
Maruyama Matsuyuki
Masui Tsuneo
Matano Tarō
Mizusawa Toshitada
Naitō Konan
Nitta Daisaku
Nitta Kōji
Noguchi Sadao
Ōshima Riichi
Otake Fumio
Otake Takeo
Rai Tsutomu
Shirakawa Shizuka
Takeda Taijun
Takeuchi Hiroyuki
Takeuchi Teruo
Tanaka Kenji
Yoshida Kenkō

Sino-British Relations

Inoue Hiromasa

Sino-Japanese Cultural Relations

See also "Sino-Japanese Historical Relations" and "Sino-Japanese Rela-
   tions-Modern" below;   also, "LITERATURE: Sino-Japanese Literary
   Relations," "JAPAN: History," and "HISTORY: China"
Iida Sugashi
Iikura Shōhei
Inoue Masamichi
Jinnouchi Yoshio
Nakajima Kenzō
Nakayama Kyūshirō
Ōta Shōjirō
Sakai Tadao

Shibata Minoru
Tadokoro Yoshiyuki
Yoshii Taijun

Sino-Japanese Historical Relations

See also "Sino-Japanese Cultural Relations" above; "Sino-Japanese
    Relations-Modern" below; also, "THOUGHT: Neo-Confucianism," "JAPAN:
    History," and "HISTORY: China"
Akiyama Kenzō
Bitō Masahide
Doi Akira
Endō Motoo
Fujita Motoharu
Hayashiya Tatsusaburō
Higaonna Kanjun
Higo Kazuo
Ichimura Kisaburō
Imai Keiichi
Imazeki Toshimaro
Inoue Mitsusada
Ishihara Michihiro
Ishii Masatoshi
Ishii Takashi
Iwai Hirosato
Kajima Morinosuke
Kawazoe Shōji
Kitō Kiyoaki
Kyōguchi Motokichi
Matsuura Akira
Mori Katsumi
Noguchi Tetsurō
Ōba Osamu
Ogino Minahiko
Ōmori Shirō
Ono Katsutoshi
Saeki Arikiyo
Sakamoto Tarō
Seki Akira
Shikata Hiroshi
Sono Toshihiko
Suenaga Masao
Suzuki Takeju
Takahashi Zentarō
Takakura Shin'ichirō
Takeuchi Rizō
Tanaka Takeo
Ueda Masaaki
Ueda Toshio
Umehara Takeshi
Ura Ren'ichi
Wada Hironori
Yamada Nakaba
Yano Jin'ichi

Sino-Japanese Relations – Modern

See also "Sino-Japanese Cultural Relations" and "Sino-Japanese Histori-
cal Relations" above; also, "INTERNATIONAL RELATIONS" (especially
"Contemporary Sino-Japanese Relations"), "JAPAN: History," and
"HISTORY: Modern-China"
Abe Hiroshi
Andō Hikitarō
Arao Sei
Banno Junji
Bamba Nobuya
Eguchi Keiichi
Endō Saburō
Hashikawa Bunsō
Hō Takushū
Iriye Akira
Ishikawa Tatsuzō
Itō Takeo
Katayama Sen
Kobayashi Hideo
Mitani Taichirō
Nagai Kazumi
Ogata Sadako
Sanetō Keishū
Satō Saburō
Shinobu Seizaburō
Tabobashi Kiyoshi
Uchiyama Kanzō
Usui Katsumi
Watanabe Ryūsaku
Yamaguchi Ichirō
Yamane Yukio

Sino-Korean Historical Relations

Fujizuka Chikashi
Hō Takushū
Shikata Hiroshi

Sino-Russian Historical Relations

Mikami Masatoshi
Mizuhara Shigemitsu
Ōhashi Yoichi
Sakamoto Koretada
Yoshida Kin'ichi

Sino-Vietnamese Historical Relations

Fujiwara Riichirō
Gotō Kimpei
Kawahara Masahiro
Takeda Ryūji
Wada Hironori
Yamamoto Tatsurō

East-West Historical Relations

Enoki Kazuo
Fujita Toyohachi
Ise Sentarō
Ishida Mikinosuke
Iwamura Shinobu
Iwao Seiichi
Kobayashi Takashirō
Kuwata Rokurō
Maejima Shinji
Masuda Wataru
Mori Masao
Nagasawa Kazutoshi
Sōma Takashi
Sugimoto Naojirō
Suzuki Osamu
Tamura Shunsuke
Yamada Kentarō
Yano Jin'ichi
Yazawa Toshihiko

HONG KONG

See also under "HISTORY": "Asia," "East Asia," and "China"; cf. "OVERSEAS
  CHINESE"
Kani Hiroaki

Hong Kong - Economy

See also "ECONOMICS: Asia"
Kobayashi Susumu
Nihei Yasumitsu

HUMOR

See "MISCELLANEOUS: Humor"

INDIA

Anthropology / Ethnology - India

See also "ANTHROPOLOGY: Asia"
Matsumoto Nobuhiro
Nakane Chie

Art - India

See also "ARCHITECTURE: Asia," "ART: Asia," and "ART: Buddhist Art
  History"
Ono Gemmyō
Takada Osamu
Ueno Teruo

Economic History - India

See also "ECONOMICS: Asia"
Edayoshi Isamu

History – India

See also "HISTORY: Asia"
Ara Matsuo
Etani Toshiyuki
Ishida Moriaki
Karashima Noboru
Suzuki Chūsei
Wada Hisanori

Thought and Religion – India

See also "THOUGHT: Asia"
Ara Matsuo
Honda Megumu
Kanakura Enshō
Kitagawa Hidenori
Miyamoto Yūshō
Nakamura Hajime

Buddhism – India

See also "BUDDHISM" (especially "Buddhist Studies*")
Fukihara Shōshin
Hadano Hakuyū
Hirakawa Akira
Nagao Gajin
Takahata Kanga
Watanabe Shōkō
Yamada Ryūjō

Hindi Language and Literature

Doi Hisaya

Pali Language and Literature

Maeda Egaku
Mizuno Kōgen

Sanskrit Language and Literature

Ashikaga Atsuuji
Nakano Gishō

INNER ASIAN STUDIES

See "CENTRAL/INNER ASIAN STUDIES"

INTERNATIONAL RELATIONS

Amenomiya Yōzō
Gushima Kenzaburō
Hanai Hitoshi
Kajima Morinosuke
Otani Hidejirō
Tanaka Naokichi

International Relations - China / Asia

See also "CONTEMPORARY CHINA"
Aoki Shigeru
Ashizawa Shinji
Etō Shinkichi
Fujii Shōzō
Gushima Kenzaburō
Hata Ikuhiko
Irie Keishirō
Itō Shūichi
Izumi Takayuki
Kawada Tadashi
Kikuchi Masanori
Osanai Hiroshi
Otani Hidejirō
Ōyama Azusa
Sakamoto Tokumatsu
Sasaki Masaya
Seki Hiroharu
Shiranishi Shin'ichirō
Somura Yasunobu
Tanaka Naokichi
Yamagiwa Akira
Yanai Kenji

Contemporary Sino-Japanese Relations

Inoue Kiyoshi
Kajima Morinosuke
Kamei Katsuichirō
Kimura Hiroshi
Kimura Kihachirō
Satō Shōji
Shiraishi Iwao
Tagawa Seiichi
Utsunomiya Tokuma
Yoda Yoshikata

Sino-Soviet Relations

Hirano Yoshitarō
Itō Shūichi
Kimura Hiroshi

Sino-Southeast Asian Relations

Ashizawa Shinji

ISLAM - including Islam / Muslims in China

See also "MINORITIES," "RELIGION," and "HISTORY: China,"
Imanaga Seiji
Iwamura Shinobu
Izutsu Toshihiko
Kobayashi Hajime

Kuwata Rokurō
Nakata Yoshinobu
Saguchi Tōru
Tasaka Kōdō

JAPAN

Anthropology / Ethnology - Japan

See also "ANTHROPOLOGY: Asia" and "OKINAWA: Anthropology"
Ishida Eiichirō
Nakane Chie
Wakamori Tarō

Archaeology - Japan

See also "ARCHAEOLOGY: Asia"
Ishida Mosaku
Matsumoto Masaaki
Mitsumori Sadao
Nagata Toshio
Saitō Tadashi
Suenaga Masao
Tazawa Yutaka
Yagi Sōzaburō

Art and Art History / Artists - Japan

See also "Cultural History: Japan" below; also, "ARCHITECTURE: Asia,"
    "ART: Asia," and "ART: Buddhist Art History"
Akiyama Terukazu
Higashiyama Kaii
Hijikata Teiichi
Ishida Mosaku
Kobayashi Takeshi
Nishikawa Yasushi
Oketani Hideaki
Satō Yūgō
Shimada Shūjirō
Shimomise Shizuichi
Sugiyama Nobuzō
Tanaka Ichimatsu
Tani Shin'ichi
Tazawa Yutaka
Yonezawa Yoshiho
Yoshizawa Chū

Bibliography - Japan

See "BIBLIOGRAPHY: China/Japan"

Cultural History - Japan

See also "Art: Japan" above; "History: Japan," "Literature: History-
    Japan," and "Thought: Japan" below; also, "HISTORY: Sino-Japanese
    Cultural Relations," "LITERATURE: Sino-Japanese Literary Relations,"
    and "MUSIC: East Asia"

Haga Kōshirō
Hayashiya Tatsusaburō
Higo Kazuo
Ishida Ichirō
Kamei Katsuichirō
Katō Shūichi

Economics / Economic History / Economic Thought - Japan

See also "ECONOMICS: Asia"
Furushima Toshio
Hiraoka Kentarō
Iuchi Hirobumi
Kobata Atsushi
Kondō Yasuo
Miyake Takeo
Nomura Kentarō
Ōuchi Tsutomu

Geography - Japan

See also "GEOGRAPHY"
Nakamura Seiji

History - Japan

See also "Cultural History: Japan" above; "OKINAWA: History"; and the
    following sections under "HISTORY":   "Asia," "East Asia," "Sino-
    Japanese Cultural Relations," "Sino-Japanese Historical Relations,"
    and "Sino-Japanese Relations-Modern"
Aoki Shigeru
Banno Junji
Bamba Nobuya
Eguchi Keiichi
Endō Motoo
Fujii Matsuichi
Fujimura Michio
Haga Noboru
Hatada Takashi
Hora Tomio
Horie Eiichi
Ichimura Kisaburō
Imai Keiichi
Inokuma Kaneshige
Inoue Kiyoshi
Inoue Mitsusada
Iriye Akira
Ishii Takashi
Iwao Seiichi
Kajima Morinosuke
Katayama Sen
Kitō Kiyoaki
Kyōguchi Motokichi
Matsumoto Masaaki
Mitani Taiichirō

Mori Katsumi
Murakami Naojirō
Ogata Sadako
Ogino Minahiko
Ōrui Noboru
Ozaki Hotsumi
Ryō Susumu
Saeki Arikiyo
Saitō Hishō
Sakamoto Tarō
Seki Akira
Shinobu Seizaburō
Suenaga Masao
Suzuki Takeju
Tabobashi Kiyoshi
Takakura Shin'ichirō
Takeuchi Rizō
Tanaka Takeo
Tōyama Shigeki
Tsuda Sōkichi
Ueda Masaaki
Wakamori Tarō
Yamada Nakaba
Yamaguchi Kōsaku
Yamamoto Noritsuna
Yanai Kenji

International Relations - Japan

See "INTERNATIONAL RELATIONS: China/Asia" (including "Contemporary
   Sino-Japanese Relations"), "HISTORY: Sino-Japanese Historical Relations," and "HISTORY: Sino-Japanese Historical Relations-Modern"

Language - Japanese

Arisaka Hideyo
Kamei Takashi
Kanazawa Shōzaburō
Kusakabe Fumio
Shibata Minoru
Watanabe Mitsuo

Law - Japan

See also "LAW: East Asia"
Fukushima Masao
Ichien Kazuo
Inada Masatsugu
Ōhira Zengo
Takikawa Masajirō

Literature: Authors - Japan

Chin Shunshin
Fuji Masaharu
Fukada Kyūya

Haniya Yutaka
Inoue Yasushi
Ishikawa Tatsuzō
Kaionji Chōgorō
Kawarazaki Chōjūrō
Nakajima Kenzō
Satō Haruo
Shiba Ryōtarō
Takahashi Kazumi
Takeda Taijun
Takeuchi Yoshimi
Yoda Yoshikata

Literature: History - Japan

See also "Cultural History: Japan" above; also, "HISTORY: Sino-Japanese Cultural Relations," "KAMBUN STUDIES," and "LITERATURE: Sino-Japanese Literary Relations"
Asō Isoji
Ishida Hiroshi
Kanda Hideo
Katō Shūichi
Kojima Noriyuki
Konishi Jin'ichi
Matsushita Tadashi
Nakamura Tadayuki
Nakanishi Susumu
Nemoto Makoto
Ogata Korekiyo
Oketani Hideaki
Sasaki Kiichi
Sayama Wataru
Sugimoto Yukio
Toki Zenmaro
Yamagishi Tokuhei

Music - Japan

See "Cultural History: Japan" above, and "MUSIC: East Asia"

Mythology / Legend / Folklore - Japan

See "MYTHOLOGY: East Asia"

Okinawa

See "OKINAWA"

Political Thought - Japan

See also "Thought and Religion: Japan" below
Hashikawa Bunsō
Mitani Taichirō
Watanabe Ryūsaku

Politicians / Diplomats / Journalists - Japan

Ikeda Daisaku
Ishibashi Ushio

Kamei Katsuichirō
Satō Shōji
Shiraishi Iwao
Tagawa Seiichi
Utsunomiya Tokuma
Yoshino Sakuzō

Science - Japan

See "SCIENCE: East Asia"

Sino-Japanese Historical Relations

See "HISTORY: Sino-Japanese Historical Relations"

Sino-Japanese Literary Relations

See "LITERATURE: Sino-Japanese Literary Relations"

Sino-Japanese Relations - Modern

See "HISTORY: Sino-Japanese Relations-Modern"

Sociology - Japan

See also "SOCIOLOGY"
Hayashi Megumi

Thought and Religion - Japan

See also "Cultural History: Japan" and "Political Thought: Japan"
above; also, "BUDDHISM: Ch'an/Zen," "BUDDHISM: Buddhist Studies,*"
"HISTORY: Sino-Japanese Cultural Relations," and "RELIGION"; and
the following sections under "THOUGHT": "Asia," "East Asia," and
"Neo-Confucianism"
Abe Ryūichi
Abe Yoshio
Akamatsu Toshihide
Araki Kengo
Banno Junji
Bitō Masahide
Harada Toshiaki
Hashikawa Bunsō
Inoue Tetsujirō
Ishida Ichirō
Maruyama Masao
Morimoto Jun'ichirō
Rai Tsutomu
Tsuboi Yoshimasa
Tsuda Sōkichi
Umehara Takeshi
Watanabe Hiroshi

Buddhism - Japan

Akamatsu Toshihide
Fujiwara Kōdō
Hanayama Shinshō
Kamata Shigeo

KAMBUN STUDIES - including Traditional Chinese Studies in Japan

See also "JAPAN: Literature-History," "LITERATURE: Sino-Japanese Literary
Relations," and "THOUGHT"
Haga Kōshirō
Ishida Hiroshi
Ishida Kōdō
Nakanishi Kiyoshi
Okai Shingo

KOREA

Anthropology / Ethnology - Korea

See also "ANTHROPOLOGY: Asia"
Akiba Takashi
Mishina Shōhei

Archaeology - Korea

See also "ARCHAEOLOGY: Asia"
Arimitsu Kyōichi
Fujita Ryōsaku
Karube Jion
Mikami Tsugio
Saitō Tadashi

Art - Korea

See "ART: Asia" and "ART: Buddhist Art History"

Economics / Economic History - Korea

See "ECONOMICS: Asia"

History - Korea

See also under "HISTORY": "Asia," "East Asia," and "Sino-Korean His-
torical Relations"
Aoyama Kōryō
Aritaka Iwao
Hatada Takashi
Ikeuchi Hiroshi
Inoue Hideo
Kitayama Yasuo
Mishina Shōei
Naitō Shumpo
Oda Shōgo
Okamoto Yoshiji
Shikata Hiroshi
Suematsu Yasukazu
Sutō Yoshiyuki
Tabobashi Kiyoshi
Takeda Yukio
Tanaka Katsumi
Tanaka Takeo
Ueda Masaaki
Yamamoto Noritsuna

International Relations - Korea

See "INTERNATIONAL RELATIONS: China/Asia" and "HISTORY: Sino-Korean Historical Relations"

Language - Korean

Kōno Rokurō

Law - Korea

See "LAW: East Asia"

Literature - Korea

Itō Toramaru

Music - Korea

See "MUSIC: East Asia"

Mythology / Legend / Folklore - Korea

See "MYTHOLOGY: East Asia"

Science - Korea

See "SCIENCE: East Asia"

Sino-Korean Historical Relations

See "HISTORY: Sino-Korean Historical Relations"

Thought - Korea

See also "BUDDHISM" (especially "Buddhist Studies*")," "RELIGION," "THOUGHT: Asia," and "THOUGHT: Neo-Confucianism"
Abe Yoshio
Kamata Shigeo

LABOR HISTORY

See "MISCELLANEOUS: Labor History" and "HISTORY: Modern-China"

LANGUAGE AND LINGUISTICS

Kindaichi Kyōsuke
Kiyose, Gisaburo N.
Yamamoto Kengo

Chinese Lexicography

Harada Minoru
Imaizumi Juntarō
Kanegae Nobumitsu
Kōsaka Jun'ichi
Kuraishi Takeshirō
Morohashi Tetsuji
Ogawa Tamaki
Ōta Tatsuo
Shinohara Hisao
Sumita Teruo
Takeda Sakae
Tōdō Akiyasu

Toki Zenmaro
Uchida Michio
Yoneyama Toratarō

Chinese Language and Linguistics

Arisaka Hideyo
Arita Tadahiro
Fujii Eizaburō
Fukuda Jōnosuke
Furuya Tsugio
Harada Matsusaburō
Hatano Tarō
Hattori Shirō
Hayakawa Michisuke
Hayashi Yukimitsu
Hirayama Hisao
Honda Megumu
Hosokawa Haruma
Iida Toshiyuki
Ikeda Takeo
Ishida Takeo
Kaga Eiji
Kamei Takashi
Kanamaru Kunizō
Kanda Kiichirō
Kawamoto Kunie
Kitamura Hajime
Kitō Yūichi
Kōno Rokurō
Konose Tsuneyasu
Kudō Takamura
Kuraishi Takeshirō
Kusakabe Fumio
Matake Naoshi
Matsumoto Akira
Miyata Ichirō
Mizutani Shinjō
Mochizuki Yasokichi
Morohashi Tetsuji
Murakami Yoshihide
Nagao Mitsuyuki
Nagashima Eiichirō
Nakajima Kanki
Nakano Miyoko
Nakayama Tokiko
Nishida Taichirō
Nishida Tatsuo
Nishitani Toshichirō
Nomura Masayoshi
Nomura Zuihō
Ogaeri Yoshio
Ogata Kazuo

Ogawa Tamaki
Ōhara Nobukazu
Okai Shingo
Ōshima Shōji
Ōta Tatsuo
Ozaki Yūjirō
Rai Tsutomu
Sakai Ken'ichi
Sakurai Akiharu
Sanui Tadahai
Satō Akira
Suzuki Naoji
Takahashi Hitoshi
Takahashi Kumpei
Tanaka Ari
Tanaka Kazuo
Tateishi Hiroo
Tōdō Akiyasu
Torii Hisayasu
Tsuchiya Shin'ichi
Tsujimoto Haruhiko
Uchida Michio
Uemura Kōji
Ushijima Tokuji
Watanabe Mitsuo
Yamada Katsumi
Yamagishi Tokuhei
Yamaguchi Kakutaka
Yamaguchi Zuihō
Yano Mitsuji
Yokoyama Hiroshi
Yoshida Megumu

Modern Chinese Language and Linguistics – including Language of Vernacular Fiction

Aiura Takashi
Araki Osamu
Araya Junkō
Harada Minoru
Hasegawa Hiroshi
Hasegawa Ryōichi
Hashimoto Mantarō
Hattori Masayuki
Hishinuma Tōru
Ichimura Kinjirō
Idachi Yoshitsugu
Imaizumi Juntarō
Imatomi Masaki
Inokuma Fumiaki
Itō Keiichi
Iwasaki Fukuo
Kakei Kumiko

Kanegae Nobumitsu
Kaneko Jirō
Kawaguchi Akira
Kawakami Kyūju
Kikuta Masanobu
Kōsaka Jun'ichi
Koshimizu Masaru
Makita Eiji
Matsuda Kazuo
Matsui Takeo
Mizuno Suzuhiko
Mochizuki Yasokichi
Morikawa Kyūjirō
Nakano Tatsu
Nakazawa Shinzō
Nasu Kiyoshi
Niijima Atsuyoshi
Nōmi Tōru
Nomura Zuihō
Ōkawa Gansaburō
Ōkōchi Yasunori
Osada Natsuki
Ōyama Masaharu
Rokkaku Tsunehiro
Sakamoto Ichirō
Sakamoto Koretada
Sambō Masami
Samejima Kunizō
Sanetō Keishū
Shibagaki Yoshitarō
Shibata Minoru
Shiga Masatoshi
Suenobu Yasuo
Suganuma Masahisa
Sumita Teruo
Suzuki Takurō
Takebe Yoshiaki
Tanaka Hiroshi
Tanaka Masumi
Torii Katsuyuki
Ueno Keiji
Yamaguchi Kazuko
Yoshida Megumu
Yoshida Sachio
Yoshimura Gorō

LAW

   Iida Tadao
   Nomiyama On
   Ōhira Zengo

    Law – East Asia

      See also "JAPAN: Law"
      Hiroike Chikurō
      Inokuma Kaneshige
      Shimada Masao

      Law – China

        Aritaka Iwao
        Asai Atsushi
        Asai Torao
        Fukushima Masao
        Hattori Unokichi
        Hiranaka Reiji
        Ichien Kazuo
        Iida Tadao
        Ikeda On
        Ikegami Teiichi
        Inada Masatsugu
        Kumashiro Yukio
        Mukōyama Hiroo
        Naitō Kenkichi
        Nakamura Shigeo
        Nemoto Makoto
        Niida Noboru
        Nishida Taichirō
        Ōba Osamu
        Ōhira Zengo
        Okamoto Yoshiji
        Ōtsuka Katsumi
        Shiga Shūzō
        Takahashi Yūji
        Takikawa Masajirō
        Ubukata Naokichi
        Uchida Tomoo
        Watanabe Ryūsaku

LEGEND

   See "MYTHOLOGY"

LINGUISTICS

   See "LANGUAGE AND LINGUISTICS"

LITERATURE - China

See also "KAMBUN STUDIES" and "MISCELLANEOUS: Children's Literature"
Andō Takatsura
Aoki Masaru
Arai Toshio
Asakura Hisashi
Chūbachi Masakazu
Ezure Takashi
Fuji Masaharu
Fujita Toyohachi
Gōyama Kiwamu
Hashikawa Tokio
Hayashi Morimichi
Iriya Yoshitaka
Ishida Hiroshi
Itō Tomio
Kamachi Kan'ichi
Kanamaru Kunizō
Kano Naoki
Kimishima Hisako
Kōma Miyoshi
Kondō Haruo
Kudō Naotarō
Kudō Takamura
Kuwabara Takeo
Kuwayama Ryūhei
Makio Ryōkai
Matsueda Shigeo
Matsumura Takashi
Mekada Makoto
Miyauchi Tamotsu
Muramatsu Ei
Nagasawa Kikuya
Nakajima Toshio
Nakatsuhama Wataru
Nakayama Tokiko
Ogaeri Yoshio
Ogawa Tamaki
Okuno Shintarō
Rei Ha
Suzuki Shūji
Takahashi Kazumi
Takahashi Kumpei
Tanaka Kazuo
Tanaka Kenji
Tanaka Toshiaki
Yokoyama Hiroshi
Yoshikawa Kōjirō

Literature - China - thru Han

See also the sections below arranged by subject, including "Poetry:
   thru Han"
Abe Shōjirō
Asano Michiari
Fujino Iwatomo
Imaeda Jirō
Imahama Michitaka
Imataka Makoto
Inahata Kōichirō
Kojima Masao
Machida Saburō
Nakagawa Kaoru
Nemoto Makoto
Nishioka Hiroshi
Okamura Sadao
Okamura Shigeru
Ōno Takashi
Sakai Takeo
Shimizu Kiyoshi
Shimura Ryōji
Shirakawa Shizuka
Takeda Sakae
Togawa Yoshio
Tsuneishi Shigeru

Literature - China - Six Dynasties

See also the sections below arranged by subject, including "Fiction:
   Six Dynasties"
Abe Shōjirō
Ami Yūji
Andō Makoto
Fukui Kōjun
Furuta Keiichi
Hashikawa Tokio
Hirano Kenshō
Imaeda Jirō
Imahama Michitaka
Imataka Makoto
Inahata Kōichirō
Inami Ritsuko
Ishida Kōdō
Itō Masafumi
Kano Naosada
Kataoka Masao
Kimata Tokuo
Komatsu Hideo
Konishi Noboru
Kōzen Hiroshi
Morino Shigeo
Nemoto Makoto

Nishino Teiji
Nishioka Hiroshi
Obi Kōichi
Ōgami Masami
Ogasawara Hirotoshi
Okamura Sadao
Okamura Shigeru
Ōyane Bunjirō
Shiba Rokurō
Shimizu Kiyoshi
Shimizu Yoshio
Shimura Ryōji
Takahashi Kazumi
Takahashi Kiyoshi
Takahashi Minoru
Takashi Masao
Takeda Akira
Takeda Sakae
Takizawa Seiichirō
Tominaga Kazutaka
Toppata Shigenao
Toyofuku Kenji
Ueki Hisayuki
Yahagi Take
Yajima Tetsusuke
Yamada Katsuhisa
Yamaguchi Tamehiro
Yokoyama Hiroshi

Literature - China - T'ang

See also the sections below arranged by subject, including "Fiction:
   T'ang" and "Poetry: T'ang"; also, "TUN-HUANG TEXTS"
Abe Kaneya
Ami Yūji
Hashikawa Tokio
Hirano Kenshō
Hiraoka Takeo
Ichihara Kyōkichi
Imai Kiyoshi
Itō Masafumi
Kataoka Masao
Kawachi Shōen
Kawai Kōzō
Moroi Kōji
Nemoto Makoto
Nishimura Fumiko
Nishioka Hiroshi
Okamura Sadao
Okamura Shigeru
Ono Shihei
Ōta Tsugio
Ryū Sampu

Shimizu Kiyoshi
Shimizu Shigeru
Shimura Ryōji
Shinkai Hajime
Sugaya Gunjirō
Tominaga Kazutaka
Wada Toshio
Yamada Katsuhisa
Yamazaki Jun'ichi

Literature - China - Sung

See also the sections below arranged by subject, including "Poetry:
    Sung"
Abe Kaneya
Asakura Hisashi
Gōyama Kiwamu
Hoshikawa Kiyotaka
Kakei Fumio
Nishino Teiji
Shimizu Shigeru
Sugaya Gunjirō
Uemura Kōji
Ueno Hideto

Literature - China - Chin / Yuan

See also the sections below arranged by subject, including "Poetry:
    Chin/Yuan"
Nakano Miyoko
Oguri Eiichi

Literature - China - Ming

See also the sections below arranged by subject, including "Poetry:
    Ming"
Akiyoshi Kukio
Chūbachi Masakazu
Hoshikawa Kiyotaka
Ichihara Kyōkichi
Kamachi Kan'ichi
Kuramitsu Uhei
Tsuru Haruo
Uemura Kōji
Yokota Terutoshi

Literature - China - Ch'ing

See also the sections below arranged by subject, including "Fiction:
    Ch'ing" and "Poetry: Ch'ing"
Inaba Seiichi
Itō Sōhei
Kuramitsu Uhei
Matsuzaki Haruyuki
Nakamura Tadayuki
Satō Ichirō

Sutō Yōichi
Tsuru Haruo
Yamaoka Riichi

Buddhist Literature - China

See also the sections above arranged by dynasty; also, "BUDDHISM"
    (including "Ch'an/Zen Buddhism") and "TUN-HUANG TEXTS"
Fukui Kōjun
Hirano Kenshō
Iriya Yoshitaka
Kanaoka Shōkō
Kawachi Shōen
Nagao Mitsuyuki

Drama - China

See also the sections above arranged by dynasty, and "Poetry: Ch'ü"
    below
Abe Yasuki
Adachibara Yatsuka
Aoki Masaru
Denda Akira
Hama Kazue
Hara Sanshichi
Hashimoto Takashi
Hatano Tarō
Iriya Yoshitaka
Iwaki Hideo
Kim Bunkyō
Nozaki Shumpei
Oka Haruo
Okuno Shintarō
Shionoya On
Takahashi Shigeki
Tanaka Issei
Tanaka Kenji
Ueno Keiji
Yagisawa Hajime
Yoshikawa Kōjirō

Fiction - China

Cf. "Fiction: Vernacular" below; see also the sections above arranged
    by dynasty
Maeno Naoaki
Sawada Mizuho
Shimizu Eikichi
Uchida Michio

   Fiction - China - Six Dynasties

      Kominami Ichirō
      Sawada Mizuho
      Takahashi Minoru
      Takeda Akira

Toppata Shigenao
Yagisawa Hajime
Yanase Kiyoshi

Fiction - China - T'ang

Hirai Hidefumi
Imamura Yoshio
Inui Kazuo
Kondō Haruo
Matsumoto Yukio
Mizuno Yoshitomo
Moroi Kōji
Nakamura Takashi
Nishioka Haruhiko
Osada Natsuki
Ōtsuka Shigeki
Shiroki Naoya
Takahashi Minoru
Uchida Sennosuke
Uchiyama Chinari
Yagisawa Hajime
Yanase Kiyoshi

Fiction - China - Ch'ing   (Liao-chai chih-i)

Fujita Yūken
Shibata Temma

Fiction - Vernacular - China

Cf. "Fiction" above; see also the sections above arranged by dynasty;
   also, "LANGUAGE: Modern Chinese Language (including Language of Ver-
   nacular Fiction)"
Abe Kaneya
Abe Yasuki
Adachibara Yatsuka
Aiura Takashi
Arita Tadahiro
Ashida Takaaki
Chida Kyūichi
Chūbachi Masakazu
Doi Akira
Fuji Masaharu
Furuya Tsugio
Hagio Chōichirō
Hashimoto Takashi
Hatano Tarō
Hattori Masayuki
Iida Yoshirō
Iizuka Akira
Imamura Yoshio
Inada Osamu
Inada Takashi
Inomata Shōhachi

Iriya Yoshitaka
Itō Sōhei
Kaneda Jun'ichirō
Kaneko Jirō
Kim Bunkyō
Komada Shinji
Kōsaka Jun'ichi
Masuda Wataru
Matsueda Shigeo
Miyata Ichirō
Miyauchi Tamotsu
Mizukami Sanae
Mugifu Tomie
Murakami Tomoyuki
Muramatsu Ei
Nagao Mitsuyuki
Nakajima Toshio
Nakano Miyoko
Nishino Teiji
Nozaki Shumpei
Oda Takeo
Ogaeri Yoshio
Ogawa Tamaki
Okamoto Ryūzō
Okuno Shintarō
Ono Shihei
Ono Shinobu
Onoe Kanehide
Osada Natsuki
Ōta Tatsuo
Ōuchida Saburō
Ozaka Tokuji
Rei Ha
Saitō Kiyoko
Satō Haruo
Shida Fudōmaro
Shionoya Kan
Shionoya On
Shiroki Naoya
Shōji Kakuichi
Sugimori Masaya
Suzuki Naoji
Takahashi Shigeki
Takashima Toshio
Takeuchi Minoru
Tamori Noboru
Tarumoto Teruo
Tatsuma Shōsuke
Torii Hisayasu
Tsukamoto Terukazu
Tsuneishi Shigeru
Ueno Keiji

Yamamoto Tetsuya
Yoshimura Gorō
Yoshimura Hisako

Literary Theory / Poetics - China

Aoki Masaru
Arai Ken
Funatsu Tomihiko
Furuta Keiichi
Hayashida Shinnosuke
Hoshikawa Kiyotaka
Ichinosawa Torao
Kobayashi Takeshi
Konishi Jin'ichi
Kōzen Hiroshi
Matsushita Tadashi
Mekada Makoto
Mizuhara Ikō
Nakazawa Mareo
Ōta Hyōzaburō
Ozaki Yūjirō
Shiba Rokurō
Suzuki Torao
Takagi Masakazu
Takamatsu Takaaki
Toda Kōgyō
Yokota Terutoshi

Poetry - China - Traditional

See also the sections above arranged by dynasty
Abe Seitoku
Arai Ken
Fukumoto Masakazu
Funatsu Tomihiko
Hama Ryūichirō
Hanazaki Saien
Hattori Yasushi
Hayashida Shinnosuke
Hosoda Mikio
Ikkai Tomoyoshi
Imazeki Toshimaro
Inada Takashi
Iritani Sensuke
Ishikawa Umejirō
Kamata Tadashi
Kezuka Eigorō
Kitō Yūichi
Kondō Mitsuo
Kuwayama Ryūhei
Maeno Naoaki
Matsumoto Masaaki
Matsumura Takashi

Matsuura Tomohisa
Mekada Makoto
Misawa Reiji
Mizuhara Ikō
Mizukami Sanae
Mori Akira
Nagao Sadao
Ogawa Tamaki
Sakata Shin
Saku Setsu
Satō Haruo
Satō Tamotsu
Shionoya Kan
Suzuki Shūji
Suzuki Torao
Takeji Sadao
Tamori Noboru
Toki Zenmaro
Uchida Sennosuke
Yamamoto Kazuyoshi
Yokoyama Eizō
Yoshikawa Kōjirō

Poetry - China - thru Han

See also "Literature: thru Han" and "Poetry: Traditional" above
Fujita Hideo
Fukushima Yoshihiko
Hashimoto Jun
Hoshikawa Kiyotaka
Nakajima Chiaki
Ryūkawa Kiyoshi
Sugimoto Yukio

Poetry - China - Shih-ching

Inoguchi Atsushi
Inoi Makoto
Inui Kazuo
Ishikawa Misao
Kaneda Jun'ichirō
Kondō Hideo
Kuroiwa Yoshinori
Matsumoto Masaaki
Murayama Yoshihiro
Nakajima Midori
Ozaki Yūjirō
Sakai Takeo
Sakata Shin
Sawada Masahiro
Shiomi Atsurō
Shirakawa Shizuka
Yoshida Megumu

Poetry - China - <u>Ch'u-tz'u</u>

Asano Michiari
Fujino Iwatomo
Kominami Ichirō
Kuwayama Ryūhei
Ōki Harumoto
Takeji Sadao

Poetry - China - <u>Fu</u>

See also "Literature: thru Han" and "Literature: Six Dy-
nasties" above, and "Poetry: Six Dynasties" below
Fujiwara Takashi
Inahata Kōichirō
Nakajima Chiaki

Poetry - China - Six Dynasties

See also "Literature: Six Dynasties," "Poetry: Traditional," and
"Poetry: <u>Fu</u>" above
Fuji Masaharu
Fujii Mamoru
Fujita Hideo
Fukushima Yoshihiko
Funatsu Tomihiko
Gotō Akinobu
Hanabusa Hideki
Hashimoto Jun
Hayashida Shinnosuke
Hoshikawa Kiyotaka
Ikkai Tomoyoshi
Ishikawa Tadahisa
Komori Ikuko
Konishi Noboru
Masuda Kiyohide
Matsumoto Yukio
Mukōjima Shigeyoshi
Nakajima Chiaki
Nakazawa Mareo
Numaguchi Masaru
Ogawa Shōichi
Ryūkawa Kiyoshi
Shiba Rokurō
Shiomi Kunihiko
Sugimoto Yukio
Takagi Masakazu
Takizawa Seiichirō
Tsuge Masanobu
Tsuru Haruo
Yamada Hideo

Poetry - China - <u>Yueh-fu</u>

See also the "Poetry" sections below arranged by dynasty
Fujii Mamoru
Konishi Noboru
Masuda Kiyohide
Nakatsuhama Wataru
Okamura Sadao
Sawaguchi Takeo

Poetry - China - T'ang

See also "Literature: T'ang" and "Poetry: Traditional" above,
    and "Poetry: <u>Tz'u</u>" below
Andō Shunroku
Ashidate Ichirō
Doi Kenji
Fujita Hideo
Fukino Yasushi
Fukuhara Ryūzō
Fukushima Yoshihiko
Hanabusa Hideki
Harada Norio
Hashimoto Jun
Hoshikawa Kiyotaka
Ichinosawa Torao
Ikkai Tomoyoshi
Kakei Fumio
Kakei Kumiko
Kamio Ryūsuke
Karashima Takeshi
Katayama Tetsu
Kawakita Yasuhiko
Kobayashi Nobuaki
Kobayashi Taichirō
Kobayashi Takeshi
Komatsu Tadashi
Kondō Haruo
Kudō Naotarō
Kunieda Minoru
Kurokawa Yōichi
Kusamori Shin'ichi
Maegawa Yukio
Maruyama Shigeru
Masuda Kiyohide
Matsuura Tomohisa
Mukōjima Shigeyoshi
Murakami Tetsumi
Murayama Yoshihiro
Nakatsuhama Wataru
Nakazawa Mareo
Nishi Giichi
Nishimoto Iwao
Ogawa Shōichi

Ōno Jitsunosuke
Saitō Shō
Satō Tamotsu
Shinkai Hajime
Tadokoro Yoshiyuki
Taguchi Nobuo
Takagi Masakazu
Takagi Shigetoshi
Takebe Toshio
Taki Shigeru
Tanaka Katsumi
Tarunaga Hidehiko
Toki Zenmaro
Tsuru Haruo
Tsutsumi Tomekichi
Yamanouchi Masahiko
Yamauchi Haruo
Yoshikawa Kōjirō

Poetry - China - Sung

See also "Literature: Sung" and "Poetry: Traditional" above
Kakei Fumio
Kanaoka Shōkō
Kurata Junnosuke
Murakami Tetsumi
Satō Tamotsu
Yamamoto Kazuyoshi
Yokoyama Iseo

Poetry - China - Tz'u

See also "Literature: T'ang" and "Poetry: T'ang" above,
and the "Poetry" sections below arranged by dynasty
Aoyama Hiroshi
Hanazaki Saien
Murakami Tetsumi
Nakata Yūjirō
Suda Teiichi
Tamori Noboru

Poetry - China - Chin / Yuan

See also "Literature: Chin/Yuan" and "Poetry: Traditional" above
Fukumoto Masakazu
Nakamura Yoshihiro
Oka Haruo

Poetry - China - Ch'ü

See also "Literature: Drama," "Literature: Ming," and
"Literature: Ch'ing" above; and "Poetry: Ming" and
"Poetry: Ch'ing" below
Hayashi Yukimitsu
Oka Haruo
Tamori Noboru
Tanaka Kenji

Poetry - China - Ming

See also "Literature: Ming" and "Poetry: Traditional" above
Fukumoto Masakazu
Oka Haruo

Poetry - China - Ch'ing

See also "Literature: Ch'ing" and "Poetry: Traditional" above
Fukumoto Masakazu
Hashimoto Jun
Kakei Kumiko
Kurata Sadayoshi
Murayama Yoshihiro

Modern Literature - China

See also "MISCELLANEOUS: Popular Culture" and "U.S.S.R.: Soviet Sinology (on Modern Chinese Literature)"
Abe Tomoji
Abe Yukio
Aiura Takashi
Akiyoshi Kukio
Andō Yōko
Araki Osamu
Araya Junkō
Ashida Shigeyuki
Ashida Takaaki
Chida Kyūichi
Hasegawa Ryōichi
Hatano Tarō
Hattori Ryūzō
Higuchi Susumu
Hishinuma Tōru
Hiyama Hisao
Hosoya Sōko
Iida Yoshirō
Iikura Shōhei
Iizuka Akira
Imamura Yoshio
Inaba Shōji
Inokuchi Akira
Inomata Shōhachi
Inuki Gunji
Ishida Takeo
Itō Katsu
Itō Keiichi
Itō Sōhei
Itō Toramaru
Jinnouchi Yoshio
Kaji Wataru
Kakei Fumio
Kakei Kumiko
Kamaya Osamu
Kamio Ryūsuke

Kaneko Jirō
Karashima Takeshi
Katayama Tomoyuki
Kawakami Kyūju
Kikuchi Saburō
Kitaoka Masako
Kiyama Hideo
Komada Shinji
Komine Kimichika
Konishi Noboru
Korenaga Shun
Kōsaka Jun'ichi
Kure Shichirō
Kuwayama Ryūhei
Maeda Toshiaki
Makito Kazuhiro
Maruo Tsuneki
Maruyama Matsuyuki
Maruyama Noboru
Masuda Wataru
Matsuda Kazuo
Matsueda Shigeo
Matsui Hiromitsu
Miyazaki Hiroshi
Miyoshi Hajime
Muramatsu Kazuya
Murata Toshihiro
Nagasue Yoshitaka
Nagumo Satoru
Nakagawa Toshi
Nakajima Midori
Nakajima Osafumi
Nakamura Tadayuki
Nakano Miyoko
Nakayashiki Hiroshi
Nakazawa Shinzō
Nara Kazuo
Niijima Atsuyoshi
Nozawa Toshitaka
Oda Takeo
Okada Hideki
Okamoto Ryūzō
Okazaki Toshio
Oketani Hideaki
Ōmura Masuo
Ono Shinobu
Onoda Kōsaburō
Onoe Kanehide
Ōshiba Takashi
Ōta Susumu
Ōtaka Iwao
Ōtsuka Shigeki

Ōyama Masaharu
Ozaka Tokuji
Saitō Akio
Sakaguchi Naoki
Sambō Masami
Sanetō Keishū
Sasaki Kiichi
Satō Haruo
Satō Ichirō
Shiga Masatoshi
Shimada Masao
Shimada Yukiko
Shimizu Eikichi
Shimizu Yasuzō
Shimmura Tōru
Shinkai Takaaki
Suda Teiichi
Sugano Shunsaku
Sugimori Masaya
Sugimoto Tatsuo
Sutō Yōichi
Suzuki Masao
Suzuki Takeshi
Suzuki Takurō
Tada Yūkei
Takabatake Jō
Takada Shōji
Takakura Katsumi
Takashima Toshio
Takeuchi Minoru
Takeuchi Yoshimi
Takeuchi Yoshirō
Tanaka Issei
Tatsuma Shōsuke
Tsukamoto Terukazu
Uda Rei
Ueda Atsuo
Ueno Kōshi
Yamada Keizō
Yamada Norio
Yokoyama Eizō
Yoshida Megumu
Yoshida Sachio
Yoshida Tomio
Yoshimura Hisako

Modern Poetry - China

Ishida Takeo
Kamachi Kan'ichi
Kurata Sadayoshi

Sino-Japanese Literary Relations

See also "HISTORY: Sino-Japanese Cultural Relations," "JAPAN: Cultural
     History," and "KAMBUN STUDIES"
Asō Isoji
Furusawa Michio
Hayakawa Kōzaburō
Hino Tatsuo
Iida Yoshirō
Itō Toramaru
Kanda Hideo
Kawaguchi Hisao
Kojima Noriyuki
Komada Shinji
Konishi Jin'ichi
Kurokawa Yōichi
Kuwayama Ryūhei
Matsueda Shigeo
Matsushita Tadashi
Nakamura Tadayuki
Nakanishi Susumu
Ogata Korekiyo
Okazaki Toshio
Ōta Hyōzaburō
Ōta Tsugio
Ōtsuka Shigeki
Sayama Wataru
Sugano Shunsaku
Sugimori Masaya
Sugimoto Yukio
Toki Zenmaro
Tokuda Takeshi
Yahagi Take
Yamagishi Tokuhei
Yamaguchi Kakutaka
Yamamoto Kenkichi

MANCHURIA

Anthropology / Ethnology - Manchuria

See also "ANTHROPOLOGY: Asia"
Akiba Takashi
Torii Ryūzō

Archaeology - Manchuria

See also "ARCHAEOLOGY: Asia"
Mikami Tsugio

Economic History - Manchuria

See also under "ECONOMICS":   "Economic History-Asia," "Economy-
     Modern/Contemporary-China," and "Economic History-China"
Edayoshi Isamu
Ishida Kōhei
Nakanishi Tsutomu

History - Manchuria

See also "Economic History: Manchuria" above; and the following sec-
tions under "HISTORY": "Asia," "East Asia," and "China"
Anami Korehiro
Hagiwara Jumpei
Haneda Tōru
Hara Kakuten
Hashimoto Masukichi
Hino Kaisaburō
Imanishi Shunjū
Itō Takeo
Kanda Nobuo
Katō Kyūzō
Kawakubo Teirō
Mitamura Taisuke
Moriyasu Takao
Nishimura Shigeo
Nomiyama On
Ogata Sadako
Oshibuchi Hajime
Tamura Jitsuzō
Tanaka Katsumi
Tezuka Takayoshi
Umemoto Sutezō
Wada Hironori
Wada Sei
Yamaguchi Osamu
Yamamoto Mamoru
Yanai Wataru

Language - Manchu

Watanabe Shigetarō
Yamamoto Kengo

MATHEMATICS

See "SCIENCE"

MEDICINE

See "SCIENCE"

MINORITIES - China

See also "ISLAM"
Ayabe Tsuneo
Hatada Takashi
Iikura Shōhei
Kambe Teruo
Kaneko Noboru
Sakamoto Koretada

MISCELLANEOUS

Aromatics / Spices - China / East Asia

Yamada Kentarō

Children's Literature - China

Kimishima Hisako

Clothing, History of - China

Harada Yoshito

Economic History - England

Nomura Kentarō

Film - China

Ōshiba Takashi

Food, History of - China

Aoki Masaru
Shinoda Osamu

French Literature

Kuwabara Takeo

Genealogy - China

Taga Akigorō

Great Wall - China

Uemura Seiji

History - European / Western

Ōrui Noboru
Saitō Hishō
Ukita Kazutami

History - Western Asia

Maejima Shinji

Humor - China

Shimizu Eikichi
Shōji Kukuichi
Uemura Kōji

Labor History - China

Furumaya Tadao
Mukōyama Hiroo
Suzue Gen'ichi

Paleosiberian Languages

Takahashi Moritaka

Popular Culture - Modern China

Muramatsu Kazuya
Suzuki Takeshi

Sex / Sexuality - East Asia

Ishihara Akira
Suzuki Akira

Tea, Works on - China

Nakamura Takashi
Nunome Chōfū

Water Control - China

Morita Akira
Nagase Mamoru
Satō Taketoshi

MONGOLIA

Geography - Mongolia

See also "GEOGRAPHY"
Oda Takeo

History - Mongolia

See also "HISTORY: Asia" and "HISTORY: China"
Aoki Tomitarō
Aritaka Iwao
Ebisawa Tetsuo
Etō Toshio
Gotō Tomio
Hagiwara Jumpei
Haneda Tōru
Hatada Takashi
Iwamura Shinobu
Kobayashi Takashirō
Mitamura Taisuke
Moriyasu Takao
Murakami Masatsugu
Naitō Chōhō
Naka Michiyo
Oshibuchi Hajime
Saguchi Tōru
Sakamoto Koretada
Tamura Jitsuzō
Tayama Shigeru
Tezuka Takayoshi
Uemura Seiji
Wada Sei
Yamada Nakaba
Yamada Nobuo
Yamaguchi Osamu
Yamamoto Mamoru
Yanai Wataru

Languages - Mongolian / Altaic

Fujieda Akira
Hattori Shirō
Murayama Shichirō
Nomura Masayoshi
Osada Natsuki
Watanabe Shigetarō
Yamazaki Tadashi

Literature - Mongolia

Kobayashi Takashirō

Religion - Mongolia

See also "RELIGION: East Asia"
Nagao Gajin

MUSIC

Nakajima Kenzō

Music - East Asia

Hayashi Kenzō
Kishibe Shigeo
Koizumi Fumio
Taki Ryōichi
Tanabe Hisao

Music - China

Mizuhara Ikō
Muramatsu Kazuya

MUSLIMS

See "ISLAM"

MYTHOLOGY / LEGEND / FOLKLORE

Mythology / Legend / Folklore - East Asia

See also "RELIGION: East Asia"
Matsumoto Nobuhiro
Matsumura Takeo
Mishina Shōei

Mythology / Legend / Folklore - China

See also "RELIGION: China"
Inada Takashi
Itō Seiji
Izushi Yoshihiko
Kimishima Hisako
Kumagai Osamu
Mitarai Masaru
Mori Yasutarō
Okuno Shintarō
Sawada Mizuho

Suzuki Takeshi
Takahashi Moritaka
Takizawa Toshiaki
Tetsui Yoshinori
Tochio Takeshi

NATURAL SCIENCES

See "SCIENCE"

OKINAWA

Okinawa - Anthropology / Ethnology

See also "ANTHROPOLOGY: Asia" and "JAPAN: Anthropology"
Mabuchi Tōichi

Okinawa - History

See also "HISTORY: Asia" and "JAPAN: History"
Higaonna Kanjun

ORACLE BONES

See "EPIGRAPHY"

OVERSEAS CHINESE

See also "ECONOMICS: Asia," "HONG KONG," and "SOUTHEAST ASIA"
Kamioka Kazuyoshi
Kani Hiroaki
Kawabe Toshio
Kurai Ryōzō
Nakagawa Manabu
Nakamura Takashi
Ogiwara Hiroaki
Sakurai Akiharu
Suyama Takashi
Tai Kokki
Tanaka Hiroshi
Uchida Naosaku
Wada Hisanori
Yonezawa Hideo
Yū Chūkun

PALEOSIBERIAN LANGUAGES

See "MISCELLANEOUS: Paleosiberian Languages"

PHILOSOPHY

See "THOUGHT"

POLITICS

See "CONTEMPORARY CHINA," "INTERNATIONAL RELATIONS," and "THOUGHT: Political-China"

POPULAR CULTURE - Modern China

See "MISCELLANEOUS: Popular Culture," "MISCELLANEOUS: Film," "CONTEMPORARY CHINA," "HISTORY: Modern-China," "LITERATURE: Modern-China," and "MYTHOLOGY"

RELIGION

Furuno Kiyoto
Moroi Yoshinori
Oguchi Iichi

Religion - East Asia

See also "Taoism: East Asia" and "Christianity" below; also, "BUD-
DHISM" (especially "Buddhist Studies*")," "ISLAM," "JAPAN: Thought
and Religion," "KOREA: Thought," "MYTHOLOGY: East Asia," and
THOUGHT: Asia"
Iwai Hirosato
Saeki Yoshirō

Religion - China

See also "Taoism: China" and "Christianity" below; also, "BUD-
DHISM," "ISLAM," "LITERATURE: Buddhist-China," "MYTHOLOGY:
East Asia," and "THOUGHT: China"
Akita Shigeaki
Asai Motoi
Fukui Fumimasa
Harada Toshiaki
Ikeda Suetoshi
Itō Takao
Kaneko Noboru
Kubo Noritada
Kuwata Rokurō
Makino Tatsumi
Mano Sen'ryū
Miyakawa Hisayuki
Miyazawa Masayori
Moroi Yoshinori
Murakami Yoshimi
Nishi Junzō
Nishioka Ichisuke
Ōbuchi Ninji
Sakai Tadao
Sanaka Sō
Sawada Mizuho
Shigematsu Shunshō
Shiratori Kiyoshi
Sōda Hiroshi
Suzuki Chūsei
Uchida Tomoo
Yasui Kōzan

Taoism - East Asia

Fukui Kōjun
Furuno Kiyoto

Taoism - China

Those with an interest in <u>Chuang-tzu</u> are listed under "THOUGHT: Classical"

Akizuki Kan'ei
Amano Shizuo
Fukunaga Mitsuji
Ishihara Akira
Ishijima Kairyū
Izutsu Toshihiko
Kimura Eiichi
Kōma Miyoshi
Kubo Noritada
Ōbuchi Ninji
Sakai Tadao
Sanaka Sō
Seimiya Tsuyoshi
Shiomi Takao
Yamada Toshiaki
Yoshioka Yoshitoyo

Christianity - China / East Asia

Itō Takao
Kuwata Rokurō
Saeki Yoshirō
Yamamoto Sumiko
Yazawa Toshihiko

RUSSIA

See "U.S.S.R."

SCIENCE - including Astronomy, Botany, Geology, Mathematics, Medicine, and Natural Sciences

Kamo Giichi

Science / History of Science - East Asia

Chikashige Masumi
Ishihara Akira
Mikami Yoshio
Mochizuki Katsumi
Nakamura Seiji
Nakayama Shigeru
Ogura Kinnosuke
Yabuuchi Kiyoshi
Yoshida Mitsukuni

History of Science - China

Hashimoto Keizō
Horiike Nobuo
Keimatsu Mitsuo
Kojima Masao
Mizukami Shizuo

Shinjō Shinzō
Tsuge Hideomi
Yamada Keiji

SEX / SEXUALITY

See "MISCELLANEOUS: Sex/Sexuality"

SOCIOLOGY

See also "SOCIOLOGY: Japan"
Baba Akio
Fukutake Tadashi
Furuno Kiyoto
Hidaka Rokurō
Nakane Chie
Oguchi Iichi
Shimizu Morimitsu
Toda Teijō

Sociology - China

Fukutake Tadashi
Hatada Takashi
Hayashi Megumi
Makino Tatsumi
Shimizu Morimitsu
Uchida Tomoo

SOUTHEAST ASIA

See also "OVERSEAS CHINESE"

Anthropology / Ethnology - Southeast Asia

See also "ANTHROPOLOGY: Asia"
Ayabe Tsuneo
Mabuchi Tōichi
Matsumoto Nobuhiro
Shiratori Yoshirō

Economy - Southeast Asia

See also "ECONOMICS: Asia"
Kawano Shigetō
Nihei Yasumitsu

Historical Geography - Southeast Asia

See also "GEOGRAPHY"
Bekki Atsuhiko

History - Southeast Asia

See also "HISTORY: Asia" and "HISTORY: Sino-Vietnamese Historical
    Relations"
Fujiwara Riichirō
Itō Takao
Iwao Seiichi
Kawabe Toshio

      Kawamoto Kunie
      Kuwata Rokurō
      Nakamura Takashi
      Ogiwara Hiroaki
      Sugimoto Naojirō
      Wada Hironori
      Wada Hisanori
      Yamada Kentarō
      Yamamoto Tatsurō

Languages - Southeast Asia

      Kawamoto Kunie

Sino-Southeast Asian International Relations

      See "INTERNATIONAL RELATIONS: Sino-Southeast Asian Relations"

SOVIET UNION

   See "U.S.S.R."

SPICES

   See "MISCELLANEOUS: Aromatics"

TAIWAN

Anthropology / Ethnology - Taiwan

      See also "ANTHROPOLOGY: Asia"
      Kano Tadao
      Mabuchi Tōichi
      Segawa Kōkichi
      Torii Ryūzō

Economics - Taiwan

      See also "ECONOMICS: Asia"
      Ishikawa Shigeru
      Miyake Takeo
      Nihei Yasumitsu

History - Taiwan

      See also under "HISTORY": "Asia," "East Asia," and "China"
      Kawabata Genji
      Nakamura Takashi
      Tai Kokki
      Takekoshi Yosaburō
      Tanaka Hiroshi

Folksongs - Taiwan

      Inada Osamu

Literature - Taiwan

      Tsukamoto Terukazu

Night Life - Taiwan

      Suzuki Akira

TEA - Works on

    See "MISCELLANEOUS: Tea"

THOUGHT

    Andō Takatsura

        Thought - Asia

            See also "THOUGHT: China" and "Neo-Confucianism" below; also, "BUD-
               DHISM" (especially "Buddhist Studies*") and "RELIGION: East Asia"
            Fukui Kōjun
            Ikeda Daisaku
            Maruyama Masao
            Nakamura Hajime
            Uchino Tairei
            Ueyama Shumpei
            Watanabe Hiroshi
            Yamaguchi Kōsaku
            Yoshikawa Kōjirō

        Thought - China

            See also "THOUGHT: Asia" above; also, "BUDDHISM," "KAMBUN STUDIES,"
               and "RELIGION: China"
            Akita Shigeaki
            Araki Kengo
            Fujisawa Makoto
            Fukui Fumimasa
            Fukushima Shun'ō
            Fumoto Yasutaka
            Gotō Motomi
            Harada Masami
            Hattori Unokichi
            Hirata Sakae
            Hirotsune Jinsei
            Honda Shigeyuki
            Hozumi Fumio
            Inoue Gengo
            Inoue Tetsujirō
            Ishida Ichirō
            Ishikawa Umejirō
            Izutsu Toshihiko
            Kano Naoki
            Katō Shūichi
            Kimura Eiichi
            Kobayashi Nobuaki
            Kojima Masao
            Kudō Toyohiko
            Kuwabara Takeo
            Makio Ryōkai
            Mitarai Masaru
            Miura Kunio
            Mizoguchi Yūzō

Nagase Makoto
Nakae Ushikichi
Nakamura Shōhachi
Nakata Katsu
Nemoto Makoto
Nishi Junzō
Nitta Kōji
Ojima Sukema
Ōrui Jun
Ōtsuki Nobuyoshi
Sanaka Sō
Shiraishi Yoshio
Takase Takejirō
Tanaka Toshiaki
Tsuda Sōkichi
Umemoto Katsumi
Yajima Genryō
Yamashita Ryūji
Yamazaki Jun'ichi
Yanagimachi Tatsuya
Yokomatsu Takashi

Classical Thought (thru Han) - China

See also "RELIGION: Taoism"
Abe Yoshio
Abe Yukio
Akatsuka Kiyoshi
Amano Shizuo
Anazawa Tatsuo
Asai Shigenori
Asano Yūichi
Chihara Katsumi
Ebata Shin'ichirō
Endō Tetsuo
Fujii Sen'ei
Fujikawa Masakazu
Fujiwara Takao
Fujizuka Chikashi
Fukatsu Tanefusa
Fukino Yasushi
Fukuhara Ryūzō
Fukui Fumimasa
Fukui Shigemasa
Fukunaga Mitsuji
Hara Tomio
Harada Taneshige
Hashimoto Takakatsu
Hayashi Hideichi
Hihara Toshikuni
Hiraoka Teikichi
Honda Wataru
Horiike Nobuo

Ichikawa Mototarō
Ichikawa Yasushi
Ikeda Suetoshi
Ikeda Tomohisa
Imai Usaburō
Inoguchi Atsushi
Inoi Makoto
Inoue Masamichi
Inui Kazuo
Ishiguro Noritoshi
Ishiguro Shun'itsu
Itano Chōhachi
Itō Tomoatsu
Kaga Eiji
Kaji Nobuyuki
Kamata Tadashi
Kanaya Osamu
Kaneto Mamoru
Kasahara Chūji
Katō Jōken
Kawasaki Takaharu
Kobayashi Toshio
Kodama Rokurō
Kominami Ichirō
Kondō Yasunobu
Kurihara Keisuke
Kurita Naomi
Kusuyama Haruki
Machida Saburō
Maruyama Matsuyuki
Matano Tarō
Matsuda Hiroshi
Matsuda Minoru
Matsumoto Masaaki
Matsushima Takahiro
Mikami Seijirō
Miyamoto Katsu
Mizuhara Ikō
Mori Mikisaburō
Morohashi Tetsuji
Nakamura Shun'ya
Niimi Yasuhide
Nishioka Ichisuke
Nitta Daisaku
Nomura Gakuyō
Nomura Shigeo
Numajiri Masataka
Ogawa Haruhisa
Ogura Yoshihiko
Ōhama Akira
Okada Osamu
Ōkubo Takao

Ōmuro Mikio
Ōno Jitsunosuke
Ōno Takashi
Onozawa Seiichi
Ōsawa Kazuo
Ōtaki Kazuo
Ōtsuka Tomoshika
Sagawa Osamu
Satō Ichirō
Satō Kyōgen
Sawada Takio
Seimiya Tsuyoshi
Senō Shigemori
Shigezawa Toshio
Shima Kunio
Shimizu Kiyoshi
Shimomi Takao
Shimotomai Akira
Sugimoto Tatsuo
Sugiura Toyoji
Suzuki Kiichi
Suzuki Yoshijirō
Tadokoro Yoshiyuki
Takada Atsushi
Takada Shinji
Takagi Tomonosuke
Takahashi Hitoshi
Takahashi Susumu
Takahata Tsunenobu
Takeoka Yatsuo
Takeuchi Teruo
Takeuchi Yoshio
Tanaka Hakashi
Tanaka Masami
Teraoka Ryūgan
Tezuka Yoshimichi
Toda Toyosaburō
Togawa Yoshio
Tokiwai Kenjū
Toyoshima Mutsumi
Tsueshita Takayuki
Tsutagawa Yoshihisa
Uchida Ryū
Uchino Kumaichirō
Uchiyama Toshihiko
Uehara Tadamichi
Ueno Kenchi
Uno Seiichi
Uno Tetsuto
Watanabe Takashi
Yagimoto Minoru
Yamada Katsumi
Yamada Sumeru

Yamada Taku
Yamaguchi Yoshio
Yamamoto Iwao
Yamamuro Saburō
Yamaoka Riichi
Yamashita Minoru
Yasui Kōzan
Yasumoto Hiroshi
Yoshida Kenkō
Yoshihara Fumiaki
Yoshii Taijun
Yuasa Yukihiko

Six Dynasties Thought - China

See also "BUDDHISM" and "RELIGION: Taoism"
Fukui Fumimasa
Hachiya Kunio
Hiraki Kōhei
Honda Wataru
Itō Fumisada
Kaga Eiji
Kimata Tokuo
Kobayashi Noboru
Matsuda Minoru
Mori Mikisaburō
Murakami Yoshimi
Nakajima Ryūzō
Sanaka Sō
Satō Ichirō
Seimiya Tsuyoshi
Seki Masao
Shimizu Kiyoshi
Shimomi Takao
Shiomi Atsurō
Wakatsuki Toshihide
Yamada Toshiaki
Yoshikawa Tadao

T'ang Thought - China

See also "BUDDHISM" and "RELIGION: Taoism"
Inaba Ichirō
Shimizu Kiyoshi
Yamada Toshiaki

Sung Thought - China

See also "BUDDHISM" and "RELIGION: Taoism"
Fujisawa Makoto
Imai Usaburō
Morohashi Tetsuji
Shimada Kenji
Shōji Sōichi
Takahata Tsunenobu
Yamanoi Yū

Neo-Confucianism - China / East Asia

See also "Thought: Asia" above; "Ming Thought" and
    "Ch'ing Thought" below; also, "JAPAN: Thought," "KO-
    REA: Thought," and "HISTORY: Sino-Japanese Historical
    Relations"
Abe Yoshio
Araki Kengo
Fumoto Yasutaka
Gotō Shunzui
Hirata Sakae
Ichikawa Yasushi
Ishida Ichirō
Kimura Eiichi
Kinami Takuichi
Kondō Yasunobu
Kusumoto Masatsugu
Mano Sen'ryū
Miura Kunio
Okada Takehiko
Ōtsuki Nobuyoshi
Rai Tsutomu
Shimada Kenji
Shimotomai Akira
Shionoya On
Suzuki Kiichi
Suzuki Yoshijirō
Tadokoro Yoshiyuki
Takahashi Susumu
Tomoeda Ryūtarō
Tsuboi Yoshimasa
Uno Tetsuto
Watanabe Hiroshi
Yamaguchi Yoshio
Yamamuro Saburō
Yamane Mitsuyoshi
Yamazaki Michio
Yasuda Kiyoshi
Yuasa Yukihiko

Ming Thought - China

See also "Neo-Confucianism" above
Iwami Hiroshi
Mano Sen'ryū
Mizoguchi Yūzō
Okuzaki Yūji
Ono Kazuko
Otake Fumio
Sano Kōji
Shimada Kenji
Teraji Jun
Yamanoi Yū
Yamashita Ryūji

Ch'ing Thought - China

See also "Neo-Confucianism" above, and "Modern Thought" below
Ishiguro Noritoshi
Iwami Hiroshi
Kawata Teiichi
Kondō Mitsuo
Kurosaka Mitsuteru
Mano Sen'ryū
Ogawa Haruhisa
Ono Kazuko
Otake Fumio
Ōtani Toshio
Sakade Yoshinobu
Sano Kōji
Shimada Kenji
Yamanoi Yū
Takada Atsushi
Yoshida Kōhei
Yuasa Yukihiko

Modern Thought - China

See also "Ch'ing Thought" above;   "Political Thought" below;
    also, "ECONOMICS: Economic Thought-Modern/Contemporary-China"
Araki Osamu
Arita Kazuo
Fujii Shōzō
Fujiwara Tei
Gotō Nobuko
Harada Masami
Harada Minoru
Itō Teruo
Kamio Ryūsuke
Kamiya Masao
Kanamaru Kunizō
Kaneko Noboru
Katayama Tomoyuki
Kawata Teiichi
Kobayashi Fumio
Kobayashi Takashi
Kondō Kuniyasu
Konose Tsuneyasu
Kumano Shōhei
Kurosaka Mitsuteru
Maruyama Matsuyuki
Matsumura Kazuto
Nakayama Yoshihiro
Nakayashiki Hiroshi
Niijima Atsuyoshi
Nomura Kōichi
Ono Kazuko
Onogawa Hidemi

TUN-HUANG TEXTS

    See also "CENTRAL/INNER ASIAN STUDIES," "BUDDHISM," "HISTORY: Asia," "HISTO-
      RY: T'ang," "LITERATURE: Buddhist Literature," and "LITERATURE: T'ang"
    Dohi Yoshikazu
    Fujieda Akira
    Hatano Tarō
    Kanaoka Shōkō
    Naba Toshisada
    Teraoka Ryūgan
    Yamamoto Tatsurō

U.S.S.R.

    Economy - U.S.S.R.

        Fujimoto Akira

    History - Russian / Soviet

        See also "HISTORY: Sino-Russian Historical Relations" and "HISTORY:
          Asia"
        Fujii Matsuichi
        Fujimura Michio
        Saguchi Tōru

    Siberia

        Katō Kyūzō
        Mikami Masatoshi
        Takahashi Moritaka

    Sino-Soviet Relations

        See "INTERNATIONAL RELATIONS: Sino-Soviet Relations"

    Soviet Sinology - on Modern Chinese Literature

        Kawakami Kyūju

WATER CONTROL

    See "MISCELLANEOUS: Water Control"

WOMEN'S STUDIES - China

    Ono Kazuko
    Yamazaki Jun'ichi
    Yuasa Yukihiko